Pioneer Surveyor - Frontier Lawyer

O. W. WILLIAMS

from a photograph of 1879

Pioneer Surveyor
~
Frontier Lawyer

The Personal Narrative of O. W. Williams

1877~1902

Edited with Annotations by
S. D. MYRES

Introduction
C. L. SONNICHSEN

EL PASO : TEXAS WESTERN COLLEGE PRESS

1966

RESEARCH

Clayton W. Williams

MAPS AND SKETCHES

José Cisneros

TYPOGRAPHY

J. Ed Davis

DESIGN

Carl Hertzog

PREFACE

HE LAST QUARTER of the nineteenth century (1875-1900) was a period of remarkable change in the American Southwest. During those twenty-five years, the way of life and the institutions peculiar to the frontier reached their highest point of development. They then declined rapidly as more and more settlers from the North and East brought in their traditional values, customs and law.

In Texas, the defeat and pacification of the Comanches during 1872-74 made it safe at last for homesteaders to establish themselves on the High Plains. Almost immediately, aggressive land agents and hard-working surveyors, moving in advance of waves of immigrants, made ready the virgin lands of Northwest Texas for the newcomers.

Vast stretches of this near-level terrain, over which the remnants of buffalo herds still grazed, would soon be occupied by ranchmen and their cattle. Surprisingly, in a few years farmers would discover ample sources of underground water — and the rich soil of the Texas Plains would produce abundantly. Towns would grow, and a stable economy would be established.

The Territory of New Mexico, farther west, was more remote and undeveloped — less organized politically and socially at the beginning of the twenty-five-year period. Apache warriors were still at large here and they periodically ravaged the white men's settlements. Billy the Kid and other outlaws made life unsafe for the law-abiding residents.

Even so, an increasing number of stouthearted men entered the Territory — miners, ranchers, merchants, adventurers — attracted by its great natural wealth. Of special importance, mining regions like those in and around Silver City acted like magnets, pulling in settlers. Although much turmoil still lay ahead, New Mexico would become relatively civilized and safe by the end of the century.

A third region of the Southwestern frontier was the Big Bend of Texas. An almost incredible wasteland on the Rio Grande border with Mexico, it remained largely unexplored. Its many gnomelike peaks and the valleys below were shrouded in mystery as heavy as the clouds hanging over them.

Along the Rio Grande, a few sleepy villages — Presidio, Redford, Lajitas — marked the western limits of the Big Bend. Far to the north and east were the outposts of Marfa, Fort Davis, Alpine and Marathon. The great expanse between the two thin lines of settlement was essentially a void, occupied only by a few Apaches, Mexicans and desperadoes, plus a handful of intrepid American ranchers.

Towards the end of the quarter-century period, the quicksilver mines at Terlingua, near Lajitas, were brought into production; but they did not materially change the primitive economy of the region. The Big Bend would continue for many years as it had been — mostly unoccupied and untamed — and it would be called properly "The Last American Frontier."

Much has been written about these early times in Texas and New Mexico. In fact, no other period in the history of the American West has contributed more to our folklore, traditions and literature. The lusty, adventuresome life of the era has caught the imagination of the American people; and the stirring accounts of Indians, miners, cowboys, outlaws and lawmen seem destined to be told and retold for generations to come.

Unfortunately, many of these accounts are inaccurate and exaggerated — more imaginative than factual by far. One reason for this phenomenon is that the frontier produced few reliable historians. Most frontiersmen were unlettered; and those who could write had little time or incentive to do so.

A notable exception to the rule is the subject of this book. Oscar W. Williams was not only highly educated; he also took the trouble to record his experiences and observations. Viewed as a whole, his writings reflect with uncommon clarity much of the history of the Southwestern frontier.

Williams came to Texas in 1877, and he went almost immediately to the High Plains as a surveyor. Three years later he began work as a miner in the silver region of Shakespeare, New Mexico. Afterwards, he undertook surveying assignments in the Texas Big Bend. Keeping a diary and recording field notes from day to day, he was able later to write detailed first-hand accounts of his observations. These accounts, because of their immediacy, constitute source material of unique value.

In recording his story, Williams experienced many interruptions and setbacks. Life on the frontier was hard, and he had only limited time for writing. As a result, he worked sporadically. Instead of planning a full, orderly review of his experiences and observations, he limited himself to narrating selected episodes as they occurred to him. These he recounted in personal letters, articles to the town newspaper, and locally printed pamphlets.

Given this discursiveness in Williams's writings — plus a number of gaps in their continuity — the first task of the editor was to establish their sequence and to supply the missing information. This objective was accomplished by resorting to Williams' diary and personal letters, by examining many supplementary sources, and by getting assistance from Williams' son Clayton, who has an intimate knowledge of his father's life. In the pages that follow, all editorial matter is printed in larger 11-point type (like this), while Williams' text appears in 10-point (smaller but spaced). Also, Williams' pieces are introduced by small drawings made by José Cisneros, suggesting their respective themes.

Since Williams' view of the Southwest is panoramic, the editor decided to add essential details to the narrative in the form of explanatory notes at the end of each major division. It is hoped that these notes will place Williams' writings in their proper historical context; also that they will assist the reader in understanding better the persons, locations and events that figure in the text, and will suggest reliable sources for further study.

The original materials — chiefly pamphlets and letters — were usually written in haste and printed carelessly, with no revision or proofreading. Editorial discretion has therefore been exercised to correct occasional factual mistakes and various errors in typography, spelling and punctuation. In addition, certain repetitious and irrelevant passages have been omitted. A list of Williams' writings, including those published in this volume, will be found in Appendix III.

The editor is indebted to a number of persons in Texas and New Mexico whose lively interest and expert advice helped make this study possible. Their names are listed, with sincere thanks, in the Acknowledgments at the end of the book.

S. D. Myres

Texas Western College
January 1, 1966

Table of Contents

Photographs and Maps

Introduction

by

C. L. SONNICHSEN

INTRODUCTION

NOT MANY PEOPLE during Judge Oscar Waldo Williams'
lifetime realized what an extraordinary man he was. It was
not merely that this Harvard law graduate had come West in the
seventies and lived through the American Heroic Age — the time
we have transmuted into a national myth. Other cultivated men
have done the same and been forgotten. But he was one of the
few with first-hand experience who could and did tell, expertly
and vividly, what those times were like.

As the slender, white-haired old man in the rumpled business
suit went about his legal and personal chores in Fort Stockton,
Texas, he did not seem much different from other pioneer citizens.
His rather stately manner and his excellent spoken English entitled
him to respect, but his real distinction was appreciated by very
few indeed.

His relative obscurity was his own fault. He was innocent of
literary ambition, and it seems never to have occurred to him to
try to sell his stories to a commercial publisher. He paid country
printers to set his letters and essays in type, and he "published"
them by handing them to his sons and grandsons and to a few
friends who might be interested.

Keeping the family record seemed to him a matter of first importance. More than once he recalled the case of his uncle Oscar
Waldo from whom he got his name, a forty-niner who died in
California. "So the story of my uncle's last days is not only lost,
but the very name of the site of the place has perished," he once
wrote. "Now I do not want this to happen to my descendants, and
as far as I can I am trying to carry to them the family story."[1]

The urge to communicate and inform, however, was more than
a family matter, and it had always been a part of him. As the psy-
chologists say nowadays, he was remarkably "verbal," and from
his youth he was continually writing — letters, diary entries, articles
for the hometown newspaper. When his children were old enough
to be interested, he began reminiscing in his letters to them. After
the year 1900, when he was well into his middle age, he made a
habit of exploring systematically in writing his recollections of early
times, and during the twenties and thirties he printed a great

number of these explorations. But he never tried to "write" in the
ordinary sense of the word, and while he was alive only a few
specialists realized what a good writer he was.

Ironically, his descendants were slow to appreciate the full value
of what he offered them so freely. "Everything which the Judge
treated," says his grandson,[2] "became as dust. The age of Richard
the Lion Hearted, I'm afraid, seemed closer at hand and more real
than the age of Billy the Kid. . . . It is true that the Judge, when he
reached his 'anecdotage' (a smart-alec grandson, namely me, applied the term at college age) became so enmeshed in detail that
he seemed to destroy the anecdotal beauty of his tales, buried their
drama and overrode their humor. . . . How could we know that he
bracketed within some thirty-odd brochures (the whole have never
been gathered together) one of the most exciting and rapidly
changing periods of our history. . . . Little wonder that we only
discovered, much later and older — as it was pointed out by out-
landers to the family circle — that the brochures the Judge published at his own expense, circulated only among friends and relatives, never publicized in any way, were vigorous contributions
to Southwestern nature study, history, folklore, and literature."

The recognition which he never sought was slow in coming, but
it came. Collectors of Texana began to watch for his pamphlets
and snapped them up when they could be found. As a result a sort
of *sub rosa* distinction accumulated like moss on an oak tree about
these unpretentious jottings. J. Frank Dobie remarked in his *Guide
to the Life and Literature of the Southwest* (1943): "Few men
have known and understood the natural features of the Southwest
as well as he. Some day his scattered writings will be put into an
enduring book." Dobie himself included Williams' description of
a buffalo stampede as the best thing of its kind when he published
On the Open Range in 1951. In 1964 Williams was anthologized
again when the Texas Surveyors Association included three of
his pamphlets in *One League to Each Wind*.[3]

From all this it is obvious that a collection of the writings of
O. W. Williams has long been overdue. Publication might have
been delayed indefinitely, however, had it not been for E. R. Wyatt
of Pleasanton, Texas, a connoisseur of Texana who for years has
been assembling the Judge's scattered publications. In a letter to
me dated June 15, 1963, he wrote as follows:

I am interested in trying to get someone to gather up and put into
book form the various writings of Judge O. W. Williams of Fort Stock-

ton. Nothing has come out of West Texas, in my poor opinion, that equals any of his articles. They cover every phase of the country and to me are the most interesting tales — factual — no fiction — and his experiences as an early-day surveyor, lawyer, county judge, and everything else, make you sit up and want more of them. Book dealers are listing his pamphlets, some as small as four pages, at prices ranging from $30 to $100. Frank Dobie in his list mentions a 96-page item that I would give my right leg for. . . .

Editor S. D. Myres and the Editorial Board of the Texas Western College Press agreed that here was a book that needed to be published. Dr. Myres accepted a Research Professorship to get the job done, and his enthusiasm for his project grew as he got deeper into it. Judge Williams' unique life experience unfolded before him in fascinating detail. Clayton Williams, the Judge's son, worked with him, and sheaves of writing hitherto unsuspected came to light. The information which Myres accumulated appears in notes and linking passages in the pages which follow. This introduction will take account of Judge Williams' youth, background, education, and experiences before he came to the Southwest; will summarize his career in Texas and New Mexico, concentrating on chapters which he could not, or did not, put into print; and will discuss his special qualities as a writer.

Williams was proud of his family background, which included many names famous in the annals of early America. The first Williams ancestor, David, who spoke Welsh in his home all his life, settled on the Delaware-Maryland border in 1690. In the decades which followed, David's descendants married into such families as the Holders, Callaways, Graveses, and Colyars, and figured prominently in the French and Indian War, the Revolution, and a hundred skirmishes on the Indian frontier. Richard Callaway, financial backer of the Transylvania State, commander of a fort during the French and Indian War, and a colonel during the Revolution, was one of his forbears. So was John Colyar, who was present at Braddock's defeat in the capacity of drummer boy, fought through the Revolution, and carried seventeen bullet scars with him to his grave. There is a monument to him in the town of Culpeper, Virginia.[4]

O. W. Williams' grandfather, Richard Gott Williams, made news in 1826 by outfitting a caravan of twelve prairie schooners and embarking on a trading venture to the Spanish Southwest. The expedition pushed on as far as El Paso and Chihuahua and would have proved profitable, but on the return trip the Arapaho Indians robbed Richard of horses and other property worth $100,000.[5] It may be worth noting also that the Juárez Archives show that when he was in El Paso del Norte in the fall of 1826, Williams filed a complaint in the Mexican court against a *ladrón* (thief) for stealing some of his goods.[6]

Oscar's father, Jesse Caleb Williams, was a prosperous merchant of Mount Vernon, Kentucky, at the time of his son's birth on March 17, 1853; but four years after this event, with a number of Kentucky families from the Mount Vernon-Crab Orchard neighborhood,[7] he moved to Carthage, Illinois. There he set up a general merchandise store and engaged in other business ventures, including a pork-packing plant at Keokuk, Iowa.

Young Oscar's earliest memories were fond recollections of this prairie community and the life which went on in and around it — the neighbor boys and girls, Johnnie Appleseed's orchard legacy, the fish in the ponds, the strawberries in the tall grass, the prairie chickens and passenger pigeons, the nut-gathering and hog-killing times, the fine old Campbellite preachers who were entertained in the Williams home.[8] He could recall in vivid detail events and personalities which caught his attention when he was no more than four or five years old.

Abraham Lincoln, for instance, made an appearance on the courthouse square in 1858 and little Oscar was there. "A platform was erected against the building and covered by a brush arbor from which small limbs and branches projected out and down," he wrote seventy years later. "Father and I were standing on the southeastern edge of the crowd, near some large trees, cottonwoods, I believe. We saw Mr. Lincoln come out from the crowd and step up to the platform. He presented a long, angular figure, dressed in a long-tailed black coat, and topped by a tall, stiff hat which was known in those days as a stovepipe hat because it had a narrow brim and a long upper story. As Mr. Lincoln stepped up to the platform, this stovepipe hat struck one of those projecting branches and in trying to catch it, he made an awkward grab for it, which made it extremely funny for my young eyes. I do not remember a word that he said, but the picture of that frantic grasp for the wandering stovepipe will remain in my mind to my dying day."[9]

To Jesse Caleb Williams and Mary Ann Collier were born seven children, of whom five grew to maturity. William D. came to Texas

in 1873, practiced law in Austin, and was an early-day mayor of
Fort Worth. Joseph J. became a leading lawyer of Kansas City,
Missouri. Susan took care of her parents, never married, and spent
her last years in Alpine, Texas. Jessie became Mrs. A. E. Hart and
moved to Los Angeles. Jesse Caleb Williams, the father, died in
1917 at the age of ninety-eight.[10]

O. W. Williams says very little in his reminiscent writings about
his family's position during the Civil War. He does comment on
"the bitterness of partisan feeling" in Carthage during those days.
Once, speaking of a lecture by Wendell Phillips which he attended,
he said: "Because my family was Southern and Democratic I had
been reared with a certain amount of prejudice against him and
his co-workers."[11] Add to this the fact that at Harvard he was
"pitched into" on account of his Southern views[12] and we have a
good idea of the feelings of the Williams family during the great
conflict.

Jesse Williams had to dispose of the pork-packing business when
his Southern markets were cut off. Otherwise the family emerged
from the war with health and property intact. Their main hardship
may have been the loss of contact with their close relatives, with
whom their ties were warm and tender. An uncle of Oscar's named
John Berry started out from his home at Liberty, Missouri, almost
as soon as peace was established, to learn the fate of his kinsmen
in Kentucky and Illinois. About the first of September, 1865, he
appeared at the Williams home in Carthage, satisfied himself of
their prosperous condition, and proposed at a family council to
take Oscar back to Liberty with him to enroll in William Jewell
College. Oscar had spent six years in the public schools and had
had some tutoring at home (his mother started him in Latin when
he was six).[13] Going to school away from home sounded exciting.
When John Berry left, he took the boy with him.

The trip by steamboat down the Mississippi and up the Missouri
remained vividly in Oscar's mind for the rest of his life and is the
subject of one of his most interesting letters to his children.[14] He
tells little of what happened to his mind during this school year,
except that he began the study of Virgil; but he did see a band of
outlaws in the act of robbing the local bank and had his first close
contact with death when one of his schoolmates was accidentally
killed by the robbers. "I had not thought," he remarked of the boy's
appearance in his coffin, "that death could show so much beauty
and distinction."

When his year at William Jewell was up, Oscar could not wait to get back to Carthage, but he did not stay long. In 1868 he sallied forth again in search of educational opportunities — this time to Christian University (now called Culver-Stockton College) in Canton, Missouri. In one of his reminiscent letters he explained that the College was reopened after the Civil War by two old classmates from Bethany College in West Virginia — Benjamin H. Smith, preacher, and Oval Pirkey, teacher. These men were leaders in the Christian Church, of which Oscar's parents were devout members, and when Benjamin Smith came to Carthage in the summer of 1868 to recruit students for the institution, the result might have been foreseen. "It was but natural," Williams recalled, "that my parents should determine to send me as an offering to that school. With me went several other boys whose antecedent history had run very closely on a line with mine."[15] The college was only forty miles from Carthage and therefore quite accessible.

Oscar spent two years at Christian University, where he studied Latin and Greek, Astronomy and Higher Mathematics, and Chemistry. He pursued the Classical Course, which, as he says, emphasized the "dead languages." There was also a "Scientific Course" which was followed, to the surprise of Williams and his fellow males, by a female student named Alice Staples.

Extra-curricular activities included flute-playing in a five-man band, baseball, and practical jokes — like the one played on Glenn Schofield, an admirer of Miss Julia Nesmith. He was indoctrinated with the idea that he might be in danger from any one of several ferociously jealous suitors. Somewhat nervously he went to call. On his way home he was accosted by a masked figure with a shotgun. After some preliminary remarks the assailant fired his weapon (over Schofield's head, of course), at the same time shouting, "You'll not call on that young lady again!" The terrified youth broke all records getting back to his room.

Sixty years later Williams tried to arrange a reunion of his surviving classmates on the college campus. The idea filled him with special rapture. "No spent soldier of Xenophon's Ten Thousand," he wrote, "could have been more delighted at the far sight of the Euxine than I was pleased at the promise, even in 'make-believe,' of lying down with the old boys on the hillside in the shade and on the grass of that springtime which had been dead for sixty years." He succeeded only in meeting two of his one-time associates —

David J. McCanne and Judge W. C. Ellison — in El Paso, Texas.[16]

After two years at Christian University, with his senior year ahead of him, Oscar left the campus and went elsewhere. He explains what happened in rather non-specific terms which are nevertheless full of overtones:

In the summer of 1870 my father decided to send me to Bethany College in West Virginia [he begins]. He had come to believe that I had spent too much money and had paid too little attention to my studies at another school, so he thought it would be best to take me away from the associations of my previous years there. He had selected the Virginia school, partly because, being a devout member of the church organization known as Disciples of Christ or Christian Church, he had turned naturally to the school founded by Alexander Campbell, its great protagonist; but partly also because the school itself was located in the wooded hills far from the temptations of a large city. Then too a "House of Poverty" should be a good place in which one would learn that practice of self-denial and patient persevering aims so useful in after life.

Knowing the high moral standards upheld by O. W. Williams in later years, his dismay at any form of dissipation, his quiet but real piety, one need not take too seriously the implication that the seductions and pitfalls of city life had been too much for him. Many fathers besides his own have been overly cautious in arranging their children's lives.

The year which Williams spent at Bethany is the subject of one of his most frank and charming little pamphlets. He describes his arrival in the wooded, hilly country, so different from his prairie home. As a baseball player he noted at once the consequences of laying out a diamond on a hillside: "Whenever a ball was knocked out of the infield it took to a long descent, and for a time the farther it went the faster it moved, so that no fielder could catch up with it before it came to the end of the slope. When finally in hand, it usually required relays of two or three players to get it back into the pitcher's base." Scores, as a result, tended to be astronomical. In one intercollegiate game, says Oscar, his team scored eighty runs.[17]

It was no particular strain for the newcomer to make the first team as pitcher, but pitfalls awaited him as a member of the Senior Class. In Latin and Greek he passed his qualifying examinations. In Astronomy and Mathematics he did likewise. President Pendleton got satisfactory answers out of him in other areas which he does not specify by name. In Chemistry he failed miserably, partly because the subject had never interested him; partly because it had not interested his teachers at Christian University. As a result he took up civil engineering instead of laboratory science — a fact which had a determining influence on his later life, since he made his living for many years as a surveyor.

The Christmas holidays that year were too short for a visit home. Instead, Oscar made a trip to Pittsburgh. Lotta Crabtree, the joy of so many Western audiences in those days, was to play there for a whole week. Oscar loved her as Little Nell. "She took the house with her at the begining and kept it with her to the close," he says. But three days of Pittsburgh "smoke and smut" were all he could take and he went back to Bethany, falling into the icy Ohio River up to his neck on the way back and getting a severe chill.

In June he boarded the stage for home, stopping off in Springfield, Illinois, where his father was in residence as a State Senator. The two of them attended a performance of *Henry the Fifth* in which Edwin Forrest starred as Jack Cade. A few hours later he was back in the old familiar surroundings looking for something to do.

The job he found in that summer of 1871 put to practical use the engineering knowledge which he had accumulated at Bethany. He was employed as a civil engineer by the Mississippi Valley and Western Railroad Company, a misguided venture which "broke up in disaster" in the fall of that year.

Back home in Carthage, Oscar picked up a job as deputy county clerk of Hancock County. How long he held it or how he spent his idle time we have no way of knowing. He must have thought long and seriously about his prospects — or lack of them — in Illinois, and in 1873 he determined, with his father's blessing, to get a legal education. He could have done it by "reading law" in some country judge's office, but he had bigger ideas. In the fall of 1873 he matriculated at Harvard.

During his first year in the Harvard Law School he was a serious and successful student. According to the records he "had a very high mark in Real Property" at the end of the year and "did very well in Torts and Criminal Law."[18] Unfortunately little more can be learned about his first year in the East. He kept a diary describing his experiences day by day, but somehow, in his moving from place to place, the volume was lost. He told his family that he knew

Alice Longfellow in a Cambridge literary society and used to see Henry Wadsworth Longfellow in his old age taking a daily walk. He had a napkin ring made out of the "spreading chesnut tree." And that is about all we can salvage from those far-off days. The diary covering his second year has been preserved, however, and it reveals the Judge as he was in his youth with the world before him, a curious, sensitive, fastidious, perceptive young man, by no means provincial, who went his own way and cast a critical and independent eye on the scenes which unfolded before him.

His second year at Harvard promised to be more rewarding than the first, and in some ways it was. Always curious and eager for new experiences, he took his time on the return journey. He attended church in Wheeling, West Virginia; visited the Mint, the Corcoran Art Gallery, the Smithsonian Institution, and the Capitol in Washington. He called on his father's sister Fanny in New York and had "a pleasant time" with her and his cousin Mary. On October 8, after a week on the road, he reached Boston and fell back into the routine he had established the previous year.

He lived comfortably, as he had during his first year, with the Arnold family, but boarded at various places around the Square. He took his studies rather casually, frequently making such notations as "Missed the lecture on Equity." He took time for a wide variety of diversions — trips to the beach, to baseball games, to art galleries and museums, to lectures. He heard Henry Ward Beecher (was "disappointed in his oratory but liked his matter") [19] and listened to music. A Theodore Thomas matinee at the Music Hall did not please him [20] but he enjoyed a concert of the Hampton Institute colored students ("The bass, especially, was magnificent") [21] and was astonished at the virtuosity of Blind Tom, Negro pianist. [22] He liked to make music himself — did some singing and bought a tuning fork so he could set a pitch; and he rented a piano on which he performed for his own amusement. Occasionally he went to the theatre. He saw Madame Januschek as Lady Macbeth and Queen Elizabeth, [23] and Ristori as Marie Antoinette. [24] He gave neither of them his unreserved admiration, but he thought Joseph Jefferson's performance "the most natural I ever saw on the stage" and "enjoyed the acting of Miss Charlotte Cushman very much." [25]

When there was an especially interesting trial, he and his friends attended in the courtroom, and they kept two or three clubs going in which they practiced legal procedure. On at least one occasion

Oscar functioned as Chief Justice.[26] But he was always looking for new experiences. He saw the inside of two prisons,[27] went through the mills at Lowell, Massachusetts,[28] visited an operating theater and the anatomy laboratory at the Medical School,[29] and made the rounds of the churches when there was hope of hearing a better-than-average sermon. When it rained or he had nothing better to do, he read — *Swiss Family Robinson,* Bulwer-Lytton's *The Caxtons,* Buckle's *History of Civilization,* the poems of Scott and Shelley, even *Gil Blas* in Spanish. At the same time he was going to parties, visiting friendly families, and forming a friendship with two Miss Waltons on whom he was calling every evening toward the end of the term.

It was a full year and an enjoyable one, perhaps too enjoyable, for the day of reckoning came. On June 27, 1875, he wrote:

> Saw that I did not get my degree, & went to see Langdell. He gave me no encouragement. Formed the resolution to stay in Boston until I did, or at all events not to let my parents know of my failure. Spalding & 10 others failed. However after considering the matter, I thought that I ought not to conceal the fact from my parents, & concluded to go to Chicago, go into business & then return in June '76 for my degree. . . .

> I was surprised at the result, & so were the "boys." In fact some of them (Edson & Wald) wouldn't believe it until they saw it for themselves.

Seventy years later Oscar's grandson noted that in his own mind "it was a cause of some sort of perverted satisfaction to learn that the Judge, in whom we children could discover no human frailty, washed out of law school in 1875. The nearest approach in all his writings to discharging a personal emotion is a diary passage describing the incredulity with which he received the news that his test paper was not acceptable. But in the same passage he suddenly became stoically philosophical and set down his plans to return in June, 1876."

The year of waiting was one of frustration. He had difficulty finding a place for himself in Chicago and when he finally went to work in the law office of John N. Jewett, his employment, much of it copying legal documents, proved to be confining and monotonous. He went to church and taught a Sunday School class. He called on various young ladies. He took his bar examinations. But in October he left his employment for reasons which he does not mention and went back home to Carthage. After a few days there he boarded the train to Clayton, Illinois, where he had an interest in a store, and took over the management.

The establishment was in debt to the extent of $10,000 and business was "dull." Life was dull too. One could go to church and one could go squirrel hunting, and that was about all. The diary reflects his ennui:

> Wednesday, Nov. 10. Store all day. Quiet.
> Thursday, Nov. 11. Quiet in the store.
> Friday, Nov. 12. Same tale as on yesterday.

Josh Billings lectured at Carthage and Oscar went to hear him, recording no opinions in his diary. There was a little law business. In April he sold his interest in the store and by the first of May was on his way back to Cambridge to try again to pass his examinations. This time he succeeded.

For a brief interval he thought of settling in the East and actually spent a week at Portland, Maine, with a classmate named Grant, who was a potential partner. On July 1 he gave it all up: "Bid Grant goodbye and left on the boat for Boston at 7 P.M." He does not say why.

On the way home he paused in Philadelphia to see the Centennial Exposition. The mechanical exhibits impressed him, as did the natural-history collections. The torchlight processions and the fireworks left him cold.[30]

Back in Illinois, he found himself again nowhere. He ran for prosecuting attorney and lost. He fished and played baseball and went to church. But his life was so lacking in variety that he could comment on August 23, 1876: "Classically engaged in hauling manure from barn yard to make up a tulip bed." A job at the courthouse working on the tax records did little to inspire him.

All this while his health was suffering. He had had constant colds during his stay in Cambridge and had developed a condition which in those days was called "catarrh." We should call it chronic sinus infection now. He tried every cure, including Dr. Sage's Catarrh Remedy and smoking cubeb cigarettes, but nothing helped much. The chances are he was in the first stages of tuberculosis. On Monday, February 19, 1877, his diary records: "Handed over my Preston Estate Suit to Charley Schofield in view of my approaching departure for Texas."

There was some background to this drastic decision. He explains in his best-known pamphlet (*In Old New Mexico*) that after his return from Harvard "I had found that I had some lung trouble, and the doctors had decided that I must go to some arid country, so in 1877 I landed in Dallas, and, finding the legal fraternity in that town of 2,500 people already far too numerous to give me any hope of success in some years, I fell back on an earlier avocation of mine and got employment as a Surveyor of Public Lands."[31]

For three years he made his living in this fashion, alternating between the Texas Plains and the settlements — Dallas, Kansas City, Chicago, Carthage — where he sought buyers for the land he had assisted in surveying. The three expeditions he made to the wild, deserted, and potentially dangerous reaches of West Texas are described in the pamphlets included first in the present volume. The annotations and linking passages recount in detail what went on in Williams' life, and we need only mention here that this chapter came to an end in 1879 when the Texas Legislature passed a law reserving unappropriated lands from further private location. Williams remarks in the pamphlet which describes his next move, "I could well say with Othello, 'My occupation is gone.'"[32]

The new occupation was an excursion into the mining industry in the wilds of New Mexico, a particularly hazardous venture since Victorio and later Nana were lifting hair right and left. Here again his own account, supplemented by the editor's annotations and family correspondence, appears in the text.

One part of his life at this time which he did not write up was his romance with Miss Sallie Wheat. Sallie was the attractive daughter of a prominent and prosperous Dallas family. Her father was Clayton Miller Wheat, a Kentuckian who came to Dallas in 1873 and grew up with the town. He served as president of the Board of Trade and was a public-spirited and charitable man. One of a family of four boys and two girls, Sallie was pretty and talented. She was a graduate of Christian College in Columbia, Missouri, where she won prizes for English composition and took leading roles in the college musical entertainments. Back home in Dallas she continued to use her fine soprano voice and her talents as an actress, on one occasion singing the part of Queen Esther in an oratorio.

Perhaps music brought her and Oscar together. It could have been their loyalty to the Christian Church. The fact that they both had Kentucky backgrounds may have helped. It seems not to have made any difference that she was very much at home in the little city and Oscar was heading for a career on the frontier. When he left for New Mexico, they were deeply interested in each other, perhaps engaged, and wrote to each other frequently.

Oscar located at Shakespeare, now a ghost town in southern New Mexico, then a typical frontier mining community. The boy who had trodden in the footsteps of Longfellow and Agassiz now followed the traces of Russian Bill and Billy the Kid, adjusting to the rough manners of prospectors and teamsters and filing away in his capacious memory the way things looked and sounded and happened in that extraordinary time and place.

He prospected all over the country, with one eye out for Indians and the other intent on minerals. Nothing good turned up, but he completed his frontier education and recorded his impressions in his diary, his letters, and later on in printed brochures. No better first-hand account of actual conditions in the Wild West can be found anywhere. "This is not the best country in the world for personal safety," he wrote to Sallie. "Many a man is killed here in some mountain 'arroya' [sic], and no one ever hears of him afterwards. I buried once the bones of a human being in a wild place in this country. I never could find out anything about who it was, and suppose I never will."[33] The indifference of his fellow frontiersmen toward death under such circumstances was natural, but Williams could not help taking special notice. "People will jest and laugh over a dead body here with the most charming indifference," he noted in his diary. "Sitting up with a corpse, when such a thing is done, the watchers will vie with each other in telling good jokes on the deceased, and the story goes that one fellow was so absentminded after telling a good story as to poke the ribs of the corpse in a jocular manner, as if to remind it to laugh at that stage."[34]

Some aspects of life in this predominantly male society he never could accept. Whisky he regarded as the root of all evil on the frontier, and a saloonkeeper as a man without a soul.

Always he was the observer and recorder, and we should never know that he was yearning for something different if it were not for his letters to Sallie. To her he wrote: "Your letters are about the only things that come to me as a matter of rejoicing. So much bad luck has happened to me lately that every letter which I receive — excepting those which have your well known handwriting — seems to announce beforehand evil news."[35]

On the positive side he spoke of "longing to sit once more with you in that pleasant parlor. . . . Letters are far better than silence, but how tame and quiet beside the pleasure of those times when we sat in the moonlight on the steps, or when you gathered roses that summer night so long ago. The summer roses have now bloomed twice since then, but we have not gathered them. . . . But not another summer shall pass — Deo Volente — without buds blooming for us. And if Dame Fortune just gives me the suspicion of a smile, the orange blossoms shall be ours."

A lawsuit finished him in the mining business, litigation over a mine which he thought he owned, but which somebody else, partly through his carelessness, got title to. The story is fully covered in the text and notes which follow in Part III relating to the dispute over the Last Chance Mine.

While this matter was being decided, his money ran out and he was glad to pick up a job as assistant postmaster in Silver City.

A little later he became deputy district clerk for Grant County and observed the last months of the Apache wars from the comparative safety of his Silver City offices.

His new employment gave him peculiar opportunities for observing the kaleidoscope of life in a frontier community. "In the town there were two places where all such men met on common ground — the gambling house and the post office," he wrote; "and before my eyes passed in turn in front of the little delivery-box most of those characters in rapid succession." In A City of Refuge he described them along with the Chinamen, the prostitutes in silks and diamonds, the aristocratic-looking gamblers, the cavalry officers in gilt and blue, the silent Apache scouts with restless, glittering eyes.

His father was anxious for him to get out of what Oscar calls "that feverish little city," and offered to set him up as a merchant in Rich Hill or Nevada, Missouri, but he could not leave his lawsuit and his mining claims, he thought. With steady employment in Silver City, however, he did feel able to abandon his bachelorhood. On December 1, 1881, he boarded the stage and headed for civilization. He took the Santa Fe to Kansas City, probably visited briefly in Carthage with his father and mother, and was back in Dallas in time for his marriage on December 15.

It was a sumptuous wedding, conducted at the Wheat home by Elder J. H. Skiles of the Christian Church. The newspaper story gave it the full-organ treatment — "the fair bride, than whom a sweeter, more intelligent girl is rarely met" — the pearl-white satin — the attendants "elegantly and becomingly dressed" — the tables "loaded with all that could tempt the appetite to rare indulgence" —the presents. "And thus one of the loveliest of our social garden withdraws from us the golden sunshine of her presence, leaving but the silver dew of memory to sparkle in the tide of unforgetting love and friendship."[36]

The contrast with what followed was severe. The newlyweds took the Texas and Pacific to Sierra Blanca, a work train to El Paso, the stagecoach to Silver City. It was all "foreign to the environment and the surroundings in which Mrs. Williams had been reared and she was never quite satisfied while so far away from friends of youthful days in Dallas" — so said her son many years after her death.[37]

The following year, 1882, saw the end of the New Mexico adventure. The New Mexico courts decided against Williams in the Last Chance litigation and he was at the end of his rope. There was nothing to do but go back to Dallas, and back to Dallas he and Sallie went. They stayed with her parents while Oscar made a new start, and in the Wheat home their first child was born. This was Oscar Waldo Williams, always known as Waldo. Two years later Mary Ermine made her appearance in the same house. The rest (Susan Kathryn, Clayton Wheat, and Jesse Caleb) were born at or near Fort Stockton.[38]

During the years when necessity forced them to take refuge in Dallas, he made a living in the East Texas timberlands examining titles and estimating timber for a Michigan lumber company. It was a living, and perhaps not much more, but the time came when even that economic security had to be abandoned. The mouse in his lungs, to quote Ralph Waldo Emerson (who had one of his own), commenced gnawing again. It was necessary for him to get to a drier climate and he began to look westward once more.

His opportunity came in 1884 when the commissioners of Pecos County found themselves in need of a new deputy surveyor. In those days the surveyors were elected and not much was expected of them, but the deputies were appointed and had to know something about the business. In Pecos County at this time Deputy Surveyor Durrell had offended some of the big cattlemen by surveying blocks in their favorite pastures and opening them up to settlement. Durrell had to go. Somehow Williams heard of the opening, applied, and was hired.

He had brought his family to a historic spot. Fort Stockton grew up beside a great spring which gushed out of the ground where Indian trails crossed and where American emigrants braving the Texas wilderness found rest and relief. The first Williams home was in the town jail, the only vacant building. They lived afterward in abandoned quarters at the Fort, and still later in a tent on acreage which they were opening for irrigation.

It was ranching country with only limited farming possibilities, but Williams tried to make the most of what he found. He was one of the earliest irrigators on the Pecos. Within a year of his arrival he had taken over the assets of a project thirty miles north of Fort Stockton known as the Austin Colony. In 1889 and 1890 he was building ditches. In 1891 he acquired eight surveys of land. The venture never paid off, but it kept him busy for several years.

An enterprise of this sort needs money, and money was something Williams saw little of. It was necessary to pick up cash wherever it could be found. Lawyers in new counties in those days usually held, or tried to hold, public office, and he was at home in the courthouse. He was County Judge of Pecos County from November, 1886, to November, 1888, and from November, 1892, to November, 1900 — hence his title of Judge. After 1902 he edged over into the practice of law, and for a good many years was in partnership with Judge W. C. Jackson. He maintained a law office until the end of his days.

All through these years he spent much of his time out of doors. His surveying activities took him all over the Big Bend and the wild country which surrounded his home. It was now that his work as a naturalist was done. "If he had forgotten about the law, and applied his Harvard studies to zoology and botany and *then* traveled west," says his grandson, "he might have become the Southwest's Audubon-without-pictures. As it was, he brought to the field a great fund of scientific knowledge through study, and then applied to the flora and fauna of the area the same keen observation with which he watched the men who first settled in it. . . . He was presented with one of the best of untouched laboratories — all of the Southwest outdoors — and the time and occasion to make researches in it. So the amateur became the expert, through background and chance. . . ."

THREE GENERATIONS, *circa* 1901
Jesse Caleb Williams, Oscar W. Williams and O. W. (Waldo) Williams

PECOS COUNTY OFFICIALS, 1898

Bottom row: John M. Odom, Treasurer; O. W. Williams, Judge; Frank Rooney, Clerk; James Rooney, Commissioner. Top row: George P. Hawthorne and Morgan Livingston, Commissioners; W. P. Ratchford, Surveyor; Tom J. Ray, Commissioner; W. C. Crosby, Deputy Sheriff.

FORT STOCKTON IN 1884

View is from the steeple of the original Pecos County Courthouse. In the fore-ground is the Friedlander store. On the extreme right are the horse barns. Officers' quarters are on the extreme left. Near the center are the parade ground and the guardhouse.

His mind was never limited to any set of interests. He was curious about whatever came his way. And so he became a folklorist. Among his companions on the trail was an old leather-faced, red-headed Mexican named Natividad Luján who knew all the legends of the Chisos Mountains and the Big Bend country. Williams wrote the stories down and sent them home to the children in the form of letters.

Natividad was the party tale-teller [according to Oscar Williams]. And when the campfire flickered low at night after long hot hours of dragging chain, transit, and axes, he would begin one of his long ancient stories — chiefly to the amusement of my grandfather, who seemed to be able to translate his every phrase with a Hemingway-like agility. Week by week, my grandfather would write letters home 'to his children' . . . and he guessed that these stories of Natividad would amuse them more than any of his other experiences. So down they went, along with his usual observations about place-names, the cacti of the Big Bend, Apache graveyards, and fatherly counsel to "study hard."

He had no particular feeling of ownership about these tales and he shared them with Carlysle Graham Raht when that indefatigable gatherer of Big Bend lore was preparing his *Romance of Davis Mountains and Big Bend Country,* published in 1919. Five of the Natividad tales appear in the book, and possibly for this reason the first edition was copyrighted jointly by Raht and Williams. He had no particular pride, either, in his skill as a writer, though he did value himself as an observer and tried to train his sons to see — really see — what they were looking at. It has remained for others to point out how well he was equipped for his task and how effectively he developed his talents.

His equipment included, at the start, a capacious memory and a penetrating curiosity about everything from cactus to Comanches. He was besides a keen student, deeply read in many specialties, and his observations are informed and accurate.

His special tools, in addition to his eyes and ears and his curious mind, were a sense of humor and a good narrative style. The humor is usually quiet, barely dimpling the placid surface of his prose, but he could be sharply ironic, was aware of the ridiculousness and incongruity of life, and displayed a considerable vein of caustic wit.

The style seems straightforward and simple, but it is well modulated and pleasantly cadenced, carrying the reader along at a good

pace, avoiding all pretentiousness and affection. It is the style of
a civilized amateur, which is exactly what Williams was, and
although there is a trace of formality in the even flow of his periods,
there is also a strong suggestion of the spoken word. Often the
Judge seems to be talking rather than writing. The effect is strangely pleasing. Walter Prescott Webb tried once to describe it in a letter to Williams himself. "Each time I receive something of yours,"
he said, "even a short letter, I am struck with the crystal quality of
your style. In some way your sentences set the emotions vibrating.
They cause me to feel the personality behind them. Though your
style is characterized by remarkable clarity — fundamental to good
writing — it has the addition of a sort of luminosity which holds
the reader like a mild magnet."[39]

Almost the only embellishment in these limpid lines is an occasional literary allusion. "I know few writers who so richly and
variously called up Greek and Roman mythology and Shake-
spearean characters and set them down on the West Texas stage,
their togas getting caught in the catclaws and *tasajilla*"— so writes
his grandson, who adds that the Judge's allusions are usually apt
and amusing.

"My grandfather," he continues, "catered to Shakespeare and
to the Frenchmen who write of battles. But his great old library
testifies to his taste — history, natural history, the 'classics' (largely
Greek and Roman) and more history. He counseled me to read
Tacitus for style . . . Herodotus for adventure, Cicero for vocab-
ulary, Shakespeare only because he was an accepted classic."

A man with such gifts, with such a background and with such
objectives could hardly have fallen in with the writing formulas
of his time. He could not have written like Zane Grey, or even like
Andy Adams or Charlie Siringo, even if he had wanted to. His
formula had to be his own. And there, perhaps, we have the explanation for his avoidance of the literary marketplace.

The training and background which sets him apart may account
also for his great handicap as a writer — his inability or unwilling-
ness to explore his own feelings, his human reactions to what he
saw. Born in the middle of the nineteenth century, he arrived
before it was respectable to expose too much of the human interior,
particularly one's own. His Harvard experience, his profession as
a lawyer, his sense of personal dignity — all had something to do
with his reticence. However we add it all up, we face the fact that
he told much of what he experienced, little of what he felt.

He had the reportorial outlook [his grandson comments]. He wanted only to set things down as they were or as he saw them, and never as he felt about them. . . .

This clear-cut objectivity is encountered throughout, even when he reported what happened to *him*. So much so that taken in large doses, it is like a disembodied voice of history speaking to you as he travels down the Missouri, climbs the Chisos, listens to Lincoln, describes an Indian ambush.

The fifty years which O. W. Williams spent in the town of Fort Stockton could not have offered much in the way of drama — except for three or four years in the 1890's when trouble stalked the streets. As a brave and public-spirited man County Judge Williams had to bear a part in it.

The central figure in the feud (for that is what it was) was Sheriff A. J. Royal, an Alabama product who had grown up in Texas. As a young man he had operated a saloon in the cedar-brakes town of Junction and allegedly had been indicted for murder when he and his partner got into an argument with one of their patrons. This was in 1884. In 1889 he had moved to the Pecos country, buying some farm-and-ranch property eight miles west of Fort Stockton.[40]

Royal had many good traits. He was an excellent family man and agreeable in company. He was quick-tempered and aggressive, however, and after he became sheriff in 1892, his conduct in office aroused a great deal of opposition. Reportedly, he killed at least one man, and there were rumors of others. His constituents began to wonder who would be next. They resented his manner, which they described as overbearing.

He came to blows with Judge Williams. At the beginning of his term of office, he asked the Judge to keep his books for him. Williams agreed and named a price which Royal said was too high. He undertook to keep the books himself but found himself unequal to the task and approached Williams again. Williams agreed as before, but named a price twice as high as his first one. Without argument Royal accepted this figure, but later when the Judge presented his bill, Royal struck at him. Williams was slender but tough and in excellent shape. In the bout which followed he gave as good an account of himself as he could, but he finally yielded to superior weight and muscle. He naturally harbored resentment.[41]

The Rooney brothers, James and Frank, who made their headquarters at Koehler's store (which James Rooney and H. H. Butz later owned) were heavily involved in the bad feeling against Sheriff Royal. Frank was county and district clerk and had crossed swords with the sheriff in the courthouse. By the summer of 1894 a great deal of tension had developed. Shooting had been narrowly averted more than once. An outbreak was expected at any moment. On the sixth of August it almost came. Sergeant Carl Kirchner of the Rangers reported four days later on the facts as he understood them:

The trouble is between Sheriff Royal and the Rooney brothers. They were on opposite sides in the last election and have had trouble ever since. Royal being a very overbearing & dangerous man when under the influence of liquor. It seems some one told Rooneys Royal was coming to clean them out & a short while after Royal stepped in pistol in hand & Rooney fired a load of shot at him but missed. Royal returned the fire but he also missed. Royal then tried to get a posse to arrest the Rooney boys but he could only get four or five men. Rooneys are law abiding men & would have given up but say they are afraid of being murdered. However they only remained in the house a short while when they agreed to surrender if they were protected which they were and gave bond to await the action of the next Grand Jury.[42]

The battle at the store had its comic aspects. Rooney fired from a storeroom at the rear of the building just as Royal appeared at the door. Royal ducked sideways and reached around the door frame to return the fire, not risking a look at his target.[43] Shortly afterward he rode out of town.

Word was sent to the ranch headquarters of County Judge Williams, and he too got on a horse, making a dash to Monahans, fifty miles away, where there was a telegraph station. He wired Adjutant General Mabry to send Rangers lest there be open war. A company was stationed at Ysleta near El Paso, 250 miles west, and on August 9 Sergeant Kirchner and four privates got off the afternoon stage at Fort Stockton, finishing a four-day trip.

In view of the seriousness of the situation, Williams considered it necessary to report periodically to the Adjutant General by letter. On August 12 he told how he had appointed "some armed and determined men peace officers" and thereby held the lid on until the Rangers arrived. He noted that the trouble had been building up for something like four years and was too deep-seated to be eliminated at once. The Rangers, he thought, would be

Pecos County Jail and Courthouse, 1883

O. W. Williams lived in the jail for a short time after arriving in Fort Stockton. Later, as County Judge he occupied an office and conducted much business in the courthouse.

O. W. Williams in 1903

Picture was taken soon after Williams had settled down at Fort Stockton to practice law. He was now approxmately fifty years old.

MAIN STREET OF FORT STOCKTON, 1908
Williams' office was the adobe building on the extreme right.

CROSSING OF COMANCHE CREEK
Business center of Fort Stockton (1908) is seen in background. Rear of Williams' office is shown on the left. The main springs are below this crossing, which is relatively shallow.

needed for several months, since there was an election coming up in which Royal was expected to run. "Under such circumstances it seems to me that we ought to have this protection. If we do not, blood is almost certain to flow and it may come anyhow."[44]

It was expected that whatever was going to happen would occur on August 20 when Royal was to appear before Judge Williams in County Court to answer charges that had been made against him. Other charges were to be heard in District Court on September 4. Williams wrote to Mabry on August 20 that "people have been very careful — yet today we are on the verge of serious trouble at County Court, and to-morrow may witness a killing. Everybody goes armed, and shotguns and rifles are a common sight in hands of citizens ordinarily peaceable and law abiding. The feud is liable to become open war at any time & is certain to continue with deepening intensity until after the November election. . . . Now finally let me add that the county clerk is afraid to go to his office in the courthouse—for the liability to assassination,—& that some of our citizens have refused lucrative employment & are preparing to move and you have some idea of the terrorizing that is going on."[45]

Thanks, probably, to the Rangers, the break did not come in August. It still had not come at election time when Royal lost out at the polls. On November 21 it came.

What happened has been an undiscussable secret for seventy years, but the lore of Pecos County says that nine prominent men of Fort Stockton banded themselves together for the purpose of eliminating the ex-sheriff. They ate together, slept together, and planned together until they found a way.[46] The fact that everybody who visited Fort Stockton was apt to bed down with a blanket on the floor of Koehler's store may be behind this bit of folklore.

Another tale which has circulated *sub rosa* says that three of the men drew straws to see who would kill Royal. The one who drew the short straw turned pale and said, "I cannot do it." One of the others thereupon said, "I can." And he did.

A third rumor which has been passed down "on good authority" reveals that those whom Royal had threatened got up a purse of $500 and paid one of the Rangers to do the job. Those who believe this tale point out that Kirchner's men did not try very hard to identify the killer.

On November 21 County Court was in session and Royal appeared before it. It is said that the sheriff asked Judge Williams if he should disarm the prisoner. Williams looked around and said he guessed not. "If you do," he remarked, "he will be the only unarmed man in my court."

Royal succeeded in getting his case continued, and at four o'clock in the afternoon court was adjourned. Judge Williams stayed at his desk to write up a few notes. Royal walked down the hall to the sheriff's office beside the east door of the courthouse and sat down to confer with his attorney, a schoolteacher-lawyer named H. L. Hackette. A third man, a deputy sheriff, was also in the office.

The nine men are said to have been stationed from top to bottom of the courthouse to be sure their victim did not escape. As if to make things easier for them, Sergeant Kirchner and Private Schmidt, in the words of Kirchner's report, "had stepped down to a saloon nearby to see if everything was quiet."[47]

At that moment somebody — we shall never know who he was — came to the door of the sheriff's office with a shotgun in his hand. Royal was sitting with his back to the door but turned partially around when he heard his name called. The charge of buckshot cut him across the back at the height of his shoulder blades, ranged upward, broke his neck, and killed him instantly. The assassin put the gun down by the door and vanished. The nine men, if there were nine men, and if the nine men were in the courthouse, came running from all directions asking what had happened. Judge Williams saw nobody when he got out into the hall. He remembered later that the washroom door was slightly ajar as he passed it. Somebody may have been inside.

The feud went no farther. Royal had nobody close enough to him to take it up. But it is still best not to talk too much about it in Pecos County.

After the Royal business was over, the years passed more or less peacefully. The children grew up, went away and came back periodically. Oscar and Sallie Williams passed middle age and began to feel the infirmities of advancing years. Sallie developed a heart condition and weakened perceptibly. In the summer of 1925 what seemed to be an obstruction in her throat put her in the hospital at Alpine, but she responded to treatment and came home. Then, suddenly, on August 25, she was gone. Her husband described her passing in one of his most touching letters to his son in China.[48]

One can imagine his loneliness when she left, but he refused to leave his home. His son Clayton made a place for him at his own house, but the old man would not occupy it though he ate his meals there. Eventually Waldo and his wife moved into the old place to look out for him, but the time came when Waldo began to die slowly with cancer and needed all the care his wife could give him. The Judge gave them a farmhouse and once again he was alone — and he remained alone until a broken hip sent him to the hospital just before he died.[49]

In the years after Sallie's passing he began to live almost entirely in memory. "When you have come to white hairs," he wrote to Jesse on March 10, 1930, "you will understand the longing with which old men look back on the friends and scenes of the golden days of youth." In his own case the longing was accompanied by a compulsion to record. It was an obsession with him, but there was so much to write about that he never got through it all. "I must write it up some time, as I believe I am the only living actor on the stage," he remarked in 1930 about the Last Chance mining litigation.[50] The need to get it all down was constantly on his mind.

He must write up so much [his grandson is speaking] — *must*. No one felt quite as strongly as he did the necessity of perpetuating the old days. He had no time, himself; was growing too old. *In Old New Mexico* concludes with "to be concluded later," as many of his brochures did, but I don't think it ever was concluded. There was too much to "write up" as he grew older, his pen hand shakier; and as he saw his oldest comrades dropping off around him, he felt even more "the only living actor on the stage." There was little he could do about it, however, but trust that his descendants would grasp the tales as he told them, store and file away the facts and the dates and the names and carry them on for posterity. And so he passed out his pamphlets; and so he droned his long stories. . . . His purpose was purely impersonal but urgent; what he had seen and done, and what he knew, were worth passing on, and by thunder he was going to pass it on!

He might have passed on much more if time had not run out on him.

At ninety [the grandson remembers], the bright, hard mind began to show the cracks and strains of age, though the eyes were still piercing under the bushy white brows, the complexion brick red with health, the walk upright. Deterioration of body followed hard upon the decline of his mental capacities; so at 93 we had to face a sight that none of his admiring and often intimidated grandchildren ever believed possible: Oscar W. Williams, stock of the family, prototype of the scholarly, strong-willed man who faced west, now a bowed and halting nonagenarian so meandering in his mind that he would say to me, his namesake grandchild: "Oscar, you say? Why, isn't that strange? The name Oscar runs in our family too . . . a long way back."

Until this dotage crept upon him, memory sustained my grandfather. He indulged continuously in recapturing the past and marching it before his mind as an army. This repetition of things that had been finally served to blot out things that are; so while he would forget what was told him fifteen minutes ago, he could recall in sharply outlined detail the happenings of his childhood in old Carthage, Illinois, decades before. And on whatever pretense, he would begin to call up the dead for us, and for all visitors, with stately address, distant gaze, as if what he told were being unreeled on an inward screen before him.

Memory was all he had left. He even stopped reading his great books in the months before his death on October 29, 1946. "In the years when he gradually dropped his practice, and could have delved into many an uncut tome, we find him reading pulp adventure magazines picked up at the corner drugstore."

Why not? His work was done. He had told much of what he knew; and if he never went back and finished his recollections, he had done far more than most men of his day to inform posterity of what went on at a time and place about which we can never cease to be curious.

NOTES

(for the Introduction)

1 O. W. W. to Captain Jesse C. Williams, Hong Kong, China, July 28, 1935.

2 Oscar Williams III, *My Grandfather and the Tales of Natividad,* unpublished essay submitted as a class exercise at Texas Western College in 1944. Oscar was an El Paso newspaperman who died suddenly and unexpectedly in El Paso, August 24, 1948. His sensitive and perceptive discussion of his grandfather's work and personality will be quoted frequently in this introduction.

3 Austin: Von Boeckman-Jones Company, undated.

4 DAR Lineage Chart of Jesse Caleb Williams and Mary Ann Collier; Clayton W. Williams to Samuel D. Myres, June 23, 1964.

5 O. W. W. to Captain Jesse Williams, Shanghai, China, March 8, 1931.

6 Juárez Archives (microfilm, Texas Western College), Reel 50, 0-116, 0-123, 0-131.

7 O. W. W. to Mrs. Fernando Sanferd, Palo Alto, Calif., undated.

8 O. W. W., *An Old Carthage Home.*

9 O. W. W. to Mrs. Jessie Williams Hart, Carthage, Ill., June 11, 1928.

10 Undated biographical sketch of O. W. Williams, author unidentified, in possession of Clayton W. Williams.

11 *An Early College Year in the Hills* (pamphlet). See also *An Old Carthage Home.*

12 *Diary,* Tuesday, February 3, 1875.

13 *An Early College Year in the Hills.*

14 O. W. W. to Captain Jesse C. Williams, Hankow, China, June 3, 1925.

15 O. W. W. to Mrs. Jacob Pirkey, June 10, 1930.

16 O. W. W. to Captain Jesse C. Williams, Shanghai, China, March 10, 1930.

17 *An Early College Year in the Hills.*

18 Austin W. Scott (retired law professor), Cambridge, Mass., to Clayton W. Williams, June 4, 1964.

19 Wednesday, November 4, 1874. (All dates refer to entries in Williams' diary.)

20 Saturday, December 5, 1874.

21 Monday, December 21, 1874.

22 Monday, November 16, 1874.

23 Saturday, March 13, 1875; Saturday, March 20, 1875.

24 Saturday, April 3, 1875.

25 Saturday, May 8, 1875; Wednesday, May 5, 1875.

26 Saturday, December 5, 1874.

27 Saturday, February 6, 1875; Monday, March 29, 1875.

28 Monday, March 29; Tuesday, March 30, 1875.

29 Saturday, March 6, 1875.

30 Monday, Tuesday, July 3-4, 1876.

31 *In Old New Mexico* (pamphlet).

32 *Ibid.*

33 Letter dated May 4, 1881.

34 Clayton W. Williams, Notes to *In Old New Mexico*, MS.

35 *Ibid.*

36 Undated clipping in possession of Clayton W. Williams.

37 Clayton W. Williams, Notes to *In Old New Mexico*, MS.

38 Waldo died on August 10, 1946, in Fort Stockton. Mary Ermine, born February 21, 1885, died on November 21, 1950, at Fort Stockton. Susan Kathryn (Mrs. F. G. Walker) lives at Alpine, Texas. Clayton Wheat, whose years of research have provided much of the information used in annotating this volume, was born April 15, 1895, and lives in Fort Stockton. Jesse Caleb was born April 15, 1899, and now lives in Fort Stockton.

39 Webb to Williams, Austin, March 14, 1942.

40 O. C. Fisher, *It Happened in Kimble.* Houston: The Anson Jones Press, 1937, 234-235.

41 Interview with O. W. Williams and Waldo Williams, Fort Stockton, July 29, 1944. This was Waldo's story. He had been interested in Clyde Royal, the Sheriff's daughter, and may have had it from her family.

42 Kirchner to Mabry, Adjutant General's Files, Texas State Archives, August 10, 1894.

43 Clayton Williams, El Paso, Texas, December 7, 1964.

44 Williams to Mabry, August 12, 1894, AGF.

45 Williams to Mabry, August 20, 1894, AGF.

46Mrs. Laura Ratchford Fromme, Elgin, Texas, June 6, 1943; Waldo Williams, July 29, 1944.

47 Kirchner to Mabry, November 22, 1894, AGF.

48 August 30, 1936.

49 Clayton Williams to S. D. Myres, December 1, 1964.

50 Letter to Mrs. John Muir, 1930, quoted by Oscar Williams.

Part I

Surveyor
on the Staked Plains

From Dallas to the Site of Lubbock

"Muddy" Wilson and the Buffalo Stampede

The Big Snow of 1878

SURVEYOR ON THE STAKED PLAINS

From Dallas to the Site of Lubbock

HEN OSCAR W. WILLIAMS, fresh from Harvard, arrived at the town of Dallas, Texas, in the early spring of 1877, a new and distinctly different life opened up to him.

A young man of twenty-four, possessed of superior intelligence and a burning curiosity, he reacted at once to the unique character of the Southwestern frontier; and for his remaining sixty-nine years he manifested an ever-growing interest in the area he had chosen for his home — in the land itself, in its animal and plant life, in its people and their history.

At the time of Williams' arrival in Dallas, it was the center of a rich farming area and the gateway to the western Plains country of Texas with its extensive sweep of cheap virgin lands. The town on the banks of the Trinity had already achieved remarkable growth and now proudly bore the name "Queen of the Prairies." Its population had by then increased from 403 persons in 1855 to approximately 7,000 in the town limits and 15,000 in the county as a whole.[1]

The railroads, which had reached Dallas in 1872-73, were chiefly responsible for this development. Yet, in addition, there was a significant and ever-expanding "wagon trade" with the counties to the west that stimulated the economy.[2] During 1877, sales of cotton in Dallas amounted to $3,500,000. Total sales of wheat came to $2,500,000; jobbing and retail drygoods, $2,518,000; groceries, $2,231,000; hardware and implements, $1,300,000; drugs, $500,000; lumber, $1,000,000; and hides and wool, $500,000.[3]

Williams doubtless considered these factors in deciding to seek his fortune here. Soon, however, he became disenchanted with Dallas and the opportunity it offered. On March 24, the day after his arrival, he noted in his diary that the streets of the town were "very muddy with very few and very poor pavements. The ground is sandy and I fancy there is an abundance of dust here where the soil dries." Even worse, from his standpoint, was the fact that Dallas had almost sixty lawyers already, all competing aggressively for the limited business available.[4] And finally, Williams

soon learned that in spite of his LL.B. from Harvard, he could not
qualify for a license to practice law in Texas.[5] On April 16 he noted
in his diary: "Every day I become more satisfied that Dallas is
much overdone in the line of lawyers and that I . . . would have a
hard time settling here."

He was thus obliged to find other employment in Dallas, move
to another place or return to his home in Illinois. Fortunately, an
opening materialized almost at once. Less than a week after he
had arrived, he began negotiating with J. S. Daugherty of the firm
of Daugherty, Connellee and Ammerman, land agents, for a "position on a surveying and land locating party starting for Western
Texas in May." On April 18 he noted in his diary: "Finally made
arrangements with Daugherty, by which . . . I am to go West to
the Pan Handle [sic] with their party. We are to be gone about
three months." The next day he began getting together equipment
for the journey.

This decision was one of the most important of Williams' life.
It introduced him to the unexplored Southwest — to its rawness,
vitality and challenge. It led to experiences that few men have
lived through and recounted. These experiences broadened his
horizon as only life on the Plains of Texas could. They matured
him and made him more tolerant of his fellowman, while they
confirmed and strengthened his deep moral convictions.

The purpose of the trip to the Panhandle that Williams and his
companions would soon undertake was to survey some of the vast
public lands of Texas, in order that they could be sold to homesteaders. To encourage the building of railroads and to promote
the settlement of people, the State of Texas issued land certificates
to the railroad companies entitling them to survey, and to register
in the General Land Office, sixteen sections of public land for each
mile of trackage built; provided the land had not already been
appropriated.[6] Having on hand an abundance of these certificates,
the railroad companies disposed of many to land agents such as
Daugherty, Connellee and Ammerman, by whom Williams was
now employed. The agents bought the certificates at $40 to $50 a
section, surveyed and filed on the land, then sold it for $160 to
$200 a section. For some time the agents found this business to be
quite profitable.[7]

At the time of Williams' journeys to the High Plains in 1877-79
— he made at least three — the region was largely unsurveyed and
unsettled. Remnants of the rapidly diminishing buffalo herds still

ranged over the grasslands; a few bands of Indians not yet effectively confined to reservations, especially numbers of Comanches, were still at large. Several ranchmen like Charles Goodnight had established themselves as far west as the Palo Duro Canyon. But for the most part, the area was open country, and in the years immediately ahead it would be occupied only by herds of cattle.[8]

A high tide of settlement in Northwest Texas had been reached in 1876, when more than 400,000 persons entered and established homes, chiefly in three tiers of counties. The top tier was composed of Cook, Montague, Clay and Archer counties; the middle one, of Wise, Jack and Young counties; and the bottom one (irregular and farther south), of Comanche, Mills, and Brown counties. Most of the land in these counties had been surveyed, preempted and sold, or was being held for sale.[9]

Williams' activities as a surveyor centered in a zone to the west of this group of counties — that is, considerably beyond the points of sparsest settlement. On their first trip, the surveying party moved north along the east line of Archer County; west along its north line, and on west along the north lines of Baylor, Knox, King, Dickens, Crosby and Lubbock counties. After arriving at their destination, the party worked within the great square composed of Crosby and Lubbock counties on the south and Floyd and Hale counties on the north.

According to the report that Williams later made to the General Land Office ("Crosby County, Sketch 5," included in this book as Appendix I), the survey involved a meander up and down Blanco Canyon from Dewey's Lake, and down Yellow House Creek from the north line of Lubbock County to the site of the present city of Lubbock.[10] The survey extended to the mouth of Plum Creek and included Block C in Floyd County, Block R and others in Hale County, and Blocks A, B and O in Lubbock County. "Sketch B," which Williams filed with the Land Office on November 7, 1877, indicates that the surveying party was charged with the responsibility of correcting errors in an earlier survey.[11]

Block O of Lubbock County, which Williams and his companions surveyed, is of special interest, since the city of Lubbock is located within it. The block is near the center of the county; it is relatively narrow but long, measuring only one section from north to south and six sections from east to west.

The surveying party traveled slowly overland by wagon, with some members riding their own horses. They took along a minimum of equipment and food; they camped in the open and lived to a considerable extent off the country.[12]

In carrying out their assignment, the surveyors operated deep in buffalo and Indian country largely unknown to white men. A decade would pass before the area would have sufficient population to justify the organization of county governments.[13] Williams regarded this first trip to the Plains as high adventure. His story about it is significant, not only for the incidents themselves, but also for his fresh and discerning way of viewing and describing them in the account that follows.

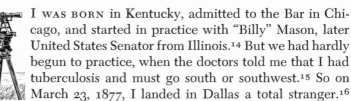

I WAS BORN in Kentucky, admitted to the Bar in Chicago, and started in practice with "Billy" Mason, later United States Senator from Illinois.[14] But we had hardly begun to practice, when the doctors told me that I had tuberculosis and must go south or southwest.[15] So on March 23, 1877, I landed in Dallas a total stranger.[16]

I had planned to start there in the practice of law for a livelihood while recovering from my lung trouble. But I soon learned that there were then many people in Dallas afflicted as I was, and also that I could not get a license to practice until I had lived in the State of Texas for a year or more. So my plan had to be changed. I made this change very satisfactorily, due to two features of my former life: first, because of my birthplace; and second, because I had had training in civil engineering under Professor Wilson Harding, uncle of Richard Harding Davis.[17]

At that time there was a firm in Dallas known as Daugherty, Connellee and Ammerman, who had been comrades at the University of Kentucky, and Kentucky-born.[18] They were engaged in "locating" lands out of the then unlocated public domain in the ancient Llano Estacado and selling them, principally to people from the states of Kentucky, Illinois and Missouri. Some of the prospective buyers went out to view the lands with the surveying parties. The firm was about to send out such a party, and needed a transitman; so I was employed.[19]

On the 29th of the following May the first part of our proposed surveying party left Dallas and camped for the night on a creek fourteen miles out.[20] Here we had a general introduction to each of the six members. B. B. Cork, a hard-featured but good-tempered man, a son of West Virginia, reported himself as an ex-Texas Ranger, stationed at Camp Radziminski when the Civil War broke out in 1860, and later a

Confederate soldier. He proved to be one of the best men of our party. Grovner and Pyle came from the pine woods of Michigan, Grovner being our future cook, energetic and high tempered but a good cook. Young Pyle was a placid, patient boy, ruled by Grovner. Then Sweatt told us how staunch a member he was of the Christian Church at Dallas, but his camp stories always carried him into drinking saloons and disreputable dances, never into any church.[21]

Pierson was our wagon driver. He was a small, lean, dark-featured man, who gave us a high-quality story of countries and adventure, and complacently patted himself on the back. He was a Gascon, he said, and, after listening to his yarn, we believed the secondary meaning of that name could well be claimed by him. A French soldier in Algiers, he had fought the Arabs and Bedouins in African deserts. Later as a soldier in Mexico he served under Maximilian;[22] he had barely saved his life by getting into Texas. He now lived in Eastland, Texas, where he was a kind of protection against the Indians of the Plains. He had handled all kinds of war horses; we could have had no safer driver.[23]

On June 1 we crossed the Brazos without needing a ferry, as the river was low and the bottom hard. We passed through Granberry, and made our night camp about eleven miles beyond the town.[24] About six the next morning we came to a small store and post office on the north side of the stage road, which was named to us as Bluff Springs.[25] Here I had a short talk with an individual who, I learned afterwards, was the claimant of a notorious name.

Coming to the little store, three of us were discussing the unusual pronunciation of some English words used by people whom we had met on the road. Such words as settlement, government, and cantonment were spoken by them with the stress on the last syllable. Just as we came to a man standing at the end of a small sidewalk facing the road, the suggestion was made that this might be due to the presence of Mexican people, whose language favored such an accent. This man called out to us: "No, gentlemen! They are native here and to the manner born."

Now a year before this I had heard Edwin Booth in *Hamlet* and I recognized the quotation. So I stopped to hear the stranger's argument, while my companions went on. I saw a man of about forty years, a little above medium height, with long black hair and whiskers, black eyes and dark complexion, dressed in a rather shabby suit of black clothes — quite a remarkable figure for those days and that country. His argument was not very cogent and was larded with quotations from Shakespeare and Sheridan. I could not stay to hear him through, but I was interested and put to him a question impolite for those days in West Texas: "Where did you come from?" I long remembered his hesitancy in answering, "From Georgia." Many years later I understood that hesitancy, when I read a book written by a Texas lawyer setting him up as John Wilkes Booth, resurrected from his grave in the Potomac.[26]

After passing Stephenville[27] we left the old stage road and headed towards Eastland, where we arrived on June 4.[28] This town was a kind of frontier headquarters for Daugherty, Connellee and Ammerman. Here we found awaiting our arrival two gentlemen who soon afterwards did much to start the first migration of white settlers into the Yellow House and Canyon Blanco country.[29] Paris Cox was planning to find homes for Quakers from Indiana and other states.[30] E. M. Powell, of the Dallas firm of Powell and Gage, was an agent seeking to sell land to immigrants going to the Plains of West Texas.[31]

It was decided here at Eastland to change our party's original plan of work. Our party, headed by Ammerman, was to go northeast to Jacksboro[32] for some necessary information and to survey a line running between several counties due west to the border of New Mexico. Connellee was to take Cox and Powell, with any other land prospectors, northwestward by way of Fort Griffin to the Canyon Blanco country.[33]

The two parties were to meet somewhere on the South Plains. In Eastland we lost our man Sweatt and gained some new members for our work ahead: the two Davis brothers, the two Martins and Willis. We could have had others at the same wage of $20 per month and cartridges *ad libitum,* as the town seemed overcrowded. The three doctors were certainly physic enough for a population of less than two hundred people, and the eleven lawyers alone would have filled up the courtroom in the log courthouse. The single well of water in a nearby creek bottom furnished the water for the entire town, but not all the liquid refreshment.

Tuesday, June 5, 1877: Beef soup for breakfast — so the day opened for us. Most of the day was spent in a bustle incident to a start. Ammerman busied himself laying in a few supplies and hiring some additional hands. In the afternoon I went out to the country to get a horse that had strayed away. I had to ride about five miles out on a sandy road, through heavy timber and under an extremely hot sun, on a slow horse. This was bad, and I am afraid I said some bad words when I rode back — through that same sandy road, under the same heat, and through the same timber — but riding a slow horse and leading a slower one. I have never been hotter, I think. For twelve or fifteen hours afterwards, the backs of my hands sweated and ached from the sunburn which they had received.[34]

On our way to Jacksboro, on June 7, we camped for the night three miles out from Breckenridge, and the next morning went into the bustling little town on a beautiful knoll, covered with a few houses and many tents.[35] We were offered town lots for sale by a zealous agent at $50 to $100 each, all on the Public Square, but we had no time for dickering and no money for buying. We camped that night on bad water and in the teeth of our first norther. On the ninth I saw my first sod house enclosed by a sod fence, just before we again crossed the Brazos River; and, at 3:00 P.M., we came to Graham, which was a small town of good houses, good-looking citizens, and no saloon.[36] A cold night, added to the snoring of our Gascon, gave us ten bad hours.

On the 10th, about ten miles out from Graham, our party camped on Rock Creek, while Ammerman, Kyle and I went into Jacksboro to get necessary information from the office of the surveyor of the Jack Land District[37] concerning the work ahead of us. Mr. Callaway, the surveyor, carried the records of all surveys made under State authority up to that time in a strip two counties wide, extending from Archer County to the eastern border of the then Territory of New Mexico.[38] That night we went to sleep in camp west of Jacksboro, with the sound of the bugle from old Fort Richardson in our ears. We had heard during the day that a band of Comanches had left the Reservation at Fort Sill and were on the warpath in the very country in which we were to do our work. A detachment of soldiers from Fort Richardson was then out on a scout for them. So the sound of that bugle rather helped us to get a good sleep.[39]

The next day, June 11, after work in Surveyor Callaway's office, we took our dinner of the three frontiersman's foods — bacon, beans, and bread — in a little valley east of the town, out of which runs a beautiful spring in an old deserted ranch. The story goes that it was an early cattleman's ranch headquarters, built to serve against Indian attacks. The ancient stone house is very solidly built around the mouth of the spring, and contains loopholes for defense against attacks from every quarter.[40]

The next day, the 12th, Ammerman went to the Keechi Valley[41] to find a guide to pilot us to the old Initial U. S. Monument on Red River so that we could check our own work with it, but the price set ($125) was too heavy, and he came back alone. So we went back to our party's camp on Rock Creek to enjoy a good supper of wild turkey and to welcome a stray dog to our party as a night sentinel against Indian attack.[42]

On the 13th of June we began to run a northerly course, formerly marked by Surveyor Callaway for the west boundary line of Jack County,[43] in order to locate the northeast corner of Archer County, from which our survey was to be made due west to the New Mexico boundary.[44] But owing to transit trouble and to our Gascon driver and wagon becoming lost for a time, it was not until noon of the 19th that we came to that corner of Archer County and began to go west.[45]

By this time our boys were taking much interest in the animal life of the country, principally for food but also for experiments and tall stories. Cork killed a rattlesnake, skinned it, and put the skin fresh on the back of his saddle, where it stuck as well as if held by Spaulding's Glue. Douglas Davis caught a live prairie dog by pouring a stream of water into its hole; on a similar later attempt, he brought to the surface a skunk, which he declined to bring into camp. For several nights thereafter he slept by himself and ate away from the common table. Murdock Martin caught a small green snake in his arms, scared our Gascon, and finally tied it around the dog's neck, with the result that Martin was thrown to the ground by the dog's frantic moves. At another time I saw Martin catch a medium-sized coachwhip snake by the tail, whirl it around his head a few times like he might whirl a whip, and then with a jerk — off went the snake's head.

On the 19th of June we ran our line six and a third miles west from the northeast corner of Archer County, and on the 20th, about 9:00 A.M., we came to a very large prairie-dog town.[46] At our noon hour we camped near a large trail going east, over which at that time passed two wagons to the east, one carrying two men and the other three. In spite of this assurance, we kept a guard out at night.

On the 21st we were passing over a beautiful country tenanted by prairie dogs, antelope and jackrabbits galore, and at about 1:00 P.M. we came to the Big Wichita, which gave us some trouble. We finally camped on a small island during a heavy rain, which caused more trouble.[47] The rising waters forced us to move back to the river bank from our island, and we had to wait there until noon of the 25th before we could get our wagon to the other side.[48] A blue catfish made our only fresh meat, and the party was given only two meals a day. This caused the two Martins and Willis to saddle up and leave us short in our working force.

Nevertheless, we took up our line again after crossing, and ran west about three miles to the northwest corner of Archer County. The next morning (26th) we ran eight miles by noon through a country marked by a great number of glistening skeletons of buffaloes, apparently slaughtered one or two years earlier. There were two spots of ten acres each, on which we estimated that there were about a hundred skeletons lying closely together, as the result of a hunter's getting what was called a "stand."[49] After noon of that day we ran eight and a half miles into the edge of what was in those days known as the "Hades" of the Wichita, and about 6:00 P.M. crossed a big trail, which our boys from West Texas called "The Famous Colorado Cattle Trail."[50]

On the 27th we ran fourteen miles into the outskirts of the Wichita Hades and were told by some cowboys of that trail that there were buffaloes around us, which news greatly interested those of our party who had never killed one. That day I killed a rattlesnake, put its head in an ant bed at night, and the next morning got its fangs clean of flesh. After a run of fourteen miles we camped at night at the northwest corner of Baylor County,[51] with a damaged transit.

Delay in repairing the transit allowed us only seven miles of run on the 28th. At the second mile on the north line of Knox County,[52] the needle showed strong signs of mineral attraction to the south and southeast of us. The next day we crossed the Salt Fork of the Wichita into a country of high rocky points marked by cedar or juniper trees. All morning of the 30th we were along that Salt Fork. Here we saw our first buffaloes; Grovner and Kyle each killed his buffalo, and the party laid off work to save the meat.[53]

We put in all of July 1st salting meat, but started our line again on the 2nd, and ran through several herds of buffalo and one herd of wild horses. We got in the afternoon our first good drinking water in some days, but camped that night at the foot of a high hill without water or good grass. On the 3rd, at the Fifth Mile Post, between Cottle and King counties, we came on some hunters' wagons in camp near some fine springs, and afterwards passed by some high mountains.[54]

On the morning of the 4th we came to a stretch of small oaks three to six feet high and known to hunters as a "shinnery." At dinner we learned that Grovner and the Gascon, with the aid of our dog, had caught a buffalo calf. Not being able to coax it with them, they had tied it behind the wagon, where of course it was choked to death. We stopped work early to hunt for water, which we at last found two and a half miles from our line, tenanted by two sets of buffalo hunters. As it was a favorable spot to check up on our work, we spent the 5th trying, without success, to find as a landmark some corner of the Jonathan Burleson Survey.[55]

The next day we again ran west and made night camp on what we suspected to be a headwater of Burford's Creek. The little antelope

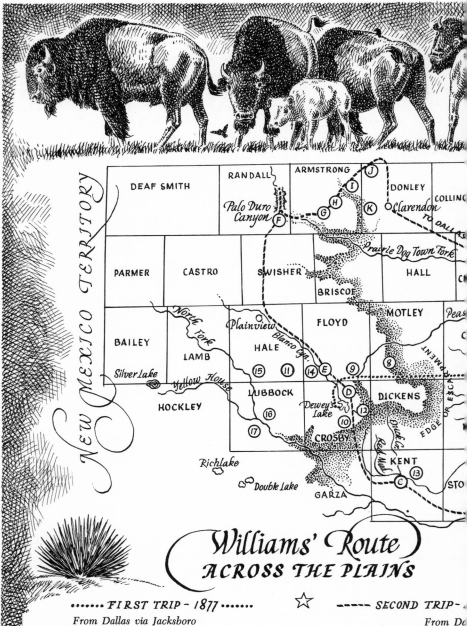

Williams' Route
ACROSS THE PLAINS

•••••• *FIRST TRIP - 1877* ••••••   ☆   ----- *SECOND TRIP -*

From Dallas via Jacksboro

(1) Set mount at NE corner of Archer Co. (2) Wichita Hades. (3) Colorado Cattle Trail. (4) Indication of minerals, S and SE. (5) First buffalo sighted. (6) Several buffalo herds. (7) Buffalo hunters in camp. (8) Edge of Escarpment. (9) Survey south to Dewey's Lake. (10) Turn north up Blanco Canyon. (11) Locate land for Judge Good. (12) Back to Dewey's Lake and down Blanco Canyon. (13) Turn back to Floyd County. (14) Set S.W. corner, Floyd County. Survey west. (15) Down Yellowhouse to Blocks A, O, S, Lubbock Co. (16) J. R. Cook comes to Williams' camp. (17) Survey around site of Lubbock. Return to Dallas via Rath's Station and Ft. Griffin. (See Williams' text.)

From D

(A) Pass
belt. (C
(D) Sto
into Cro
Palo Du
(H) Cau
ranch. (J
Co. (K)
Return t

OKLAHOMA TERRITORY

Red River

EMAN | WILBARGER | WICHITA | CLAY
⑤ ④ ③ ② | ① MONTAGUE
Henrietta
Montague

a River | BAYLOR | ARCHER
IOX

KELL | THROCKMORTON | YOUNG | JACK | WISE
Ft. Richardson | Decatur-1878
Brazos R. | Jacksboro

Sta. | Ⓐ | Graham
Cn. | PARKER
Ft. Griffin | Weatherford

STEPHENS | PALO PINTO
Breckenridge | Palo Pinto
PALO PINTO

iffin | Eastland | Granbury
| HOOD 1877

buffalo hides. (B) Enter gypsum
n of Salt Fork and Duck Creek.
ch. (E) Begin surveys extending
e and Lamb counties. (F) Enter
"Muddy" Wilson joins party.
mpede. (I) Pass over Goodnight
ray Co. Turn south into Donley
y rain and flood at Clarendon.
om account of George A. Grant.)

Stephenville
ERATH

J. CISNEROS

which I had caught yesterday was not faring well, as we had no milk and it would not take cornmeal with water as a substitute, nor would it drink fresh animal blood. On the 7th, Douglas Davis caught a buffalo calf and gave it to Ammerman, who hoped to carry it back to Dallas with him. But his calf and my fawn died in our camp that night in a shinnery, and were buried in the sands. The following day we ran five miles, and then tied up a connection with Jackson Springs, where we spent the remainder of the day.[56] Here I caught my first sight of the Llano Estacado.[57]

Standing out against the western sky there was an immense barricade, level with that sky — stretching north and south, and marked by recesses, parapets and peneplain like a Middle Age fortification of Vauban design. The great fault appeared so abrupt to us that at first thought it seemed impossible for us to carry our wagon and equipment up to its top. And had our line been carried a little farther north, it would have been a serious task. But, as we later found, that line carried us up a long and comparatively easy ascent to the level top, and most of the way we had no more trouble than in the lower country.

On the 9th we ran some eight miles over a rather rough country, and camped near a good spring which dripped with a noisy splash from a rock ledge into a nice pool. We named it Jessamine Springs, but later I was told it was known as Roaring Springs.[58] Near it there were still standing in conical shapes the poles of some Comanche tepees, probably abandoned a year or two earlier.

Here we began to notice trees and plants which we had not seen in our survey up to this point, such as maidenhair ferns, grapes, wild currants and black walnuts. At this spring we enjoyed eating wild plums of a different species from those of our earlier days on the survey. We took this to mean that our continued rise in altitude had the same effect on vegetation that would appear in a level country from a difference in latitude.

After a sharp chase in the afternoon, Ammerman and I caught a buffalo calf. Again he planned to bring a calf back to Dallas as a pet intended for his Kentucky sweetheart, and again he lost out. The calf died that night. He then abandoned the plan, much to the relief of our Gascon, who had handled all kinds of war horses but never had had to ride in the same wagon with a buffalo.

On the 10th we passed some good springs about 10:00 A.M. and took dinner on the edge of the high plain of the Llano Estacado, here somewhat rough on the surface. Here the party caught sight in the distance of four animals supposed to be buffaloes, one of them white. So an elaborate plan was made to surround and kill a white buffalo while work was suspended. After two hours of wasted time, we closed in on three horses and a *white mule* bearing a Mexican brand. During the next two days several buffaloes were killed while our party was engaged in checking our line with surveys made the previous year by Ammerman.[59]

On the 13th we continued our county line west on the Plains until approximately north of the old Dewey's Lake corner on the lower end of Blanco Canyon, then ran south to it.[60] The lake was very small and seemed to me to be a remnant of an old beaver dam. We found there an old but well-marked wagon road, which someone told us was the Fort Concho and Fort Sill road.[61] It ran up Blanco Canyon, and later we learned that it was on the Mackenzie road of 1872.[62] We camped there for the night, and the next morning went back to our line on the High Plains.[63] On the 14th we continued our county line to Canyon Blanco, and with much difficulty got our wagons down the breaks, and went into camp some two miles below an unfinished house, generally described as Tasker's Ranch.[64]

We lay in camp all of the next day, and found camping halfway between us and Tasker's Ranch a family from Erath County,[65] going to New Mexico. Seeing our lights in camp the night before, they became alarmed and put out night guards, in fear of Indians. They now decided to travel with us as far as possible. This greatly pleased our boys, as there were two good-looking girls in the party whom they could visit for a time.[66]

On the 16th and 17th we ran up Blanco Canyon to where it ended at the foot of a high bluff. Here waters of rainfall dropped into it from a wide ravine running through the Plains in Hale County.[67] The Mackenzie road ran up the canyon also; but close to Tasker's Ranch where Crawfish Canyon comes into the Blanco, the road took up to the Plains for maybe twelve miles. It then came down into Blanco Canyon, crossed it, and then went out on the Plains, turning then to the north and west until it crossed the wide ravine.

On the 17th we camped with the Erath County family at the road-crossing near the Canyon head, where they had dug a well of good water. On the 18th we ran out on the Plains along the Mackenzie road, headed generally northwest. At the place where we crossed that ravine in Hale County, we "located" at the request of Cork, as agent for Judge Good of Dallas,[68] four sections of land by virtue of I. & G. N. Railroad certificates, to my best recollection.

In the afternoon a herd of buffalo, running fast upwind, crossed the road ahead of us, and our horsemen of course took after them. The buffaloes stopped in a lake of water; while they were drinking, four were killed. The country was dry and parched; we thought that the herd had scented water, had come on the run and refused to leave it until their thirst was alleviated. This was the only water we had seen in the twenty-two miles of our day's run, and we camped there.

The next morning we decided to go back to Blanco Canyon, as the country appeared to be exceedingly dry and we had not been able to learn, from any source, anything about it.[69] Our Erath County family left us to follow the road going north. The next year, in 1878, when I came to the end of that road on the western breaks of the Palo Duro Canyon,[70] I wondered how they fared, but hoped that the good lord of that canyon, Goodnight, had come to their rescue.[71] We camped that night where the road crossed the Blanco.

On the 20th we went back to Tasker's Ranch, and found the two masons who were working on the house to be much excited over the sight that morning of four Indians riding on the High Plains. We were now supposed to be on our way back to Dallas, leaving the masons alone in the Blanco Canyon — much to their discontent.

On down the Mackenzie road, buffalo were often in sight. In the afternoon I killed a two-year-old animal.[72] On the next day our Mackenzie road continued in a southerly direction through a large prairie-dog town; and in places through air loaded with stench from the carcasses of buffaloes recently killed, especially so between Catfish and Red Mud creeks. We passed through a large shinnery bearing acorns in sight. That night a buffalo plunged through our camp, fortunately doing no harm to any one of the prostrate men, but creating quite a panic among the animals and men, in which panic our Gascon jumped the highest and swore in two known and several unknown languages very fluently.[73]

The next day about dusk,[74] in the valley of the Salt Fork of the Brazos, we were surprised at meeting J. S. Daugherty, coming out with three land prospectors: Tyree of Gallatin, Tennessee; Daniel Boone of Eastland, and Hostetter of Pennsylvania. We camped at that spot without water, and after some discussion it was decided that our party would go back for more work on the Plains. So after a night's sleep we went back to Duck Creek, where we sent the two Davis boys and the Gascon and his wagon back to Eastland, and others of us took the road back to the Plains for more work.

A few days later, on the 25th, we camped in Blanco Canyon about a mile below Tasker's Ranch and laid over there a day preparing to continue our proposed county line to the New Mexico line. On the 27th we began running this line, beginning where it crossed the Mackenzie road on the Plains west of Blanco Canyon. At night camp we built an earth mound for the southwest corner of Floyd County.[75]

We found no water up to noon of the 28th, then left the line and took a course of north 42° east for the lake we had found on the 18th of July. We camped dry the night of the 28th. About 11:00 A.M. of the next day we came to the lake.[76]

On the 30th, while the party was getting prepared with water supply, I started afoot to follow our wagon tracks back to our county line and got there, hot and thirsty, about 2:00 P.M. I was worried because I had not been able to catch sight of our wagon, since I was following over a level plain where the wagon could be seen seven or eight miles away. When 3:00 P.M. came, with no wagon in sight, I knew something had gone wrong.

With the idea of "safety first," after some hesitancy I turned back on the county-line wagon trail, for that way led to the Tasker Ranch. It was a lonesome walk under a hot sun without water. When a coyote jumped out of a hole near me, I shot it with my pistol for its blood. But when I looked on a very scabrous skin, I turned away. At about sunset I caught sight of wobbling figures away ahead and something being waved high in the air. It was the men with the wagon and a flagman waving his rod. The party had lost the proper backtrack but had kept on south until they caught our county-line trail.[77]

On the next day about 9:00 o'clock, we got back on running our line and ran some seven miles, stopping east of a large ravine which appeared to course a little west of south. On August 1 we ran our county line into the ravine, then left it and surveyed down the ravine itself, which we decided later was the North Fork of Yellow House Creek. At nightfall we came to some springs around which were a great number of buffalo and antelope. There were many relics of Indian camps here, rather recently abandoned, and I picked up an odd saddle supposed to have been used by Indians, which I have kept to this day.[78]

During the next morning we surveyed to the west, on land now located in Block O of Lubbock County,[79] and found what we called the West Fork of Yellow House Creek. About a mile south of us and across that fork from us, we saw a herd of a thousand or more buffaloes stretched out a half mile long parallel to us, in the height of mating season. We quietly watched them for a short time; but suddenly, from end to end, that long line started a stampede away from us. We could see no cause for this, but the hunters had told us of the poor vision and acute scent in the animal. There was a light breeze blowing over us toward the herd; so we supposed our presence was detected from the air.[80]

We continued on down the valley below the junction of the two forks of Yellow House Creek, finding the stream bed furrowed in stretches to a depth of three feet and a width of five feet, while in other parts there was a wide, unfurrowed bed, with occasional dry ponds choked with the skeletons of buffaloes. In some places good springs fed the bed, and a great abundance of small catfish was to be seen. Some of these springs came up in the creek bed, but others came into it from the high hills of the Plains in the north.

About noon of August 3, as our wagon halted for dinner, our rear chainman raised a panic by running toward the party, pointing back up the mesquite-clad valley and yelling, "Indians!" Looking back I could see nothing moving, save a glimpse now and then of something red moving rapidly toward us. We promptly unhitched our animals, got out arms and cartridges and under our wagon lined our guns on the spokes of the wheels, ready for good shooting.[81]

But we were greatly relieved when we saw some horsemen clad in ragged clothes, one in a red undershirt, coming into an open glade and yelling, "Friends!" Their animals were staked on grass, the cook began to prepare a large dinner, and our party gathered around these new "friends" to listen to a rather dramatic story of a chase after Mescalero Apaches, ending in the death (as it then appeared) of a number of United States soldiers and some hunters, due to lack of water on the desert. The chief narrator was the red-shirted horseman, who gave the name of John R. Cook and later told the story in book form under the title *The Border and the Buffalo*.[82]

As I recall the story he gave, it ran about as follows: The Indians, returning from a raid in Texas, stole a number of horses from the hunters, who saddled to pursue them and joined a detachment of Negro soldiers from Fort Concho, following them under Captain Nicholas Nolan. The combined party had crossed the Yellow House above us and had been in a desert seventy-five hours with no water for beast or man; and the big trail had dwindled to a small one, owing to little detachments splitting off to one side or other.

So Captain Nolan called them to a conference. The captain explained to the men that the party was in a serious situation; that he was responsible for the movements of his men and officers, and that he had brought the officers and a scout into council for their advice. But he had no such authority over the hunters; he had asked them to the

SURVEYING PARTY, 1876

Surveyors like this group, headed by C. F. H. von Blucher, were har-
bingers of civilization on the High Plains. Permanent settlers followed
close behind. Williams' party was similarly dressed and outfitted.

CHUCK WAGON GANG ON HIGH PLAINS

During the 1880's cattlemen and their herds moved in and occupied
vast stretches of grassland. In a few years much of the area would be
fenced in and converted to farms.

HEADQUARTERS, TASKER'S RANCH

Oldest house on High Plains. Located in Blanco Canyon, about fifty miles northeast of Lubbock. Henry Clay ("Hank") Smith obtained the property from Charles P. Tasker, after the latter became insolvent.

MASONIC HALL, OLD FORT GRIFFIN

Erected in 1853. Photo taken in 1928. Williams stopped at the fort on his second trip to the Plains, in 1878.

council for such information as they could give, especially because some of them might have been in a battle with the Comanches two months before, somewhere in that neighborhood. He told the hunters that they were at liberty to guide their own movements.

The Army captain then called on the scout, José Tafoya[83] of Fort Concho — now San Angelo, Texas[84] — and asked him what he thought about the movements of the Indians. Tafoya replied that he believed that all of the diverging trails the soldiers had found would lead to a common point where there was water — that it was probable they would meet at the "Lost Lake." Had he ever been at that lake, and if not, what did he know about its location? Nolan inquired. Tafoya had not been there; and then he gave a story on which he based his theory.

Tafoya said that in 1859, when the Federal Government was having the boundary line between Texas and New Mexico established from the northwest corner of the Texas Panhandle to the southeast corner of New Mexico, his father was a scout for the party of soldiers and surveyors. After crossing the Canadian River and coming up on the South Plains, the party was halted because no water had been found ahead. José Tafoya was with his father when the latter was called on by the commanding officer for information. His father was asked the location of the nearest water on the route. He replied that he thought it was the Lost Lake, but could not be certain.

Tafoya said that the lake was about a mile long and one fourth as wide, with a draw containing springs and cottonwood trees coming into it. He had once been with a party long ago that had come down the Canadian River some distance and turned south on the Plains to the lake. He thought it lay southeast of them and close by, or it might have been east and farther away. Captain Nolan then ordered a further search, which was unsuccessful and was abandoned. This development gave the officer no hope of finding the Lost Lake.

Nolan then brought out an Army map, which he said carried notations of Bull Mountain as a camp on some military expedition, presumably with water. As near as he could estimate, it was not over thirty miles from them, and no better promise existed. So Nolan ordered his troops to march in that direction, as he took it from the map. The hunters after some debate took the back trail to Yellow House Creek, possibly a longer distance but with a certainty of water at its end. So it proved, but it was a long and bitter trail for men weak and harassed by thirst, some afoot and others on weakened or crazy horses.

Two men, mounted on the strongest horses of the party, got to the creek and took water and a short rest. Seeing an antelope nearby, they lay down in the ruts formed by buffaloes trailing into water; and by kicking up their legs high in the air, they tolled the animal close to them and killed it. They skinned it in such a fashion that they could use the skin as a canteen, and cooked some of its meat. After eating and resting a short time, the two hunters returned with water and food for their comrades, all of whom they rescued, save one who could not be found and was believed to be hopelessly lost.[85]

When Cook's whole party had rested at the water, they crossed to the north side of Yellow House Creek; they soon caught our wagon trail and followed it down the creek. When they came to our wagon, they felt safe. The saga of the hunters was then told. But not that of the soldiers. It was some time later when we learned that the command got to Bull Mountain water, with four men having died of thirst. So far as I know, no one has ever found that securely hidden Lost Lake.[86]

One of those hunters — red-shirted Cook — later came into the lime-light to tell the hunters' story in his book. But this happened only after I had heard a tragic report about him. In 1881, when I was in charge of the post office at Silver City, New Mexico,[87] there came into the office one day two men of that 1877 band of hunters — "Boston Charley" and "One Thumb" Foley, a former soldier. I knew their names and found that they had no mail. So when they came to my window, and before they gave their names, I told them that there was no mail for either.

Angrily one of them said, "How in the hell do you know?" I told them.

The other said, "That beats the devil!" — they still used hunter's language. I asked them about Cook, and was told that all they heard was "he had been hung for horse-stealing."

Some years later, in an English catalogue of second-hand books I saw listed *The Border and the Buffalo,* by John R. Cook, a story of the last days of the buffalo in the Texas Panhandle. Of course I sent for it. He could hardly have written it after a fatal contact with a rope's end, and Boston Charley's report was another case of a "Lost Lake."

On the 4th of August we continued our line down to what we knew as Plum Creek, a dry ravine coming down from the escarpment of the Plains to the north of us. All afternoon we had been hearing the boom of Sharps rifles.[88] At a pond on the lower end of Plum Creek we came to another band of hunters bathing in the water. From there, we went up the draw and north on the Plains, and camped for the night on a sandy stretch covered with large shin oaks, a growth known to the hunters as shinnery. The name originated with French trappers and derived from the French word *chene,* an oak tree.

That night in the shinnery was a very uncomfortable night for me. For more than two weeks we had had no horses with us other than the two wagon animals, owing to the uncertainty of finding water. On Plum Creek I had sprained my ankle and could not keep up with the wagon; so at nightfall I lay down to sleep in the sand, intending to get up early next morning in time to get to the wagon for breakfast. But my ankle was sore, and the sand did not make a good bed for an all-night sleep.

Sometime toward midnight I heard some noises like the grunting of hogs. Looking around in a dim moonlight, I saw near me a buffalo, apparently grazing and giving an occasional snort of some kind. Having in mind the danger of a stampede, I rolled over and got close to the nearest and largest shin oak as quietly as I could; but not quietly enough. The stampede came at once: for fifteen minutes I fairly hugged a very small oak. About 4:00 A.M. there was a repetition. When it was over, I got up and found our wagon tracks in the deep sand. I followed them in the faint moonlight until I got to the wagon. I then woke up the cook for a very early breakfast, just as Pyle was starting back to hunt for me.[89]

That day, August 5, we made Blanco Canyon, three or four miles below Tasker's Ranch. After leaving the shinnery, we came to a level grass plain, where our stray dog made his last play for camp favor. He was a stately animal of solid black color and fine form — a useful guard at night. He soon developed a habit of charging after fleeing buffaloes and throwing them into somersaults by pulling their snouts to the ground. After this he would set back on his haunches with his red tongue dripping, apparently laughing at the clumsy animal trying to regain its feet.

Then the dog would come back to wag his tail over the petting given him by the men, which appeared to give him great pleasure. The men came to give more attention to his performances than to anything other than the daily appearance of signal smokes in the high air, supposed by us to be sent up by the Comanches. It went so far that there was a nightly argument in camp over his name. Should we call him Crusoe or Jack?

But pride goes before a fall. Crusoe was no exception to the rule, and his fall came literally at the heels of a wounded buffalo — a kind of poetic justice. I think that even Davis found no pleasure in the event. His companions called it hard luck, while Grovner appeared to consider it as a special affront to him. It came after we had left the shinnery and were crossing a plateau, the last eastern point of the Llano Estacado jutting out high above the broken terrain below.

Ahead of us on the smooth plain we caught sight of a dark body apparently pressed close to earth and motionless. In that country in those days the buzzard was unknown and the coyotes were few and far between. We had found several carcasses of animals with the same odd appearance, with dried brown skin — almost mummified, covering fleshless bones — apparently undisturbed since the bodies were laid down in death. At first sight we thought that this was another story of the same kind, a desert burial under sun and air. But when we were about one hundred yards away, the dark body arose and took the shape of a huge buffalo bull with shaggy head facing us in battle mood.

The dog on first sight charged out from the wagon, and with a harsh growl headed straight for his hereditary foe; so we looked forward to another series of somersaults. But for the dog to bring this into play, it was necessary that the bull run from him; instead of doing so, the beast stood his ground and shook his head up and down in an angry invitation to close combat. The dog did not see fit to take this challenge. He swerved to the left and, catching a view of a short tufted tail wagging high in the air, made a leap after his enemy's plume. The bull turned to follow the dog's motion.

As the buffalo did so, we saw that he was somewhat crippled from a wound. He had been lying in a puddle of water not much larger than his body but large enough to give some relief from the fever caused by his injury. The wound slowed up his movements so that in turning to follow the dog's attack he was able to turn only fast enough to keep the dog at his rear end. There followed a circling movement of both animals for ten or more revolutions, the dog jumping for the tail, and the bull occasionally varying his turning motion with a vigorous kick at the dog. While this was going on, our wagon and party had passed by the scene of combat and were leaving it behind us.

We were possibly fifty yards away and moving on, when somehow the bull landed squarely against the side of the dog a tremendous kick that threw Crusoe fully twenty feet in our direction. He fell on his feet, running toward our party but looking backwards at his enemy. As the buffalo took no steps after him, he turned his head to face us and stopped as if in mute interrogatory about what he should do. But no sign or sound came back to him other than our continued movement away from him. After a few moments of pause, he came trotting to us, head hung low, tail dragging on the ground, and a trick of the eye that seemed to say, "Do not blame me."

"Jack is giving up his fight," said Davis.

"Better say that Crusoe could not basely desert his masters," countered Grovner.

Now the dog never again met a buffalo in war, and from that episode to our arrival at Eastland he was "Jack" to our party. There we turned him over to Charley Connellee as "Jack." Several years later he went to the Indians' "Happy Hunting Ground," where he may have found the wild white cattle that Crusoe's ancestors hunted so long before Jack was born. If so, it was Crusoe who came "home from the hills," and we fancied that some Army officer at Fort Richardson was long lamenting the mysterious loss of a scion of ancient nobility.[90]

On the 6th of August, Daugherty, Ammerman, Boone, Hostetter and I went down to Mamie's Brook to look at some land that Hostetter might want; from there, on the 7th, the others took the road for Fort Griffin, while I went back up Blanco Canyon under directions to survey out for Tasker the upper and lower leagues of Eastland County school lands. I did this work and set stone corners on the 8th and 9th. On the 10th I surveyed out the section on which lay the ancient beaver dam known as Dewey's Lake.[91]

Somewhere on this stretch of road I saw a mode of hunting which I had never seen before and will never see again. We came to the top of a low ridge overlooking a valley with a small creek, fringed with cottonwoods and bordered toward us with open prairie. Looking down on that prairie we saw two horsemen riding at full speed, one going east, the other west. Each rode fast some distance, slowed down, stooped down by his horse's neck and then raised back in the saddle. The two rode to a common point where we then caught sight of a wagon top under the trees, leaving us much puzzled. But when we came to the wagon, we were shown two wild turkeys caught afoot by the riders, exhausted by their long flight of about a half mile.[92]

A few days later, our party took the road back across Rock, Red Mud and Duck creeks to camp one night by a clear gypsum spring on Double Mountain Fork, some two miles out from a kind of hunters' headquarters known as Rath City, consisting of one store, two saloons and a dance hall.[93] Early the next morning we heard some shots fired at some point between us and the "City." On our way in, we came to a bend in the road where there were signs of recent bloodshed. In the town we were told that "Spotted Jack" had been killed that morning at that spot, but no one was able or willing to tell us why or by whom he was slain. Later we learned that he was a noted horse thief; but that was all we got out of the story.[94]

Passing on by Flat Top, near California Creek we met a band of Tonkawa Indians sporting highly colored calicos by the yard in the breeze, with squaws and horses.[95] They claimed to be going on a buffalo hunt. At the Clear Fork we met a small herd of cattle being driven, it was said, to the canyon ranch of Tasker. On the 17th we got into Fort Griffin and camped close to the wigwams of the Tonkawa Indians.[96]

Before going into the fort, we had at the noon camp a visitor in the shape of an Indian, who introduced himself to me as Peter Punk, "whiteman's friend," asking gifts. He handed me a dirty letter of introduction signed by an Army officer. It ran after this fashion: "Peter Punk asks me to give him a letter to all white people, as a friend of theirs. Maybe he is; maybe not. But certainly he is the damndest thief in Texas, so watch him like a hawk." As a token of our kindness we gave him some tobacco, and honored him with Tyree as a special guard to set him on the road in the proper direction for the old fort.[97]

Here at Fort Griffin, I met Tasker, owner of Tasker's Ranch, mentioned earlier — a young man of about twenty-eight, a good-looking blond, scion of the house of Morris Tasker & Co. of Philadelphia, whose exhibit of a pipeline water delivery system I had seen at the Centennial Exposition in that city in 1876. Touched with tuberculosis, he had come West for a cure; but instead of taking the outdoor route, he was specializing in cards and drink, I was told.

On the 18th we took the road for Dallas, via Eastland and Granberry, and arrived there August 28 with some forty buffaloes and eighteen antelopes to our credit as hunters.[98]

"Muddy" Wilson and the Buffalo Stampede

FOLLOWING HIS RETURN to Dallas at the end of August, 1877, Williams spent a few days drafting field notes relating to the survey just completed. On September 3, he took the M. K. & T. train to St. Louis, thence on to his home in Carthage, Illinois.

His diary from September 6, 1877, through February 11, 1878, records: numerous visits with relatives and friends; the sale of three sections of land along the "Doub Mt Fork [sic] of the Brazos";[99] work on tax titles for a local law firm; work at abstracting; side trips to Keokuk, Quincy and Indianapolis, and to Mount

Vernon, Kentucky; gay parties at Christmas and New Year's; regular attendance at church on Sundays; and two visits to the doctor, who informed Williams that his lungs were sound but that he had bronchitis.

On the trip to Indianapolis, December 15, Williams met a former roommate from Harvard, George A. Grant, who promised to join him later in Dallas. On February 11 the two met a second time in Indianapolis, and the following day they left together by train for St. Louis; from this point they came on to Dallas, arriving at 9:30 P.M., February 15, via the M. K. & T.

For the next several days Williams was occupied in various ways. He made maps, read law, attended a sale of horses, went to church, and planned a trip to Fort Concho. His diary for the period from March 3, 1878, to June 2, 1879, has been lost. Fortunately, however, his companion George A. Grant gives us an adequate account of their visit to the Staked Plains in 1878.[100]

Williams undertook this second surveying expedition for the Dallas real-estate firm of Powell and Gage. The objective was to "locate" public lands in an area north of the territory Williams had covered the previous year.

E. M. Powell and E. L. Gage were land agents operating somewhat like the first agents with whom Williams had been associated — Daugherty, Connellee and Ammerman. A broadside published at the time by Powell and Gage shows that they were alert and aggressive in locating, surveying, patenting and selling public lands.[101]

The most desirable area available at the time consisted of some thirty thousand miles of rolling grassland, an area about the size of Indiana. The land was situated west of the Indian Territory between the 33rd and 36th parallels. Powell and Gage described it as "a gently rolling prairie . . . generally a black loam of great depth and fertility, and well suited to the growth of grain, vegetables, and fruit, as well as one of the finest grazing regions of the United States. These lands are free from swamps and miasma, and the climate equals that of Colorado for health." The price asked was $200 a section or 31¼ cents an acre.[102]

The surveying party consisted of ten men: E. M. Powell of Dallas; M. A. Frazell of Kirkwood, Illinois; O. W. Williams of Carthage, Illinois; Dennis Varcoe of Honesdale, Pennsylvania; J. H. Myers, S. A. Thompson and Richard Grayson, all of Philadelphia; G. H. Kent of Davenport, Iowa; F. H. McQuestion of

Manchester, New Hampshire; and George A. Grant of Meriden, Connecticut.

The party got under way early in April, 1878. Heading westward, the small wagon train passed through Grand Prairie, Decatur, Jacksboro, Graham, Fort Griffin and Reynolds City (Rath's Station), then went on to a point some fifteen miles south of the junction at the fork of Yellow House Creek. Here the men began their survey. The survey, according to Williams' report to the General Land Office in "Crosby County, Sketch 5," extended down Yellow House Canyon in Lubbock County and up the North Fork of the Yellow House into Lamb County. As a result of the survey, certain blocks in Lubbock, Hale and Lamb counties were tied to a point 650 varas south of the southeast corner of Dewey's Lake.[103]

While on this assignment, Williams saw one of the last large herds of buffalo on the Plains. The preceding winter thousands of buffalo hunters had come to Texas from the north, where many of the herds had already been destroyed. Using their perfected techniques of wholesale slaughter, the hunters during the months of December, 1877, through June, 1878, literally decimated the animals that had roamed the extensive prairies of Texas.

In the following pages Williams describes the stampede of the buffalo herd he encountered and his subsequent meeting with "Muddy" Wilson, one of the last buffalo hunters on the Plains.

 ON A HOT SUMMER DAY in 1878, our surveying party, with G. H. Kent, Dennis Varcoe, M. A. Frazell and other tenderfoot prospectors,[104] came out of the head of Crawfish Canyon, going west to start surveying at a small rock corner in Block O, Lubbock County. I had built this corner the year previous, on a survey in that block some two or three miles east of the present town of Lubbock.

Some time in the afternoon we caught sight dimly of some objects moving north across the bare horizon to pass our forward march at a right angle. Soon after, we could make out a man on a gray horse with a gray dog following, and an open wagon drawn by gray or white oxen. When in line with our path of progress, the procession stopped. On coming up to it, we found the solitary horseman to be a rather handsome red Indian of about thirty-five years, who greeted us in English of as good grammar and pronunciation as we could boast.

He explained that he was a buffalo hunter now on the road to Omaha, Nebraska. The big Southern herd, he said, was now either killed out or scattered into such small fragments as to make his business an unprofitable one, and after considerable time spent in vain in the search for what might remain of that herd, he was then abandoning the range.[105]

The hunter further said that he had been feeling somewhat bad that morning, and upon catching sight of our approach, decided to wait for us in the hope that someone of our party might have some kind of medicine suitable for his trouble. Here G. H. Kent, one of our band of prospectors, became much interested. On starting out, he had loaded up a huge valise with specifics for every disease imaginable in our country, even for yellow fever; he was especially proud of his collection of remedies for hydrophobia and the bite of rattlesnakes. Up to this time there had been no call for anything out of his apothecary's shop, and the great inconvenient piece of luggage had caused much ridicule to be aimed at him.

So it was with much satisfaction that Kent heard the hunter's statement. The march of our party was halted while Kent made a diagnosis of the Indian's troubles and ransacked his drug store in a learned search for the proper specific. The Indian was much pleased with his zeal in the matter, and upon learning that our course for the next three or four days would probably carry us to the north, much on the line of his route to Omaha, he yielded to the earnest solicitations of Kent and announced that he would travel with us for several days.

That afternoon we came to our proposed starting point at the little rock corner on the boundary of the survey in Block O, Lubbock County. With the transit and chain we turned north to meander the course of the shallow ravine, which we knew as the North Fork of the Yellow House, a typical Arabian wadi in which the water never ran except just after a heavy rainfall.[106]

The second night we camped at a pond of water about a hundred yards in diameter. On our arrival, a drake and a duck were seen swimming in the very center. The Indian got out his heavy Sharps rifle, the customary arm of the buffalo hunter, and after a quick aim over his "sticks," shot off the head of the drake.[107] The duck arose and, after a short circle in the air, landed in the water near the body of the drake. Again the rifle was laid over the sticks — and then the head of the duck floated beside that of the drake, and the big gun was put back in its sheath. Then the gray dog went into the water and brought out the bodies of the two birds. After this exhibition of skill, we were willing to admit, first, that the Indian was entitled to call himself a hunter and, second, that Kent's thaumaturgical specifics had not ruined the hunter's skill with the rifle.[108]

It was not often in those days on the Llano Estacado that a trail made by wild animals could be found. But there was a well-beaten narrow trail of that kind plainly visible for nearly a mile down the wadi from this pond. The existence of other signs, such as a small growth of tules, or reeds, and marshy ground, led us to believe that this was a permanent watering place fed by some kind of spring. We also found a very dim, slightly worn trail of a wagon leading up the ravine from the spring at least as far as the Sand Hills.

Later we learned from hunters we met east of the Cap Rock that this watering was known to them as "Las Aguilas," which might be termed in English, "Eagle Springs." We had found on coming to the Llano Estacado that a line of Spanish names marked the natural objects along the eastern border of that great plain, from the Canadian River on the north to Tobacco Creek in the south. There were in succession the Cañoncito Blanco, the Palo Duro Canyon, the Tule Canyon, Blanco Canyon and the Casas Amarillas (Yellow Houses) on that fringed border; while out on the plain itself were the Lagunas Rica, Tahokia, Azul, Negra and Lobo — and other names of Spanish origin.

East of the plain this type of name disappeared. It seemed to us that the eastern "rim rock" of that Staked Plain was the "Ultima Thule" of the Spanish-speaking peoples of the valleys of the Pecos River and the Rio Grande in their exploration towards the east. Their prerogative of names began with the western edge of the plain itself and ended with its precipitous wall on the east, where they could look down on the great valleys of fertile soil that were in time to become the domain of the Anglo-Saxon invader.[109]

We camped at Las Aguilas that Saturday night. At supper time a rather violent sandstorm blew up. To protect his cuisine, the Indian laid his big wagon sheet in a drapery from the front to the rear wheels of his wagon, and on the leeward side of that bulwark he cooked and dined on the fruit of his rifle. He had refused our invitation to eat with us. After our supper that evening, George Grant and I went over to his campfire, and behind that shelter of the draped wagon sheet, we drew from him as much of his story as he saw fit to relate to us.

His English name was "Muddy" Wilson. He was born in the north-eastern part of the then Indian Territory, a member either of the Wyandot or of the Delaware tribe.[110] I do not recollect now which of the two tribes claimed him, but his father was a chief or an influential man of one or the other tribe. At an early age he and a sister had been taken from their people and placed for education in Oberlin College in Ohio, where his sister had taken to books and the white man's ways very thoroughly. She had married some naval officer; at that time she and her husband were stationed on an island on the New England coast at the mouth of a New Hampshire river, where many years later at President Theodore Roosevelt's invitation the Treaty of Peace between Russia and Japan was drawn up and signed.[111]

But, as Muddy said, there was too much "hell" in him to endure the humdrum life of the schools. He finally ran away from the college, and after some years of wandering became a scout for the Army at some of the posts in Kansas. After that, he had become a buffalo hunter. When the Southern herd was cut off in Kansas and driven south, he had followed the drift and had come down into Texas. He had made his headquarters for two years past at Fort Concho (now San Angelo), and had been associated with Charlie Vroman, who had each year outfitted him for his winter's hunt. The last winter's hunt had not been very successful, and the prospect ahead was even less promising; so he was on his way out for some other occupation.

On the next day, Sunday, we remained in camp all day at the springs and gave our jaded animals a rest. Myers and I took our rifles and went out afoot to hunt. About two miles from our camp we caught sight of a pair of buffaloes slowly making their way toward the spring. Being blessed with great good luck, we managed to kill both of them. This brought much contentment to our party. For many days we had been without fresh meat and vegetables; bacon, coffee and bread only, three times a day, had become quite monotonous. But the Indian shook his head. To him the fact that the two lone buffaloes were wandering about together at a season of the year when these animals ordinarily gathered in great herds meant that here was added proof that there were no more big herds to be found, and his occupation was gone.[112]

On Monday the transit and chain began to lead our wagons up the wadi of the North Fork through the southwest corner of Hale County and into Lamb County.[113] We were getting into lands virgin to the surveyor. The section of land which we here surveyed out was afterwards patented to William M. Weber of Mount Vernon, Kentucky. It was the first tract of land in Lamb County on the patent rolls of the State. Up to that time the map of that county in the General Land Office was only a blank sheet.

We had found no water on the surface after leaving Las Aguilas; but on coming to the dry, bare bed of a pond in the wadi, which appeared to have been filled with water at one time, we dug down a short distance and found water. It had a bad taste, as it was shallow water in an arid country. We then surveyed out Weber's section to include the dried-up bed.

Here we turned north, and after passing over some miles of sand dunes covered with a growth of quite small shrubs, we came out on a wide bare plain. We had no knowledge whatever of the country ahead of us, and we were somewhat alarmed lest we suffer for water. Then we came to a depression in the plain, which seemed to run east and west, and down which surface water might run after rains. Searching along this draw, we came again to a dry bed of a former water hole. At one end there was the round hole of a crawfish. Dropping into it a particle of the hardened mud brought out by the crawfish, I heard it strike water. Here we camped for the night, using the underground water.

This stretch of valley land pleased our prospectors. We therefore went east, following the course of the wide, shallow ravine and coming, after some miles, to a spring of sweet water rising from a sand-rock stratum and running as a small stream some miles farther east until the earth finally swallowed it. Later we learned that this stream was sometimes described as "Running Water," and sometimes as "Upper Catfish Creek." Its course led to the head of Blanco Canyon to the east, while to the west the source of that wide shallow draw was to be found over in New Mexico, surprisingly far away. It was always with us in those days a matter of curious speculation how such long, dry water channels as the North Fork of the Yellow House, the Running Water, the Tule and others could exist in such a desert country, pitted and pockmarked with what we called "dry lakes," and bearing no evidence of running in full length at any time.

Although there was a gracious promise in this warm red soil of bountiful harvests in the long years of the future, yet I believe that I have never looked upon any other country as destitute of the graces which go to make up what we call scenery as this plain which then lay before our eyes. The blue sky met the horizon of brown grass, then in the sere of a long drought, in a circle unmarked by tree, stone or hill, save a little undulation in the southwest where the sand dunes under the eternal southeast wind had risen in small waves. The margin of sky and earth danced up and down in heat waves just enough to throw doubt upon the wavering outlines of the dunes. But away from that margin there was no movement; even the birds of the air were not to be seen. Nor was there sound. There was no hum of bees — no chirping of crickets — no swish of a bird's wing — no rustling of leaves.

It might have been a dead world. But we could not consider it a desert, in the modern use of the word, so long as that spring kept up its flow and that grass sward lay so solidly on the dark red earth. With better grace we might have called it a desert (in the ancient sense of a country deserted by its former inhabitants), for of life and motion there was little evidence. Yet it was only a few hours until we saw animal life passing over it in great mass and swift motion, with the sound of falling water.

We ran our line of meander down the creek on the north side — two chainmen and two flagmen afoot — while I carried the transit from station to station on a gentle horse — wise to frontier life, as we soon learned. We had come some six or eight miles down the watercourse when, as I was setting up my instrument, the flagman asked if I had not heard a peculiar sound. I stopped my work to listen and caught a faint throbbing sound of somewhat irregular cadence such as I had heard two years before, when twenty miles away from Niagara Falls. It came from the north, and looking in that direction, we could make out what seemed to be a low-lying cloud sweeping down on us quite rapidly.

It was late July, so it could hardly be a norther. There was nothing in its appearance to lead us to suspect it might be a rain cloud. We were for a moment at a loss to account for it. Then we caught sight of dark objects showing up on the ground-front of the grayish white cloud and then dropping back from sight everywhere along its width from the eastern sky to the western horizon. Almost at once the cry went up, "Buffaloes! A stampede!" Immediately, we began to prepare to meet the storm. Looking back, we saw our wagon and our ambulance (passenger wagon) about half a mile away, apparently being lined up to meet the charge with the smallest possible front, but too far away for us to join them in time. So we prepared our little party to face the stampede on our own ground.[114]

We stood in single file, facing the oncoming herd. Our transit was set up in the middle of the file, with the last man holding the reins of my saddle horse. With the only rifle in the party, naturally I was at the head of the file, in order to split the passing animals by the firing of the gun — if they did not divide to either side on catching sight of us. There was no greater danger at the head of the file than at its foot; for once broken at the head, immediately the whole line would go down. It seemed to me inevitable that the mere sight of us would divide the herd; however, I might have been wrong on that point

We were not long in getting set for the rush of the buffaloes. But we were barely ready, when they were on us with a swirl of dust and a thunder of hoofs — yet so far as I could judge, they were absolutely mute. The front line was thickly packed shoulder to shoulder, and the eyes of the animals were cast back as if trying to see something behind them. When I realized this attitude of the buffaloes, I began firing the gun — although they must have been one hundred feet away — because it began to look as if they might run over us without seeing us.

The shot had no effect; I do not think the sound of the gun was heard by the animals. I concluded that we could not split them by sight; so I commenced to shoot as rapidly as possible, but without effect until they were a distance of about thirty or thirty-five feet. At this point I saw some of the animals in front of me begin to push their neighbors to one side or the other to make an opening in that crowded front line. That opening must have been about twelve feet wide when the front line passed us, although it seemed to me that I could touch a buffalo on either side with the point of my gun.

Behind this dense line there was no regular formation; the animals came on in loose order, gradually thinning out to the rear. As soon as I felt safe in doing so, I turned back to see in what shape the onrush had left our party. During the terrific uproar of the passing multitude, I had dimly made out sounds which might have come from the men or the horse behind me, and when I turned I greatly feared to find that some calamity had befallen us. But beyond a horse that was trembling, a party of four men exceedingly dust laden and full of strange oaths, there was nothing to show that we had been in any danger.[115]

After the big bodies had passed us, they plunged through the small tule-bordered creek. The water and mud lay spotted on the brownish-yellow grass for some forty yards out, while the banks and bed of the creek were streaked with the marks of the huge briskets and cloven feet. The water for a few minutes ceased to run. We saw no animals mired or bogged down; but if the stream had been wider, we were certain, some of the weaker lagging ones would never have gotten out to hard ground. We had seen along the larger streams numbers of places in boggy ground where the carcasses of these beasts were locked up thickly in dried mud, and we could now understand the reason.

As soon as the last of the animals had passed us, our vision opened to the west. We could see that our main party had weathered the storm and was begining to get ready to follow our march. We learned later that the herd was not so dense and heavily packed with buffaloes as at our point of contact; but the estimate made by members of our main party as to the number of animals in the stampede ranged far higher than ours: it was set by some of them at fifty thousand. It was impossible for us to make any reliable estimate, however, because neither party could determine the end of the flanks on the east and the west. But the herd was almost surely the last great herd of the Southern buffaloes after they had been cut off from any migration to the north, and after five years of the Sharps rifle in the hands of the professional hunters.[116]

We were getting ready to continue our meandering course; the forward flagman had started ahead when our attention was directed to some unexpected action on the part of our rear column. Wagons, animals and men had ceased moving, except only the Indian, who was walking rapidly away from them with the big rifle on his shoulder and the "sticks" in his hands. Some fifty or a hundred yards away he lay down on the ground, set up his sticks, and in the crotch placed his heavy rifle, pointing to the south. Something seemed to be in the air.

Looking to the south along the path of the departed herd, we were surprised at the sight of buffaloes turning back toward us. A small band of about one hundred had fallen out from the rear of the frantic herd when out of our view, and — led by thirst, apparently — were making their rather leisurely return to the waters of the creek. The Indian had noted this and, having halted the motion of our rear guard, was getting ready to go into action as a hunter.

We had noticed in places in that country the carcasses of buffaloes in large numbers lying in a small space — sometimes as many as fifty or more lying on a plot of ground not exceeding ten acres. The hunters explained this to us as the site of a "stand" gained on the animals, where they were shot down one after another without attempting to flee; but the explanation seemed to us almost unbelievable.[117] Now it began to appear that we might have the story illustrated before our eyes; so we sat down in quiet to wait on the play.

The waiting was rather dreary. When first seen, the little herd was more than a mile away and was coming towards our party of five in such a course as to present to the waiting Indian a side shot at the marching file. The animals moved along in a very deliberate manner, cropping at times the short grass. Now and then, a cow would stop to give nurse to a calf. But there were three or four large ones, apparently bulls, in the lead and they seemed to decide the general movements of the herd. When the leaders stopped to graze, the rest of the animals would gather together around them while feeding; and when they began to move, gradually the others would fall into a single file behind them.

The Indian was just as deliberate; it was not until the leading bulls were slowly moving in line about a half mile away that he fired. I was looking at the forward bull coming straight toward me and I had the illusion for a moment that I saw the bullet coming out of the beast on the side opposite the Indian. I really saw some piece of flesh or bone following out the bullet. The animals began to run, but speedily slackened up behind the wounded one. As it stood for a moment and then began to walk around in a gradually narrowing circle, the others here and there began feeding on the grass. In a short time it lay down. Some of the others came up to it, and then began bellowing, just as I have heard tame cattle bellow at the sight or smell of the blood of another of their kind.

As this ceased and the grazing began again, the large bulls strung out once more in procession toward the water until finally they were followed by the other animals. Then the big gun boomed; the big herd began to run, and this time they did not stop. Just after the big gun spoke, there followed the whip-like cracks of a Winchester rifle in rapid succession four or five times. Looking back, we saw the Indian with his rifle high in the air apparently about to strike Kent, who was backing away with a Winchester in his hands. The big gun, however, did not fall.

Muddy Wilson must have remembered in time the kindness of Kent when they first met. He stayed his hand, but we heard from our rear guard that evening that he cursed Kent bitterly as the cause of breaking the stand which he was about to secure. Successive shots had ruined a chance for us to witness a vivid example of the buffalo hunter's skill at his game. So we took up again our line of meander, while the Indian got his outfit together and began a lone trail after his prey.

We never saw him again, but once more he was brought to our mind about a month later when we got back to the nearest post office on our frontier. The postmaster told us that there was a reward of some fifteen hundred dollars offered by the Government for the capture of one Muddy Wilson, wanted for the killing of two Negro soldiers at some Army post in Kansas. When he asked us why we did not bring him in, we offered two reasons in explanation: first, that we knew nothing of the offer at the time and, second, that we had seen two headless ducks floating in the spring at Las Aguilas. Either excuse was sufficient, the postmaster agreed.

EARLIEST VIEW OF LUBBOCK

This photo was taken in the early 1890's, shortly after North Town and South Town were consolidated on Section 1, Block O, which Williams had previously surveyed.

LUBBOCK IN 1907

Rapid growth of the town is indicated. Yet horses and wagons are still important. First courthouse is seen on right, behind windmill.

REMNANTS OF BUFFALO HERD

On Goodnight Ranch. Williams saw the last herds on the High Plains and was caught in, and survived, the last buffalo stampede.

CHARLES GOODNIGHT

First rancher in the Palo Duro Canyon area (1876). He controlled an extensive spread centering on Armstrong County. As time passed, his holdings decreased.

The Big Snow of 1878

O SCAR W. WILLIAMS made a final visit to the Panhandle during the winter of 1878-79. He acted in this instance as a deputy surveyor of Texas, under authority of the Commissioner of the General Land Office. His primary assignment was to correct errors in surveys that had been made earlier in Hale and Swisher counties.

The surveying errors had led to conflicting claims among three groups of land agents, including the two firms for which Williams had previously worked. The Commissioner indicated that Williams must look to the agents for his pay. After the assignment was completed, he filed his sketch and field notes of the re-survey at the office of the Jack Land District, with headquarters at Jacksboro, on February 17, 1879.[118]

During this winter journey, Williams experienced a phenomenon of the Plains that had become well known to the people of Texas and to many outside the State — the sudden bone-chilling blizzard. Newcomers like Williams were especially impressed by this peculiar feature of Texas weather.[119]

The northers that plague the Panhandle result from the sweep of three distinct air masses into the region. One group of winds, cold and dry, comes in from Canada and Hudson Bay, along an unimpeded route over the Central Plains toward the south. Other winds — arriving from the Rocky Mountains — may range from warm to cold, and from moist to dry. The third component of Plains weather — the currents from the Gulf of Mexico — is usually warm and moisture-laden. The collision of these winds, varying in intensity and humidity and temperature, produces weather of great extremes, subject to rapid changes. Thus, a blizzard may arrive almost without warning and then disappear in a matter of hours.[120]

Williams recounts an experience on the Plains in 1878 during the coincidence of a blizzard, a buffalo hunt and a "brush with the Indians."

WE WERE A PARTY of surveyors seeking, under instructions from the General Land Office, to make connections on the ground between a corner near what was then known as Dewey's Lake in the lower end of Blanco Canyon and corners set along the region of Upper Catfish Creek in Hale County about a year before. The Dewey's Lake corner was tied to surveys along the upper tributaries of the Brazos River, while the Hale County corners were located by connections with surveys on the upper waters of the Red River. We were to determine the borderline of these different sets of surveys in Hale County.

Leaving the Dewey's Lake corner, we went up Blanco Canyon along an old wagon trail known as the Mackenzie Trail, said to have been made by Colonel Ranald S. Mackenzie in 1872 in his campaign against the Comanches and Kiowas. This led us to the mouth of Crawfish Canyon (coming from the west) and thence up on the Plains for a distance of some twelve miles, where we crossed the main canyon to its north border. From that crossing we followed the trail on the High Plains to a point somewhere near the southwest corner of the Callahan County School League No. 3.[121]

Here we left the trail and went in a northwesterly direction. Our immediate object then was a surveyor's corner, given in the field notes as an earth mound containing a bottle enclosing a paper which carried the words, " Center of Hale County." We arrived on a bright warm day near the supposed site and began search on an open plain covered with a well-matted sod of short grass. We searched diligently for that mound for nearly a whole day without success; later we were told that the surveyor had postponed erecting it until a convenient day, which had not arrived.[122]

That night a cold wind blew from the west, and the next morning we stepped out of our big tent into a deep snow and a frigid air — nothing in sight other than clouds above and snow below. We could make no search, so we waited for better weather. But the next morning brought no change except for the worse. Our horses, staked out for the night, were gaunt and shivering; our mules, tied to the wagon, had eaten up the wagon box, part of the sideboards, and as much of our tent ropes as they could reach. And the same lowering clouds hung over us. We had to make a change of site, and there was then in Hale County no house for ready shelter.[123]

The nearest refuge which we could gain was some twenty miles away at the head of Blanco Canyon. It cut deep back into the plain to end in a cove, two hundred feet deep and a mile wide, in which cottonwoods and willows would give us fuel and would furnish limbs and bark for our animals in lieu of grass. So back we started on a long, slow journey of a day and a night, trusting to our needle alone to guide us through the waste of snow; for we could not possibly follow the trail back to our wagons under the fourteen inches of snow.

It was a dreary ride until we caught sight of a small herd of buffalo slowly coming toward us a mile away and halting now and then, apparently to scrape into the snow so as to get a little grazing.[124] Then the cold was forgotten as we planned to lay in fresh meat for our appetites when we could find fuel. But that wide, level open plain did not promise success, because we had to stalk in the open; our weak, starved riding horses could not run down such hardy beasts in the chase.

We drove the wagon into a low swale ahead of us, hoping to avoid being seen by the buffaloes while we made our plans. Finally we decided that our only chance of laying in fresh meat rested in stalking the animals by the method known to the buffalo hunters as "wolfing." Summerfield and I were selected as wolves. We made up hats of suitable material as nearly white as possible. Next we got out our "slickers" — long coats made of waterproof materials of very light yellow color. Equipped in these garments and with each carrying his rifle, we started on foot, one behind the other, towards the game.

We wanted the meat; soon we got down on hands and knees and, one might say, "hobbled" along with the rifle in one hand, and the other hand helping the body movement. This movement is laborious under any circumstances; in the deep snow, Summerfield called it erroneously "hell" — the temperature was not fitting. I think we were about a hundred and fifty yards from the herd of some eighty animals scattered loosely in halting movements, when we saw some commotion among them.

Immediately they lined up to face us, bulls and cows in a front face, heads high in the air, and the calves behind them. We knew that we must act at once; so we rolled over on our backs in the snow, feet towards the animals. Laying our rifles against us, at the word we fired together. Instantly the herd was in flight, leaving one animal on the ground and another limping behind and badly wounded.[125]

We went up to the carcass, signalled to the wagon to come up and prepare the meat for use, and then turned to investigate how the buffaloes could have gotten any grazing under the deep snow. In doing so, we saw twelve to fifteen coyotes sitting on their haunches in a half circle around the dead body, waiting for their turn at the feast. They had probably sneaked along behind the herd for many miles on the chance of catching a forlorn weakling calf. As we went back over the trail looking at the signs of grazing, they scuttled away from us but kept within scent of the blood.

We found along this trail round holes in the snow, sometimes as large as a tub and often going down to the soil, which had been made by the buffaloes as they slowly moved forward. This discovery puzzled us until we went out into the snow away from the buffalo trail. There we found, standing out above the snow, tops of stalks in clumps of a grass known as sedge grass, which grew sparsely scattered among the low-lying grass known to us as buffalo grass. Then we understood that the animals began grazing on these tops and continued grazing down to earth.

One of our four men, Charlie, came up to us tbout this time, and after telling us that he had never killed a buffalo, asked permission to go after the crippled animal. After warning him not to get lost and to remember that our wagon trail lay to the left of the direction taken by that animal, we gave the permission, and off he went with his horse at a keen gallop.

When the meat had been cut and loaded in the wagon, we took up again our easterly course.[126] We had not gone far when we caught sight of a large number of objects moving westward on a course parallel to and not far from our own, and behind them three men on horseback. One of them rode over to us and told us that he and his comrades were driving a *caballada* of horses over the Plains to the Chisum Ranch on the Pecos River in New Mexico.[127] In order to have fuel for campfire and to carry some forage for saddle horses, they had cut willows and cottonwood limbs, and in travois fashion had loaded them on horses to meet the emergency of continued deep snow. They had heard our shots and had come to us in the hope of getting fresh meat. Their leader galloped on to the dead buffalo, drove away the coyotes, cut out some meat and rode off towards his comrades. Our Charlie, keen on the trail of the wounded buffalo, missed this byplay.

Our progress was slow. We pitched our tent early, because we feared that our Charlie was lost and that we must make a search for him. But our tent poles were barely covered, when in he came, much excited and declaring that Indians were close at hand. The boys laughed at this and accused him of trying to play a prank on them. This excited him more, and he said that he had found the trail of a large party within a mile of camp, had seen the trail of Indian tepee poles and knew that

Indians had passed quite recently. He offered to show us that tepee trail. The wink passed between the men, and one of them rode back with him to verify his story.

They came back with the word that the trail of the tepee poles was there, as Charlie claimed. Then, as the plan had been laid while the two men were away, it was agreed that fires would be extinguished and two guards set out at night. Much to his disgust, Charlie was told to be on guard on the south until about one o'clock, while another stood watch on the north. About midnight, back to the tent came Charlie, shivering with cold — to make a report, which was cut short on finding his comrade of the night-watch contentedly snoring in his blankets. This ended the play, and Charlie went to bed, sullen over the joke but inwardly rejoicing that he could sleep without being troubled by nightmares dragging tepee poles "travois fashion."[128]

The next day we moved down the canyon to await the melting of the snow and turned our animals loose under charge of one man to get such grazing as they could find in bushes or on grass under snow-laden brush, in addition to the night feed of corn. The next evening at sundown I looked out from our tent, expecting to see our animals being driven in for the night feed by the guard. Much to my alarm I saw our stock heading, not for our tent but for the pass out of the canyon which led to the south. They were taking the back track, a movement that travelers always feared when conditions did not promise the stock a full stomach. The guard was far behind in deep snow, with small chance of heading them off from the pass.

I thought that I could intercept them if I started at once; so I picked up a rope and off I went hurriedly, without extra wraps or even gloves. But when I got to the foot of the pass, they were halfway up. Night had come with a cold wind and a cloudy sky, so cloudy that at times I could hardly make out the forms of the animals. It was some six or eight miles farther before I could get ahead of them and catch the gentle old black mare that always led them. I put a nose-hitch on the mare and got on her bareback. I was very cold. For a time I tried to drive the other animals. But it was too dark to drive safely, and my only sense of direction came from the wind. So finally I put the old mare in the lead, trusting the others to follow.

I looked for a light, after a time, but saw none. I had about decided that I was lost, when I heard what was a most musical sound to me, the bark of our dog. Passing over a hill I came in sight of a small fire and coals of a beautiful red tint. After I had literally fallen off the old mare, I went into the tent to receive a dousing of snow and to thaw out in our tub, with the satisfaction of knowing that the mare (not I) had brought back every one of our animals. But I myself brought back a frostbitten right hand and right side of the face, and a case of chilblain.[129]

Some three or four days later, the snow had melted so much that we took our way back through slush and mud to the place where the deep snow had fallen on us. And again we searched for the fabled earth mound and storied bottle — again without success; we had to connect with another corner of equal significance. So it comes that at this good day, fifty-four years later, I have never seen that mound and bottle officially designated as "Center of Hale County."

NOTES

(for Part I)

1 On October 14, 1876, the *Dallas Weekly Herald* spoke of Dallas in these terms: "The Queen City — The Foundations of the Young Giantess of North Texas Laid Broad and Deep." The newspaper estimated the population to be four thousand. However, an estimate made the previous year was more optimistic: twelve thousand people in the town and twenty thousand in the county as a whole. *Directory of the City of Dallas for the Year 1875* (St. Louis, n.d.), 13. The figures in the text are an approximation based on these estimates.

2 *Ibid.*, 12.

3 A. H. Hill (ed.), *A History of Greater Dallas and Vicinity* (Chicago, 1909), II, 123; C. D. Morrison (ed.), *General Directory of the City of Dallas, 1878-79* (Marshall, Texas, 1878), 193-212. The leading newspaper of the town published other favorable reports about the flourishing community. *Dallas Weekly Herald*, May 30, June 20, 1874; Oct. 10, Nov. 4, 1876; March 31, Oct. 27, 1877; Jan. 19, 1878.

4 *General Directory of the City of Dallas, 1878-79*, 193-94.

5 A year of residence in the State was required for a license.

6 The management and mismanagement of public lands in Texas is a challenging story about which much has been written. For brief accounts, see A. S. Lang, "Financial History of the Public Lands in Texas," *The Baylor Bulletin* (No. 3, July, 1932), XXV; Curtis Bishop, *Lots of Land* (Austin, 1941), *passim*. The part that O. W. Williams and other surveyors played in the story is told interestingly in Sue Watkins (ed.), *One League to Each Wind* (Texas Surveyors Association, Austin, n.d.), *passim*.

7 C. U. Connellee, "Some Experiences of a Pioneer Surveyor," *One League to Each Wind*, 223-24.

8 Because Williams was on the Texas Plains during this important transitional period, he was later able to write authentic accounts of what he saw and experienced. This chapter of the book is concerned with the details of these early episodes in Northwest Texas. For a general account of the period and the area, see R. N. Richardson, *The Frontier of Northwest Texas, 1846 to 1876* (Glendale, Calif., 1963).

9 R. N. Richardson and C. C. Rister, *The Greater Southwest* (Glendale, Calif., 1935), 349-52; W. C. Holden, "Immigration and Settlement in West Texas," *The West Texas Historical Association Yearbook* (June, 1929), V, 66-86. (Publication hereinafter cited as *West Texas Yearbook*.)

10 The town of Lubbock was established on the plot that Williams had surveyed in 1877: Survey 11,523 (Section 1, Block O), near the center of Lubbock County. General Land Office, Map of Lubbock County, 1915. After completing the survey, Williams had visited his hometown of Carthage, Illinois. There, according to his diary for Oct. 16, 1877, he had sold this land to H. G. Ferris, a local banker and

investor. In June, 1891, the organizers of the town of Lubbock, who had succeeded in combining the settlements of old Lubbock (North Town) and Monterey (South Town), bought Section 1 of Block O from Ferris for $1,920 and moved the two communities to a place near its center. An election to organize the county had been held the preceding March. From that date until the town was incorporated, March 10, 1891, the commissioners' court of Lubbock County governed the town as well as the county. S. V. Connor, "The First Settlers," in L. L. Graves (ed.), *A History of Lubbock* (*The Museum Journal,* Lubbock, 1959-61), III, 45-81.

11 General Land Office, "Sketch B, Crosby County," Sk. File B, Jack District.

12 Surveying was essentially outdoor work. Moreover, the surveyors were constantly on the move; any unneeded equipment and provisions served only to impede their progress. For pictures of typical early surveying parties and their equipment, see *One League to Each Wind,* between pp. 260 and 261.

13 R. P. Smythe, "The First Settlers and the Organization of Floyd, Hale, and Lubbock Counties," *West Texas Yearbook* (June, 1930), VI, 17-34; C. V. Hall, "The Early History of Floyd County," *The Panhandle-Plains Historical Review* (1947), XX, 3-140. (Publication hereinafter cited as *Pan-Plains Review.*) After the Red River War in the autumn of 1874, the High Plains were regarded as relatively safe for white settlement. For an authoritative account of the pacification of the Indians in this area, see Ernest Wallace, *Ranald S. Mackenzie on the Texas Frontier* (Lubbock, 1965), *passim.*

14 William Ernest Mason was born in New York, July 7, 1850. He moved to Chicago in 1872, where he was admitted to the bar and began practicing law. He later served in the state legislature and in the United States Congress. James L. Harrison (comp.), *Biographical Directory of the American Congress* (Washington, 1950), 1343, 1512. Williams and Mason were briefly associated as young lawyers in the Chicago office of J. N. Jewett; they did not establish a law firm together. Williams, *Diary,* July 14-October 12, 1875. (Hereafter referred to as *Diary.*)

15 Williams' diary contains no entries indicating that he was dangerously ill. He did suffer from chest pains during cold and rainy weather, especially in a humid climate; however, he seemed normally healthy and energetic in the arid Southwest. Even so, he was always obliged to take good care of himself, since his respiratory system was inherently weak.

16 By 1877, when O. W. Williams arrived, Dallas had become a thriving town, boasting a new city hall and courthouse, running water supplied through underground wooden pipes, an artificial gas supply, and three mule-car lines providing rapid transportation over unpaved streets. W. P. Webb (ed.), *The Handbook of Texas* (Austin, 1952, 2 vols.), I, 456; II, 366-67. (Hereinafter cited as *Handbook of Texas.*) On the early history of Dallas, see J. H. Brown, *History of Dallas, Texas, from 1837 to 1887* (Dallas, 1887) and L. B. Hill (ed.), *A History of Greater Dallas and Vicinity* (Chicago, 1909).

17 In Williams' library at Fort Stockton will be found the textbook he used in the engineering course: John Gummere, *A Treatise on Surveying* (1853). The book is inscribed, "Oscar W. Williams of Carthage, Illinois, a student at Bethany College." From the standpoint of earning a living, the course in engineering proved to be one

of the most important in Williams' college career. Richard Harding Davis (1864-1916) was a Philadelphia-born journalist, novelist, playwright and social figure who enjoyed great popularity for a time. See S. J. Kunitz and Howard Haycraft (eds.), *Twentieth Century Authors* (New York, 1942), 351-52.

18 The firm maintained an office at 507 Camp Street, Dallas. *General Directory of the City of Dallas, 1878-1879*, 74. The partners were J. S. Daugherty, C. U. Connellee and J. B. Ammerman. *Handbook of Texas*, I, 393, 466. Connellee has left an interesting record of his activities as a surveyor on the Plains. *One League to Each Wind*, 217-28; also, see 318-20.

19 In preparation for the journey, Williams "bought a Sharps needle gun and a small Smith and Wesson pistol . . . got the rifle, belt, scabbard, box of caps, shells and mould for $10." *Diary*, March 29, 1877. Since Williams lacked money to buy a horse, he rode out in Daugherty's wagon; in exchange for transportation, he was to help the wagon master take care of the horses. Anticipating the return trip, he noted: "But coming back with Powell, I'll have to foot it, as the main party with the wagon will be out until October. . . . I am to get $15 per month. . . . In the afternoon I dressed up in frontier styles . . . broad-brim hat, gray flannel shirt, worsted coat, pants and vest and stoga boots." *Ibid.*, May 21-28.

20 The day was cloudy and windy. Williams found the water in camp to be "warm and bad"; so he drank the first coffee "that had ever passed my lips." *Ibid.*, May 29.

21 Throughout his life, Williams retained strict views respecting morals and temperance. On meeting men like Sweatt, he always expressed his disapproval, at least to the *Diary*.

22 Archduke Maximilian (Ferdinand Joseph) of Austria (1832-67) ruled as Emperor of Mexico from 1864 until his death. Captured by the Liberal troops of Benito Juárez, he was executed by a firing squad near the town of Querétaro in 1867. J. J. Kendall, *Mexico Under Maximilian* (London, 1871); W. H. Chynoweth, *The Fall of Maximilian* (London, 1872).

23 On May 29, the first day in camp, Williams saw his first scorpion. He also went with B. B. Cork to the creek for some fishing. "I didn't even get a bite (fish bite, although I got numerous mosquito bites) and left in disgust. Just about dusk two wagons came up and camped on the opposite side of the river. When supper was over and night came on, we laid down our blankets and slept in a row on the ground, except Sweatt who lay in the wagon on some four flour sacks. The wind blew heavy and cold all night, and I got no sleep until later and then very broken. Some of the boys were nervous about centipedes." *Diary*, May 29.

24 Granberry (Granbury), Texas, about sixty miles southwest of Dallas, is located on the Brazos River in the center of Hood County. It was first settled in 1854 by Thomas Lambert, whose colony united with the Stockton colony to form the nucleus of the town. Granbury, named in honor of General Hiram B. Granberry, became the county seat. A college was chartered here in 1873. By 1877, the town had a public school, a Methodist church and a newspaper. T. T. Ewell, *A History of Hood County, Texas, from its Earliest Settlement to the Present* (Granbury, Tex., 1895); Texas Historical Survey, *Inventory of the County Archives of Texas: Hood County* (San Antonio, 1940). Williams noted: "At 9 we reached Granbury and took on 1000 lbs.

of flour, for which I paid $45 leaving in my hands $5 for D. C. & A. Camped at a well for dinner and soon after starting again struck sandy post-oak lands, known as Cross Timbers. The travel through this was extremely warm and uncomfortable. In the evening we camped near a big spring about 11 miles from Granbury. Ate at supper a cake, which our cook made by aid of turtle eggs." *Diary*, June 1.

25 There is a Bluff Dale located in Erath County about fifteen miles southwest of Granbury, which probably is the place Williams referred to.

26 Williams made much of this story, retelling it in several of his letters. Although the story was widely current at the time, it is now generally discredited. Even today, however, the story is occasionally resurrected. See *San Angelo Standard*, June 27,
[1965.
27 At six in the afternoon of June 2 the party arrived at Stephenville "and camped about two miles beyond on edge of sandy country. S. is a nice place. In the evening heard a whippoorwill for 1st time on trip." *Diary*, June 2. Stephenville is located in the center of Erath County; it was named for John Stephen, who settled there with his brother in 1854. Vallie Eoff, *A History of Erath County, Texas* (M.A. Thesis, University of Texas, 1937).

28 Eastland, Texas, is located in north-central Eastland County, which was organized in 1873. Mrs. George Langston, *History of Eastland County, Texas* (U. S. Department of Agriculture, Washington, 1917); R. Y. Yancy, Jr., *A History of Eastland, Texas* (M.A. Thesis, University of Texas, 1940). The county seat was established originally at Merriman in 1874, but C. U. Connellee arranged to have it moved to Eastland in 1875, where he, J. S. Daugherty and others were responsible for building the courthouse there. Connellee sold enough building lots to erect "the finest jail west of Fort Worth," as leading citizens of the town boasted. *One League to Each Wind*, 221, 224, 319.

29 Yellow House Creek and Blanco Canyon are located about two hundred miles northwest of Eastland, near Lubbock. The Yellow Houses, in western Hockley County, were so named because they consisted of caves on a high bluff of yellow clay that resembled a city when seen through a mirage. J. E. Haley, *Charles Goodnight, Cowman and Plainsman* (Norman, 1949), 74-75. Blanco Canyon breaks into the Staked Plains (Llano Estacado), extending from southern Floyd County into northeastern Crosby County for about twenty-five miles. For a number of years preceding its settlement, hunters and traders used the canyon and the White (Blanco) River flowing through it. W. S. Mabry entered this area in 1873, going on north into the country of the Kiowa Indians. See "Early West Texas and Panhandle Surveys," *Pan-Plains Review* (1929), II, 22-42. Operating from his base at the mouth of Blanco Canyon, located southeast of present Crosbyton, Col. Ranald S. Mackenzie led successful campaigns against the Comanches in 1872 and 1874. In the spring of 1875, Lt. Col. William R. Shafter conducted an important military expedition to the Blanco Canyon in search of Indians. During the summer he touched on the site of Lubbock and moved on to the Casas Amarillas Lake in northwestern Hockley County. J. E. Haley, *Fort Concho and the Texas Frontier* (San Angelo, 1952), 199-203, 216-26, 231-33. Henry Clay Smith, the first resident, built a rock house in Blanco Canyon in 1877. *Handbook of Texas*, I, 172; II, 943. H. C. Smith, "Northwest Texas," *Texas Almanac, 1883*, 119. The operations of Colonel Mackenzie were especially significant. Wallace, *Ranald S. Mackenzie*, 60-91, 128-68.

30 Paris Cox was a Quaker from North Carolina who went to Boxley, Indiana, where he set up a sawmill. This he traded for fifty thousand acres of land in Crosby County, Texas, some of which he sold to settlers at twenty-five cents an acre. He established a settlement in the northwest part of the county in 1879, naming the central town "Marietta" in honor of his wife. After many hardships, the colony was eventually able to provide for some two hundred settlers; however, it was abandoned in 1891. Hall, "The Early History of Floyd County," *Pan-Plains Review*, XX, 66-68. See also *Plainview Herald*, Sept. 18, 28, 1930; M. P. Ziegler, *Colonel R. P. Smythe, Pioneer Surveyor and Organizer of West Texas* (M.A. Thesis, Texas Technological College, 1932), Chapter II; R. A. Burgess, *The History of Crosby County, Texas* (M.A. Thesis, University of Texas, 1927), Chapter VI.

31 Williams joined Powell and Gage, Dallas land agents, for his second trip to the Plains, as explained in the following section of this chapter.

32 Jacksboro, the county seat of Jack County (named for W. H. and P. C. Jack, two brothers active in the Republic of Texas), was the headquarters of the extensive land district in which Williams and his party operated. All surveys in the area had to be cleared and registered here with W. Callaway, who represented the General Land Office. C. U. Connellee, "Some Experiences of a Pioneer Surveyor," *West Texas Yearbook* (June, 1930), VI, 80-93; W. S. Mabry, "Early West Texas and Panhandle Surveys," *Pan-Plains Review* (1929), II, 22-42. Jacksboro was established in 1855. Fort Richardson was built near the site in 1867. By 1871 the town — with flour mills, brickyards, gristmills, sawmills and a cotton gin — was a thriving trading post. For accounts of Jack County, see T. F. Horton, *History of Jack County* (Jacksboro, 1932); Gilbert Webb (ed.), *Four Score Years in Jack County, 1860-1940* (Jacksboro [?], 1940); D. W. Whisenhunt, *Fort Richardson, Frontier Post in Northwest Texas* (M.A. Thesis, Texas Technological College, 1962).

33 Fort Griffin was established in 1867 and named for Maj. Gen. Charles Griffin, Commander of the Texas Department. The troops stationed here escorted government mail, surveying parties and cattle drivers. A town in northeastern Shackelford County grew up around the military post and bore the same name. During Williams' time on the Plains, Fort Griffin and the adjoining village served as headquarters of American troops and buffalo hunters. The place, one of the toughest on the frontier, consisted of a saloon or two, a dance hall and an eating place. The fort was closed in 1880, and most of the merchants moved to the nearby town of Albany. C. C. Rister, *Fort Griffin on the Texas Frontier* (Norman, 1956), *passim;* B. O. Grant, "Life in Old Fort Griffin," *West Texas Yearbook* (Oct., 1934), X, 32-41; Wayne Gard, *The Great Buffalo Hunt* (New York, 1951), 218-21.

34 This paragraph is interpolated from the *Diary* of the same date.

35 Breckenridge is the county seat of Stephens County, which was established in 1876. L. W. Hartsfield, *A History of Stephens County, Texas* (M.A. Thesis, University of Texas, 1929). The town is named for John C. Breckinridge (1821-75), once Vice President of the U. S. and later a Senator from Kentucky. It was a small village until the 1890's, and really did not grow appreciably until oil was discovered nearby in 1918. "The county court prescribed that the land be bought at public cost and resold in the form of lots at public auction." *Handbook of Texas*, I, 212. While in the Breckenridge area, Williams noted: "In the afternoon saw a fawn, and later 4

antelopes which I gave chase to, getting a shot at them, but without success. Took a bath before retiring and in the teeth of a heavy Norther which blew up in the evening." *Diary,* June 8.

36 Graham, founded in 1872 in southeastern Young County by Gustavus and Edwin Graham, became the county seat in 1874. Local business enterprises consisted of a saltworks, a sawmill, a gin and gristmills. C. J. Crouch, *Young County: History and Biography* (Dallas, 1937). Williams noted: "This is a very neat, nice town, good location, good houses, better class of citizens than usual for a frontier town. Lots 26 x 150 ft. on corner square opp. hotel worth $250. Dwelling lots worth $25. . . . Camp about 2 miles from town. A very cold night, and I needed more blankets than I had. Pierson snoring during the night made me think that a snake was on my bed." *Diary,* June 9.

37 Jacksboro: see note 32, preceding.

38 In reaching Jacksboro, the party had passed through Hood, Eastland, Stephens and Young counties. The surveyors would proceed to the northeast corner of Archer County then turn directly west, heading for Crosby County.

39 Williams could see Fort Richardson from Jacksboro but lacked time for a visit. The fort, named for a casualty of the Civil War, Israel B. Richardson, was located one-half mile south of Jacksboro. It was established in 1867 for the protection of the frontier and the Butterfield Overland Mail route. At the height of its activity, the fort maintained a garrison of some three hundred soldiers, who were available as escorts on the cattle trails and for expeditions against the hostile Indians. The fort was abandoned in 1878 after the Indians of the area had been brought under control. Donald W. Whisenhunt, "Fort Richardson," *West Texas Yearbook* (Oct., 1963), XXXIX, 19-27. In March, 1877, the Indians had defeated a large party of buffalo hunters on the Yellow House near present Lubbock. On May 1, a band of Apaches and Comanches had stolen all the horses from the hunters at Rath's Station, a trading post. The buffalo hunters, now equipped with new mounts, were searching the Plains for Indians or missing horses. P. I. Wellman, *Indian Wars of the West* (Garden City, 1947), 167-98; J. R. Cook, *The Border and the Buffalo* (Topeka, Kansas, 1907), 185-239. Williams understandably found comfort in the resounding bugle: "We camped that night in a mesquite prairie west of town, and went to sleep to the sound of the bugle from the Fort." *Diary,* June 10.

40 Williams added that a "thick cluster of surrounding brush" made this a "model hiding place. In the afternoon we loaded up with some additional flour and meal, and went out to the mesquite flat where we camped for the night." *Ibid.,* June 11.

41 The Keechi Valley referred to was probably the basin of the Keechi Creek running from south-central Jack County to about seven miles northwest of Mineral Wells. Other areas bearing the same name were located too far southwest to apply. *Handbook of Texas,* I, 940; J. C. McConnell, *The West Texas Frontier* (Palo Alto, Texas, 1939, 2 vols.), II, 112, 299.

42 The stray dog was a "large black mastiff" who "came up to us in a friendly way, and as we were in need of a friendly dog, we insinuated him into the bed of our wagon. Then we drove on, very rapidly, for the image of a pursuer with a double-barrel gun occasionally crossed our mind. No such incident occurred, however, and

at 6 we rolled into camp, hungry, and feasted on some wild turkey. Yesterday the boys killed a young antelope and ate him up, leaving us only the melancholy satisfaction of looking at its hide." *Diary,* June 12. Dogs were frequently companions to early explorers, buffalo hunters and surveyors. See Gard, *The Great Buffalo Hunt,* 185-86; R. W. Strickland (ed.), "The Recollections of W. S. Glenn, Buffalo Hunter," *Pan-Plains Review* (1949), XXII, 31-32.

43 The founding of Jack County in north-central Texas began when immigrants settled near a salt mine (Salt Hill Community) in 1854. Troops from Fort Richardson located in Jack County played a part in arresting and bringing to trial Indian leaders responsible for the 1871 Salt Creek Massacre. C. C. Rister, "The Significance of the Jacksboro Indian Affair of 1871," *Southwestern Historical Quarterly* (No. 3, Jan., 1926), XXIX, 161-80; Wallace, *Ranald S. Mackenzie,* 30-38.

44 In this vicinity on June 13 Williams' group lost their line and "then started to find wagons. But when we got to the edge of the prairie we could see nothing of them, and sent Dan to hunt them. After waiting some time and seeing nothing of them, we went back to morning camp and trailed them until 4 P.M. when we caught up with them in camp near Belknap road. We ate our dinner and camped where we were. Guard was kept this night. Circle around the sun, cloudy and other indications of rain." *Diary,* June 13.

45 Archer County, in north-central Texas, was named for Dr. B. T. Archer, Commissioner of the Republic of Texas to the U. S. The county was created from the Fannin Land District in 1858, but no permanent settlement was made until Dr. R. O. Prideaux arrived in 1874. A year later the Kiowa and Comanche raids ceased. See Winnie Nance, *A History of Archer County, Texas* (M.A. Thesis, University of Texas, 1927). Here the surveying party suffered intense heat, swarms of mosquitoes and homesickness. *Diary,* June 15-17. On June 18 Williams noted: "Had to bridge the Wichita here in order to carry our wagons across. About 5 we ran across a prairie-dog town, the first I have seen. Owls and dogs were conspicuous. The holes are dug at an angle of about 45°. Camp on open prairie. Ammerman and I are running transit alternately." To the north of Archer County was the unorganized county of Wichita, where Tom Burton's family had located in the 1860's at the present site of Wichita Falls. The McFarlins were at McFarlin Springs on the Red River by 1875. The Waggoners had started their ranching operations in the southern part of Wichita County in 1872. J. R. Morgan, *The History of Wichita Falls* (Oklahoma City, 1931), *passim.*

46 Williams further commented: "While running through the prairie-dog town we had a good opportunity to observe some of their habits. When we would come into their sight some self-constituted sentinel would get out over his hole, stick up their [*sic*] black stumpy tails, shake them and whistle a short, sharp whistle improperly called a bark, just as they are incorrectly called dogs. . . . Today's rain is the first which has fallen on us since we left Dallas. This is certainly a dry country. Camped at night in a low prairie by a creek. Our guard was kept up tonight. I ran the compass (transit) today and set it up to take another observation tonight, but failed to take one because of the clouds." *Diary,* June 20.

47 According to Williams' diary, on June 22 a "big rain storm blew up from the West about 7 P.M. Cork and I made down our bunk under the best wagon and very

soon Ammerman, D. Davis, Willy, and Murray made down theirs. This rain was so heavy that it forced Ammerman, Davis & Cork into the wagon, but I lay all night in water and wet blankets. About 9 o'clock an alarm of Indians was raised, but it proved to be false. Pierson, our gallant ex-French soldier, at the rear of 'three or four men, charged a mesquite bush and came near riddling it with bullets. This was a very unpleasant cold night." *Ibid.,* June 22.

48 Here they camped on a high mesquite prairie. "About midnight Ammerman and I took an observation on the Eastern Elongation of Polaris, which showed a variation of needle 14º 57′ E, manifestly wrong, and indicating presence of mineral." *Ibid.,* June 25.

49 Now in buffalo country, Williams wrote: "Saw 3 buffalo-hide wagons going North this afternoon. The freighters with wagons report no Indians about and only a few 100 miles West. About 6 P.M. we passed (crossed) the famous Colorado Cattle Trail. Just at dusk I killed a large diamond rattlesnake with 6 rattles. Douglas Davis took the skin, and I the rattler. Our camp was made in a low valley, rather unsafely, as it promised rain. However, it did not rain, and at 12¾ A.M. Ammerman and I got another observation, which showed a variation of 11½ E, again plainly wrong." *Ibid.,* June 26. Regarding buffalo "stand," see note 117, following.

50 Doubtless Williams referred to the Western Cattle Trail, which extended from San Antonio northward, passing through Baylor County. Regarding this trail and others, see C. A. True, *Development of the Cattle Industry in the Southwest* (M.A. Thesis, Texas Christian University, 1928); also Jack Potter's *Map of Cattle Trails, 1866-95,* Archives, University of Texas.

51 Baylor County, named for Dr. Henry W. Baylor, a surgeon in the Mexican War, is located on the north-central Plains of Texas. It was an Indian stronghold in 1853 when the first surveys were made. Large herds of buffalo were in the area as late as 1870, and the Indians strongly resisted white encroachment. C. C. Mills tried to settle in the southeastern part of the county in 1855, but the Indians kept him out until 1875, when other white men, such as the Millett brothers and John W. Stevens, arrived in force. *Handbook of Texas,* I, 124-25; S. A. Britton, *The Early History of Baylor County* (Dallas, 1955), Chapter I. At this camp Williams noted: "Observation at 2 A.M. showed a variation of 12º 23′ — wrong again." *Diary,* June 27. The reader may have noted that, writing from memory years after his visits to the Plains, Williams was not always entirely accurate in referring to locations and to distances.

52 Knox County in Northwest Texas was named in 1858 for Henry Knox, who was Secretary of War in George Washington's first cabinet. Three rivers run through the county or along its border, which make it good farm country. *Handbook of Texas,* I, 972.

53 Near the Salt Fork, Williams, riding Cork's mare, bogged down in a gully, "and only got out by carrying away a great deal of mud." The party "closed at a high mesquite-topped hill, and camped in a prairie-dog town. Took another observation and reading by a dim light, made a variation of 13º 53′, again too much & we let the instrument stand in order to read by daylight, but the boys disturbed it, and we lost our sight." *Diary,* June 29. "Among other dissipations of the afternoon, took a bath in the Salt Fork." *Ibid.,* June 30.

54 Cottle County is located on the rolling prairies of Northwest Texas. The county was created in 1876 and named for George W. Cottle, who came from Tennessee in 1832 and died defending the Alamo on March 6, 1836. King County, situated on the lower Plains of West Texas, was also created in 1876. It was named for William P. King, also of Alamo fame. *Handbook of Texas*, I, 420, 960-61.

55 The Jonathan Burleson Survey is located in northern King County, about two miles south of the border with Cottle County. Consisting of four sections, it encloses a part of the Buford Ranch on the North Fork of the Wichita River. The town of Guthrie is ten or twelve miles to the south. General Land Office, Map of King County, 1905. "While I was running the line for this purpose I caught a young antelope and brought it into camp, intending to save it for my sisters. That night the hunters gave us an Indian scare, but without any effect, as we didn't scare." *Diary*, July 5.

56 Jackson Springs, evidently intermittent in action, originates in the northwestern part of present-day Dickens County. The waters flow northeast for three miles into southern Motley County.

57 Llano Estacado refers to the Texas portion of the great high plains at the base of the Rocky Mountains. This area in Northwest Texas came to be known by the Spanish term for Staked Plains. The origin of the name "Llano Estacado" is disputed. Some hold that when Coronado crossed this grassy area, he staked out the route to guide him on his return. Others believe that the name refers to the land topography, which resembles a palisaded or staked area. *Texas Almanac, 1964-1965*, 294. Josiah Gregg insisted that the early Mexican hunters and traders marked a route across the Plains to avoid getting lost; hence the name. *Commerce of the Prairies* (Cleveland, 1905), 239-40. (The first edition of Gregg's book — in two volumes — was published in New York in 1844). Haley describes the region, as it was then, as "that great plateau of New Mexico and Texas, a wilderness, arid, unsettled, and then almost unknown. . . . Traditionally, it was the Great American Desert." *Charles Goodnight*, 276-77. Bartlett's map of 1850-53 designates the area thus: "The whole country from the headwaters of the Red, Brazos and Colorado Rivers to the Rio Pecos is a sterile and barren plain without water or timber producing only a few stunted shrubs which are insufficient to sustain animal life." J. R. Bartlett, *Personal Narrative of Explorations and Incidents in Texas, New Mexico, California, Sonora, and Chihuahua* (New York, 1854, 2 vols.), I, facing xv. See also J. E. Haley, *The XIT Ranch of Texas and the Early Days of the Llano Estacado* (Norman, 1953), 35-37.

58 Williams and his party were in the future Motley County, where within the year Henry Campbell selected a spot on the edge of the escarpment, built a dugout, and started his Matador Ranch. At this place a natural spring (Roaring Springs) falls to a creek below. *Handbook of Texas*, II, 481-82; W. M. Pearce, *The Matador Land and Cattle Company* (Norman, 1964).

59 After eating at a pond and observing that Grovner had killed a "big bull buffalo," Williams noted that they were on the trail again. "About 4 P.M. Douglas Davis succeeded in killing a buffalo. About 5 we saw the same wild horses with the white mule that we saw several days ago. I got 2 square shots at an old bull at 150 yds. distance & missed him. Slipped up on him by leading the horses. Cork killed a calf by running it on horseback. Coming into camp late I killed a rattlesnake, & brought it into camp at Henderson's Springs for Cork." *Diary*, July 12.

60 The party was now at the point near the center of Crosby County, east of present-day Lubbock, where Williams would soon spend much time surveying, both on this trip and the two to follow soon. On Crosby County, which was named for an early Texas Land Commissioner, Stephen Crosby, see R. A. Burgess, *The History of Crosby County, passim;* N. W. Spikes and T. A. Ellis, *Through the Years: A History of Crosby County, Texas* (San Antonio, 1952), especially Chapter I.

61 Mackenzie used this road in 1872 and 1874 for the movement of troops and wagon supply trains. After the battle of the North Fork of Red River on Sept. 29, 1872, he transferred the Comanche captives to Fort Concho in wagons over this route. Wallace, *Ranald S. Mackenzie,* 165.

62 The trail was actually made in July and August, 1872, as Col. R. S. Mackenzie pursued the Indians from his headquarters on Bull Creek into the area of the Blanco and Palo Duro canyons, through the Quitaque country, and on to Forts Sumner and Bascom in New Mexico. He thus proved that troops could be moved successfully across the Staked Plains, a feat previously considered impossible. On September 29, 1872, he captured a sizeable number of Indians on the North Fork, seven miles above the mouth of McClellan Creek. Wallace, *Ranald S. Mackenzie,* especially Chapters IV and V.

63 Williams noted: "Mosquitoes bad and smoked them out with buffalo chips fire." *Diary,* July 13.

64 Charles P. Tasker was a young spendthrift from Philadelphia who in 1877 had Hank Smith of Fort Griffin select a ranch site for him in the Blanco Canyon. Tasker named the ranch "Hacienda Glorieta," and it seemed to live up to its name until Tasker fell deeply into debt and left suddenly. Smith, who held a lien on the ranch, took over and operated it. His house was thus the first in the Blanco Canyon area. H. C. Smith, "Along the Reminiscent Line," *Crosbyton Review,* Feb. 29, 1912; Haley, *The XIT Ranch,* 44; Martin Hornecker, *Buffalo Hunting on the Plains in 1877* (Geneseo, Ill., 1929), 20.

65 Erath County, named for George B. Erath, a frontier Indian fighter, is located in the Grand Prairie region of the north-central Plains, about fifty miles southwest of Fort Worth. *Handbook of Texas,* I, 569-70. Erath was also one of the early surveyors in Texas. *One League to Each Wind,* 204-16, 284-85, 325-26.

66 Here in the afternoon, "Murray and I went after buffalo but didn't get any." *Diary,* July 15.

67 Hale County, named for John C. Hale, a Texas hero killed at the battle of San Jacinto, is located in the center of the Llano Estacado about sixty-five miles south of Amarillo. In 1877 the Indians had left this area of the Plains after the extermination of the buffalo, and the ranchers had not yet arrived. M. L. Cox, *History of Hale County, Texas* (Plainview, Tex., 1937); H. Ford, *History and Economic Development of Hale County, Texas* (M.A. Thesis, University of Colorado, 1932). Connellee had entered Hale County ahead of the Williams party and located the Bottle Corner. *One League to Each Wind,* 228.

68 Judge Good (John Jay Good), born in Mississippi in 1827, came to Texas in 1851 and the next year participated as commander in the Hedgcoxe War involving the

Peters Colony. He later became presiding judge of Confederate military courts in the South. When he returned to Texas, he was elected district judge in Dallas, but General Sheridan removed him as "an impediment to Reconstruction." Good practiced law and became mayor of Dallas in 1880. On the side, he bought and speculated in public lands. Brown, *History of Dallas*, 80-81.

69 On the 19th Williams noted: "Made a corner 5 ft. high about 65 varas west of the large pond, with 2 buffalo heads facing N and S at top. I intend taking these sections coming at this mound for Pa. . . . Camped for the night at the well dug by our New Mex. friend Keith in the canyon below the trail crossing." *Diary*, July 19.

70 Palo Duro Canyon begins east of Canyon, Texas, and extends southeastward through Randall, Armstrong and Briscoe counties. The stream it contains, Prairie Dog Town Fork, flows into the Red River. *Palo Duro*, meaning "hard wood," refers to the strong cedar brush growing profusely in the area, from which the Indians made their arrows. Water from the northern part of the Staked Plains drains into the canyon. It is almost a thousand feet deep, varying in width from a few hundred yards to fifteen miles. The canyon provided shelter from northers; offered water and grass for cattle; and the varied trees gave fuel and shade to the Indians. After 1874, when Col. Ranald Mackenzie defeated the Indians in the canyon, Anglo-American settlements were begun. Charles Goodnight and John Adair founded the JA Ranch at Palo Duro Canyon in 1876. *Handbook of Texas*, II, 328; Haley, *Charles Goodnight*, 283-84. On the geology of the Plains country, see Fred Rathjen, "The Physiography of the Texas Panhandle," *Southwestern Historical Quarterly* (No. 3, Jan., 1961), LXIV, 315-32.

71 Charles Goodnight was one of the fabulous men of the period. Born in Illinois in 1836, he came to Texas in 1846 with his mother and stepfather. After experience as ranger, Indian scout, and guide for a frontier Civil War regiment, Goodnight entered the cattle business before the lands of the West were fenced in. His ranch extended over an almost limitless range on the Staked Plains. With Oliver Loving, he marked out a cattle route from Fort Belknap, Texas, to Fort Sumner, New Mexico, which became the famous Goodnight-Loving Trail. Goodnight's later partners included John Chisum and John G. Adair. There is no evidence that Williams personally met Goodnight, although he passed over Goodnight's spread. The standard work on the colorful rancher is Haley, *Charles Goodnight, passim*. See also W. P. Webb, *The Great Plains* (New York, 1931), 205, 264-65; C. C. Rister, *Southern Plainsmen* (Norman, 1938), 120; C. C. Rister, *The Southwestern Frontier* (Cleveland, 1928), 277; L. F. Sheffy, "The Old Home Ranch Site," *Pan-Plains Review* (1946), XIX, 11-17; L. S. Kinder, "A Chapter in the Life of Charles Goodnight," *West Texas Yearbook* (June, 1930), VI, 112-23. Especially interesting is Goodnight's own description of the early Panhandle: "It was absolutely a trackless, roadless territory, filled with lawless people unusual in number even for a wild country." "Sketch of Panhandle's First Settlement," *Frontier Times* (No. 3, Dec., 1929), VII, 113-16.

72 In addition, Williams commented: "Threatening rain. 4 Indians seen this morning at Dewey's Lake. John and I caught in a rain and don't get to camp until late. Sleep under wagon and do pretty well." *Diary*, July 20.

73 No mention is made in Williams' diary of this incident. All recorded is: "Dry, and 20 miles without water. Camped at night on a high mesquite prairie. A buffalo came by at night grazing." *Diary*, July 21.

74 On the 22nd the surveyors "traveled all day in a great prairie-dog country. Owls, rabbits and occasionally rattlesnakes in their holes." *Ibid.*, July 22.

75 Floyd County, named for Dolphin Ward Floyd, killed at the Alamo, was created in 1876. The Arthur Duncan family became the first permanent settlers in 1884. The county is located just northeast of Lubbock County and due north of Crosby County, where Henry Clay (Hank) Smith settled in 1878. Smith was a government contractor at El Paso and Fort Quitman after the Civil War. *Handbook of Texas*, I, 613; II, 624. For a full account of the area, see Hall, "The Early History of Floyd County," *Pan-Plains Review*, XX, 3-140; Smythe, "The First Settlers and the Organization of Floyd, Hale, and Lubbock Counties," *West Texas Yearbook*, VI, 17-34.

76 "Reached the lake about 11 o'clock. Laid there all day. Got a full supply of rain water. Slept on damp ground." *Diary*, July 29.

77 The *Diary* for the 30th says simply: "I got lost but about 4 o'clock to my surprise ran onto our party."

78 "About dark saw springs and great many buffalo. Camped for night." *Ibid.*, August 1.

79 Lubbock County, named for Col. T. S. Lubbock, co-organizer of Terry's Rangers in the Confederate Army, was one of the counties created from Bexar Territory in 1876. Buffalo hunters frequented the area in the 1870's, but no permanent settlers arrived until George W. Singer and his wife in 1879 put up a merchandise store five miles northwest of the site of Lubbock. In 1887 the Legislature included the county in the so-called Crosby District of ten counties, which were counted as one judicially. In several of these counties there would not be a single resident taxpayer for some time to come. Smythe, "The First Settlers and the Organization of Floyd, Hale, and Lubbock Counties," *West Texas Yearbook*, VI, 17-34; Graves (ed.), *A History of Lubbock, passim.*

80 "Saw about 1000 buffalo. Very sore and tired. Signs of Indians. Good camping place at foot of hill." *Diary*, August 2.

81 "At noon the boys were scared to death by what they thought were Indians, but which proved to be hunters coming back from Indian hunt. Have had a hard time, nearly starved for water." *Ibid.*, August 3.

82 This book became a classic. It is full of Western lore, including many details of Indian life and buffalo hunts that were contemporary with Williams' surveying activities on the Plains.

83 As a *comanchero* (Indian trader), José Piedad Tafoya had learned the Plains thoroughly. He became a scout for the detachment at Fort Concho after his capture by Mackenzie in 1874. Haley, *The XIT Ranch*, 28-29, and *Fort Concho*, 246-51. Charles Goodnight declared that as a guide, "Tafoya was a wonder, and knew the Plains from the Palo Duro to the Concho by heart." Haley, *Charles Goodnight*, 196.

84 Fort Concho was one of a series of military posts set up to protect settlers and travelers in the South Plains area of Texas. Located on the Concho River, it was at the junction of, or near, several important early trails: the Comanche, Marcy's, Ford and Neighbor's, the Goodnight-Loving, the Lower Road and connecting routes. Because of the strategic position of the fort, its troops could strike out in several directions against any threat to the whites in the great West Texas area. The fort, established in 1867, was deactivated in 1889. Famous soldiers who campaigned from it against the Indians included Ranald S. Mackenzie, William R. Shafter, Benjamin H. Grierson, and Nicholas Nolan. The soldiers involved in the near-fatal incident discussed here were on a scouting expedition from the fort at the time. Haley, *Fort Concho, passim;* Susan Miles, "Fort Concho in 1877," *West Texas Yearbook* (Oct., 1959), XXXV, 29-49.

85 Cook, *The Border and the Buffalo*, 260-73. The buffalo hunters from Rath's Station had joined up with Captain Nolan's company of Negro soldiers (cavalry) from Fort Concho at Mucha Que (in present-day Borden County) on July 20. In search of the marauding Indians, the combined party made a dry march to the salty and scarce water of Cedar Lake (in present-day Gaines County). Seventeen miles west, their scouts found a large Indian trail heading northeast toward Double Lakes (in Lynn County). With little water in their canteens, the group rode out on the trail and made a dry night camp. While traveling another twenty-five miles northeast in the sizzling sun, two men suffered sunstroke. After three days without water, drinking horse urine and blood, and with some men affected with blind staggers, the expedition disbanded to seek water — everyone for himself — on July 28. The hunters went northeast, missing Silver Lake, but reaching the Yellow Houses. Nolan and six troopers pushed on to Double Lakes, about thirty-five miles south and a little west of where Williams' survey party was working. Nolan was severely criticized for the way he handled this assignment and he barely missed court-martial and dismissal from the Army. At best, he was never able to overcome the stigma of his misadventure. Haley, *Fort Concho*, 244-61. M. L. Crimmins, "Captain Nolan's Lost Troops on the Staked Plains," *West Texas Yearbook* (Oct., 1934), X, 68-73; H. Bailey Carroll, "Nolan's 'Lost Nigger' Expedition of 1877," *Southwestern Historical Quarterly* (No. 1, July, 1940), XLIV, 55-75. For a list of the men with Nolan, see "Recollections of W. S. Glenn, Buffalo Hunter," *Pan-Plains Review*, XXII, 63-64.

86 The so-called Lost Lake seems to have been a surface collection of water that rapidly disappeared, from drainage or evaporation. Such lakes were common on the High Plains of Texas. There is a Lost Lake just west of Tatum, N. M.

87 Williams became assistant postmaster at Silver City after he had failed in his mining ventures around Shakespeare. See III, following.

88 Sharps rifles were favorites with buffalo hunters because of their accuracy and deadly effect. They were made by Christian Sharps at Hartford, Connecticut, and came in three calibers: .44, .45 and .50. The Sharps gun was popular because of its long range and lethal power. It was fast also, firing up to eight shots a minute. But the gun was heavy, weighing up to sixteen pounds; so hunters supported its barrel with cross-sticks or a tripod. It fired with a loud boom, as Williams notes. Gard, *The Great Buffalo Hunt*, 97-98; Mari Sandoz, *The Buffalo Hunters* (New York, 1954), 97-98; E. D. Branch, *The Hunting of the Buffalo* (Lincoln, Nebr., 1962), 160.

89 The *Diary* does not mention this incident.

90 Although nothing about this episode is recorded in the *Diary,* it made a lasting impression on Williams, since he later elaborated the story in a separate pamphlet, *Crusoe or Jack.*

91 See "Crosby County, Sketch 5," Appendix I. The survey included a meander up and down Yellow House Canyon from the north line of Lubbock County to the mouth of Plum Creek; also a survey of Block C in Floyd County, Block R and others in Hale County, and Blocks A, B and O in Lubbock County.

92 The *Diary* is silent at this point.

93 Rath City (also known as Reynolds City) was a small supply depot that Charles Rath of Dodge City operated on the south side of the Double Mountain Fork of the Brazos River in Stonewall County, twelve miles northwest of the present site of Hamlin. In 1877, $100,000 worth of buffalo hides were handled here. The place had become the headquarters of some eighty buffalo hunters, including such outfits as John Cook's and the Mooar brothers', during the last months of the Southern herd. Some of the hunters also campaigned against the Indians from this location. By the mid-summer of 1879, after the herd had been destroyed, Rath abandoned his store, and the settlement disappeared. Naomi Kincaid, "Rath City," *West Texas Yearbook* (Oct., 1948), XXIV, 40-46; I. D. Rath, *The Rath Trail* (Wichita, Kan., 1961), *passim.*

94 Spotted Jack was a scout and guide who briefly joined Captain Nicholas Nolan in pursuit of the Indians. Haley, *Fort Concho,* 257-58. "Recollections of W. S. Glenn, Buffalo Hunter," *Pan-Plains Review,* XXII, 31-32, 48-49.

95 These Indians, a small remnant tribe, had settled near Fort Griffin for protection against the Comanches, their deadly enemies, who had practically wiped them out. They were friendly to the whites and served them as scouts on raids against the Comanches. Haley, *Fort Concho,* 188; Branch, *The Hunting of the Buffalo,* 189.

96 "Got no dinner. Team gave out. No money from Tasker. Sent order for provisions. Got $16.45 worth. Camped near Tonk wigwams. Heavy dew." *Diary,* August 17.

97 The *Diary* does not mention Peter Punk.

98 The *Diary* for August 18 to 28 records the return trip through open country, the party camping en route. Place-names mentioned are N. Hubbard, Lynch's, Gonzales Creek, Eastland, Maisico Settlement, Hog Creek, Stephenville, Granbury, Brazos River, Fall Creek, and Fort Worth. Back in Dallas, Williams made this entry in his diary of August 29: "Daugherty gave me a $45 check for my three months' work. Cheap enough! Proposes making me a Deputy Surveyor of Jack District. I can sign the field notes. Loaf all day."

99 This was the land that Williams sold to H. G. Ferris, on part of which the town of Lubbock was later located. See preceding notes 10, 11 and 79. "Doub(le) Mountain Fork of the Brazos" in this passage refers to the same stream called Yellow House Creek by Williams elsewhere, and by others. The buyer of the three sections was a banker in Carthage, Illinois, and a recognized pillar of the community. See Williams' pamphlet, *An Old Carthage Home* (reprinted from *The Carthage Republican,* Dec. 6, 1922), 10-11.

100 George A. Grant, "Surveying Trip to the Staked Plains, 1878," manuscript in the O. W. Williams Collection.

101 The real-estate firm of Powell and Gage maintained an office in the center of the Dallas business district, at 507 Main Street. The partners were quite active in promoting their business. In addition to sending out numbers of broadsides to prospective customers, they ran a series of advertisements in the *General Directory of the City of Dallas, 1878-79*, with headings like these: FOR INFORMATION ABOUT STATE LANDS, ASK POWELL AND GAGE. . . . POWELL AND GAGE HAVE LANDS IN ALL THE WESTERN COUNTIES.

102 Broadside, "Powell and Gage, Land Agents and Locators, Dallas, Texas."

103 Because of the great areas which early surveys in Texas covered, they were frequently defective. A popular method, both rapid and cheap, was "reconnaissance surveying," but it caused many difficulties. In his career as surveyor, Williams spent much time making re-surveys to correct surveying errors. Regarding this problem, see W. D. Twichell, "Surveying in Texas," *One League to Each Wind*, 134-42.

104 Williams, having survived the rigors of his first trip to the Staked Plains, now considered himself no tenderfoot, and in many respects he was not. But as we shall see, the Southwest would continue to test his vigor and resourcefulness for many years to come.

105 The big herd of buffalo in Texas had been thinned out in the wholesale killings of 1874-78. Concerning the extent of this slaughter, which is almost unbelievable, see Cook, *The Border and the Buffalo*, 113-291; Gard, *The Great Buffalo Hunt*, 4, 182-234; Richardson and Rister, *The Greater Southwest*, 297-300; Sandoz, *The Buffalo Hunters*, 172-73, 315-25; Branch, *The Hunting of the Buffalo*, 124, 127-47, 156-70.

106 The North Fork of the Yellow House, as used here, is apparently the North Fork of Double Mountain branch of the Brazos River.

107 The hunter used "sticks," often cut from the forked branch of a tree, on which to rest his heavy Sharps rifle. See note 88, preceding.

108 Excellent marksmanship was common among buffalo hunters. With their Sharps rifles they could fell an animal almost a mile away. A good hunter could occasionally kill more than a hundred animals in a day. Gard, *The Great Buffalo Hunt*, 98, 128-29; Sandoz, *The Buffalo Hunters*, 97-98.

109 This barrier to communication was real. With the passing of time, however, the two cultures have blended considerably; yet the Spanish influence is still great in the Southwest, especially on the High Plains, in the El Paso area of Texas, and in New Mexico and Arizona. Regarding Spanish place-names in the Panhandle, see Frank P. Hill, "Plains Names," *Pan-Plains Review* (1937), X, 36-47.

110 By 1867 the Delawares, who had occupied the basin of the Delaware River, had been removed to the Indian Territory and incorporated with the Cherokee Nation. The Wyandots were a branch of the Hurons who lived in the Great Lake country. F. W. Hodge, *Handbook of American Indians North of Mexico* (Washington, 1907, 1910, 2 vols.), I, 385-86, 584-91; J. C. Wise, *The Red Man in the New World Drama* (Washington, 1931), 22-24, 146 ff. Bartlett encountered Delaware Indians in Texas

near Fredericksburg on the first leg of his surveying mission along the Mexican border. *Personal Narrative,* I, 59.

111 Williams refers to Seavey's Island, a part of the harbor of Kittery, Maine, site of the Portsmouth Navy yards. The treaty ending the Russo-Japanese War was negotiated here in 1905.

112 The last great slaughter of buffalos in Texas occurred in the winter of 1877-78. Only small and scattered herds remained in 1879. By this time, the buffalo hunters had left for the Middle West, where some herds were still intact until they too were exterminated (by 1884); or the hunters remained in Texas but switched to freighting, ranching or other activities. Cook, *The Border and the Buffalo,* 291; Sandoz, *The Buffalo Hunters,* Ch. XV; Gard, *The Great Buffalo Hunt,* 253-73; Branch, *The Hunting of the Buffalo,* 202-21; C. C. Rister, "The Significance of the Destruction of the Buffalo in the Southwest," *Southwestern Historical Quarterly* (No. 1, July, 1929), XXXIII, 34-49.

113 Regarding Hale County, see note 67, preceding. Lamb County, authorized by the Fifteenth Legislature in 1876, was named for Lieutenant George A. Lamb, who came to Texas from South Carolina in 1834. He was killed at the Alamo. The site of Lamb County was deep in buffalo and Indian country. An early *comanchero* trail crossed its southwest corner. The Legislature later appropriated much of the county to help pay for the State capitol; the land became part of the huge XIT Ranch extending along the northwestern line with New Mexico. Lamb County had no organized government until 1908. Haley, *The XIT Ranch, passim; Handbook of Texas,* II, 15-16; *Lamb County Leader,* March 31, 1955.

114 Buffalo herds tended to stampede at the slightest provocation. Once under way, a stampede became a peril to all persons and things ahead. The herd, consisting of thousands of animals and extending as far as the eye could see, moved with irresistible force. Indians, who knew the animals' traits intimately, were extremely careful to anticipate and avoid stampedes. Sandoz, *The Buffalo Hunters,* 103-04; Gard, *The Great Buffalo Hunt,* 11-12.

115 Leaders of a herd in stampede instinctively avoided any object that would impede their progress. Since the stampede moved with such bounding force that its momentum could not be arrested, the herd often divided to avoid collision with an object in its progress, merging after the object was passed. Williams' experience thus confirmed the recognized pattern of buffalo behavior. Homer W. Wheeler, *Buffalo Days* (Indianapolis, 1923), 88, 162-63; Gard, *The Great Buffalo Hunt,* 11-12; Sandoz, *The Buffalo Hunters,* 231-32.

116 Williams was apparently correct in this sumise. He had probably witnessed the last buffalo stampede to occur on the Plains of Texas.

117 The buffalo was an extremely stupid animal. Physically it was sluggish, except when the herd was in full flight. Once the hunters located and killed the leaders, which were usually found at the head and edges of the herd, the other animals stood helpless in a "stand" and could be picked off with ease. W. C. Holden, "The Buffalo of the Plains Area," *West Texas Yearbook* (June, 1926), II, 8-17; Homer W. Wheeler, *Buffalo Days,* 81-82; Branch, *The Hunting of the Buffalo,* 58, 165-68.

118 In making this survey, Williams and an associate, John Summerfield, acting on the authority of the Commissioner of the Land Office, made another correction of conflicting lines. To do so, they established a base line running from Dewey's Lake to Blocks K and JK in Hale County, which line the Land Office accepted as final for determining locations in the northwestern part of Hale County. General Land Office, Jack Land District, Sketch and Field Notes of Connections, File 11,386, Fannin Script.

119 See "Weather on the Plains," *The Texas Almanac, 1873,* 97-98.

120 The reasons for the eccentric and severe weather on the Plains are discussed in Webb, *The Great Plains,* 21-26; C. F. Kraenzel, *The Great Plains in Transition* (Norman, 1955), 12-23.

121 Williams was now in southeastern Hale County near the border of Floyd County. The Callahan County school land lay in both counties. General Land Office, Map of Hale County, 1900; Map of Floyd County, 1904.

122 Williams' associate, C. U. Connellee, had established this point in the fall of 1877, but did not clearly mark it. *One League to Each Wind,* 217-28, 318-20.

123 Blizzards were one of the worst hazards to life on the Plains, especially when no shelter was available. John R. Cook probably expressed a common view when he said: "I will put the Panhandle of Texas against any other 180 square miles of territory in America for spasmodic, erratic weather." *The Border and the Buffalo,* 73. Northers unexpectedly overtook many persons on the Plains — soldiers, buffalo hunters, ranchmen, surveyors, and settlers — who suffered severely. The blizzards were equally damaging to animal life, especially to buffalo and cattle. For some typical examples, see Haley, *Fort Concho,* 187, and *Charles Goodnight,* 320-21; Gard, *The Great Buffalo Hunt,* 92, 282-85; Sandoz, *The Buffalo Hunters,* 44, 175, 321.

124 Because of the construction of their hoofs, which were cloven, narrow and sharp, buffalos experienced much trouble in the snow. They were often stalled in their tracks until the snow hardened to ice or melted. While thus handicapped they were especially vulnerable to attacks by Indians and wolves. Sandoz, *The Buffalo Hunters,* 45; Branch, *The Killing of the Buffalo,* 40.

125 Some Indians theoretically regarded sneak attacks such as this one to be unsporting, if not cowardly. Believing the buffalo to be a "brother" by nature, they held that the animal should have at least the appearance of a chance. One Indian code required that the buffalo be attacked in the open and killed in close personal encounter, not by stealth or by powerful guns at a distance. However, most Indians used the ambuscade or other stratagems for the kill. Plains Indians used deception to kill buffalo as early as the time of Mendoza (1598). Herbert E. Bolton (ed.), *Spanish Exploration in the Southwest, 1542-1706* (New York, 1916), 230. See also Gard, *The Great Buffalo Hunt,* 27-42; Branch, *The Killing of the Buffalo,* 30-46, 163-64; R. N. Richardson, *The Comanche Barrier to Southern Plains Settlement* (Glendale, Calif., 1933), 26-27.

126 Williams does not explain how much buffalo meat they took. Buffalo hunters often wasted great quantities of meat. Frequently, after the animals were skinned, their carcasses were left to the wild animals. At times, the buffalos were killed for

their humps and tongues only. "The Recollections of W. S. Glenn, Buffalo Hunter,"
Pan-Plains Review, XXII, 24-25.

127 John S. Chisum was a famous cattleman who moved from Texas to New Mexico,
where he established permanent residence, with headquarters on South Spring
River near Roswell. He left behind unpaid notes which could not be collected because he was beyond the jurisdiction of the Texas courts. His herds increased
rapidly in New Mexico, where his spread extended from Fort Sumner to a line near
the Texas border. Chisum should not be confused with Jesse Chisholm of the famous
Chisholm Trail. Haley, *Charles Goodnight,* 231-33; Wayne Gard, *The Chisholm
Trail* (Norman, 1954), *passim;* H. B. Hinton, "John Simpson Chisum, 1877-84,"
The New Mexico Historical Quarterly (No. 4, Oct., 1956), XXXI, 310-37.

128 The Indians tied poles to the sides of horses or dogs, which dragged the poles
and their loads along the trail in travois fashion. Practical jokes were common among
frontiersmen. Such jokes were a means of compensating for the long and boresome
days in the open country or small town. Favorite jokes in the Southwest, elaborately
planned and executed with much gusto, included the "snipe hunt" and "badger
fight." These were usually employed to initiate tenderfeet into the manly ways of
the local community. See R. E. O'Neil, "Good Badger Puller Keeps Fight from
Going to Pot," *The Southwesterner* (No. 10, April, 1965), IV, 1, 7.

129 Severe frostbite and chilblain could lead to serious consequences. Often persons
caught in blizzards on the Plains were poorly clothed for cold weather; also, medical
help was far distant and frequently incompetent. In the blizzard of 1873 a man
named Riney lost both feet from exposure. Sandoz, *The Buffalo Hunters,* 170.

Part II

Miner in Early New Mexico

MINER IN EARLY NEW MEXICO

B Y THE SPRING of 1879 Oscar W. Williams was back in Dallas and confronted with another decision regarding his future. On February 20 the Legislature at Austin had passed an act setting aside 3,050,000 acres of land in the Panhandle to provide for the construction of a new capitol. This land, later incorporated into the huge XIT Ranch, lay immediately to the west of the area in which Williams had surveyed during a part of the preceding two years. In effect, the State of Texas thus suspended its sale of public lands; as a result, Williams was obliged to look in another direction for employment.[1]

With characteristic resourcefulness, the young man decided to act at once. This time he headed even farther west — to the mine fields of Leadville, Colorado. Abe Lee's discovery of gold there in 1860 had opened a mining district that rapidly expanded. By 1879, the Carbonate regions around Leadville were producing huge quantities of silver and lead. Stories of strikes by men who became rich overnight — H. A. W. Tabor, Thomas Starr, Charles Mater, W. P. Jones and others — were widely circulated.[2] Hearing these accounts, Williams concluded that Leadville offered a man of his abilities an unusual opportunity; therefore on June 9 he and several companions set out overland by wagon with Colorado as their destination.[3]

Williams covers only the highlights of the trip in the published account that follows. His diary, however, gives many more details, the most important of which are incorporated in the annotations to this chapter. The *Diary* also reveals that the party changed their plans on July 6, 1879, after encountering two sheepmen from Colfax County, New Mexico. It is likely that these men, coming from the west and being acquainted with mining conditions there, described the intolerable lawlessness prevailing at Leadville and recommended the better prospects around Santa Fe.[4]

At any rate, Williams' party, joined by the sheepmen, changed their course. On July 25, the Texans arrived in Carbonateville, a mining camp twenty-five miles southwest of Santa Fe. Although the party soon disbanded, Williams did not leave the camp until October 5. Meanwhile, he prospected in the area, bought and

worked a small lead-and-silver mine (which seemingly never produced), learned something about the mining business, and began
to collect impressions and stories he would later set down in
writing.[5]

After spending some two months prospecting at Carbonateville,
Williams returned to Dallas. Afterwards, he visited his brother
Will in Austin and then the Williams family back in Illinois. While
away from New Mexico for six and a half months, he received
occasional reports from associates in the mining fields.[6]

In April, 1880, Williams returned to New Mexico and took up
residence in the mining town of Shakespeare, located some fifty
miles southwest of Silver City, near the railroad stop of Lordsburg.
At the time, favorable reports of silver strikes in the vicinity of
Shakespeare had aroused much interest among prospectors. Williams joined the influx of miners who hoped to find fortunes by
sinking shallow shafts in the surrounding hills.[7]

As a matter of fact, however, the mines around Shakespeare
were highly overrated — at least so far as the ordinary miner working with pick and shovel was concerned. The available ore was
mostly low-grade and costly to refine. Commercially, only the mining of copper was to prove profitable in the area, and such mining
would require ample capital and the use of advanced techniques.
In effect, Williams and the other placer miners at Shakespeare
had chosen to operate in a territory that produced much less than
it promised.[8]

Reviewing Williams' career as a miner, we are led to conclude
that from a business standpoint it was none too impressive. In all,
he devoted two and a half years to various phases of mining.
During this time, despite great effort on his part, he did not make
a single important strike or organize a single effective business
operation. And in the end, as indicated later, problems of all kinds
overwhelmed him, and he was obliged to surrender his mining
interests as a dead loss.

Yet, when Williams' mining years were over, he was still a
young man — only twenty-eight years old. The rigorous outdoor
life he had been obliged to lead had improved his health and
doubtless prolonged his life. He had gained invaluable experience
in a business that was highly competitive and sometimes cut-
throat. His mind had been sharpened, his character strengthened.
The lessons he had learned would serve him well during the sixty-
five years still ahead of him.

And, after all, so far as mining is concerned, Williams did strike a rich lode in New Mexico — the materials for the narratives that follow. The reader of this account as Williams later wrote it may well conclude that the young miner's efforts in Shakespeare were not wasted, but resulted in a legacy in some respects more important than any silver mine.

To New Mexico by Chance

☙ IN THE SPRING of 1879 I could well say with Othello, "My occupation is gone." I was then living in Dallas, Texas, and was engaged in locating lands out of the great unappropriated public domain of Texas in the Panhandle and disposing of my locations to investors at a small profit. But recently the Legislature had passed an act reserving those unappropriated lands from further private location, for the purpose of raising funds to erect a new capitol building.

When my occupation was lost, it was up to me to hunt for something else to do, but always with the limitation that the scene of action must be in the arid West. In those days when the arid West was mentioned, it was tied up necessarily with three main items: the buffaloes, the Indians and the great mines. Just then, the public attention was very much taken up with the discovery of the immense beds of carbonate ore being opened up at Leadville, Colorado. I made up my mind to try for health and occupation in that place.

Very quickly I got together a party of five to make the overland journey with me. We were rather a motley party. N. B. Laughlin, an attorney of Dallas, threw his lot in with us; in time his decision carried him to wealth and to the office of Associate Justice of the Supreme Court of New Mexico.[9] J. W. Bell, an ex-Texas Ranger, joined us. But for him the fates began here to spin a thread of life with a tragic ending. He was killed by Billy the Kid at the Lincoln County courthouse two years later.[10]

N. J. W. Fish and G. W. Irving were Harvard boys, just out of school, seeking adventure in the West. This desire must have come to Fish easily, as he received his given names from his great uncle, Nathaniel J. Wyeth, a pathfinder in the West a hundred years ago, much of whose story is told in Washington Irving's *Astoria and Captain Bonneville*.[11] Fish was an engineer by education, and when I last saw him in Boston some ten years ago, he was serving as mayor of the quiet old town of Taunton, Massachusetts. After an active life in foreign countries and

many states as an engineer, the slim youth had widened greatly, physically as well as mentally.

Irving had been a fellow student with Fish in the Lawrence Scientific School at Harvard, and had been stroke oar in the Harvard crew
of eight. He was quite a powerful youth. Shortly after our party disbanded at Santa Fe in the summer of 1879, he became a member of
some engineering corps of the Union Pacific Railroad and died a few
years later in the service of the same company.

For the purposes of our trip, James Martin, an ex-Confederate soldier,
was the most important member of the party. He served as Cook. I write
it with a big "C," because I shall never forget the pleasure I had in
eating his hot sourdough bread after a dry, warm, fatiguing ride of six
or seven hours, often into the night. He never served it cold.[12] He drove
our wagon also,[13] and during a terrible hailstorm on the Plains, when
our mule team was about to desert us under the sting of the hailstones,
it was good old Jim Martin who held up the mules at the risk of his life
and saved the day. I have heard that he died in Santa Fe County some
twenty years ago or more.

This writer made the sixth member. We took our route northwest
along a line quite closely paralleled now by the Fort Worth and Denver
Railway. We struck no town after leaving Henrietta[14] until we came
to a small settlement at Tascosa, consisting of a post office, two stores,
and the house and corrals of Casimiro Romero, a Mexican freighter.[15]
One of these stores was owned by a man named Edwards, who some
two years later came to Silver City, New Mexico, and promoted the
building of a custom mill, which later burned down.[16] It was at this
place, Tascosa, that we learned from two Englishmen, Rogers and
Cottle, of the discovery of a new mining district near Santa Fe in the
Cerrillos Mountains which was reported to be rich in carbonates. As
the result of this information we changed our plans and made Santa
Fe our destination.[17]

A mail line of recent establishment operated with buckboards and
small Mexican mules from Fort Dodge, Kansas, to either Fort Bascom
or Fort Sumner, New Mexico. The line supplied Tascosa communication with the outside world. For all that, it was an isolated spot in a
desert, if that can be called deserted which had never been inhabited.
It lay several miles south of the Canadian River on the northern slope
of what we knew as the Staked Plains, but which is now better known
as the South Plains — a bare, treeless plateau, then destitute of human
life and almost so of birds and mammals. The advent of the traveler
made the spice of Tascosa's life. As we laid over a day to rest up our

OLD TASCOSA

Now a ghost town in Northwestern Panhandle of Texas near border with New Mexico. Williams and party passed through enroute to New Mexico.

SANTA FE, NEW MEXICO

A view of the town as Williams saw it during his visit in 1879.

THE COPPER MINE AT SANTA RITA

An operation of historic importance, located east of Silver City.
The Apaches often raided the mining settlement.

CHIEF GERONIMO

He and his Apache band were a constant danger to
Williams and other miners as they prospected for silver
and gold in Southwestern New Mexico.

animals, we found ourselves quite popular, until it was learned that there was no one of our number disposed to join the party of six or seven men who seemed to devote their full time to drinking and gambling and who constituted the entire floating population of the village.

We had left Tascosa and crossed the Canadian River to take the ancient road from Fort Smith, Arkansas, to Santa Fe,[18] when we were overtaken by the little buckboard carrying mail, that had followed us out of Tascosa. The driver, of course, stopped to swap news with us, according to time-honored custom. He told us that on the day of our departure a fight occurred among the gentry of the cards and bottles, in which two of them had been killed; and that the barkeeper, struck in the abdomen by a spent ball which had passed through the wooden bar-counter and landed against his bare skin, had shriekingly announced his departure from the Staked Plains to a hotter and better-inhabited country. Later, after examination, he postponed the trip.

In reply to our inquiry as to the cause of the trouble, we received a terse answer: "Drinking and Gambling." During the next three years of my acquaintance with the Territory of New Mexico, there were many, many similar incidents within my knowledge, and the answer of the stage driver was stereotyped. Looking back over nearly fifty years of life on the frontier, I am astonished even yet to consider the enormous waste of time, money and life due to one or the other, or both, of these evils, during the years 1879 to 1882 in New Mexico.

There was an Indian war going on at the time, and it was deadly. In total deaths, there were possibly more outright and immediate killings by Indians than resulted in the same period from drinking and gambling among the whites; but in the measure of waste of time and money and in the shortening of life at its latter end, I am sure that the Indian record was left far behind. An old-time miner of Shakespeare, when asked by me if he drank in the early days, said "Never, that's why I am here yet." Certainly the lives of many that I knew in those days were shortened from these causes.

We continued our journey up the Canadian River, then along the barren stretches of Pajarito Creek[19] and over the divide down to the little village of Anton Chico[20] on the banks of the Pecos River. The river borders of green gardens and truck patches made it seem to us a veritable oasis. There we stopped over a day to rest and feed man and beast. But we did not appear to be welcomed by the Mexican population. They eyed us with hostile glances from the time that we six heavily armed men rode into the village until we left, and now and then we heard something about *tejanos diablos* ("Texan devils").

There was in the place a Jewish merchant from whom we made some purchases to replenish our commissary. After we had made good with him by paying him some sound American money, he called me to one side and told me that the Mexicans believed us to be members of the gang of Billy the Kid and, furthermore, that there was talk of waylaying us in some canyon ahead on our road. This was the first time that we had heard of this distinguished son of New Mexico; so, after learning something of that gentleman's career from the merchant, we moved out on the road with a scout in front on each flank. But we were not attacked. Possibly the fact that we had paid for everything we laid in at this oasis may have had something to do with our freedom from ambush. When Billy paid, he too was probably safe from these people.[21]

When next we halted our jaded animals for prolonged rest, it was at our journey's end, at the foot of the Cerrillos Hills near an ancient turquoise mine (with some history and much fable hanging on it)— in a very small cluster of tents, shacks and dugouts trying to live up to the name of Carbonateville. Here our party disbanded.[22] Laughlin left with fifty cents in his pocket for Santa Fe, twenty-five miles away. Fish and Irving, using Carbonateville as headquarters, began to roam the adjacent country and ended by buying five thousand Mexican sheep for shipment east. Martin procured employment nearby in some kind of mining work.

Bell and I established camp among the other tents and shacks, acquired some mining prospects and, with some little expeditions into foreign territories and occasional visits to Santa Fe, put in there the remainder of the summer.[23] Near us was the headquarters of five men known as the "St. Louis bunch" headed by Captain Moore.[24] Every Sunday or two, Governor Lew Wallace would come out from Santa Fe in his ambulance[25] to spend the day with those boys in particular, and with the balance of us in general. He was a very democratic, sociable man, greatly liked by us, and those Sundays were red-letter days to us. We were told that he had written *Fair God*. I have been told since that at that very time he was engaged in writing *Ben Hur,* and I believe that a room in the old Governor's Palace is still pointed out as the scene of those labors.[26] But of all this we heard nothing in those Sunday visits.

The little camp of seventy or eighty souls boasted of a weekly newspaper commensurate in size — two sheets about twelve inches square — carried on by a picturesque editor, who was called Padre Aoy. He was a dark-skinned little man of nervous manner and voluble speech who was generally referred to by the Mexicans as a *gachupín* — that is to say, in English, of Spanish birth. Because of a camp tradition that he had been formerly a priest, he was commonly called "Padre."[27]

Now the Padre made a scanty living by camp subscriptions and by advertisements, the latter coming largely from Santa Fe business houses. But he had a soul for larger achievements and for adventure far beyond the limits of the camp. He made me the confidant of these ambitions and soon enlisted me in one of his schemes. It was founded on one of those hazy stories of the discovery of New Mexico by the Conquistadors and of the early wanderings of the Franciscans in their attempts to delimit the bounds of the Indians of the Pueblos.[28]

At this time (1879) the maps of New Mexico contained a spot marked "Gran Quivira," some eighty miles south and east of Santa Fe. This was then supposed to mark the site of the Indian town of that name, which the Turk described to Coronado as the chief city of a kingdom abounding in gold and silver, and for which the Spaniard searched and Padilla died.[29] Padre Aoy believed in the truth of this conjecture and that he held the key to the discovery of its hidden treasures.

The Padre described to me a desolate place, where the ruins of an ancient city of adobes were interlaced with the threads of canals and *acequias,* dimly margined now by worn borders almost effaced by the hand of time, within which no waters had run for hundreds of years at the will of man. There were to be found there the fragments of a large Franciscan mission abandoned by the Fathers in haste at the time of the great Indian Rebellion of 1680.[30] They hid the gold and silver plate of the mission service and all other treasure accumulated during a hundred years of occupation. This had never been recovered. The Padre had formerly been a Franciscan, knew the rules and practices of that order, and believed that he could promptly lay his hands upon the spot where the Fathers should have deposited their treasures.

The story was of course very plausible to me, as at that time I knew but little of the early Spanish explorations in New Mexico. When the Padre proposed that I join him in a trip to prospect the ruins of this fabled town of the New Mexican Eldorado, I eagerly accepted. However, I was called back from that country before the old man was ready to undertake the journey. It was at least as enticing to me as the promises of Leadville were when I left Dallas, and I greatly regretted losing the chance to make that trip. But when the investigations of Bandelier and others later clearly demonstrated that the only possible foundation for the imaginary city of the Turk lay in grass-covered villages of wandering Indians on the far Kansas plains, there was some solace to me for the loss of the Padre's "Gran Quivira."

During the summer months of 1879 I began to get interested in reports from the mines in Southern New Mexico, particularly in reports from Shakespeare, a camp in the Pyramid Hills being opened for the second time, the first attempt having been made in the late 1860's by William Ralston, of the Bank of California, and his associates. When Ralston waded out into the Bay of the Golden Gate at San Francisco the end of August, 1875, and closed his career, the town of Ralston, on the site later to become Shakespeare, ceased to exist. Recently, it had begun to come up out of its ashes, under a new name and backed by a St. Louis syndicate.[31]

So I decided to grubstake some prospectors and send them down to the new camp. For that purpose I enlisted two men, Grady and Pettie.[32] They brought to me a third applicant. He was a tall, gangling man of blond complexion, who said that his name was William Rogers Tettenborn; as I recall, he was about twenty-five years old. He had much more to say about himself. His mother was the daughter of a Scotch sea captain named William Rogers, who plied his trade in the Baltic Sea; Tettenborn's father, a Teutonic subject of the Russian Czar, lived in some port of the Baltic Provinces. Bill's own career in the United States had been extremely hectic. He had a bullet in his leg, received in Fort Worth, and he bore a scar from a knife slash in the shoulder as a receipt for a difficulty in Denver. Many had been his marvelous escapes. But I was employing prospectors, not gunmen, so I did not take him.

These men left for the south about the time that I was called back to my Dallas headquarters.[33] Although Tettenborn was much disliked on account of his vaporing braggadocio and his capacity for soldiering in camp, yet he insinuated himself into the party and lived on their provisions all the way down. This was an art at which he was a past master, as shown by his subsequent career in Grant County. Yet his conduct was tempered by a high degree of regard for his personal safety. In those days of peril from Indians, when mineral strikes were made in dangerous territory and the inhabitants would flock to the new find, he was never known to work himself in with a small party; it was always the largest group that was honored by his presence. He was not of the class that rush in where angels fear to tread.

Later in Southern New Mexico he became well known as "Russian Bill." There was a gang of outlaws at that time domiciled in the San Simon Valley, across the line in Arizona, many of them noted as dangerous and desperate characters. With his desire to be regarded as a bad man, it was natural that he should want to be looked upon as a strong man in that crew. He might have served as a spy for them, but it was generally believed that he was not admitted to full fellowship with them because of his lack of courage. However, because of his association with these outlaws, and probably to some extent also because of his evident wish to be considered a wild, woolly man, and his reckless assertions along that line, Bill came to the end of a rope. Somebody believed his statements.

Quite early in 1881 the Southern Pacific Railway was being hurriedly built across the plains at the foot of the Pyramid Hills to the east, and the company constructing it used a large number of horses branded "P. I." Repeatedly, these horses were stolen in small numbers at night. One day some of the "P. I." horses were stolen in broad daylight, and not long afterwards Russian Bill in a saloon in Shakespeare was heard to boast of being one of the heroes in the action.

About that time Sandy King, a much worse man than Bill, showed up in that town, and Bill immediately fell on his neck. King had committed a murder, but had quite recently been given freedom on what was then known as "straw bail," a bond signed by irresponsible parties. On arriving in Shakespeare he and Tettenborn became brothers of the blood and slept together in a room attached to the hotel of "Bean Bellied" Smith. After they had dropped off to sleep one night, a small crowd went into their room and with short shrift hung them both to the roof supports. It was said that King cursed his captors but that Russian Bill wept and begged for mercy, but without avail.[34]

Later in the winter of 1881 and 1882 while I was employed in the post office at Silver City, a letter came to that office from the Russian consul at New York City, stating that he had been asked by the mother of William Rogers Tettenborn to inquire as to the whereabouts of her son, from whom she had last heard in a letter written by that son under the postmark of Silver City. It fell to me to answer the consul's letter. Considering the feelings of the mother, I wrote the consul that Tettenborn had met with a serious accident sometime before at Shakespeare and thereafter died. If Russian Bill has a tombstone on that Baltic shore erected by a mourning mother, it probably carries as true a story as many of our American gravestones tell.

Santa Fe lay only twenty-five miles away from our headquarters in the Cerrillos Hills, and during the early days of my sojourn there, I made several brief visits in the town. It was a place of much interest to me. It laid claim to be the oldest white settlement in the United States. Around it for a center there rested as a corona the mystery of the decayed pueblos, the romance of their Spanish conquerors and the tragedy of the great Indian Revolt of 1680 — about all of which my

gachupín friend Aoy had much to tell, gathered from Franciscan man-
uscripts and the reports of Spanish officials. And I had a personal
interest in the storied town which appealed to me even more than its
historic record.[35]

My grandfather, Richard Gott Williams of Richmond, Kentucky, in
1826 led a trading expedition from St. Louis, Missouri, to Taos and
Santa Fe. Finding the market for his goods at the latter places too
small, he carried his caravan down to the city of Chihuahua for final
disposition.[36] He brought with him from Missouri a youth of seventeen
years, who left the party either at Santa Fe, or at El Paso to return to
Santa Fe, and who later became the most noted of the early American
settlers in New Mexico. More stories of frontier adventure have been
built up around his name than can be claimed for any frontiersman
excepting Daniel Boone.

Kit Carson was born near Richmond, Kentucky, about the year 1809.
His birthplace was only a few miles distant from the town of Boones-
borough, founded by Boone and made famous by his exploits in its
defense. So Carson may be said to have been born under the aegis of
Daniel Boone and to have carried on the career of that famous adventurer. His parents moved to Missouri following the trail of the great
scout when Kit was only two years old, and he came to youthful manhood on the banks of the Missouri at or near the town of Old Franklin.

When my grandfather's expedition came to this last-named place,
it was halted for a short period, because this town was the last place
where preparations could be made for entering the "Great American
Desert," as the Western Plains were styled on the maps of that day.
Kit Carson was at that time apprenticed for an unexpired term to a
saddler of the town, after the custom of early times. He must have met
in the party old friends of the family from the Richmond neighborhood.
At any rate, he desired to join the expedition and made application to
the saddler to be released from his apprenticeship. The saddler refused,
and the party left without him. Several days later, out on the Santa Fe
Trail, he caught up with the party and was made a member. The saddler
advertised Kit in the local paper as a runaway, and offered a reward
of two cents to him who would bring him back. The reward was never
paid. Kit did not go back; Santa Fe and Taos claimed him.[37]

So when my friend Danover of Dallas, Texas, a recent arrival from
Texas, proposed that we should spend a little time in Santa Fe viewing
the place "from its ground floor," as he expressed it, I accepted the
proposition. We saw it truly from the ground floor; we could not well
view it from a higher floor, since none existed, other than in one hotel.

We rented a single room, set up light housekeeping, and then explored the old place. It bore on its face evidence of its antiquity. An adobe house assumes the appearance of age within a short time, and Santa Fe was a town of adobes, from the ancient church to the latest building. But there was some color to its life. On Sundays the band from the fort came down to the plaza to a "guard mount" of swelling music and spectacular color and motion. At the Mexican *bailes*, the belles of the ball came out in laces, black *mantillas*, and a hothouse of artificial flowers of colors and shapes never designed by Nature.

Our "ground floor" experiment was not very satisfactory as to eatables. We could get Mexican dishes served in the best of Mexican style, but we had not yet been educated up to that standard. In the markets, goat meat could be found in abundance and sheep meat now and then, but here too our education was lacking. Beef was very rarely to be had, and when we did get a taste of it we felt that some family had sacrificed an old worn-out plow ox. We were able to get milk — but I must tell that story.

By dint of earnest but sadly broken Spanish, and by the aid of much gesticulation which we called sign language, one day we engaged a Mexican milk vendor to deliver to us each morning a quart of milk for a certain price. About eight o'clock the next morning a knock at our door introduced to us our Mexican, asking for a vessel. Out in the street beyond him we saw a herd of thirty or forty goats waiting to deliver milk, kept in place by two small boys. The Mexican selected a nannie with much deliberation, milked her and finished the delivery by handing in the vessel containing the milk. It seemed to be quite scant in quantity, but we now learned a curious fact of natural history — that each goat gave just a quart of milk, regardless of how high the milk might stand in the vessel. Our education was progressing, but for me the process was soon ended.

When I got on the stage bound for Las Vegas, then the terminus of the A. T. & S. F. Railroad, I found that General Edward Hatch and two junior officers were to be my fellow passengers. The Ute War had broken out in Colorado, and they had been ordered to report for duty.[38] At Las Vegas I learned that Fish and Irving had left two or three days previously with a trainload of sheep for the Kansas City market. As my train passed a siding about twenty miles out of Kansas City, on which a freight train was standing, I saw the two shippers waving at me from the caboose. After my arrival in that city I went down to the stockyards to see them.

They told me that their shipment of five thousand sheep had overstocked the market, and that they were about to divide it into two parts: one bound for Chicago and one for St. Louis. They introduced me to a plausible individual who claimed the name of Coffman and who seemed to act as adviser in the matter of shipment. They said they had picked him up in New Mexico as a kind of foreman because he was familiar with the handling of sheep — and, as they were not, he was quite useful to them. He was well versed in the art of "fleecing," as was made plain on that shipment.

After my return to Dallas on October 9, I received a letter from Fish authorizing me to shoot him, Coffman, on sight. The letter stated that the shipment had been divided as proposed when I saw them in Kansas City, one half being consigned to Chicago and the other to St. Louis; that he and Irving had gone with the St. Louis consignment, while their new foreman had taken the other to Chicago — and the proceeds of the sale to parts unknown. Fish and Irving were being educated also, but in a higher school than Danover and I — the white man's school.

Second Journey via El Paso

I SPENT THE WINTER of 1879 and 1880 in Texas and the Mississippi River states. During that time I received reports from Pettie of his progress in securing mining properties.[39] I heard nothing directly from my other prospector, Grady. From one of Pettie's letters, however, I learned that shortly after their arrival in Shakespeare, Grady had left him to prospect in that spur of the Burro Mountains which comes to an end near the site of an old stage stand known as Soldier's Farewell,[40] and was never heard of afterwards. It was later reported that a band of hostile Indians had passed through those hills shortly after he entered; it was generally believed that he had been killed by them.

The life of a prospector was very precarious at that time in that country. The very nature of his occupation kept his attention attracted to the rocks underfoot rather than to the horizon about him and left him exposed to the sly approach of lurking enemies. The Apaches of one tribe or another in succession had broken out from their reservations in raids that swung into Mexico and back again, as the pursuit on either side of the boundary might occasion.[41] Grady, a former Colorado prospector, had gone into the hills accompanied only by his burro, following his Colorado practice. Afflicted with weak eyes, he was probably an easy victim.

Pettie further wrote me that he had made a location of a claim for me on the big Shakespeare mining lode near the Superior Mine of Jim

Carroll, and had given it the name of "Joe Johnston," after the noted Confederate general. This claim was abandoned by us two or three years later when the Shakespeare camp became quite dead, because the ore was low grade and hardly justified the cost of the annual assessment. Recently I have found that it covered a part of the ground now being mined under the name of the "85" Mine, which is said to have produced an immense amount of ore from which a large sum of money has been realized.[42]

Pettie had also procured for me a half interest in a location bearing the name of "Oasis," in consideration of drilling a shaft on the vein of ore. The owners of this location were Major W. A. Downing, then running a sawmill in the Chiricahua Mountains but formerly a mining operator in Nevada; Fred W. Smith, the hotel man in Shakespeare; and Tom Dunn, a prospector, then living at Leitendorf's Wells. I took in with me on this contract Currie and McCutcheon of Dallas, Texas. We drilled the shaft and in due time received a deed to the half interest contracted.

The Oasis location lay several miles south of Shakespeare in a neighborhood generally referred to as the Leitendorf District. The shaft did not disclose any rich ore, but the location itself later proved to be quite valuable. It did not prove to be an "oasis" to us, however. It led us into a bootless lawsuit in which we lost our claim after a trial remarkable in some respects, which I will relate further on in this story.[43] Some months after the deed was executed to me by Dunn, Downing and Smith, Dunn proceeded to locate the ground in his own right individually under the name of "Last Chance," and then sold the controlling interest in it to Bement, Nisbet and Mackay of Evansville, Indiana. We did not learn these facts until much later.

In the early spring of 1880 I began my journey to Shakespeare from Dallas. On March 29 of that year, my former Harvard schoolmate George A. Grant of Meriden, Connecticut, arrived in Dallas, primed and ready for more Western experience. He was not a novice in the West. He had spent the summer of 1878 with me on the Staked Plains of Texas, at that time the last stand of the buffalo and only a few months before abandoned by the Quahada band of Comanches, who were finally brought into the fold of the Reservation by Chief Quanah Parker[44] in spite of the opposition of old Mauwe, the leader of many a raid over the Rio Grande. But Grant had never experienced the life of the miner and planned to top his trip to the Plains with one to the mountains. I was very much pleased at the prospect of the companionship of my old chum.

W. G. Currie had also decided to join the party. He was one of the most quiet, modest and unobtrusive of men. He had been a soldier in the Civil War, serving in an artillery company during some desperate battles, yet he was the "mildest mannered man that ever scuttled a ship or cut a throat." It was almost painful at times to look on at his embarrassment when he was brought to the front unexpectedly in conversation, but it was delightful to witness his cool, clear-cut presence of mind in a serious emergency. Currie had arranged to take the Overland stage with me to Shakespeare, while Grant planned to organize a company to travel over the same route by horse and wagon.

Fort Worth was then the western terminus of the T. & P. Railroad, and probably the most western railhead in Texas — certainly in North Texas. Currie and I left Dallas on April 6, 1880, and on the next day in a light sprinkle of rain we mounted the coach from the Clark House in Fort Worth and started on a long and fatiguing trip.[45] We started out, however, with little hint of that kind. It was a fine Concord coach drawn by six spirited horses; and when the driver cracked his long whiplash over their heads, we sailed up the dusty street in great style. From here we passed to an even dustier road, which ended for us nearly a thousand miles away — a thousand miles of hot sunshine and cold nights, sandstorms and snow.[46]

Although we were traveling smoothly in that Concord coach, yet we could get no sleep. So when we got to Fort Concho (now San Angelo) at 8:30 P.M., April 9, we welcomed a layover of two nights — the 9th and 10th — while Currie visited with his brother Joe.[47] On the evening of the 11th we left San Angelo, but in much less state than on our departure from Fort Worth. A priest joined us here, and our party of four was crowded on a little open buckboard drawn by two undersized half-broken Mexican mules. After we were all seated with the driver in position, the mules were led out separately, by ropes fastened by a nose-hitch, and held in place while another man buckled on the harness. When all was ready, the nose-hitches were loosened, the driver gave a yell, and away went the mules at a frantic gallop.

"*Bueno,*" said the priest. But after two or three miles of this speed, the animals began to lag, and the driver put into use the best device that I have ever seen applied to get motion out of a mule without marring the hide. At the end of his flexible whiplash he had attached just three links of an ordinary chain — he must have been an Odd Fellow. When that Odd Fellow signal dropped lightly on the withers of the mules, we always regained at once our starting speed.

Until then, I had supposed that the use of flint and steel was a thing of the long past, but we had hardly settled down to our three-links rate of travel when our priest drew out of his small baggage a little tin box, and out of it he brought his "makings." It was rare indeed in those days that Americans smoked cigarettes; never had I then seen such an elaborate set of machinery dedicated to that purpose, and not often since. First came an empty cartridge shell in which was thrust the charred end of a cotton cord some two feet in length, and colored, streaked and striped like a Joseph's coat. Next came a flint and its steel, and then a package of corn shucks cut square, and a handkerchief full of tobacco. In a deft manner he poured his tobacco, rolled his shuck, struck fire on the charred end of his cotton cord and lighted his cigarette. Then, and not till then, would he talk.

By morning's light we had come to the head of the Concho, by noon to the flats of Centralia, and shortly afterwards we passed a *tinaja* by the roadside, which the driver told us was called Flat Rock and which had been a week previous the scene of a murder by Indians. We were in a bare desert country and there was nothing improbable in the story on its face, but the driver was inclined to suspect that the Indians had been charged with a murder committed by a white man.

At sunset we came to the Pecos River and crossed on a pontoon swung by iron chains between banks, with movable platform on either side as approaches to the pontoon, to fit any stage of the water. It was an ingenious piece of work, soon to be abandoned. From the river, our road led west up a wide valley. All night the little mules danced to the music of the three links, while now and then our tired eyes brightened up at the pungent odor of smouldering corn shuck. At sunrise we passed through the beautiful water of Comanche Creek, just as we heard the morning trumpet notes from the Fort Stockton garrison.[48]

At Fort Stockton our good priest left us. He told us that we had been riding for two hundred miles through a country of mesas, but that now we were about to enter a land of sierras, and he pointed out to us the serrated top of Sierra Madera rising behind the level front of the Nine-Mile Mesa. The skyline of the mesa country was marked by horizontal escarpments, some higher, some lower, but all running smooth and parallel with the earth's surface; the horizon of the sierra country was ragged with lines dented by cones pointing upward to the sky.

When our country, after the War with Mexico, acquired its great Southwestern territory, we also took over as a prize quite a number of foreign words in use in that territory, which we have incorporated into our language. The larger part of these words were desert bred, many in Arabia — one, the word *adobe*, probably coming with Abraham from Ur of the Chaldees. These words traveled west along the arid parallel of the 30th degree of North Latitude up to the Iberian shores of the Atlantic Ocean, where they rested for seven hundred years and then came on west to America on the barks of Columbus.

These barks carried over two other words, *mesa* and *sierra*. These two words came to the Atlantic shores from the households of the early Romans, at the foot of the Apennines. In the Latin of the Romans a *mensa* was a table used for dining or other purposes, and it had an elevated flat surface. Therefore our mesas may be literally called table hills. The word *serra* in the same language meant a saw with pointed teeth, so that our sierras just as literally may be said to be elevated saw-shaped ridges with teeth facing the sky. So now at Fort Stockton we were leaving the country of Nature's cooks with the great dining tables and were entering into the land of her carpenters with the giant saws — all according to figures of speech adopted by ancient peoples.

At 9:00 A.M. of April 13 the mules were changed at the Leon Holes, and we had a short opportunity of examining these curiosities of nature about which we had heard something from nearly every driver and station keeper on the road from Fort Worth to Fort Stockton. I have never seen any springs similar to them. Two of the holes were of a circular shape, about a hundred feet in diameter; the third was of smaller size. The overflow of water from the upper hole passed into and out of the other two in succession. One of the holes was claimed by the station keeper to be 46 feet in depth, and the next to go down to 220 feet. The walls of the holes were almost perpendicular; at the top, a mat of roots of tule and other aquatic plants, of sufficient depth and strength to support a man, extended out six or seven feet from the earth margin. The water was clear and of a beautiful blue tint. This was the picture in 1880. It may interest some Old Timers to learn that these holes are now entirely filled up with sediment, and the marsh below them has become a lake. A dam built by an irrigation company formed the lake.[49]

At Fort Davis, which we reached at 9:30 o'clock that night, we found that there was considerable uneasiness about the Indians.[50] Some days before our arrival they had raided the vicinity of the fort and killed some people. It was believed at that time that another raid on the fort was about to be made, as the signs of their presence had just been detected. So I am afraid that our driver pushed the little mules to the limit of their strength in making Barrel Springs at 3:00 A.M. on the 14th.[51] It was a very cold ride. I suffered from the cold, although wrapped up in a buffalo robe. When the mules were at their best speed, it seemed to me that the cold night air literally blew through that robe as if it were no more substantial than a mosquito bar.

At 7:00 A.M. we were in El Muerto, a name that was enough of itself to raise the hair on a traveler's head in Indian times.[52] The stock tender here assured us that another week would see him out of the d---d country; a helper at the station was not going to wait even that long. At Van Horn, the next station,[53] to which the water for all purposes was hauled out of the hills two and one-half miles away, we found the same uneasiness. Eagle Springs[54] was our next stopping place, and we met here a bunch of Pueblo Indians headed by a chief whose name was Simón, to the best of my recollection. Their Spanish was bad and ours was worse, but we understood them to say that they had been trailing one of Victorio's raiding bands of hostile Indians.

During our brief stay at this last station, we were able to get the local tenders off the subject of Indians far enough to be told that a priest had located in the nearby Eagle Sierras a vein of ore ten miles long and ten feet wide. We hoped that our former *compañero* of the corn-shuck cigarette had been the finder, but we could not learn the name of the lucky person. It occurred to us that his was a pretty good-sized find, large enough to give to each of us a chance at a location, but we had heard that the Shakespeare mines near the present town of Lordsburg were as large or larger in extent. Since we thought that the hostile Indians might not be so abundant there as in these Sierras of the Eagle, we went on. Our assumption as to Indians was not correct. Also, the tender must have been in error as to the size and character of that vein of ore. Although I have seen a small vein of coal not far back of the Eagle Springs, I am told that it was not profitable.

Leaving this station, we passed into the Bass Canyon about nightfall. This was a dangerous place at that time, in which a number of men were killed in those troubled days. My friend Grant and his party passed through the canyon later and narrowly escaped an attack — so narrowly, indeed, that he was reported killed. Although he is alive to this day and persists in denying the report, yet the rumor is still in the records.

About 1:00 A.M. of the 15th we came to old Fort Quitman, in the valley of the Rio Grande.[55] In the afternoon we passed San Elizario and Ysleta,[56] where we looked on the first growing crops in the four hundred miles of travel since leaving Comanche Springs. As the river and the canals carried no running water, these crops were plainly faring badly. At Ysleta we saw some very old and large pear trees, planted along the banks of canals (known then by the Spanish name *acequias*) in accordance with an ancient obligation imposed on the owners of *solares,* or colony lots. They must have been the oldest pear trees then growing in Texas.

We were told that the crops would do no good until the snow on the headwaters of the Rio Grande melted and sent down the flowing waters of the river. The present Elephant Butte Dam has wonderfully changed the aspect of that sixty miles of sandy barrens and has built up a perennial strip of green to succeed the old alkali white-and-yellow sands.[57]

About ten o'clock the night of the 15th we arrived at the corral of the stage company in the town of Franklin, situated to the best of my recollection about where the Mills Building now stands.[58] In those days the name of Franklin was applied to the small settlement on the Texas side of the Rio Grande, which has now become a large city under the name of El Paso; opposite it in Mexico, a much larger settlement bore the name of El Paso del Norte, now known as Juárez. The Mexican town was noted for the large vineyard of mission grapes owned by an American named Dr. Alexander,[59] and for the church of Nuestra Señora de Guadalupe.[60] The American town was then noted as "the substance of things hoped for, the evidence of things not seen," but the faith of those who at that time endured the grim hardships of that desert town has been greatly justified.

There was an adobe hotel near the stage corral, and a small irrigating canal lined by a few cottonwoods ran not far south of it. The stumps of some of those cottonwoods were visible twenty years later, but the old adobe hotel did not endure long after the railroads were built into the town. Of course the stage corral passed out of use when the passenger coaches came in. There was some excitement among the natives over the approach of the two railroads from the east and the west, and we were told that town lots near where the Hussmann Hotel now stands were held at the exorbitant price of one hundred dollars a lot.[61] There seemed to be an uneasiness among the lot holders about the possible location of the depot by the railroad company, which made for tardy sales.

In the early morning we started for Mesilla. We left behind us our open buckboard and embarked in a covered hack drawn by two good horses; so we felt that we were getting up in the world again, especially because we had as fellow voyagers a lady named Mrs. Hughes and her two children, bound for some station not far from Shakespeare. We stopped for breakfast at a station where the horses were watered at a gravel pit in the river bed, sunken to catch the underflow. The keeper gave us a breakfast of burnt beans, rancid bacon and coffee grounds, for which he apologized at much length. However, he had no apology to make for his charge of one dollar for each of us. I had nothing less than a five-dollar bill, and received back in change four Mexican dollars. I demurred to the insufficiency of the change, only to be assured at great length, with citations of various authorities, that the custom of the country ran for acceptance of Mexican dollars at the same value as those of American coinage. When I arrived at Mesilla and found that the Mexican coin was received at only seventy-five cents, I began to feel that the phrase "custom of the country" might cover a multitude of sins — and subsequent experiences confirmed this feeling.

We arrived at Mesilla[62] about 8:00 a.m. and waited there for the arrival of the stagecoach coming down the river from the north. After its arrival, it was decided to hold back our departure a few hours so that we might pass through some dangerous territory in the nighttime. Some time about noon we crossed the Rio Grande, going through the first running water that we had seen in the wide bed of that stream — water, we were told, coming from melting snows at its headwaters and only that day arriving at our crossing place. Our coach was somewhat crowded, and I was riding in the boot (box) beside a rather taciturn driver and behind four good horses that easily carried a large Concord coach of the same type as that in which we had left Fort Worth.

As we passed over the river I noticed a Mexican, mounted on a small horse — thin of flank and apparently in very bad condition — following the tail of the coach. An hour later he was still hanging to our rear as closely as he could urge on his jaded animal. In reply to a question put to the driver, I learned that the Mexican was going to Fort Cummings, some forty miles away, and had taken up after us in order to get protection in case of an attack by the Indians. In answer to my suggestion that his jaded horse could not keep up with the coach, which had relays of animals every few miles, the driver simply said, "We'll see." We did. When we got to Fort Cummings,[63] the Mexican was just as close to our tailboard as when we drove through the Rio Grande water.

We had a late dinner at Mason's Station, and not long after leaving that place we passed a spot in the road which bore witness to an Indian raid. Lying in the order of their yokes were the partially dried carcasses of twelve oxen, and behind them lay in place the irons and charred fragments of a freight wagon. A little farther on in the road lay the ruins of another such wagon and its teams. They had been destroyed by the Indians several months before our arrival.

It was after nightfall, however, before we came to the scene of the recent killing about which we had heard much in Mesilla. We had been keyed up all through the afternoon and night, watching for the site.

The attack by the Apaches had taken place on the road some twelve miles east of the fort, only one or two days before our arrival at the spot. An Army officer, his son and the driver had been murdered by Indians. As the officer was a paymaster on his way to some Arizona fort, there was the possibility that he had carried money to pay the soldiers stationed there.

We had come up a long shallow canyon and out on an open stretch of country over which arose a forest of dead yucca flower stalks, when we saw ahead some white objects scattered over the broad, smooth surface of the road. As we approached nearer we saw that these white objects were papers and envelopes of various sizes and that they were scattered not only on the road but also in the yucca bushes on the south side of the road. The driver halted the horses and announced, "This is the spot."

We got out and looked around. There were many tracks of horses and men in the road where the soldiers had taken up the trail of the Indians after the attack. They had taken up pursuit on a trail leading to the southwest; looking out over that course in the faint moonlight, we soon discovered something that led to much speculation. The tops of the yucca flower stalks, standing eight or ten feet above ground, carried along the departing trail a line of white markers plainly showing the direction of that trail as far as we could see. Examination disclosed to us that these white markers consisted of large white envelopes cut at one end and thrust down on the pointed tops of the stalks. We wondered who did this and why.

After a short stop we went on to Fort Cummings, where we caught the answer to our speculations. When word of the massacre was brought to the fort, a troop of cavalry with some Yuma Indian scouts was sent out to take up the pursuit of the hostile Indians. Arriving at the scene, the troopers soon discovered that the trail of the departing Indians was clearly marked by the white papers on the dead bloom stalks — so clearly that the scouts and soldiers followed it quite rapidly. While following at considerable speed, they rode down into a shallow draw with rocky borders so low that the riders fancied no ambush was possible. Yet, once well into that depression, they were fired on by Indians from both sides. One Yuma scout was killed, several soldiers wounded, and the entire command thrown into confusion. Some of the cavalry horses had strayed back to the fort; it was therefore evident that a number of soldiers had been dismounted and the pursuit had been broken. This was the purpose of the white markers, which indicated considerable ingenuity on the part of the Indians.

Other Historic Points En Route

W We left Fort Cummings in the darkness of the night and came out on the old road leading around the southern foothills of the Cooke's Peak Range. At a distance of a few miles from the fort we came into a glade in the midst of tall pine trees scattered rather thinly on both sides of the road, with here and there a knob of ancient rock protruding through the pines in the dim light.

Our moody driver swung his hand in the direction of a point in the pines on the south side of the road and said, "Do you see that pile of rocks about three hundred yards out from the road?" I did not.

"Well," he continued, "It's there, just the same — and that's where Emmett Mills, his friends and the stage driver were taken in by Cochise and his Apaches."

At that time I had never heard this story; so I listened to our stage driver's saga with great interest, as it was well told by a man who may have carried his coach through the danger of a similar attack and who was now driving in daily risk from the same tribe of Indians. I could well understand how he was picturing to himself all the details of the hopeless fight of the driver and his passengers, putting himself in the driver's boot as he did so. His story briefly told, as I recollect it after nearly fifty years, ran as follows:

The great Civil War between the States broke out in 1861. By July of that year, Col. John R. Baylor and the Confederates under him were taking the El Paso territory and threatening to capture the Upper Rio Grande Valley, through which the Overland stage route ran. If they succeeded, it would cut off communications between Arizona and Southern New Mexico on the one side and the Northern Union States on the other.[64] Emmett Mills, a youth of eighteen years, and his brothers, W. W. (afterwards U. S. consul at Chihuahua) and Anson (afterwards a general in the Federal Army), had determined to throw in with the Union men.[65] When Emmett learned of the situation, he was at some point on the stage line. The stages were about to cease running, so he left at once on the next coach. With him on the stage were four or five other men, who were gamblers.

When the stage arrived at the glade among the tall pines, it was attacked by Indians under Cochise, the most wary and dangerous of the Apache chiefs. It was forced from the road and overturned, the horses being killed. Behind the overturned stage and later behind some nearby rocks, the party made the best defense possible. Fort Cummings had not then been established, and the sounds of the conflict could hardly have been heard by the stage employees at Cooke's Springs, nor, if heard, could any help be expected from them.

The fight was apparently hopeless from the beginning. But the party fought to the bitter end. For two days they kept the enemy at bay while they suffered from lack of sleep, food and water. At last, with ammunition exhausted, the lone survivor was killed and the Indians came to mutilate the dead.[66] But the whites had made battle so desperately and so effectively that it is said that Cochise told his braves that if they could fight as well as the men of the coach, he could whip the entire United States Army. How this speech of Cochise's came through to the whites was unknown to the narrator.

This was the driver's story, as I recollect it. But I am not quite certain whether he said Emmett Mills was going out on a westbound coach for Tucson or was coming from Tucson on an eastbound coach. My memory rather favors the eastbound route. However, later on I heard the story again — this time from the lips of G. M. Frazer, a Confederate soldier under Colonel Baylor in the Rio Grande valley at the time, or very shortly after the time, when the coach was attacked.[67] I wrote out his statement and sent it to the Silver City *Sentinel*, which published it some time between 1884 and 1886, but I have never seen that statement since to verify any of the details. Someone should hunt out all that is on record about the fight and put it in print, as it is a classic in the annals of Southern New Mexico and should not be lost to posterity. If that rock mound near the old Overland stage route still lifts its front in the remains of that thin forest of pines on the south flank of the Cooke's Peak Range, it is probably the sole tribute paid in stone or paper to a gallant band making a hopeless fight.[68]

The road over which we were then traveling was possibly the route of General Philip St. George Cooke during the War with Mexico, when he carried an expedition from Santa Fe through to California. Certainly Cooke's Peak derives its name from that officer.[69] Later, during the Civil War, an expedition was organized in 1861 by the Federal Government in California to march through Arizona and New Mexico for the purpose of defeating the efforts of the Confederates to occupy the Rio Grande Valley. As this detachment of soldiers passed over this road from the Mimbres to Mesilla, it is probable that the cairn of stones referred to by the driver was erected by them. I subsequently passed over this part of the road and saw several times from the coach a pile of rocks south of the road, about where the driver had pointed it out.

The soldiers who comprised this expedition from California were commonly spoken of by the inhabitants of New Mexico and Arizona as the "California Column."[70] Many of them remained in the country, and when I was living in Shakespeare and Silver City from the spring of 1880 to the fall of 1882, there were still quite a number of them to be found in various parts of Southern New Mexico and in the valley of the Rio Grande, but principally in the valley from El Paso up to Albuquerque. A few had drifted farther east into Texas, among them a local celebrity named Roy Bean, who for a time, as justice of the peace near the mouth of the Pecos River, claimed to be the "Law West of the Pecos," and published that claim by a painted sign hung up over the door of his saloon.[71] His brother, Sam Bean, however, remained in New Mexico and, at the time of which I am writing, resided on the Mimbres River, above the stage crossing.

This crossing was our next stopping place.[72] There was a station here for changing animals, kept by a stock tender who also served as postmaster for the people of the lower Mimbres Valley. If the story told me here by the driver was correct, the stock tender could hardly have qualified for the position under the present Civil Service rules. The local mail destined for delivery at the post offices between Mesilla and Silver City was carried in a single sack, and each postmaster along the way opened it and sorted out the mail for his office.

On one such occasion, the Mimbres postmaster brought out to the driver for inspection a letter which had strayed into the wrong sack, addressed to "John Harris, Tucson, A. T." — Arizona was then a territory. The postmaster said he had never heard of any "Tuckson," but that did not bother him half as much as the fact that the "damfool writer" did not put down the place AT which "Tuckson's" letter was to be delivered — as he did not know the names of all the ranchers on the Mimbres, it might be intended for some one of them. He learned then from the driver that A. T. stood for Arizona Territory.

From Mesilla to this crossing of the Mimbres, we had traveled on the Overland route — known also, I believe, as the Butterfield route — as it existed before the Civil War.[73] The report of Col. Benjamin L. E. Bonneville of the Third Infantry, dated at Santa Fe, New Mexico, on July 15, 1859, shows that he left old Fort Thorn on May 13 of that year and proceeded by Mule Springs to a "quagmire called Cooke's Spring," where he found a station of the Overland Mail route. It was kept by four men in a little hut. Similar stations along the whole route were found "at from eighteen to twenty miles apart, with four men each."[74]

But at the Mimbres crossing this mail route turned farther to the south than the route over which I was traveling in 1880. The report states that on leaving the Mimbres, the Colonel "proceeded to another quagmire called Cow Spring," which was also a station on the mail route. Here his party turned a little to the northwest and found water in a *ciénega* in the southeastern point of the Burro Mountains. From here the water was carried to supply the mail station of Soldier's Farewell and to the next station farther west, both of which lacked local water sources. The second station west of Soldier's Farewell was also without water, which was hauled to it from a hole or spring about fourteen miles southwest. This was probably the place afterwards known as Leitendorf's Wells,[75] although no name is given in Colonel Bonneville's report.

After leaving Soldier's Farewell, the Colonel's party found that "our road lay west over a valley about forty miles wide, towards Stein's Peak, which appeared in the distance. As we descended into this valley or *playa*, the mirage presented to our view lakes, harbors, bridges, ships and all manner of water scenes changing continually as we approached." I traveled this old road several times in 1880, when it was still plainly marked on the surface of the ground, from a point near where Lordsburg[76] now stands, through Soldier's Farewell to that "quagmire called Cow Springs," and I recall clearly those mirages of lakes, although I am pretty sure that I never saw any ships sailing on those waters.

Passing by the site of present Lordsburg, the Colonel's party came at sunset to Stein's Peak Station,[77] where water was so scant that they did not succeed in watering their animals until two o'clock on the following morning. Here they found about fifty Indians — men, women and children — living, apparently, on friendly terms with the station keepers. From this place the party passed out west up a canyon of Stein's Peak for several miles and then, turning south, they entered a "chasm in the mountains," with a roadway at its bottom, wide enough for two wagons. Continuing into the San Simon Valley, they came to another station at the San Simon "River." The river was dry, and water was brought to the station from the *ciénega* at its head some twelve or fourteen miles away. Beyond this, in Apache Pass, they came to another station of the mail route and again found a dry station to which water was hauled — in this case, however, from water holes in the mountains only some three miles distant.[78]

I have given these details of Colonel Bonneville's itinerary for a purpose. The memory of this mail route, over which so much of the history of the Southwest passed like a panorama, should be perpetuated by markers of stone. That could have been easily done in 1880, as the trail was marked then not only by the worn surface and the ruts of wagon wheels, but also by a parallel line of bushes growing thriftily by the roadside. I have hopes that it can be done even now. Furthermore, the road ran for long stretches in a direct line as if laid out by a transit, and this was particularly the case in the wide flats east and west of Lordsburg. Once having caught its trace, one should easily follow it.

But, coming back to the Mimbres crossing: We left that place, on the stage road of that day which led to Silver City and from there through the Burro Mountains to Shakespeare.[79] It was evident that a segment of the old mail route of 1859 had been abandoned at some later time, and a new route established from the Mimbres River as far as the Pyramid Hills.[80] This must have happened about the years 1871 and 1872 when the mines near Silver City and Pinos Altos began to be largely developed. At the time of Colonel Bonneville's journey, these mines could hardly have been in active operation, as he makes no mention of them, while he gives considerable attention to the copper mines "towards the head of the Mimbres," by which phrase he referred to the district known as the Santa Rita copper mines.[81] He says that these mines employed 180 men; that the owners desired to increase that number to 400; and that the laborers were chiefly Mexicans from Chihuahua, who were viewed from old times by the Indians as enemies.

As the ancient trail from those mines to Chihuahua crossed the Butterfield route at the station of Cow Spring, it is probable that what little mail and travel went from the copper mines to the United States was handled at that station. That Old Chihuahua Trail leading south from Cow Spring by the Tenaja Mountains and Carrisalillo (now Hermanas) Springs was plainly visible in 1880, when I passed over it several times.[82] There were then to be seen at Carrisalillo Springs the ruins of an old adobe house which had presumably served as a way station.

This trail was well known to the Mexicans, and on it I met in that same year, between the Tenaja Mountains and those springs, a party of five Mexicans afoot and a leader on horseback, who told us that they were escaping from peonage in Mexico and going to work in the Clifton copper mines.[83] The men on foot were dressed in cotton shirts and drawers only, wore sandals, and carried over the shoulder a thin, half-size blanket and a small sack of *pinole* (flour made from parched corn). To escape the risk of Indian attack, they traveled only by night and slept by day under the shade of a blanket thrown over a small greasewood or other bush. They were totally unarmed. The leader carried a pistol of antique design and a *machete* (a long, broad-blade knife), spoke some English and stated that he received a certain amount of pay

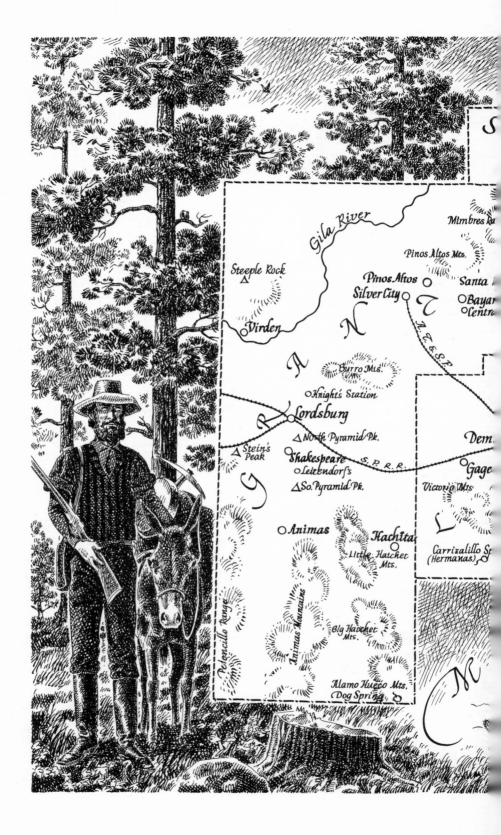

Gila River

Mimbres Ra

Steeple Rock
△

Pinos Altos Mts.

Pinos Altos ○
Silver City ○

Santa

Bayar
Central

Virden ○

S

N

A

R

G

Burro Mts.

Knight's Station ○

Lordsburg ○

Stein's
Peak
△

△ North Pyramid Pk.

Shakespeare ○
Leitendorf's ○
△ So. Pyramid Pk.

S.P.R.R.

Dem

Gage ○

Victorio Mts.

L

Animas ○

Kachita

Little Hatchet
Mts.

Carrizalillo Sp
(Hermanas) ○

Pelencillo Range

Animas Mountains

Big Hatchet
Mts.

M

Alamo Hueco Mts.
Dog Spring ○

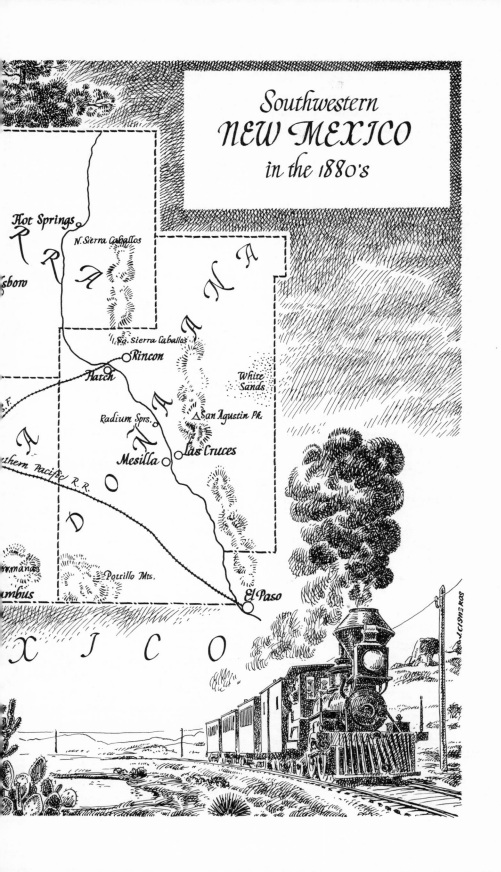

Southwestern
NEW MEXICO
in the 1880's

Hot Springs

N. Sierra Caballos

sbow

So. Sierra Caballos

Rincon

Hatch

Radium Sprs.

White Sands

San Agustin Pk.

Mesilla

Las Cruces

Southern Pacific R.R.

.F.

manas

umbus

Potrillo Mts.

El Paso

X   I   C   O

at the copper mines for bringing in these men as laborers. He was quite vain of his English and of his travels with some circus, and boasted that he had been all over the world — why, he had even been as far as St. Louis!

While I am on the subjects of the Santa Rita mines and the Old Copper Trail to Chihuahua, I may mention that some twenty-five or thirty years ago in the town of San Carlos,[84] State of Chihuahua, near the old Spanish presidio of San Carlos, I met an elderly Mexican gentleman named Flotte who told me that his grandfather, Dr. Flotte of Cincinnati, Ohio, settled in Chihuahua City, and about the year 1800 became director of the mint at that city; that a large part of the coinage at his mint consisted of *tlacos* — a copper coin valued at about two cents in American money — and that a great part of the copper coined came from the mines of Santa Rita in New Mexico. He said much of this copper was carried in packs on burros from Santa Rita to Chihuahua City. If the story of this trail and these mines could only be told from the beginning period, it would give more of the early history of Southwest New Mexico than we can ever hope to obtain from any other source. The Copper Trail is another route which merits markers.

After leaving the Mimbres Station we came through Apache Tejo, some time about midnight.[85] Against the skyline I caught sight of a large wooden wheel some fifteen or twenty feet in diameter, from the top of which there ran out north into the darkness a level line of small planks. These were supported on both sides by long stakes nearly upright in position, in pairs leaning slightly towards each other. The driver told me that this was an overshot waterwheel fed by a wooden gutter from a spring. He explained further that it was used to operate an *arrastra*, which was used by some American to crush gold ore into fine particles so that the gold might be extracted from the rock. The crushing was effected by grinding the gold-bearing rock between upper and lower stones of great hardness, much as flour was ground out even in those days, the power from the waterwheel being applied to revolve the upper stone.

This was my introduction to one of many Spanish words then current among Americans to describe materials and processes of the mining industry of those days. Later I learned others, such as *petanque, veta,* etc. — all carried up out of Old Mexico by the Spaniards in their search for mines and accepted by the Americans later. But the increase of English-speaking miners and the great improvements made in mining machinery and methods gradually led to their disuse, and now such words as *arrastra* and *petanque* are almost as obsolete in common English use as the "hides" and "carucates" of The Domesday Book.[86] And as I cannot find them in such standard dictionaries as Velázquez and Barcia, I am led to believe that they were provincial, possibly originating in Mexico and not coming from the great Latin fountain. Perhaps they came from Aztec or other Indian sources.[87]

I do not know how far back the name of Apache Tejo can be traced. It might go back to some of those scattered periods when the Santa Rita mines were worked from Mexico, but it was certainly in use just before the Civil War. It was at this place that the noted Apache chief Mangas Coloradas (Red Sleeves) was murdered in his cell by American soldiers in 1863, as I recollect. He was one of the two most noted Apache chiefs of that day, Cochise being the other.[88] Both were enemies of the Americans.

Mangas Coloradas came into Apache Tejo on some pretense of peace-making. As I recollect, General J. R. West, who was in command, for some reason had him put in the guardhouse. That night the guards murdered him in his cell. This act greatly incensed his branch of the Apache Nation; and Cochise as his successor, already an enemy of the whites, made bitter war for some years afterwards.[89]

It would seem that this place has a history that probably runs with that of the Santa Rita mines. During the intermittent working of these mines, it must have been occupied — probably for truck farming, possibly as an outpost station for soldiers. Some provision must have been necessary for the support of the workers in the mines and their families, and for that purpose the Mimbres River and other water sources must have been used for the cultivation of crops.

Quite recently in the Mimbres Valley I was shown the ruins of old houses which were thought to have been the homes of Indians of a culture antedating that of the Pueblos of Northern New Mexico.[90] Among them I noticed one or two stone foundations laid in rectangular shape, such as the Mexicans of today place for their adobe houses. So while there may be, as claimed, ruins of a very early Indian culture in that valley, I am quite sure that there must also be present the ruins of old Mexican houses which date back to the days when the Spaniards worked the copper mines only 100 to 130 years ago. In 1859 Colonel Bonneville found some settlement there.

About 3:00 A.M. on the morning of April 17, we passed a rather large spring of high temperature, known then as Hudson's Hot Spring, which was the home of a familiar character of those days named Dick Hudson. He did not own this spring, as our Government some years earlier had adopted a policy of reserving from sale mineral and warm springs, in order that they might be made of public use for medicinal purposes. But he procured a lease on the property and made his income from the use of its hot water by people afflicted with rheumatism or other diseases. Apparently, however, the disease which had sent most of the patients to this spring was the result of too much indulgence in liquor. It was quite popular in those days among the followers of John Barleycorn.

Hudson's Spring itself was rather remarkable in appearance. A cone some ten feet high, and possibly eight feet in diameter at the bottom and hardly a foot wide at the top, was the vehicle through which the water came out of the ground. This chimney had seemingly been built up by the waters of the spring in the process of precipitation during which minerals carried in solution crystallized on coming to the surface. However, the vent at that time was not found at the top of the cone but at a point about halfway from the top on the north side. It seemed probable to me that this opening had been made by the landlord for the purpose of facilitating the use of the water. I had seen several fumaroles in West Texas which delivered their waters and gas through a similar chimney at the highest point of the cone. Indeed, the cone itself could not have been originally built up in any other way.

On to Silver City and Shakespeare

Not long after leaving Hudson's Spring, we passed into a rather shallow valley coming down from the northwest. It gradually narrowed and deepened as we traveled; then, about 9:00 A.M., we came up a sharp rise in the floor of the valley where some springs broke out and two or three small irrigated plots lay on either side of the road. Just above this, we turned sharply around the site of a noisy stamp mill and came into the lower end of the town of Silver City.[91] The stage and horses were housed for the time being in Meeson and Merriage's Corral, while the passengers took breakfast across the street in a two-story brick building called the Exchange Hotel, owned by Louis Timmer. Next to the hotel there was a large mercantile house operated by W. H. Porter and C. P. Crawford.

Silver City was the most important town in Southern New Mexico. It must have had at that time a population of about fifteen hundred souls, one half American, and the other half Mexican. It was certainly the most substantially built of all the territorial towns other than Santa Fe; and while some of the towns in the Rio Grande Valley might have had a greater population, yet certainly it was only here that you could find two-story houses of brick or lumber in addition to the best class of adobe houses. It was the chief city in the development of minerals, and the production of the mines in its vicinity was greater than that of any other part of New Mexico. It was sending out much silver from its own Chloride Flat, while through its gates passed the entire output of gold mined around Pinos Altos[92] and the copper bars from the Clifton mines. With it as a center, a large number of prospectors searched for minerals in every direction through this highly mineralized country.

The location of Silver City in the first instance depended upon the discovery and working of the silver mines in nearby Chloride Flat, but its development and permanence were due to some happy features of its situation. It lay in a neighborhood where Nature had fixed the seat of many minerals in quantity, but in that neighborhood there were not many sites which could be converted into towns. It was situated along the border of the timberline which came down from the north to the edge of the great open treeless flats that mark the southern boundary of New Mexico. Timber is a most important item in the development of mines. Also, that irregular timberline border stretched across many miles of rocky fringes and rounded valleys where towns might have been built.

Although there were sites along the borderline of the timber and within the mineralized territories where towns could well be built, these sites were difficult of access. In those days of transportation by ox and mule, this was an almost fatal defect. Silver City was easily accessible. There was one necessity, however, that in an arid climate overrode all others. Distance from the timber belt and from the mineral territory, and difficulty of access might be overcome, given a great mine or group of mines. But no city could be set on a permanent foundation unless it was assured of a water supply of sufficient quantity and of reasonable cheapness. The flat above San Vicente Springs offered a location which satisfied all of these requirements. Because it was conveniently close to the silver mines being developed on Chloride Flat, it was selected as the site of the future Silver City. There may have been other neighborhoods just as happily situated; but once Silver City was established and started on its career, no rival of sufficient strength was ever able to challenge its growth.

The water supply to which the town appears to have owed its location was due to a somewhat peculiar topographical feature. Above the San Vicente Springs there was a rather level valley about a half-mile wide at the upper end of the town, but constricted just above the spring to a width of some three hundred yards. At this point, a dike of some ancient rock crossed the valley fifty or sixty feet below the surface of the valley above. This made an underground dam which backed up the subsurface waters lying in the valley above, and over it passed the spring waters that were used for irrigation and for the stamp mill. So the townsite was practically located over a natural reservoir, and there was no difficulty those days in getting good water in shallow wells within the limits of Silver City.

But some five or six years later occurred a serious change in the topographical features of this valley within the townsite. A flood, followed by another in quick succession, dug a deep ditch down one of the main streets, and now there is a canal sixty feet deep where in 1880 some of the most prominent buildings of the town were situated. Into that ditch went the Porter and Crawford store, Timmer's Exchange Hotel, the Tremont Hotel, Max Schutz' store, the Morrill store and the postoffice. A bridge now spans that ditch where the old postoffice stood in 1880. The front of a solid block of buildings formerly on each side of that street just below the bridge is now represented by willows and cottonwoods growing sixty feet below. This happening at the time must have been considered a calamity. It now is plainly seen to have been inevitable, and probably it was a solution to more serious problems of sewerage and sanitation which the people were obliged to face eventually.[93]

After breakfast I again took up my journey to Shakespeare on the same stage I had arrived on; but Currie, being a little fatigued, laid over at the Exchange Hotel for the next day's stage. So it was from him that I later learned of quite a fall of snow that night in Silver City. We had noticed on our arrival that we had come into an atmosphere keen and crisp, more so even than that of the mountains around Fort Davis. When we came up the canyon to Silver City, we were passing through a country whose waters, if they could have passed over the dry soils of the great intermountain basin of Southern New Mexico, would have come to rest in Northern Mexico in a lake having no outlet to the salt seas on the east and on the west. But on this day our coach was to travel a road which led through *arroyos* and canyons whose waters, when stripped from the clouds above in the rare rains which set the storm waters running over the arid spaces, would pass to the Gila River and the Gulf of California. For we were at the height of the Continental Divide.

It was a good road for those days, and our coach lumbered along at the rate of five or six miles an hour, with Sam Dycus driving the four well-conditioned horses. Nevertheless, it was a mountain road, and when we ceased to climb uphill, that moment we began to go down-hill — and few and far between were the compromises where we could travel on level stretches. As far as Cherry Creek, we traveled over a high rolling plateau, scantily clothed with clumps of juniper bushes, and the truncated top of Cooke's Peak was at times to be seen high in the east. This part of the road must be closely paralleled by the present highway from Silver City at least as far as the site of Hank Kramer's Station on Cherry Creek.

After passing that station on Cherry Creek, we began a long climb up towards the heart of the Burro Mountains. The higher we climbed, the denser became the scrub forest, and the higher grew the rounded mountain oak and the scarred alligator juniper, with now and then a sightly pine tree by the roadside. About 3:00 P.M. we began to travel on a roadbed rather level compared to our morning's experience, but to gain that advantage it wound in and out among the rocks and shrubbery to such an extent that we could seldom see its surface for a hundred yards in front or behind. We were going at a clipping pace when my sole passenger companion remarked that, over and above the rattle and clangor of our vehicle, he could hear the sound of the foot-steps of a running horse. It came from the front, and we leaned out of the coach windows to look forward.

There was nothing in sight on the road at first. But after a few mo-ments a horse with a Mexican rider came into view around a curve in the road, traveling at a fast gallop. As soon as the rider caught sight of our stage, he began to gesticulate furiously and to call loudly to us. As he came nearer we made out that he was crying out, "Los Indios, los Indios!"

Dycus began yelling back at him, "Where? Where?" But he got no answer other than "Los Indios, los Indios!" as the Mexican and his horse shot by at a hard gallop with never a moment's slowing up, and with the rider's eye apparently fixed on the roadside ahead of him regardless of us. Dycus called down to us from the boot, "Get ready, I am going to drive like the devil for Knight's Ranch four miles away."

Of course, we began to "get ready" — after our idea of what that meant. We both carried rifles; and naturally, as we had in our minds the expectation of an ambuscade from the roadside, we seated ourselves so we could scan both sides of the road for shooting. I took a seat op-posite my fellow passenger, with my back to the way we were going, in order that, being right-handed, I could shoot towards the right-hand side of the road, while he could cover the left-hand roadside from his position on the rear seat. We hurriedly set in reach all the cartridges we could get out. Then we put in our time gazing out at the trees, bushes and rocks as they rushed past, fearing every moment to see a dark face peering at us from the cover of some tree or rock.

By this time the driver had gotten his horses up to about the best speed he could expect, considering the weight of their load and the character of the roadway, which was fairly level but crossed by water-worn dents, and winding in many a serpentine curve like the trail of a rattlesnake. About this time we who rode in the body of the coach discovered that in some respects we lacked a great deal of being "ready" for that promised devil's ride. We were tossed up and down and thrown about in the coach so that it was impossible for us to remain in shooting position, nor could we keep our guns on the cock, ready for prompt firing, for if we did so, one of us was liable to be shot.

On we went, tumbling about in the body of the coach, almost helpless in the event of an attack and wondering how it was possible for the driver to keep his seat on the boot. We were also getting bruised and hurt, but that simply served to put us in a fighting mood if it came to a point where we must make a fight. Occasionally we would fancy we saw dark faces lurking in the roadside shrubbery, but there could be no certainty of this in the fleeting vision. However, there was never a shot heard by us during that fantastic ride of four miles.

At last, our coach came to a halt in front of a high adobe corral, next to which stood a single-story adobe house, with its windows filled up with rock so placed as to allow a porthole or two through which persons inside could shoot. This was known then as Knight's Ranch, although owned and inhabited by a man named John Parks, who came to meet us at the coach steps.[94]

Upon stepping down from the coach, we saw nearby some Negro soldiers engaged in various occupations; some were shoeing horses, others cooking at a camp fire and others going over the saddles and guns. They composed a troop of the Ninth or Tenth Cavalry, and their commander, Major S. A. Purington, was going from party to party giving directions and orders. He was a man of some sixty-five years, with snow-white hair, about six feet two inches in height, and weighing well over two hundred pounds — just the physique that no one would have expected to be fit for pursuit of Indians in a rough mountain country. I met him five years later at Fort Stockton, Texas, and found him to be, even then, a hale and hearty old man, who had gone into the Regular Army from the Volunteer Service after the Civil War.[95]

I learned that the cavalry troop, led by Indian scouts on the trail of the hostile Indians, had come that morning to Knight's Ranch and had relieved the inmates from a state of siege. Fortunately, the Indians had not been able to do any damage beyond wounding a horse in the corral, but they had lurked around the house all the night before and had fired repeatedly into it and the adjoining corral. On the approach of the scouts and the soldiers, the Indians had disappeared; but the soldiers, after a hard and forced march, were not in shape to continue pursuit without resting their horses.

These Indian scouts were not of a prepossessing appearance, being long-haired specimens, rather undersized, scantily clad and generally very dirty and greasy to the eye of a white man. They were physically not men of fine shape, being quite scrawny and angular in build, with eyes that were fleeting and evasive in glance. Two or three of them were lying in the shade of a pine tree, with heads reposing in the laps of comrades who were engaged in hunting out the insects which must have inhabited their mops of coarse black hair. They may have been preparing for fight, but their appearance lacked much of giving the picture left us by Herodotus of the Spartan soldiers at the Pass of Thermopylae, dressing their long hair before the last stage of the battle.

We did not tarry long at Knight's Ranch. The Major gave us an escort of two soldiers who were to go as far as the edge of the woods, since our driver for some reason considered this stretch of the road to be peculiarly dangerous. I have been told that it was on this same stretch of road that Judge McComas and his wife were killed some three years later by the Apaches while on their way to Lordsburg;[96] so the driver must have had some knowledge of the crossing of an old Indian trail in that vicinity. It was not a long stretch through the trees to the open prairie (some three miles only, as I now recall), but we paid the closest attention to it. When we had left behind the last shrubs of a gradually diminishing and vanishing growth of trees and began to breathe naturally, we came under the afternoon sun to a landscape view which I shall never forget.

The southern expanse of the Burro Mountains shuts off the eye from east to west, so that we were looking down on a vast plain which embraced only a semicircle, but that semicircle was bounded on the southeast by the hills of the Mexican border near the present town of Hachita,[97] and on the northwest by those mountains that lay near the Box Canyon on the Gila River. Having a scope of nearly a hundred miles, this made up a tremendous amphitheater marked by an almost uniform drab yellow, but dotted here and there in the body of the arena with the pointed dark slashes of hilltops. In the background and "darkly painted on the sky" loomed up the dim bulk of the Chiricahua Mountains. To the west the view was shut in by the irregular outlines of the Dos Cabezas Mountains, with the two faces looking up to the heavens and reminding the inhabitants of those days of the stony face of old Cochise, epic hero of his people and scourge of the whites.[98]

Below and before us in the grassy heart of this plain we could see a conical peak of beautiful form in the midst of a small range of peaks and truncated cones, standing up among them like Saul among his brethren. The driver told us that the hill was known to Americans as Pyramid Peak and to the Mexicans as Piloncillo (Sugarloaf Mountain) because of its likeness in shape to the form in which brown sugar of those times was sold over the counter.[99] On the northern slope of a hill, brother to the Sugarloaf Mountain, we could dimly see some fifteen miles away a short broken line which I was told was Shakespeare, the end of my journey.

The sky was a hazy blue above the drab-colored earth, and the whole view gave me a feeling of something unreal, a picture of a dream, a vision of a fevered fancy. Over it all there hung a sinister smoke, dotted here and there with dark-blue fragments scattered through the yellow below and the lighter blue above. The dry grass in the wide basin was on fire in a hundred places. According to the driver, this was the work of the Indians who were making their way in small parties from the Arizona reservations to the Mexican border, and erasing their trail by the use of flint and steel or the more primitive fire drills. There was no fire on the road between us and Shakespeare, but on either side, and more especially on the west, there were many smoky areas, each easily defined in the absence of a driving wind.

Some Shakespearean Characters

W AT ABOUT 6:00 P.M. the stage entered the solitary street in the little town of Shakespeare and stopped at the door of a small one-story adobe hotel. A rather small man of about thirty-five years, sandy haired, blue eyed and freckle faced, came out and introduced himself as Fred Smith, the proprietor of the hotel. He had a pleasant address and some weeks later told me that he was the son of "Extra Billy" Smith, wartime governor of old Virginia. In my ignorance I had never heard of this wartime governor, nor can I now recall that I ever afterwards heard of him, but I was willing to accept anyone with the pleasant and gracious manner of Fred Smith as an Hidalgo, or son of somebody. When I learned that he was commonly known in camp as "Bean Bellied" Smith, I was surprised and inquired the occasion of the nickname. No one, however, could explain, and the general opinion seemed to be that it was a kind of expression of dislike aroused in some way by his conduct in a pistol duel with Ross Wood, which occurred not long before my arrival.

The few persons seen just after our arrival were eager to hear the latest Indian news from the Silver City country and were almost as eager to give us the latest word to be had from Shakespeare and the Gila River territory. Nearly all of the men were then out in the hills south of the town, scouting for Indian signs. The evening before, someone had reported Indians among the hills and on the plains west towards San Simon, located southwest of Shakespeare, over the Arizona border. There was a small militia organization in the town which had been commissioned and furnished Springfield rifles and cartridges from Santa Fe.[100]

These men had been out all day trying to catch and trail any Indian signs near the town, but so far the few who had returned had nothing definite to report. The next morning, however, we learned from some man who had returned late in the night that the trail of a few Indians had been followed through the camp, beginning in the direction of Steeple Rock and going south toward Mexico, but it had been abandoned twenty or thirty miles out from Shakespeare. The people were not equipped for a pursuit of more than a day's time, and moreover considered that they were organized for home protection and not for foreign expeditions.

If the census taker for 1880 got around to Shakespeare to list its population (I do not recall his appearance), then his report depended for numbers on the stage of the Indian warfare at the time. When I landed there in April there were probably a hundred and fifty men, women and children living in the place. This was the maximum population, due to the fact that the Indians were raiding that part of the country and all of the whites had gathered for safety in the town. A month later, when the crisis had passed and the alarm had subsided, the census man would have found a scant hundred in the place, because the prospectors who made their headquarters there would then be out in the hills, and others who had business elsewhere would be on the road.

This population was composed almost entirely of grown men. I can recall but very few women and no children. Fred Smith's wife; Miss Jessie, the widow of Ross Wood; and a girl about twelve, daughter of a man named Lincoln, are all of the white females that I can remember — and between the two women there stood as a bar the memory of the duel in which Ross Wood lost his life to Fred Smith.

O. R. Smythe was then building a home for his family in the north part of the burg, but he had not yet moved in when I stepped down from the stage.[101] With the exception of two or three small adobe houses lying west of the West Arroyo, the buildings of the town all lay on one side or the other of the single street which ran on the fairly smooth surface of the divide between two *arroyos* coming from the hills to the southwest and uniting just below the last house. That street is now occupied by a railroad track.

What might be called the town center, socially and in business affairs, was located in the mercantile house of Smythe, Long and Price, situated near the center of Shakespeare. Around and back of it there was a large adobe corral occupied by the stage company's horses and vehicles. The junior member of the mercantile firm, John E. Price, was superintendent of the New Mexico division of the stage company. Although at the time, the A.T. & S.F. Ry. Co. was building southward from Las Vegas, and the Southern Pacific eastward through Arizona, the Overland stage line was still a strong company, but on its last legs.

Next in importance to the general store of Smythe, Long and Price, the hotel was the center of interest when a stage from the East or the West came to a halt in front of its door. Every passenger was a possible customer for some mining claim, and the prospectors were there waiting, loaded with specimens of ore backed by the assayer's certificates and ready to seize upon a victim. The proprietor of the hotel would be taken aside by the eager ones and implored by all that was holy, to point the way for them to interview those travelers who might listen to their story of a Golden Fleece lying in the hills. Now and then a tinhorn gambler would eye the passengers with a practiced gaze, but it was not until Lordsburg came into being that this class came to the heyday of its career in those parts.

There were no churches or Sunday schools, no lodges or fraternal organizations, and no social clubs in existence at Shakespeare; so it naturally resulted that those desiring amusement or recreation gathered together at the saloon.[102] There in the evening came the miner, the prospector, the occasional settler from the Gila, the rustler from San Simon — with now and then a wayfarer on his road to other parts. It was a place where one could learn of some lucky strike in a mine or of a rich find by some prospector. Here one group would discuss the barbaric details of some Indian raid, while another argued the respective mineral merits of different geological strata with the assurance of experts. Here could be heard the camp jokes and stories of adventure.

But here also occurred the tragedies of those days. Here the miner lost his wages, and the prospector his mining claims, over the bar or at the card table. Here was planned and often carried out all that was evil in the camp. Outside or inside its doors, there came to the bitter end of death the sudden quarrels and the feuds of long standing, equally due to the liquor sold at the bar. For the saloon keeper kept his saloon, not for the rest and information of its patrons but for the purpose of making money by the sale of liquor and by the rake-off on gambling. The greater the amount of liquor sold and of gambling carried on, the larger were his profits. The results figured with him only to the extent that his pocketbook was benefited, but even had he taken concern over the welfare of his customers, he could have done little to avoid the usual consequences. The evil lay in his occupation.

In the store, the hotel and the saloon, men from all parts of the United States and Mexico met — men from Canada, England and Europe — men of different languages and of various classes and occupations. There was Vic Van Hal: his fair skin, honest blue eyes, blond mustache, and broken English significant of his descent from some ancient Batavian Islander of the country we now call Holland. One of his close friends was Don Carlos Leroy, whose black eyes, swarthy skin, and hybrid French and Spanish name warranted belief in a family origin under Southern skies.

However, Carlos Leroy's name rested under an unspoken suspicion in the camp — unspoken because it was not considered good form in those days, and liable to bring on trouble, to question any name which the wearer might see fit to fasten on himself. Nevertheless, there were suspicions about the names of more than one of the tenants of Shakespeare, arising from various causes. Since Leroy's surname was French, while his given name was Spanish, he lived under a cloud; yet there was never anything in his conduct during the time that I knew him to warrant any doubt about his character.

Louis Sicotte came to Shakespeare from California, but his family were said to be seated in French Canada. His comrade, Bob Fambro, came from Georgia and was of Huguenot extraction. James E. Carroll, owner then of the Superior Mine, was reputed to have come there from San Francisco. England had at least two representatives. Hitchens was there from Cornwall, where from the time of the Phoenicians tin was mined, and copper from the year 1700.

There were three men in camp whose surnames were Brown. One of them was commonly known as "Geological" Brown, because in the broad English of his native Yorkshire he was incessantly alluding in his conversation to the "geological formation" of Shakespeare and Leitendorf's. Returning to England later that summer, the steamer on which he embarked was sunk and he was lost. F. R. Brown, an assayer, was commonly dubbed "Simple" Brown. This was due to his remark, on being introduced to a stranger as "Mr." Brown, that the camp had three Browns — "Geological" Brown, and "Dumb" Brown — each having a title, but that he was "simple Brown." The use of an adjective instead of an adverb gave him his nickname.

A prominent member of the camp was Mr. Crosby, whose initials I believe were J. F. He represented the owners of the Last Chance Mine at Leitendorf's, Messrs. Bement, Nisbet and Mackay of Evansville, Indiana, from which town Mr. Crosby was said to have come to Shakespeare. But the part of his life which gave the color to his career was spent on the Panama Canal when it was being promoted by the French syndicate. Crosby gave us much of the story of the construction of the canal as he saw it, and his account of the vast number of deaths among the employees was so lurid that we felt like paraphrasing a famous line of Tacitus to say of De Lesseps that he made a graveyard and called it a canal.

Crosby was given to telling us that he had never been finally cured of the Panama fever incurred while working on the canal and recurring at intervals even yet, and that there was no remedy for it save whiskey. So when he appeared on the street in one of his periodical sprees, the neighbors would say each to the other, with a wink and a smile, "Crosby has another spell of Panama fever." But when the fever had been allayed by the whiskey cure, Crosby was a good man, and still in the prime of life.

Probably the outstanding development of the camp at that time was being brought about by a company having its headquarters at St. Louis, and represented in Shakespeare by General Boyle, Judge Bonnell and Major Craig. I do not remember the title of that company, nor do I recall the names of its mining claims, which lay somewhere in the neighborhood of what is called the "85" Mine at the present time. General Boyle and Judge Bonnell remained at the camp during the summer of 1880, Judge Bonnell returning East some time before General Boyle.

General John Boyle belonged to an old Kentucky family. He had seen service in the Civil War and was about fifty years old, a man of quiet manner and pleasant ways — a lawyer, I believe, by profession. Major Craig was superintendent of company work, an irascible old gentleman at times, but generally of courteous ways. He had been a resident of St. Louis before coming to Shakespeare. As well as I can recollect, Judge

THE GENERAL STORE

In Williams' day, the headquarters of Smythe, Long and Price. Now the headquarters of Mr. and Mrs. Frank Hill's ranch. On the porch is an old coach that ran from Shakespeare to Silver City.

SHAKESPEARE TODAY

Foreground: Left, General Store; right, Assay Office. Background: Left, Grant House; right, Stratford Hotel. The railroad tracks were laid in 1914. Poverty Flat is the area extending back of Grant House and Stratford Hotel.

MINERS AT ROXY JAY SALOON

Located northwest of the General Store. The saloon was closed in 1893. Materials from the building were used in constructing the first church in Lordsburg.

CEMETERY AT SHAKESPEARE

Still in use. Russian Bill, Sandy King, Ross Woods and others are buried here.

Bonnell was a St. Louis lawyer and the attorney for the mining company. These three gentlemen were the best-settled inhabitants of the burg, for while nearly every other citizen held himself in readiness to ride at a moment's notice to a mining discovery and put in good time in that occupation, these gentlemen sat in cozy content in a neat company house in the north end of town. They passed the time reading, writing and talking during the day and, for serious undertaking at night, playing whist or cribbage with such of their friends as were of like mind.[103]

Among the people of the camp, the Hart brothers made a picturesque duet, partly because they were not interested in any phase of mining, and partly because in mental and physical characters they complemented each other. They were ranchers, having cattle ranging in the south flanks of the Burro Mountains and in the vicinity of the Box Canyon. Walter was a tall, slender man of about twenty-five years, with a blond face of serious, almost grim, aspect; while his younger brother, Richard, shorter and heavier of build, carried a smiling countenance under a crown of black hair. They were almost inseparable companions and men of very correct habits and of good repute. We understood that Connecticut was their native state.

Naturally the prosperity or adversity of the mining camp had little to do with the affairs of these brothers, except so far as it had to do with their residence and with the fortunes of their friends in the camp. They continued to prosper alike when the camp was in high feather and when it was desolate, until they had accumulated quite a small fortune in cattle. Then one day they announced that their cattle and ranches were for sale at a bargain, and shortly after this they sold out at a very low figure. The two brothers had inherited such a fortune that the cattle and ranches in comparison were a mere picayune in value, and their inheritance called them back from the land of the Apache to the canyons of New York City. I understand that now only Walter is living; Richard, of the friendly face, died some years ago.

Victor Gibson came to the camp from St. Louis. The St. Louis men of the mining company made much of the fact that his father, an attorney, had been decorated with the title of Count of the Holy Roman Empire, although I never heard Victor himself mention the fact. He was a young man, evidently unaccustomed to frontier life, quite a tenderfoot in fact, but gifted with the will and ability to fit in with whatever was in order. So he soon lost his pink-and-white complexion and acquired the standard red neck and tanned face, along with some knowledge of the hills and arid flats.

While Gibson's education was going on, I met him one hot summer day on the old stage road from Soldier's Farewell, about fifteen miles out, coming back to Shakespeare. He was alone, mounted on an exceedingly deliberate old bay horse equipped solely with a bridle put together crudely with fragments of rope and leather without a bit for the mouth. He was mounted sideways like women once were accustomed to ride, and was seated on a fiery red blanket without a surcingle to hold it in place. His hands were blistered; and his face, of a deep red, wore a very woebegone appearance. When in hearing distance, he called for water.

Now, I was getting a similar education at that time and was alone, riding a fractious horse on that hot, dusty road. I was suffering from chapped lips and blistered neck and seriously pitying myself until I came to that picture of woe. But I had water, a saddle and a horse with some disposition to travel; so as a sufferer I was not in competition at all with Victor Gibson. After he had refreshed himself with water and fastened his red blanket with a girth of borrowed rope, he told me his experience of the last day and night.

Gibson had left his party, which was returning from Carrisalillo Springs to Silver City, at a point north of the present station of Gage,[104] and had cut across the country to Soldier's Farewell, where he camped for the night. During the night someone stole his saddle and saddle blanket and would have taken his bridle, but the pack rats had cut it into pieces and carried them into various holes and so-called nests. After catching his hobbled horse, he had to patch up a bridle and saddle from his outfit and to set out in this lame condition for an all-day's ride. My appearance had relieved him very much, but there were two matters yet greatly weighing on his mind. He rejoiced that he could not get to Shakespeare before nightfall (for otherwise he would be seen and laughed at), but he was unable to find words strong enough to do justice to his prejudice against pack rats.

So far as age goes, Uncle John Evenson was the Nestor of Shakespeare. He must have been over fifty years of age; it was camp rumor that he had been a sailor in his youth. I would have suspected that he had come out of that hive of Scandinavian sailors on the North Sea and had become a Viking of the Plains, but I was told that his service had been only on the inland seas, the Great Lakes. It was claimed for him that he had been a resident of the camp from the days when it was Ralston, but I never learned whether or not the claim was founded on any measure of fact. He was apparently in better finances than most of the other adventurers, as he owned a comfortable house and had an income which kept him from daily labor.[105]

Pete Graves was another character of the camp, and he held on for a good many years in Lordsburg after the Southern Pacific was built. He claimed to have been a soldier in the Regular Army, and upon his discharge at some fort in the Southwest, he had remained there in the absence of any incentive to return to his native territory. Where that native territory lay, I do not know, but from his language and from the few tales I heard him relate of the "Auld Lang Syne," I would be inclined to place it in the Mississippi Valley not far from St. Louis.

I was with Pete on two occasions when we prospected for minerals in a dangerous country, and I say for him that he did not soldier (in the current use of that expression) while with us, but was a cheerful and willing man in performing camp duties. But he was naturally indolent and had become much addicted to liquor, so that his faculties had become somewhat clouded. After the station at Lordsburg became of importance enough to call for a justice of the peace, Pete filled that position for some years and became very much impressed with the dignity of the position.

Mr. Hitchens tells the following story to illustrate what Pete thought of himself as a man entitled to wear the Ermine: On one occasion after a drinking bout with a party which included a witty Irishman, it so happened that Pete and the Irishman put in the night together in the same bed. After they were snugly under the covers, Pete, whose mind was mellow with whiskey and good comradeship, remarked to his bed-mate, "Well, Pat, you would have lived a long time in Ireland before you would have had a chance to sleep with a judge, would you not?"

"Yes," came the answer, "and you would have lived a damned long time in Ireland before you would have had a chance to become a judge." Pete's answer is not on record.

O. R. Smythe was one of the very few men who remained to the last, tied to the glebe. He brought his family to Shakespeare, and around that family and the Wood family there centered such home life as existed in that wild settlement on the frontier. After the final breakup of the town, he moved to its successor, Lordsburg, where he passed the remainder of his days in the respect and honor of his fellow citizens.

There were two young men of promise who were at various times in the employ of Smythe, Long and Price; their names were John Phillips and Tom Wood. Phillips was tall, slender and dark skinned, a youth of steady habits and good principles; the firm did not employ men of any other character. I do not know anything of the subsequent career of these young men, other than that I have heard that Tom Wood became in time a trusted official of some high-class corporation. He was one of several men of Shakespeare who have made themselves potent citizens in other communities. Out of just such narrow nurseries, inured to hardship and guarded by self-denial, many of the strong men of the world have worked their way into standing and power among other peoples.

In the cohort of soldiers of fortune gathered into the little town from the ends of the world, there was no spirit brighter or more generous than that of John E. Price. Then in the prime of youthful grace, he exhibited nothing in his conduct that would cause a mother to sigh. Although he held a position of trust and power in a country where the ordinary restraints of settled life were powerless, he used that position generously to aid those needing favor or help, and gave greater grace by the manifest pleasure he had in the act. In truth, it often seemed to me that John Price exhibited more pleasure in extending help than the recipient appeared to feel in taking it.[106]

He was of an athletic build, and his countenance was a ruddy blond under a crown of beautiful golden-red hair. He was quite a handsome man; topped with a steel morion, he might well have stepped into a frame to pose as the picture of Alvarado, the Fair God of the Aztecs. I have heard a Mexican helper describe him under the name of El Dorado, "the Gilded One." I am not certain that he had studied in Europe, but he had been in France before taking his position with the stage company.

Price once related to me an experience in Paris, as follows: He was on top of the Arc de Triomphe, looking down on the streets and buildings below, when he heard the clatter of feet and the swirl of a body passing him in rapid motion. He turned to see a man rushing to the railing and plunging down to death. The suicide, in throwing himself over the railing, had put his body in the position of a diver plunging into a bathing pool, with hands clasped together in front of the head, and the body following in a curving plunge to earth. This made a powerful impression on Price's mind, and up to the day of his death in Seattle in July, 1928, I am sure that he never forgot the weird grace of the body of the unfortunate one as it hung suspended over the railing in the moment that it turned from the horizon toward the earth.

One day shortly after my arrival, the stage from the East brought in a man who speedily became remarkable among us for his extraordinary physical energy. He was named W. B. Donoho, about sixty years of age, but still full of life and movement. Within a few days he had set out as a prospector in the vicinity of the town. About daybreak of every morning we would hear the clatter of his heavy boots on the rocks as he made his way out of the camp to his day's work in the hills. About sundown he would make his weary way back with a knapsack loaded with specimens of ore gathered during the day. No heat was great enough, no rain heavy enough, no wind furious enough to interfere with this routine.

At night Donoho would often be seen in the assayer's office where the assayer would teach him, as far as possible, how to detect valuable ore by its appearance to the eye. Sometimes he might be found by the campfire of some trained prospector, drawing out the secrets of the profession: how to follow "float" up the valleys to the hills as the hound follows a trail; how to cross-cut the hill slopes for the ore vein when the trail of the float was lost. Always, however, he would courteously apologize to those whom he thus sought, for the trouble he made. This apology would be followed by his story of having been a merchant in Memphis, Tennessee — of a man who prospered much until the bad years came, when the failure of his customers forced him down to financial ruin; but he had now come to Shakespeare to gather a grubstake to leave to his dear children and grandchildren. A high-class old gentleman of infinite courage and patience!

From the time that I first came to Shakespeare as a pilgrim and a stranger, to the day in 1881 when I passed my last day there as an inhabitant, I was out of its gates much of the time. I spent the winter of 1880 and 1881 in the East;[107] while most of the remainder of that year found me a loyal burgess, yet I was absent on prospecting trips very much of the time. It was during these trips that (as prospectors) I learned much about the men whom I have described, for the intimacy of camp life brought into strong play the good and the bad characteristics of each individual. The incidents of the trips to the hills with these prospectors, which I shall give later, are to be taken in connection with the individual pecularities of those who remained in the burg, as partially marked out above. These accounts will as a whole give the best picture that I can frame out of the air of those denizens of frontier Southwestern New Mexico.

Prospecting: Its Trials and Rewards

❦ IMMEDIATELY AFTER my arrival in Shakespeare I began to learn my bearings in the camp.[108] My associate Pettie was away at that time prospecting on the borders of Old Mexico; poor Grady was believed to have been killed by the Indians at the southeastern point of the Burro Mountains, and I had not yet made the acquaintance of his successor as our guide, Bob Fambro. On my first day's search for those mining locations in which I was interested, I was able to find the Henry Clay, the Yellow Jacket and the Atwood, in which I had no claim; but I could not find the Joseph E. Johnston, in which I was very much interested. When Pettie had made this fragment of a location, he as a loyal native of Georgia had given to it the name of this soldier of four wars, who also claimed Georgia as his native state.

On the 19th of April, Currie and I went out to the camp of Fambro and Sicotte to get Fambro to pilot us around. We found a tall, athletic young man of about thirty, cheerful of manner and jesting in speech, who readily undertook to carry us through the locations, although he admitted that he had never been on the ground of the Johnston. On the 20th, after finding the boundaries of the Superior near the top of the hill, we finally caught the stone mounds that marked the irregular outlines of the location named in honor of that famous soldier of Georgia.

On the 21st, with the same guide, we went over the locations near Leitendorf's known as the Grant, the Lee, the Johnny Reb, and the Last Chance. Fambro did not know the Oasis location, in which we owned a half interest. We were disappointed considerably, but some two months later we learned that the Last Chance was located squarely across our Oasis, and that Fambro had really shown us over its surface at that time. Tom Dunn had made both locations, the Last Chance some time later than the Oasis; and after he had joined in a conveyance to us of a half interest in the Oasis. This action of Dunn's brought about a year later a trial in Silver City having many peculiar features, which I will discuss at another place in this narrative.[109]

On the 23rd, Pettie got back from his prospecting trip, loaded with samples of ore and bristling with excitement as the bearer of good tidings — a kind of mental strain which I afterwards saw in a number of men at different times. Such men were always lifted up for a time — superlative of speech, nervous in manner, and each apparently greatly impressed with the duty of thoroughly informing every soul in the vicinity of the special magnitude of his discovery. But Pettie carried samples of ore which seemed to justify his state of mind.

The five samples which he carried were reported by Assayer Simple Brown to carry silver at the rate of 30, 52, 148, 1060 and 1846 ounces to the ton, besides a portion of other minerals. Now, in those days an ounce of silver was worth a dollar in U. S. money; so that the find must be good if the vein proved strong. We were assured that it was at least two feet in width — a true fissure vein. And for some months now the

Stonewall District at the Carrisalillo Springs in the border of Old Mexico — for so the discoverers named the new district — was the center of interest in the little burg of Shakespeare.[110]

But now came days in that lonely country when the dread of Indian warfare overshadowed everything else.[111] We faced for a year or two the incessant danger resulting from the roaming bands of the Warm Spring Apaches under Victorio — bands that had never been great in number and were split into small detatchments, shifting from Mexican territory to American and back again as the pursuit on either side of the boundary might compel.[112]

Now we were threatened with an outbreak of Apaches from the San Carlos Reservation in Arizona in much greater numbers, and the news from the Mogollon Mountains appeared to show that a large body of the savages was on its way to Mexico, on a route that must almost certainly carry them not far from the old sentinel of Shakespeare — Pyramid Peak — murdering and destroying as they went, like a scourge of the Lord. Day after day came tidings of deaths — sheepherders and sheep in the foothills, prospectors in the mountain rocks, settlers in the valleys — and always a trail of fire by night and of smoke by day. Many of the reports were not true and what was true was often much exaggerated, but even stripped of all distortion, the situation was most dangerous for the traveler and those in small settlements.

About this time an engineer corps of the A.T. & S.F. Ry. Co. camped in Shakespeare one night on its way to map the route of that railway to Guaymas in Old Mexico; and a few days later on the same site there encamped a detatchment of the Fourth U.S. Cavalry. As far as we of the uninitiated could determine, the civil engineers were as well equipped as the soldiers to meet an Indian attack, except only in the matter of horses. No one in the area went unarmed, even from the door of his home, if he had one, and outlying settlers gathered together for mutual protection.

On May 8, at night, we caught sight of signal fires burning on mountain tops in the Stein's Peak Range. While that seemed to indicate that at least one part of the Indians was passing down to Mexico on a route to the west of us, it was reasonable to infer from the fact that signals were visible from our section that there was another part passing on the side of the hills that faced us. So a keen lookout was kept for a time; but no report came of the near presence of such a band, and the excitement died down. On the 15th of May, I left Shakespeare with the purpose of prospecting for mines near the Mexican border, and especially of examining the three locations in the Tenaja Mountains, near the present station of Gage, and the eight locations at Carrisalillo springs, Stonewall District, all made by Pettie on his recent trip.

Our party was to consist of numbers sufficient to offer some protection from the danger of Indian attack. But nearly all of the party were to start from Silver City. Pettie, a man named Bryan, and one or two others were to get to Cow Spring that evening,[113] while I was to ride over from Shakespeare to join them there. This journey alone, of twenty-five or thirty miles, did not appeal to me as a pleasure trip, and it brings a smile to me now as I recall how I passed the most dangerous mile of that stretch. This lay at the extreme southeast corner of the Burro Mountains near the deserted old stage stand known as Soldier's Farewell.

Here, where the low hills of that range fall down to the open grassy plain, a line of low stunted junipers, mingled with an occasional rock of large size, crept down into the flat grasslands, offering hiding places to command the old stage trail. The name of Soldier's Farewell, added to the current tradition as to the origin of the name, was enough of itself in Indian times to fill one with about all the uneasiness the mind cares to cary. But in my case I had also very vividly in mind the tale that my partner Grady, half blind but still prospecting, had wandered into this part of that mountain range where an old Indian trail crossed out of the hills, and that the buzzards had told of his end.

As I came to this part of the road, I rode with the big rifle pointed at each rock, stunted bush and hiding place in turn as I passed — with my pistol loosened in the scabbard and my cartridge belt carefully adjusted, eyes big and wild, intent on every movement on the roadside, sure that I would never get through. If I could tell how happy I was when I got through that strip of danger, one would know how badly scared I was. After I had passed through that danger zone, I could not remember that I had seen a single living thing — rabbit or bird or other animal life — along all that part of the ancient roadway. It was as if all life there feared the coming of the Apaches.

By two o'clock in the afternoon I had arrived at the site of Cow Spring. I was greatly disappointed at the appearance of this spring. It had been noted on maps and referred to in accounts of travelers for nearly a hundred years. In the early days of the Santa Rita copper mines, it had figured as the last certain water supply on the Copper Trail going south until the water of Carrisalillo Springs was reached. About the time in October, 1826, when Kit Carson was joining my grandfather's caravan on the plains west of Kansas City, another Kentucky adventurer, James O. Pattie, was traveling over this Copper Trail from Cow

Spring to Janos for adventure in Mexico, leaving behind him an uneasy father, Sylvester Pattie, operating the copper mines at Santa Rita.[114]

Cow Spring was also an important station on the Overland Mail route from San Antonio, Texas, to San Diego, California, as it was operated by Colonel George H. Giddings about the years 1856 to 1861. The attempt of Lieutenant George N. Bascom to arrest Cochise in 1861, at a time when Cochise and his Indians were furnishing Giddings' stations with hay all the way from Mesilla to Tucson, led Cochise to believe that the people of the stage line were principally responsible for Bascom's action.[115]

That Apache warrior, as the first fruits of his war on the Americans, destroyed the station at Cow Spring and every other of Giddings' stations from Tucson to Mesilla. In this special fight made on the stage company, Colonel Giddings lost thirty-six of his employees, including his own brother, who was killed at Stein's Peak with thirteen other men. The two coaches carrying the brother and his thirteen men going to meet Cochise in the effort to conciliate him were the last coaches to pass through Cow Spring Station until the re-establishment of the Overland service after the Civil War.[116]

One might have expected something of interest in the surroundings of Cow Spring. But in a flat featureless plain, all that seemed to me worthy of note as I rode under a hot summer sun was a line of cattail rushes, known to the Mexicans as *tules,* low in height — a line only some two hundred yards long skirting a reach of stagnant water with black, boggy banks, beyond which I could see an adobe house with one or two small outhouses. Not far from the road there were some cows lying down; away to the left, four or five horses could be seen. Except for these animals and some birds fluttering among the tall rushes, there was no sign of life or activity about the scene. The days of the Copper Trail were past, and the Overland stage had deserted the place. In 1859 Bonneville described it as a quagmire. In 1880 it was still a quagmire, although harnessed slightly to man's use.

But after all, there was something of interest there. I found at the house two men who gave me their names as Jack Frost and Jim Haggerty. They told me that they had a small dairy ranch there and that their principal market was in Silver City, where they got fancy prices for butter and milk. They showed me over their milk house, a small adobe building arranged so that a current of air would continually pass through and over a framework which was covered with tin platters of milk seated on gunnysacks soaked in water. This was a frigidaire of the 1880's. The principle on which this arrangement operated to cool water or milk was well understood in that country. Gunnysacks were a part of the equipment of every kitchen service.

Subsequently, I heard more about these two bluff dairy men that was a little more in keeping with their physical appearance. Jack Frost was believed to own his name; at any rate he had come down from Montana with that name and was said to have borne it in that country without occasion to suspect any need of change. Haggerty was supposed to carry his mother's name, but he had carried it into and out of some peculiar situations. One of these was styled in newspaper headings a few years after the Civil War as the "Great Diamond Swindle." [117] As I recollect it, the details ran something after this fashion:

A tale of diamonds came up to San Francisco out of the red deserts of Arizona, and it came in such a fashion as to create considerable interest and belief. A large company was organized and chartered. As I recall, General George B. McClellan was, if not president, at least a strong promoter of the company. Parties were sent down to investigate and were taken by the discoverers to a place where in red earth some small diamonds were found. I do not remember where this place was supposed to be, other than it was somewhere northwest of Lordsburg. Later I learned from Harpending's story that the site of this alleged discovery must have been in Colorado.

Doubt was thrown on the genuineness of the discovery, and when the diamonds were finally identified as having come from Brazilian fields, the bubble burst. Before this, however, many people had invested in the stock of the company, and much money had been paid out to the alleged discoverers. Now, Haggerty was said to have been an accessory in some way, and the money gotten from this enterprise had served to carry him for some time and was still keeping him in a business of nominal profits. This was the story I heard of the two "Barons" of Cow Spring, and if not true it was at least interesting enough to gain credence in those parts. Where little was known, much was suspected.

About dusk Foote and Crittenden and their party got in, bringing with them Russian Bill Tettenborn. Somewhat later Pettie and the man named Bryan arrived from Silver City. Russian Bill was still holding forth to one or two nodding heads about his discovery of the Adams Diggings [118] and his departure from that site with Indians only a few steps behind, when I passed over to the Land of Nod, far from Apaches. When I got up the morning of May 16, Bill was following Bryan, the new man, with the same story, only a few feet farther along on his flight from the Indians but going good and strong. We took the Copper

Trail, running almost due south over an open plain towards a small range of mountains referred to by our leaders as the Tenaja Mountains. At noon we took our dinner in a pass through which the trail ran, and near a rock basin holding a small amount of rainwater.

Rock water holes of this character were often described by Americans as *tinajas,* for so the Mexicans named them to distinguish them from *charcos* or water holes in earth basins. Due to this, I suppose, the name of Tenaja came to be applied to this little range of limestone hills, on the east end of which Joe Daugherty and his associates had made a number of mining locations and styled the camp the Victorio Mining District, after the old chief of the Warm Spring Apaches.[119] I am told that later the mountains came to bear the name of the mining district. This will illustrate how fleeting and evanescent are place names in territory without fixed settlement, and it leads us to suspect that the miners of the days of James O. Pattie had an even different name for these hills on the road back to their homes in Old Mexico.

Now, in 1880 this Old Copper Trail was a distinctly marked road as far as we traveled it, and I was told that it was in similar preservation for many miles south of the Mexican boundary. It had evidently at one time been traveled by wheeled vehicles, and the two parallel lines of wheel-made ruts were visible in places for a mile or more. But the day of the two-heeled *carretas* had long passed, and the road was then marked by the trail of animals in single file, going for a time in the wheel rut on the right side, then shifting to that on the left side. This single-horse trail was broad and strong; while we met no wayfarers on it, it was in use by smugglers largely, and to a lighter degree by peons escaping from Mexico to labor in the mines of Grant County. Now and then a deserter from the Army or a refugee from justice may have headed over it towards Mexico as to a City of Refuge.

However, the silence of the plains, the blue sky of the desert, and the hills that bridled its path were all that interested us. I have never been impressed more strongly by a feeling of loneliness at any other place, unless it might have been on Broadway in New York at lunchtime when thousands met or passed me without a friendly face among them. It was a dead world along that ancient highway — no life, no trees — even the yuccas, the grass and the mesquites seemed to be void of the freshness of greenery. It was so dead that even Bill's braggadocio had fallen lifeless by the time we camped for the night at some water holes about ten miles out from the Carrisalillo Springs; so we had a quiet night and a good sleep.

About eleven o'clock on the morning of the 17th we came to Carrisalillo Springs and found prospectors there, among them a noted character of the fraternity, named Charlie Fry. But I was interested more in the mining locations than in the people in camp; I spent the remainder of the day going over the topographical features of our new mining camp of Stonewall.[120] Two natural objects were in plain evidence — the spring and a rather large hill rising from the plain at the northwest margin of the spring plateau and extending a mile or more away to the west and north. A smaller feature, but more important to us, could be made out in the shape of a low dike of rock creeping out of the spring valley towards the southeast. On this dike were our mining locations.

The spring was small: it ran only a short distance, then sank out of sight in a body of black earth. It was situated in a little circular basin of dark-colored soil, containing a few acres of earth inside a low platform of rocks extending around the north and east sides of that basin. I concluded in the course of my inspection that the rock dike, visible at the southeast corner of the basin, extended underground across the basin to the northwest, so as to bar the passage of subsurface water from the south and east sides of the basin. If so, then this basin was practically an underground lake. Not a tree, not even a mesquite shrub, grew in that level circle which presented the appearance of a new-mown meadow, except that where the waters ran, there was a clump of reeds or canes twelve to eighteen inches high and extending possibly fifty feet into the water.

This growth would very satisfactorily explain the origin of the name of Carrisalillo Springs, which the place then bore. The Spanish noun *carrizo* is derived from the Latin language and means in English a reed or a cane. The derivative *carrizal* means a "place taken up with a growth of reeds or canes." Now, if you go further and make the diminutive of *carrizal* — a "little place where reeds or canes grow" — that becomes, in New Mexican Spanish, *carrisalillo*, the name of our spring. The name of the spring has been changed; but, strange to say, the change was not made from Spanish to English, but the old Mexican name of mountains twenty five miles away has been saddled on the little basin, and it is now called Hermanas Spring.[121]

The first night after our arrival at Carrisalillo, I witnessed an incident which was characteristic of Russian Bill. We all had made camp together on the north side of the meadow, not far from the spring. My bed was made down nearer the running water than those made by others of the party and was only a few feet distant from a light buckboard in which Chamberlain, one of our miners, and Bill traveled. Some time after midnight I was awakened by the sound of horses' footsteps. I raised up, and by the faint light of a moon in its first quarter I could see two horsemen ride up in a walk to the little stream and stop to let the horses drink. I called out to them the cowboy's greeting to "light and rest your saddles," for I had no reason to suspect them of being Indians. They might be Mexicans or Americans, but no hostile Indians would approach a spring at night on a highway in any such foolhardy way. So I expected to get some kind of reply in Spanish or English.

But there came no reply. I could hear the boys in our party rustling in their blankets as they peered out into the darkness in an attempt to understand the occasion of the challenge. I saw the horsemen, after a moment's hesitation, gathering up the loose bridle reins and spurring their horses as they set off in a gallop to the south without a word. As soon as they were safely away, fifty yards on the run, up rushed Bill, with loud curses, to the buckboard. Laying a big Springfield rifle across the tire of a hind wheel, he bellowed out that he was going to shoot the liver out of the d—d scoundrels. Had we not caught and held him, he might have fired out in the darkness after the fleeing forms. The men were plainly in full flight and, as we heard later, were deserters from the Army — making for the boundary of Mexico, which was only four or five miles distant. They had given Bill a chance to play to the galleries, and he played. The next day Chamberlain took Bill back to Silver City although he, Bill, was quite reluctant to travel with only one companion through Indian country.[122]

During the 18th, 19th and 20th, Pettie, Bryan and I prospected the surface of the dike near the spring where our locations were situated and where Pettie had found some high-grade ore. We, too, found some small pieces of copper glance (ore) showing a good grade of silver content, but we could find no body of it to encourage us. The vein carried quite a width of clear quartz without a mineral stain, but the amount of worthwhile ore was small — exceedingly small.[123] So we concluded to hunt fresh fields and pastures new, after coming to a realization that many a hunter for valuable ore must have passed over the Copper Trail and paused to hunt over that dike just as we had hunted, fascinated by a few flakes of rich ore.

Early in the afternoon of the 21st, we started on a trail said to lead to Mesquite Springs; but some eight or nine miles out, we turned from the trail across some rough hills, and after camping dry that night we

made Eureka camp by noon of the next day. We had Charlie Fry with
us and he took us to the site of an old Mexican smelter which might
apparently have been in use rather recently and illustrated how skillful
an old Mexican *adobero* might become in the use of mud. Here we
left Fry and went down south to the Hachitas and camped about
4:00 P.M. on a trail.[124] Keeping on, we got to Mesquite Springs about
noon the next day and, loading up there with water, we went five or
six miles out to the foot of some hills and prospected there until our
water gave out, when we started back. By 8:00 P.M. of the 24th we
were again at Carrisalillo. Here Fry caught up with us and persuaded
us to go with him and Malone to prospect some country which Malone
considered good.

So on the 26th in the afternoon we went back on the Copper Trail
to the tank (*charco*) for the night, and the next day we went about
twelve miles west and prospected in a country of limestone, but without success. On the 28th we were back at the tank, and by night we
made the *tinaja* in the pass near Joe Daugherty's Camp.[125] Here we
found some parties at work on the east end of the mountain, but we
were just a little disgusted with prospecting by this time. After a short
search over the lime rocks of the Victorio mining camp, we were back
at the dairy farm of the Barons of Cow Spring by dark of the afternoon
of May 29.

By four o'clock on Sunday, May 30, we were getting back to our
home town. Ahead of us by the roadside we saw the little mounds of
the Shakespeare *Campo Santo* in three brown, sunburned rows. The
keen eye of Pettie caught sight of one of a dark red color, heaped a
little higher than the others and placed on the south side of the road
nearer the town. This meant a new grave made since we had left two
weeks before, so we began to speculate as to its tenant. We all finally
agreed that it must be the grave of Bill Reed.

Shortly before our trip to Carrisalillo, I had gone to Silver City on a
quick trip. I returned riding on the boot of the stage, Sam Dycus driving. Somewhere in the Burro Mountains we met the eastbound stage
driven by Bill Reed. The drivers halted their horses for a short chat,
first about Indians, and then about stage affairs. At the end of their
chat, Dycus asked Reed to call at a certain store for a package which
he, Dycus, had forgotten to bring out that morning. Bill answered, in
a weak high-pitched voice, that he could not understand why the stage
company kept in its employ a man with one leg in the grave and without any sign of a head. Sam retorted that no one but a "damfool" com-

pany would hire an infernal idiot of a consumptive with two dead feet.

After these comradely remarks, each drove away, smiling. Given a little reflection, I thought I understood that each man was condoling the other in this queer fashion over his physical ailments. Reed's appearance verified Dycus' description of a consumptive in the last stages. At one and another time we had each seen him helped from the stage by others, limp and exhausted at the end of his drive.

Feeling certain that Reed was dead, we rode up to the corral of Smythe, Long and Price. After putting up our horses, we entered the store. The first object to meet our eyes was a human body lying on the counter with a wrinkled, mummified head resting on a pillow of brown wrapping paper, hands folded over his breast. It was Bill Reed, not "in the flesh" because he was merely skin and bone, but it was Bill Reed — alive. Then we learned that it was big, rollicking Bob Fambro whose body was lying under that mound of blood-red earth in the little *Campo Santo* by the roadside.

The story of the killing of Fambro by Bill Carroll ran about as follows: Bill, a sullen man of bad temper, was believed to be weak-minded. He was keeping bar at the town saloon, where Fambro and some friends were drinking and playing cards. Unexpectedly, he and Fambro quarreled over something, and Carroll suddenly drew a knife from under the bar and stabbed Bob Fambro through the lungs. Bob was unarmed. His friends took him home, but somehow he managed to slip away from them with his rifle and started back, weak and staggering, to the saloon.

Fambro had been trained to the rifle on the Plains of Texas as a buffalo hunter in the days of the great Southern Herd and was reputed to be a dead shot. I heard a tale told on the streets of Shakespeare about his skill in killing six out of a herd of seven deer before the lone survivor got out of range. One would have expected that he would certainly have killed Carroll — and so he would, but a chair had fallen over on the floor near the door, and as he advanced, raising the gun to shoot, he fell over it. He was never able to get up again.

Bob lived about twelve hours. Towards the last, his mind began to wander. A man who attended him told me that he talked about buffaloes and several times used the word "stand" in a connection that was not understood by the nurse. The stand was an important stage in the practice of buffalo hunting, known to every hunter as the climax of a successful hunt. Bob was back on the Plains but the hunter was about to go home from the hills below the Cap Rock.[126]

Some Incidents of Special Interest

ॐ ON JUNE 1 Walter Hart and I mounted our horses to make the
ride to Silver City, and about noon the next day we rode into
town.[127] The Tremont House, run by a man named Pete Ott, was
situated on Main Street about a block north of the post office; the
Exchange Hotel lay diagonally across, a block southeast of that office,
and its proprietor was Louie Timmer; the Southern Hotel occupied a
site at the foot of the hill on the margin of the town between the other
two, and was operated by a man named Conners, who had recently
come from Longview, Texas. The floods, which I have heretofore referred to, later destroyed the Tremont and the Timmer and left the
Southern isolated from the town by a deep gulch.

Hart and I put up our horses at a corral and wagonyard owned by two
Englishmen, Meeson and Merriage, and then registered at the Timmer
House, which fronted directly on the corral. The Bremen stamp mill
was situated not far away to the south where the level flat on the townsite narrowed down to a deep gulch in which the San Vincente Springs
broke out. We could hear the ceaseless drum of the iron stamps.[128]

I made inquiry here about my old friend Grant, whom I had left at
Dallas two months earlier and who was to have left Dallas by wagon
shortly after Currie and I took up our route by stage. I had heard but
little from him during that two months. It was past the time for his party
to make its appearance at Silver City. As the Indians had depredated
along two hundred miles of his route, I was naturally uneasy about his
welfare. I derived some satisfaction upon learning that his party had
stopped at Fort Cummings to cut hay for the Government for a short
period, although that occupation could hardly be taken as less dangerous than wayfaring on the Camino Real.

While engaged in this search I fell in with a man named Edwards,
whom I had met the year before at Tascosa, Texas, while on my way
to Santa Fe. He owned one of the two stores in Tascosa, and it was
in the saloon attached to his store that the two men had been killed
in a gambling dispute on the day that my party left the place. He was
quite a handsome man of some thirty-five years, a blond distinguished
by a Van Dyke beard. As I recollect it, he was a native of Georgia but
had wandered over the Atlantic and had married, in the city of London,
a young woman connected with a variety theatre. She had been accustomed to the busy life of the metropolis, and the loneliness and mon-
otony of life in a cage set in a desert at Tascosa greatly depressed her.

Her husband sold out his store and trekked with his ox-trains into the mining territory of New Mexico.

Edwards was quite an adventurer. Within the next year he had built a custom mill in Silver City with the cooperation of Wright and Roodhouse of Roodhouse, Illinois. It was not a success, and when it was burned down, the company by which it was insured refused payment and suit followed.[129] As a witness in this suit I attended the Federal Court at Springfield, Illinois, in the fall of 1884, and while there I learned that Edwards was dead and that his widow, then living in Chicago, had succeeded to his estate. She had gotten back to the noise and crowds of her earlier life.

On the 4th, about 6:00 P.M., after having heard the evidence in the examining trial of Bill Carroll at Silver City for the murder of Fambro, Hart and I started our return journey on our rested horses. By eleven o'clock that night we were knocking at the door of Hank Kramer's house in the valley of Cherry Creek. By night of the 5th we were back in Shakespeare, after having had some trouble in crossing the low flat below town, where a heavy rain had fallen. The summer rains had begun. During the remainder of the month there was much cloudy weather and some rain; I began to suspect that the Pyramid Hills were not so very dry as reported, a suspicion which was easily and finally removed during the next three months.

During one of the dry spells between the rains, Currie made the acquaintance of some settler on the Gila who had evidently found time to leave his crops of pumpkins and potatoes to wander among the hills of Steeple Rock. After several mysterious conferences between them, Currie let me know that he was off for the hills with his new friend to do a little prospecting. When I asked him how he proposed to travel, he informed me that he had arranged to hire a burro for a riding animal, while his new friend would furnish another to carry the bedding and provisions.[130]

Now, the country about Shakespeare, over which Currie had put in his time in search for ore, had impressed him as being greatly fertile in rattlesnakes. So when I suggested the danger of snakebite where the feet and legs hung close to the ground from a saddled burro, especially during the night, he called a halt in the proceeding until his friend, ready and expedient, proposed to shorten the stirrups. When at dusk the procession moved, the last I saw of Currie as he passed out into the growing darkness was a tremendously big straw hat sitting on top of two knees at sharp angles above the withers of a squat burro. He was all knees and hat.

Five days later the knees and the hat, both somewhat dilapidated, appeared at the door of our little adobe house. After stretching, rubbing his knees, and getting a square meal, Currie enlightened us about the course of his prospecting, which like that of true love had not run very smoothly. Twice he had fallen from his animal on hillsides. Once the burro had carried him against his protest under the limb of a juniper tree and he had been knocked off, with sundry welts and bruises. Many times he had barely lifted his legs in time to escape the strike of a rattlesnake. Because of the constant strain on his knees in such unusual positions, he had suffered from cramps, and on getting off his animal he had often fallen to the ground. But the grit of the man carried him through what were to him extraordinary hardships — and he brought back with him some very promising specimens of ore. It subsequently developed that his locations were in what was afterwards known as the East Camp at Steeple Rock.[131]

So far as I know, this was the beginning of the interest in the East Camp, and Currie's locations were probably the first to be made in that camp. How it came that he and his friend of the cushaws and potatoes failed to discover the great ledge on which the Carlisle was afterwards located is to me something of a mystery, as they must have passed in sight of its outcroppings. It was but a short time afterwards that the Carlisle location was made. Its discoverer, a man named Mounts from Denton County, Texas, was even more of a tyro in such matters than Currie. Mounts had traveled out from Texas with my friend Grant, and at that very time was engaged in mowing gramma grass for the garrison at Fort Cummings. Mounts knew something about mowing grass, but nothing at all about gold or silver ore when he set up his rock corners on the Carlisle Mine.[132]

On the second day after Currie's return from his East Camp discoveries, Pettie, Carlos Leroy and Vic Van Hal took up his trail with the intention of finding the location of his discoveries and of prospecting it for their own use. This would not be difficult, barring some unusual happenings such as a heavy rain washing out tracks or a dust storm covering them up.

When the three returned some five or six days later, they claimed to have had but little trouble in following the trail out to the hills beyond the Gila River and in finding the site of Currie's locations on mining claims. They even claimed to have found the spot where he had been thrown off his animal by the limb of a juniper tree, and to have seen the print of his body in a sand bed in some *arroyo* where he had landed after a flight over the burro's head. But they had not found any of the rich ore which Currie had brought back, and believing the reported discovery to be a fake, they had made no locations for themselves.[133]

Yet, Van Hal afterward spent many months at the site of these mining locations of Currie's and pinned his faith for a time on some nearby locations of his own. He was one of the small band that kept up the life of Poverty Flat for several seasons and worked and prayed (very silently) for the success of East Camp. Along the line of tents that faced the creek bed in that camp of millionaires who gave their homes the name of Poverty Flat,[134] lived Currie, Billy Davenport, Frank Campbell, Van Hal, Kistler, Grant, MacDonald of the whispering voice audible a mile away, and for a shorter time Billy Blackburn — with others whose names I have forgotten.

So striking was the life and character of these men, so jovial and hopeful were they in the depths of hard luck, that the name of Poverty Flat was as well known to the prospectors of those days as that of Shakespeare, with all its backing of foreign money. Many were the jokes and good stories that came from that cluster of tents and dugouts to amuse the wanderers in the plains and hills on the border, and many more were charged up to it on the public ledger, in order to give them a good pedigree. I may not have occasion to mention anything further about the life of Poverty Flat, so I will relate here one of these stories. It was told to me in 1886 by Kistler, who was then almost due to abandon his old homestead in the flat.[135]

Currie was a man who had the affectionate regard of every man in the camp. However, he carried with him into the wilderness all of the little niceties of habit and manner which had been in proper play in civilization but were rather obsolete in a mining camp. He occupied the last tent in the row which fronted the *arroyo* where the camp caught its water supply and a hundred feet or so from the next tent, that of Billy Davenport. Early every morning he would appear at his tent door and snuff up eagerly the balsamic odors that filled the air from the surrounding pines, piñons and junipers. One morning this odor was badly infected by a mephitic smell that could come from only one animal, a common camp plague.

Currie saw his neighbor Billy very busily engaged in tossing out pots, pans, skillets and other utensils of his domestic use. Going over to learn the cause of such extraordinary action, he was told that Billy had heard during the night a noise among his boxes and tins where he kept his food supplies. Supposing that a dog had gotten into his tent, he had lambasted that corner with boots, hammers and rocks. The result was disastrous, and he spent the remainder of the night in Frank Campbell's tent, much to Frank's discomfort. He was now clearing out his tent and giving it a chance to shake off the aroma of the skunk, and intended to give himself the same chance later.

The camp had been much troubled by skunks, but Currie's tent had somehow escaped, and he prided himself on having successfully shunted them away. So in the goodness of his heart, he proceeded to tell Billy how he might accomplish the same end by using the same scientific methods which had helped him to secure immunity. For those were the days when Darwin's writings had come into much public discussion, and Currie always tried to keep up with the march of scientific thought.

"Billy," said he, "did you ever hear of Darwin?" Billy did not remember any such gentleman. "Well," went on Currie, "he was a great scientist, and taught many wonderful secrets of nature. He taught the doctrine of inherited instinct. Did you ever hear of it?" Billy knew that a polecat had an out-stink, but he didn't know anything about an in-stink.

"Now then," continued Currie, "what Darwin taught was that animals, after centuries of experience, passed on to their offspring as a kind of frame of mind the result of the parents' experience, so that what the parents had learned by experience to avoid, the offspring avoided even before having had any experience. This he called inherited instinct. For example, the cats learned by long experience that dogs were their enemies and that they must keep away from the dog family. Now, the young ones came to know by this inherited instinct, without any experience, that they, too, must shy away from dogs and their kin, and at first sight of a dog must take to a refuge.

"So, when I hear a polecat nosing about my grub-box in the dark, I just rise up on my elbow in my cot and say loudly 'Sic' two or three times. The cat thinks, by inherited instinct, that I am setting a dog after it, and it makes away as fast as it can, even if it has never seen a dog in its life. Now, this plan will work just as well for you as it does for me. Just try it and I will warrant that you do not have any more trouble with polecats."

But this theory came to an end before Billy could test it, and Currie's speculation was hoist by his own petard. One dark midnight shortly afterward, the tent dwellers were awakened by unusual noises and swearwords coming from Currie's tent. Looking up that way, they could see flashes of light on the canvas, followed by darkness. Since those were Indian days, Billy and Kistler, after arming themselves, cautiously made their way up to Currie's door and, gingerly opening the tent flap, peered in. They saw Currie, in the shortest of nightshirts, standing on his writing table in the center of the tent, engaged in scratching matches on the tent roof and by their light craning his neck down to look over the floor and under the table. His face wore a most serious aspect.

Rather breathlessly they asked, "What's the matter, Currie?"

His answer gave a full solution. "Nothing," he said, "only there is a dad-gasted cat in here somewhere that doesn't know what 'sic' means."

In the latter part of June, I first became acquainted with the late Judge H. C. McComas. The story of his death, along with that of his wife in 1883 at the hands of the Apaches in the Burro Mountains, and of the disappearance of their small son at the same place and time, has become quite a classic in the annals of Grant County. I had become quite well acquainted with him through the intermediary friendship of Adolphus B. Preston. At one time Preston, who died December 29, 1928, in Arnold, Kansas, was a citizen of Silver City.

Mr. McComas was a lawyer who was commonly known by the title of "Judge" and who had practiced law in St. Louis and later in Fort Scott, Kansas, before coming to Silver City. He was a man about sixty years of age, but quite active and enterprising in spirit, and suave and genial in manners. He had become interested in some mining locations at Carrisalillo Springs and was on his way to that place in company with a Mr. Hyatt (a promoter) and some others.

General Boyle, a man named McGowan, and James Carroll, owner of the Superior Mine (where the "85" Mine is now worked) and brother of Bill Carroll, came in from the west about June 26. On Sunday, July 4, we enjoyed a dinner distinguished by a great dish of fish brought back by Pettie, John Phillips and others from the Gila River. After dinner, the General and I started for Silver City in a single buggy. It was almost sunset when we left town, but the General drove a spanking team of Kentucky horses, and by bedtime we were housed at John Parks' home at the old Knight's Ranch in a room marked by portholes. These holes had been used more than once, we were told, in defense against Indians.

About noon of the next day we arrived in Silver City. Shortly afterwards I met Mr. Preston and learned from him that a man commonly known as Charlie Williams had been badly wounded and was then under medical care in town. There was a mystery about the matter, as Williams had ridden into town barely able to hold on to his dun pony but had refused to tell who had given him the gunshot wound in his left leg. He had no money and was then lying in rough quarters; he was dependent for nursing and medical attention upon the charity of friends and acquaintances. Just then there was need for someone to attend to him as a nurse during the following day. I volunteered my services; so General Boyle had another comrade behind his bay horses on his return trip the next day.

I had a very slight acquaintance with Williams, who had apparently made his headquarters at Shakespeare during part of the preceding May and June. He had no special occupation but spent much of his time at the saloon. He was reputed to be a rustler; and in common with all rustlers of the day in New Mexico, he was charged up against Texas as a debit item. For while in ordinary usage the word "rustler" is a creditable title as applied to a man, yet in New Mexico and Texas in those days — and even until now — it was a common euphemism used in toning down the harsh term "cattle thief." It was believed that Williams was independent of that formidable band of rustlers who made their headquarters in the San Simon country; at any rate, he did not appear to have any close relations with them.

Possibly as long as six weeks before this time, Williams had shot a man named Molliter at Shakespeare. As the wounded man had died the next day, Williams had been arrested for murder and taken to Silver City, where he had secured straw bail and had remained there up to that time. Molliter was, like Williams, a man of whom almost nothing was known. It was said that he came from some place in Indiana, where he was wanted for murder. But as it was certain that he was afflicted with consumption, it was highly probable that his presence in Shakespeare was due to that ailment. The act of Williams in shooting Molliter was, so far as the public knew, without cause and remains to this day an unexplained mystery, unless it can be laid solely to a frame of mind brought about by excessive indulgence in liquor.

Molliter was lying on a bench in front of the saloon in the heat of the day taking a sunbath, a habit which he cultivated as a means of fighting off his disease. Williams had been in the saloon all morning, drinking pretty heavily. About noon he walked out through the front door of the building, twirling his pistol around his head. When his eyes fell upon the prostrate man lying on the bench, he turned the pistol down on him and fired. Not a word passed at the time between them. No explanation was offered by either party later, so far as I can recollect. Molliter lived less than a day after being shot. I had these facts in mind the next day after my arrival in Silver City while I was going to the place where Williams lay, and I rather hoped to have some explanation of the two mysteries. But nothing came of that hope. Such explanation as I got was to come later and from another man.

I was taken to a freshly built house of one room, unpainted and, except for a few benches, almost bare. But on the south side of it there stood a rough frame fashioned in the shape of a bed on which lay Charlie Williams, with nothing but a blanket between him and the rough, unplaned pine boards — a pillow under his head, a linen sheet over him. To the ankle of his left foot a rope was tied; and after being carried over the foot of the bed, the rope held a rock in suspension. There was a gunshot wound in the left leg, high up towards the hip, the bullet having entered on the outside of the leg, while its exit appeared on the inside just above the knee. The rock was used to hold the leg taut.

Williams was somewhat under the influence of morphine, and we — the other attendant and I — did not engage him at once in conversation. But about a half hour later, two men, whom I understood to be gamblers, came in carrying two bottles of mixed drinks and, waking up the wounded man, informed him that they had brought him these bottles, and that they had won a certain amount of money betting on him that night. Williams brightened up and assured them that they could safely bet on him, for he was not in any danger of dying from his wound. Then we understood that these men had bet on him living through the night, and later we were informed that this had been going on for two or three days.

About eleven o'clock in the morning the doctor came in; even at that early hour, he was plainly far gone in liquor. He examined the wounds — did not dress them, but instructed us to be careful to keep moist the scant linen rags with which they were covered in order that the flies might not gain access to the raw flesh. There was no pretense of other antiseptic precautions. Lister had not been heard of in Silver City at that time. After a moment's testing of the pulse, the doctor pulled out a promissory note for $50 and asked the patient to sign it. Williams protested. His word, he said, was as good as his note, since he had nothing but a dun pony, which was to go to someone whose name I have forgotten, in case he died. But the doctor insisted. Williams finally agreed to sign, and I held up his shoulders while he wrote at the bottom of the note the name "Charlie Williams" in a bold, running hand.

Then he began to talk to us. Williams, he said, was not his name, nor did he come from Texas. He intimated that his family lived in Wisconsin. I offered to write for him any letters to friends or kinfolk which he might feel disposed to have sent out. He refused this offer and remarked that all the friends he had in that vicinity already knew of his

condition and that if he died, he hoped to God that no kinfolk of his
would ever know how or where he passed away. It is probable that
they never did.

After spending two days in attendance on him, I had to leave for
Shakespeare July 8 on the stage. When I left, Williams, a man of
about thirty, of great strength and powerful constitution, was making
a determined fight for his life, under what seemed to me to be the
worst possible conditions for recovery.[136]

Excitement in the Tres Hermanas

ON GETTING BACK to Shakespeare I found George Roberts and
Murdock Martin waiting my return.[137] They had been with me
in 1877 on the Texas Plains. For some months past, their time had been
spent near a new town named Gayleyville at the foot of the Chiricahua
Mountains, in search of mining locations. Dissatisfied with their prospects there, they were now outward bound — Roberts for no particular
spot, Martin for his old home in Texas.

I found Roberts anxious to trade off some mining location which he
owned, and which was situated not far from another location in the
Chiricahuas, known as the Texas, which at that date was believed to
hold the promise of becoming a real mine. He evidently did not consider his property very valuable, since Mr. Currie was proposing to
swap him a gun for it — a gun of ancient and doubtful history — while
he was contending only for a small sum to boot. As that kind of gun
has become almost entirely forgotten by Old Timers and is utterly unknown to the present generation, I may be excused for giving a short
account of the last days of this particular one after it had fallen from
a former high estate.

Before leaving Dallas with me for the West, Currie had asked my
opinion of a gun which he said he could get for his use. As his description of it was almost unintelligible to me, I went with him to view it.
I had never seen another like it but had heard of the paper-cartridge
Enfields. I took it to be one of that make. It was a short-barreled affair
which broke at the point of contact of barrel and breech, but it carried
a hollow nipple with the setting for a cap, like the squirrel rifle of my
youth. However, we always loaded the squirrel rifle from the end of the
barrel, while this gun was loaded with a cartridge at the breech. The
cartridge was made of paper and, when placed in the gun, was bitten
or torn off at the end, in order that the powder might be ignited from
the blaze of the cap carried down through the hollow nipple.

When I learned that only fourteen cartridges went with the gun, I told Currie that cartridges of that kind could not be found in any part of the West familiar to me, and that unless he could get quite a number in the Dallas or Fort Worth markets, it was useless for him to consider buying this gun. When he repeated that he could not find any, I thought that ended the matter. But when he came with me on the stage he carried that old fusil with him, and here it was again to the front as a weapon to be used in aid of its owner.

Finally, Roberts wanted to test the shooting qualities of the old gun. Currie hesitated at losing a precious cartridge, but at last agreed to the test. Roberts backed a marked shingle against a rock, stepped off twenty-five yards, knelt to a deliberate aim and fired. At the explosion he fell back with a loud yell. When we went up to him we found that his eyebrows and eyelashes had been almost entirely burned off. The powder had flashed up through the opening where the barrel and the breech came together.

Now after this, I was much surprised when Roberts told Currie — with much blinking of the eyes and twitching of the face — that the trade was a "go." He gave as a reason that he could sell the gun for a toy to some youngster, and at least it would cost him nothing; while to hold the location meant an expense of $100 in development work in the next five months. He really thought that Currie had made a bad bargain. But Currie only smiled. That gun had been the occasion of many a jest leveled at his head.

On Sunday, July 11, 1880, the little burg witnessed the return of Carlos Leroy from a prospecting expedition to the Tres Hermanas Mountains. Soon after his appearance at the office of the assayer, it was whispered around that he had brought back some marvelous specimens of rich ore, and immediately thereafter he became the most popular man in Shakespeare. It was only after considerable delay and by the aid of the assayer that I got the chance to see this ore, and as soon as I saw it I put in an application to be taken as a companion on Leroy's return trip.

It was a black rock — the piece that I saw — very heavy and on the outside bearing the granulated appearance of black powder. I think the assayer called it an argentite. He placed it on an iron plate and brought down his hammer on it two or three times, then called our attention to its changed appearance. He had beaten the loose, black granulations down to a polished surface, a surface almost as clear and lucent as the face of a silver dollar. A mine that furnished only a thin sliver of vein of such material would certainly be in the class of those

that paid "from the grass-roots down." Every prospector dreamed of
such a discovery. No wonder nearly every man in camp was ready to
desert his place and to follow the trail to the hills.

I do not remember that Leroy followed any definite system or plan
in selecting his comrades for the trail back to the Tres Hermanas Hills.
The men who went along were not former associates of any intimacy;
we had not been tied together in any former ventures. Indeed, I barely
knew two of the others by sight, and Leroy seemed to be even less
acquainted with them. Horton, Tomlinson, Sicotte, and I made up the
favored four who were to share with Leroy the riches of the New Ophir.
Not a one of us flinched or soldiered in camp or on the march. While
we did not meet with success, still I cannot recall a complaint or a
sharp word during the long, hard rides, nor during the wearisome night
watches. Yet, Tomlinson was a consumptive, as we soon learned, and
Horton suffered from an injury to his leg, while grey hairs grew heavy
on Sicotte's temples.

We left Shakespeare about 3:00 P.M. on July 12 and struck out on
the old stage road towards Soldier's Farewell. But after nightfall we
turned from the road and cut across the country towards the *tinaja*
on the Old Copper Trail as straight as we could make our way in the
darkness of the night. This served a double purpose: first, to shorten
our journey, and second, to throw off our trail those who, we were sure,
would follow us out from Shakespeare. After some forty miles of riding
we camped well after nightfall and slept late the following day. By
the afternoon of the 13th we were resting our tired horses and our own
weary bones at the *tinaja,* beyond the Victorio Mountains.[138]

By 2:00 P.M. of Wednesday we got to Carrisalillo Springs and laid
up for the remainder of the day and night in order to freshen up our
horses, as we expected a rather strenuous time on the last leg of our
journey to the Tres Hermanas. By nightfall two more pilgrims showed
up at the springs, having heard somehow in Silver City of Leroy's
strike. It was often a source of wonder to me in those days to learn of
the unaccountably rapid spread of the knowledge of any remarkable
discovery of mineral. Let some man make such a find, and in almost
a moment the scattered members of the prospecting fraternity — some
from the towns, some from the hills, and some from the flats — would be
found coming from every direction towards a common center. If anyone can claim foreknowledge of the radio service, the old-time prospector must be the guilty party.

On Thursday, the 15th, our party went into the Tres Hermanas,
getting our water at the Macho Spring but making our camp some

distance away after the custom of those times when Indians on the move had to come to water, no matter how much they might wish to hide out from observation. At once we went to the locality of Leroy's discovery. But although we hunted diligently, we found none of that black sulphide of silver and very little of any other kind of ore. It was rather a disheartened quintet that ate an early supper and went to bed without a light. We scattered the next morning to make separate search. When we gathered together about 3:00 P.M. on the following day, we were even more disgusted to learn that no one of us could report any success in finding good showings. Further, Horton had found fresh moccasin tracks, and Tomlinson had caught sight of a quick movement on a hillside of scattered rock and brush, which appeared to him to have been made by a human figure.[139]

So we got our traps ready, mounted our horses, and set out to leave the hills, where we had found no signs of ore and where we were in probable danger from Indians. We camped at the western foot of the Three Sisters (Tres Hermanas). But after nightfall we caught sight of fires on our side of the tallest peak of that range, fires which were plainly used for signaling purposes. The lights winked, disappearing for a short time, then blazing up for a time, much after the fashion of the dots and dashes of the Morse code. It was the Indian telegraphy that we were witnessing and, as the messages sent out might be locating our position for a band of hostile savages, we decided to change camp at once. In darkness we mounted, rode four or five miles, dismounted and made down our beds, still without light. Now and then during the night the lights flashed out from the hills repeating, we decided, the same message time and time again.[140]

Now, many years after that night I saw an ancient Spanish map of Apacheland. On it were marked the names of the subdivisions of the Apache tribe in their respective habitats, and as these names were of Spanish origin, I could easily recognize them, except one which carried no meaning to me at first. I knew the locality of the Chiricahuas; the Gileños must be the Apaches of the headwaters of the Gila River; the Mescaleros (Mescal Makers) were mapped in the White and Sacramento mountains, where they may be found today. But the Apaches Faraones, who were assigned to the territory between the Chiricahuas on the west and the mouth of the Pecos River on the east, puzzled me in my attempts to give meaning to the name.

There was nothing in the story of the Pharaoh of Egypt that seemed to have any connection with the word, even though the spelling was almost identical. The only other Spanish word to my knowledge that had any chance for a connection was the word *farol,* meaning "light-house," a word evidently derived from the name of the island and lighthouse at the mouth of the Nile in early Greek days. But how could Apaches, living in the hills far away from any body of water have any relation to a lighthouse? This remained a puzzle until I happened to call up in memory the winking and blinking of the lights of the Apache signal fires that night on the high points of the Tres Hermanas. The purposes of lighthouses on the ocean shores were better served by a blinking light, flashing and dying alternately, than by a steady glare. So this branch of the Apache family was known to the Spaniards as the "lighthouse" Apaches.[141]

Early the next morning, the 17th, we were on our way back to Car-risalillo Springs. About noon we caught sight of two horsemen coming toward us, and our glasses told us that they were white men. We knew Mr. King, who was the owner of a small mine in the Eureka District, commonly known as the King Mine, which was situated some twenty or twenty-five miles west of the springs. He introduced his companion as Mr. Crittenden and stated that they had left the springs that day to prospect in the Tres Hermanas, where they had heard that Leroy had made a discovery of rich ore.

Crittenden was a man of about thirty, of whom none of us had any previous knowledge. Upon learning from us of the probable presence of Indians in the mountains from which we had just come, he and King decided to return with us to Carrisalillo Springs. But when we came within six or seven miles of these springs, Crittenden left us, intending, he said, to try to kill a deer to bring into camp, since there were then at that place more than twenty hungry men. His last remarks were directed at King, whom he asked to lay by some bacon and bread in his (King's) saddle pockets, so that if Crittenden got back to camp after nightfall he might have something to eat without disturbing the camp and without making a light.

It was then in the afternoon of the 17th, about two o'clock, when we rode into Carrisalillo Springs. Some twenty men or more hailed us as we rode up — men who had trailed us out of Shakespeare — men from Silver City, from Central City and from Fort Cummings — all of whom came from points along the Overland stage route, and who were hard on the trail of Leroy and his mine at the end of the rainbow. John Price was there, leaving his cares to his clerks of the stage line. Deputy Sheriff Tucker left off his official duties but not his guns and, regardless of all lawbreakers who might cross his path, came hurrying down the Old

Copper Trail to hunt down the most elusive fugitive of all his experience.[142]

Among these devotees of the Goddess Fortune, we recognized the familiar face of our old friend Charlie Fry, his red face in a broad smile that could not be hidden even by his month-old whiskers. But Charlie had a diplomatic bent in that many-sided brain under a dirty, lop-eared hat, and as he came up he gave us a very enthusiastic invitation to a dinner of venison stew and potatoes, which he declared would be cooked to perfection by the time we should have taken care of our horses.

We had had only a scant breakfast, and it was then two hours after the noon hour. There and then, old Charlie won his right to all the information we could give him concerning that strike of Leroy's. And, of course, he used his right when the opportunity came. We heartily wished for our sake we could give him a good report — and for his own sake also, because that was one of the dinners that linger in my memory.

We followed him over to a small fire with a large Dutch oven in the center. With a horny left hand Charlie lifted up the top. There came to our nostrils a most delightful fragrance, and at once I saw in Sicotte's face a very eager smile, which I am sure was repeated from my own countenance. But Charlie's next move brought about great change in our facial expressions. The dirt lay deep on his hands; his fingernails were fringed with very black tips; and at the outer edge of his lips on each side a yellow tobacco streak discolored his month-old whiskers and took up the march again down the front of his shirt bosom. So when he stuck his right forefinger into his mouth, moved it back and forth in order to get it thoroughly wet, then plunged it into the boiling stew with a rapid stirring motion and brought it back to his mouth to get a good taste, there was consternation among the members of our party.

Sicotte was quite fastidious, and he drew back as if from the strike of a snake. Tomlinson had a weak stomach, and he had the appearance just then of a man about to lose his breakfast. Charlie announced that the stew was not quite "done." Looking up as he said this and noticing the flurry among his guests but mistaking its meaning, he gravely added, "Don't worry, boys. It will be ready in just a few moments."

It may be that I should leave the reader to give a kind of gastronomic credit to our party in the assumption that we did not partake of that stew. But it was no Barmecide feast. As a matter of fact when it was "done" to Charlie's taste, we set to with a vigor that soon brought us to scraping out the bottom of that oven. We quit slightly hungry. Mutual confidence brought out the facts that no one of us would admit that he had caught the slightest flavor of tobacco, and all agreed that it was one of the most satisfactory dinners we each had ever had. Hunger was a wonderful sauce in the desert, as well as in town.

During our attack upon the stew, our host kept up a continuous run of conversation between bites for the entertainment of his company. During this talk he referred to someone as a "ca-*pit*-u-list," placing the primary accent on the syllable "pit." It was mildly suggested to him that the word was properly accented on the first syllable, as "*cap*-i-tal-ist." Charlie was up in arms at once in defense.

"Don't you know the difference between a '*cap*-i-tal-ist and a 'ca-*pit*-u-list'?" We did not. He proceeded to enlighten us. He took much pride in his power to use the Queen's English with great force without having to call to his aid any low-down "cuss" words. So his explanation of that difference ran in something like the following language:

"A '*cap*-i-tal-ist' is a feller who has a dad-gummed pile of money. He comes to you and says he would like to see your mine. He goes with you to see it, takes some samples and has them assayed. Then he comes back and says he wants a working bond on your blasted mine for six months, and will pay you five hundred down if you will let him sink a shaft on it, and ten thousand more if you deed it to him on his asking for it. Then he goes to work on it and either tells you he doesn't want it, or pays you the ten thousand and takes a deed from you which says he paid ten thousand for it and not a durned cent more.

"But a consarned 'ca-*pit*-u-list' is a feller who hasn't any money but swells around like a turkey-gobbler. He comes to you, and says he hears you have a mine. You say you have more than one. He asks you to let him see the cheapest one, which you sell to him for one hundred dollars; but when you make him a deed, you find you have been horn-swoggled into saying he has paid you ten thousand. Then the dad-gasted feller goes back to the Bible class in his town and tells his friends in that class that he has bought a rich mine for ten thousand, but because of his old friendship for them, he will let four-fifths of it go to them at ground-floor prices. That snoozer is a 'ca-*pit*-u-list.'"

Since some movement of the Apaches in the neighborhood was probable, all the men then at Carrisalillo Springs agreed that we would camp without fire and closely together that night. When darkness began to fall, I made my bed down a few feet from where King was lying on his blankets, and we engaged in conversation. After a short time his friend Crittenden made his appearance. He asked King if he had laid by for him something to eat. He was told that there was bacon and bread in the pockets of King's saddle, some fifteen or twenty feet away. Against the skyline I saw his figure move away to the saddle, where he seemed to stoop for a moment. Then he jumped back with a loud yell that might have been heard a mile away.

The men in camp immediately came running up, guns in hand. Between moans Crittenden explained that as he stooped to the saddle, something jumped at him and struck him on the hand; that he had heard no rattle but it might have been a snake, as the pain from the wound was intense. We immediately lit a small fire and by its light we routed out and killed a little rattlesnake under the saddle. It had only a button on its tail and could not rattle.

We then examined Crittenden's hand and found the marks of the two fangs between the knuckle of the forefinger and that of the middle finger. We cut in with a knife, but it bled very little. Then we hunted for what was in those days considered useful in such a case, but there was no whiskey in the party. The arm was rapidly swelling to a great size, so at last we began to apply black mud from the springs. Owing to the fever in the blood, the mud caked rapidly, and we were kept busily engaged in trips to and from the water's edge.

Finally, two of us were left to nurse the victim through the first half of the night while the others went back to their blankets. Crittenden was suffering great agony and expressed the belief that he was going to die. After all others had retired, he began to intimate to me and my comrade that before he died, he had a confession to make. We tried to hold this back, but at last he would not be denied any longer. Raising on his elbow, he said that he was the man who had killed Charlie Williams, and pointing to a gun lying near the fire declared: "That is the gun I killed him with." This was the first word I had had of Williams' death.

He went on to say that Williams had wanted an interest in a mining location which he owned near Pinos Altos, but as Williams had no money and would be useless to Crittenden as a partner, he had been turned down. Later, as Crittenden was riding up along the mountain slope to his mine, his horse arched its neck to look back. Crittenden turned his eyes back also and found that Williams, on his dun horse, was trailing him to his mine. To drive him back, Crittenden turned his rifle down in the general direction of Williams and, without aiming, fired. As he did so, he saw Williams slump forward and catch the horse's mane for support. The horse turned back down the hill toward Silver City. This Crittenden declared to be the truth, adding that he had already told the circumstances to Ad Eaton, who kept a wagonyard in Silver City and would verify this confession.

After the confession was made he seemed to rest easier, and we gave way after midnight to our two successors. The next morning at Crittenden's request I went to shift his horse to a stake for a change and found the rope cut and the horse missing. Later the horse was found. By a strange coincidence it had been bitten on the nose by a snake; the horse's head was swollen as big as that of a hippopotamus. On hearing this, Crittenden, who was getting better, became very much troubled; he insisted that he be kept informed every hour of the day as to the condition of the animal. That evening he had the horse staked near where he lay, with the saddle and bridle close at hand. He let his nurses go about 10:00 o'clock that night on the plea that they were not necessary any longer.

The next morning Crittenden and his horse and saddle were missing. We trailed his horse south some four miles into Mexico, where he must have expected to get away from his confession. But he was going, sick and weak, on a disabled horse, into the worst Apache country in Mexico, and we gave him up as a man who would never be heard of again. Yet, six months later a letter was received at Silver City from him, dated at Guaymas in Sonora, in which he stated that he had gotten finally to that point after going through Hades.[143]

NOTES

(for Part II)

1 For a summary of the action taken by the Texas Legislature in the construction of the new capitol, see J. E. Haley, *The XIT Ranch of Texas and the Early Days of the Llano Estacado* (Norman, 1953), Chapter IV; Joubert Greer, *The Building of the Texas Capitol, 1882-1888* (M.A. Thesis, University of Texas, 1932). The new policy regarding public lands is explained briefly in *Report of the Commissioner of the General Land Office*, Aug. 3, 1880 - March 1, 1883, 3.

2 D. L. and J. H. Griswold, *The Carbonate Camp Called Leadville* (Denver, 1951), Chapters I and II. Williams was also doubtless influenced by this book in his library: A. D. Anderson, *The Silver Country of The Great Southwest* (New York, 1877).

6 *Ibid.*, Oct. 8, 1879 — April 17, 1880.

4 Lawlessness had reached its highest pitch in and around Leadville at the very time that Williams and his party were en route there. Griswold, *The Carbonate Camp Called Leadville*, Chapter IV. On the other hand, the mining camp of Carbonateville, near Santa Fe, was enjoying a boom, with relatively little lawlessness. General Lew Wallace, then Governor of New Mexico, often visited Carbonateville to relax and to write. O. W. Williams, Letter to Clayton W. Williams, Sept. 9, 1918.

5 *Diary*, July 25 - Oct. 8, 1879.

6 *Ibid.*, Oct. 8, 1879 - April 17, 1880.

7 Shakespeare began to attract many miners from Silver City and Pinos Altos in April, 1879, owing to favorable reports from speculators and developers. By the time Williams arrived, mining activities were in full swing. *The Grant County Herald*, April 12 and 19, 1879; Jan. 3, 1880. *Thirty-Four*, April 23, Aug. 20 and Dec. 12, 1879. General John Boyle was responsible for reactivating the mining district. For a full and somewhat glowing account of the activities and prospects in and around Shakespeare, see *ibid.*, Dec. 24, 1879.

8 Early in 1880, F. M. F. Cazin, a mining and civil engineer of Bernalillo, N. M., reported that he had examined the mines at Shakespeare and found that they did not come up to expectations. The ore was low-grade; the mines were capable at best of only a small margin of profit. *Ibid.*, Jan. 21, 1880. For another critical report, see *The Daily Southwest*, April 10, 1880.

9 N. B. Laughlin, a native of Grand Tower, Jackson County, Ill., was born July 24, 1884. After graduation from Missouri State University, he came to Dallas. He was admitted to the Texas Bar in 1876. Because of ill health, he, like Williams, traveled west. After arriving in Santa Fe, he spent the next three years in the mining camps of New Mexico. In 1880 and 1886, he was a member of the Territorial Legislature. From 1894 to 1898, he was Associate Justice of the Territorial Supreme Court, then continued the practice of law until his death in 1924. R. E. Twitchell, *The Leading Facts in New Mexican History* (Cedar Rapids, 1912, 5 vols.), I, 517.

10 On the killing of J. W. Bell, see introduction to Williams' "City of Refuge," III, which follows.

11 Nathaniel J. Wyeth was a successful ice merchant of Cambridge, Mass., who became an explorer. He organized expeditions that went into the Northwest during the early 1830's and helped establish American claims to the territory. The route he followed became the famous Oregon Trail. His diary contains much valuable information about the Northwest. T. D. Clark, *Frontier America* (New York, 1959), 458-59, 462, 489, 572; R. A. Billington, *Westward Expansion* (New York, 1949), 460, 513-14, 516.

12 "Regularly after a meal he [Jim Martin] took some of the old dough, put it in a tin bucket and mixed it to a consistency of a heavy cream with some flour and water, then hung the bucket to the rear of the wagon so that between the heat of the sun and the jolting of the wagon, it was ready for service at the next meal. Sometimes dust worked its way into the bucket; but whether the yeast was short in quantity or dirty in quality, always the bread pan was cleaned out." Letter, O. W. Williams to Clayton W. Williams, Sept. 10, 1918.

13 "Five of us rode Texas ponies, while Jim drove the team and wagon carrying our camping plunder." Letter, O. W. Williams to Clayton W. Williams, Sept. 9, 1918.

14 Henrietta is the county seat of Clay County, now on the Fort Worth and Denver and the M.K. & T. railroads. Founded in 1860, the town was abandoned during the Civil War. Reoccupied in 1865 after the War, it was again abandoned because of Indian raids. It was finally settled permanently in 1873. For some years Henrietta was the principal trading center for Fort Sill in Indian Territory. It had a population of about four hundred when Williams passed through. W. P. Webb (ed.), *The Handbook of Texas* (Austin, 1952, 2 vols.), I, 798-99. Williams' party evidently traveled from Henrietta west by a little north, paralleling the Red River, crossing the Little Wichita and Pease rivers, going up Prairie Dog Fork of the Red River, and skirting around Palo Duro Canyon, the area to which Charles Goodnight had moved his herd of cattle three years earlier.

15 The party arrived at Tascosa on July 5, 1879, after passing through open country. Here the presence of Indians was reported, but none were seen. *Diary*, June 17-July 7. Tascosa, located in Oldham County, Texas, bordering the east line of New Mexico, was settled by Mexicans from New Mexico in the early 1870's. The town sprang to life in 1877 as ranchmen moved into the area. It was known as reasonably law-abiding until it died in 1887 because the Fort Worth and Denver Railroad passed it by a mile or two to the west. Haley, *The XIT Ranch of Texas*, Chapter XIII; J. L. McCarty, *Maverick Town: The Story of Old Tascosa* (Norman, 1946).

16 A large mill built by the New Mexico and Massachusetts Mining Company was also destroyed by fire about this time. *Grant County Herald*, May 17, June 21, 1879; Feb. 7, July 3, Sept. 25, 1880; *New Southwest and Grant County Herald*, Sept. 9, 1881.

17 At Tascosa, the party changed its destination on July 6 after talking with two sheepmen, Rogers and Cottle, "who told us of a 'find' of carbonates more recent than that at Leadville, and not so far away"; so the party "decided to turn our course to the new field. The new Mecca was called Carbonateville (of course) and was

situated about 25 miles south of Santa Fe, New Mexico." Letter, O. W. Williams to Clayton W. Williams, Sept. 9, 1918.

18 The party was on the famous Santa Fe Trail followed by the William Bucknell expedition of 1821, and the great trade route until the 1860's. The most definitive work on the trail is: U. S. Department of Interior, *The National Survey of Historic Sites and Buildings . . . The Santa Fe Trail* (Washington, 1963).

19 Pajarito Creek, located about five miles north of Tucumcari in western Quay County, New Mexico, is one of the minor southern tributaries of the Canadian River. The name is Spanish for "little bird." A large ruin on the rim of Pajarito Canyon was known as Tchirage or "Place of the Bird People." C. F. Coan, *A History of New Mexico* (Chicago, 1925, 3 vols.), I, 576. New Mexico Folk Society, *New Mexico Place - Name Dictionary* (Mimeographed, 1950), 1.

20 Anton Chico, located on the buffalo plains along the west bank of the Pecos, is about thirty miles southeast of Las Vegas, N. M., and some five miles off U. S. Highway 84. Don Salvador Tapia filed a petition on Jan. 24, 1822, for the land on which the town was established. Later the land came into the possession, by grant, of Manuel Rivera and thirty-six others. From 1854 to 1860 the U. S. Army maintained a frontier post at Camp Rio Pecos nearby. Anton Chico later became a sheep and cattle center. Betty S. Rouse, "Anton Chico: Historic Village," *New Mexico Magazine* (No. 10, Oct., 1959), XXXVII, 36; H. B. Carroll, *The Texan Santa Fe Trail* (Canyon, Texas, 1951), 142-43, 186. Documents concerning the land grant are to be found in Survey-General Records, No. 29, Bureau of Land Management, Santa Fe. The Jewish merchant to whom Williams refers was apparently one of the Diffenhofer brothers sent to Anton Chico by the Spiegelberg mercantile firm of Santa Fe. See William J. Parrish, "The German Jew and the Commercial Revolution in Territorial New Mexico, 1850-1900," *New Mexico Historical Review* (No. 1, Jan., 1960), XXXV, 19-20.

21 Billy the Kid (William H. Bonney), the notorious outlaw, ranged freely over Southeastern New Mexico and West Texas during those early years. His career, especially in Lincoln County, N. M., has become a saga of the Southwest, provoking much discussion and a number of books, including P. F. Garrett, *The Authentic Life of Billy the Kid: The Noted Outlaw of the Southwest* (Santa Fe, 1882); W. N. Burns, *The Saga of Billy the Kid* (New York, 1920); G. W. Coe, *Frontier Fighter* (Albuquerque, 1934); M. A. Otero, *The Real Billy the Kid: With New Light on the Lincoln County War* (New York, 1936); W. A. Keleher, *Violence in Lincoln County* (Albuquerque, 1957).

22 The party arrived at Carbonateville on July 24 and disbanded four days later. *Diary*, July 24-28, 1879. For a brief account of conditions in the mining camp, see Erna Ferguson, *New Mexico* (New York, 1955), 304. Carbonateville, located in the Cerrillos (Galisteo) Mining District, was much alive when Williams was there. The place is the site of the ancient turquoise mine and the Mina del Terra that produced gold and silver. The town is now in ruins. F. S. Jones, *New Mexico Mines and Minerals* (Santa Fe, 1904), 29-33; G. F. Shenk, "The First Gold Mine," *New Mexico Magazine* (No. 8, Aug., 1953), XXI, 16, 55.

23 Williams traded his horse for a half-interest in two small shallow mines. He spent

considerable time working them personally and "prospecting" in the immediate area. *Diary*, July 28 - Oct. 2, 1879.

24 The "St. Louis boys" are referred to in the *Diary* of Sept. 4, 6 and 13. Williams visited Santa Fe with some of them on Sept. 13.

25 Ambulance in the sense used here was a passenger vehicle — a wagon mounted on springs — formerly used in the West. The U. S. Boundary Commission used ambulances in making the surveys along the border with Mexico in 1850-51. J. R. Bartlett, *Personal Narrative of Explorations and Incidents in Texas, New Mexico, California, Sonora, and Chihuahua* (New York, 1954, 2 vols.), I, 97. Hereafter cited as Bartlett, *Personal Narrative*.

26 Governor Lew Wallace achieved success as a military leader, lawyer, statesman and writer. He was born in Brookville, Ind., April 10, 1827. After a distinguished career in the Union Army, during which period his defense of the National Capital brought him renown, he accepted an appointment by President Hayes to become Governor of the Territory of New Mexico. Wallace confronted many difficulties, including the troubles in Lincoln County; he refused reappointment to office in 1881 when his term expired. He did, however, accept an ambassadorship to Turkey, which post he occupied with distinction until 1885. Lew Wallace, *An Autobiography* (New York, 1906), II, 847-51, 911-37; E. F. Harkins, *Famous Authors* (*Men*) (Boston, 1901), 59-74.

27 Padre Aoy, the *gachupín*, was later well-known in El Paso, especially for the founding of Aoy School. Jaime Aoy Vila was born in 1832 of noble parents in Valencia, Spain. He became a priest, migrated to Havana, left the priesthood, then joined the Mayas of Yucatán, adopting their customs and learning their language. By 1873 he was in Utah, where he became a Mormon. Later he moved to Santa Fe, then on to the mining area of Carbonateville and Silver City. By 1888 he was in El Paso, where he took charge of a small school for Mexican children. Friends aided him in keeping the school alive. He died in 1895 and is buried in the Evergreen Cemetery, El Paso. Today Aoy School, a part of the El Paso public-school system, is named in his honor. *El Paso Herald*, April 29, 1895; April 29, 1933. *El Paso Times*, April 28, 1895; *El Paso City Directories*, 1887-1888, 1888, 1889, 1895-1896. Conrey Bryson, *The Story of Mr. Aoy* (unpublished manuscript). In Carbonateville, Aoy's printing shop was a small room equipped with a few fonts of type. At the time, Aoy was a small swarthy man of about forty-five years. O. W. Williams, Letter to Clayton W. Williams, Sept. 19, 1918.

28 The most definitive listing of the Franciscans and their jurisdictions in New Mexico is to be found in Eleanor B. Adams and Fray Angélico Chávez, *The Missions of New Mexico, 1776* (Albuquerque, 1956), 328-47.

29 Padre Aoy was apparently referring to "Gran Quivira," the largest of the Piro Indian pueblos, located about eighty miles south of Santa Fe, and abandoned before the Pueblo Revolt of 1680. The mission ruins are now a national monument. See E. L. Hewett and W. L. Mauzy, *Landmarks of New Mexico* (Albuquerque, 1940), 106. The fabled city of Quivira originated in the mind of a Plains Indian living at the Pueblo of Pecos, called "The Turk" by the Coronado Expedition. In search of the wealthy city, he led the Spaniards to the Pecos and Brazos rivers and northward

into Kansas. Quivira turned out to be a collection of grass huts inhabited by the Wichita Indians. See H. E. Bolton, *Coronado on the Turquoise Trail* (Coronado Cuarto Centennial Publications, 1540-1940, Vol. I, Albuquerque, 1949), especially 282-303.

30 Father Aoy was in error, since Gran Quivira and the missions at Abo, Quarai, as well as others in the area, were abandoned before the Pueblo Revolt, probably in the 1670's. Rumors of the burial of church treasures and gold have persisted to the present, without any warrant in fact or documentation.

31 Shakespeare was originally a stage stop established in 1867 on an alternate route used to escape Indian attacks. The town first bore the name of "Grant" in honor of the U. S. Army general. In 1870, William C. Ralston, a leading financier of San Francisco, became interested in the place because of the discovery of silver nearby and organized a mining company which sold stock widely in the United States and Europe. His representatives laid out the Virginia Mining District, extending from Grant (now renamed Ralston) to Leitendorf's Wells, in which area Williams was to operate. Unfortunately, the financier became deeply involved in various costly ventures, including the Great Diamond Hoax, discussed later. On Aug. 27, 1875, his bank closed; the same day, he went into San Francisco Bay for his regular swim and drowned. The mining camp was depopulated for some time thereafter, but it reopened in the late 1870's after Gen. John Boyle of St. Louis arrived and staked out claims. Being a devotee of Shakespeare, he renamed the new settlement in honor of the poet. He also promoted the mining district energetically, and it is likely that Williams read some of Boyle's glowing reports. An excellent account of Shakespeare is found in four articles by Mrs. Emma M. Muir in *New Mexico Magazine* (1948), XXVI, Nos. 7, 8, 9, and 10. (Hereinafter cited as Muir, *Shakespeare*.) On the founding of Shakespeare, see Muir, *Shakespeare*, No. 7, pp. 26-27, 59; No. 8, pp. 27, 46. See also, G. B. Anderson (ed.), *History of New Mexico* (Los Angeles, 1907, 2 vols.), II, 723-25; Marjorie White, "Shakespeare: The West's Most Authentic Ghost Town," *New Mexico Magazine* (No. 4, April, 1962), XL, 5-9, 35.

32 In the *Diary* of Sept. 20, 1879, Williams noted that work was closing down somewhat in Carbonateville and that he was making arrangements to grubstake Pettie with a burro and other equipment so he could go to Shakespeare. Williams received money from Dallas for this new venture. *Diary*, Sept. 24, 29-30; Oct. 2-3, 1879.

33 Williams left by stage on Oct. 5. Several army officers, concerned with the Ute War then under way, were on the coach. For a contemporary account of the trouble with the Utes, see *Grant County Herald*, May 29, 1880. The trip was made overland to Las Vegas, N. M., then by the A. T. & S. F. R. R. to Kansas City. Williams then proceeded by train (M. K. & T.) to Dallas, where he spent several weeks visiting friends and business associates. He also worked for a brief period in the county tax office. Early in December he went to Austin to visit his brother Will and to look after some business in the offices of the State Comptroller and the Adjutant General. After returning to Dallas on Dec. 22 and spending Christmas there with friends, he left on Jan. 29, 1880, for his home in Illinois, where he visited relatives and promoted his mining interests. On March 23 he left for Dallas; from here, on April 6, he set out on his second overland trip to New Mexico. *Diary*, Oct. 5, 1879 - April 6, 1880.

34 At midnight on New Year's Day, 1881, the Vigilantes hung Russian Bill and

Sandy King from the rafters of the dining room of the Grant House. The bodies were left hanging until the morning stage arrived "to serve as a warning to incoming passengers that Shakespeare was a place of law and order. One of the passengers was more interested in Russian Bill's boots than the challenge of his body, for they were new and his size, so he took them off and added them to his wardrobe. Then he helped in the burial, and breakfast was served." Russian Bill was executed for the specific crime of stealing a horse, and Sandy King, a really bad man, for being "a damned nuisance." Muir, *Shakespeare*, No. 9, pp. 25-26; *The New Southwest*, Nov. 12, 1881.

35 At the time Williams was in New Mexico, Santa Fe, founded in 1610, was both the capital and the largest town of the Territory, although it had only a few thousand people. The Santa Fe Trail was opened in 1821 and had been the chief means of intercourse, both commercial and cultural. The town consisted chiefly of adobe houses, populated by a people not fully adjusted to American ways. As a result, Williams, who was not yet familiar with the mixed culture of the Southwest, found the place to be both baffling and intriguing. For popular accounts of the town, see Henry Inman, *The Old Santa Fe Trail* (London, 1897), a copy of which is in Williams' library; also Paul Horgan, *The Centuries of Santa Fe* (New York, 1916); Oliver La Farge, *Santa Fe: The Autobiography of a Southwestern Town* (Norman, 1959). A graphic account of the city, including early photographs, will be found in *New Mexico Magazine* (No. 6, June, 1960), XXXVIII, 22-28, 33-40.

36 Richard Gott Williams was born in Culpeper County, Virginia, June 23, 1812. He was of the fifth generation of his family in America. *Williams Family Genealogy* (1935), II, 424-42. During 1826, R. G. Williams spent some time in the El Paso area. See Introduction, note 6. The extent of his trading activities in the Southwest has not been determined.

37 According to Dr. Myra Ellen Jenkins, Senior Archivist, New Mexico State Records Center and Archives, official records of Santa Fe traders make no mention of a Richard Gott Williams expedition. While the details of Carson's arrival in 1826 are a bit hazy, most chroniclers, following the statement of the Carson and Bent families, believe that he was in a caravan of the Bent, St. Vrain Co. from Franklin, Missouri. See Edwin LeGrand Sabin, *Kit Carson Days* (New York, 1935, 2 vols.), I, 13, and M. Morgan Estergreen, *Kit Carson, Portrait in Courage* (Norman, 1962), 23-25. Christopher Carson (Kit), probably the most famous of the "mountain men," and the Indian scouts, was also an Indian Agent. During the Civil War and Navajo Campaign, he was Colonel of the New Mexico Volunteers, and in his last years, Brevet Brigadier General, U. S. Volunteers. He died in 1868, and is buried near his home in Taos. See also, Stanley Vestal, *Kit Carson* (New York, 1928); F. T. Cheetham, "Kit Carson," *The New Mexico Historical Review* (No. 4, Oct., 1926), I, 375-99; M. D. Moody, "Kit Carson, Agent to the Indians in New Mexico," *ibid.* (No. 1, Jan., 1953), XXVIII, 1-20.

38 The uprising of 1879, in which a group of White River Utes killed Indian Agent Nathan C. Meeker, resulted in the death of a number of Utes and soldiers. See Robert Emmitt, *The Last War Trail* (Norman, 1954). Gen. Edward Hatch was military commander in New Mexico, 1876-81. He had recently gained a reputation fighting against Victorio. F. B. Heitman, *Historical Register and Dictionary of the*

United States Army (Washington, 1903, 2 vols.), I, 510; H. H. Bancroft, *History of Arizona and New Mexico* (San Francisco, 1890), 725, 743, 746.

39 The *Diary* shows that while away from the mine fields, Williams received reports about conditions and activities there: entries of Oct. 22, 1879; Jan. 15, 26, 28, and April 1, 1880.

40 Soldier's Farewell was a stage station in Grant County, N. M., on the Overland route. Completed in Nov., 1858, it lay between Cooke's Spring, now in Luna County, and Stein's Peak Station in Hidalgo County. Traditionally, the name came from the sad farewell of a homesick man in the first companies of dragoons going west to occupy the desolate territory the United States acquired from Mexico by the Gadsden Purchase. R. P. and M. B. Conkling, *The Butterfield Overland Mail, 1857-1869* (Glendale, Calif., 1947, 3 vols.), II, 124-25.

41 Two years before Williams arrived in New Mexico, the Apache chief Geronimo and his warriors had left Ojo Caliente and depredated in southern Arizona and northern Chihuahua. During the time Williams was in the mining fields, the miners were in constant danger from Geronimo and his Apaches. A number of books deal with these times. See Britton Davis, *The Truth about Geronimo* (New Haven, 1929); Anton Mazzanovich, *Trailing Geronimo* (Los Angeles, 1926); John Bigelow, Jr., *On The Bloody Trail of Geronimo* (Los Angeles, 1958); also John P. Clum, "Geronimo," *New Mexico Historical Review* (1928), III, 1-40, 121-44, 217-64.

42 The "85" Mine, an important producer of copper, was sunk near the Superior Mine at Shakespeare in the Virginia Mining District. Thereafter, it operated successfully for a number of years. E. C. Anderson, *The Metal Resources of New Mexico and Their Economic Features Through 1954* (New Mexico State Bureau of Mines and Mineral Resources, Bulletin 39, 1957), 85-88; R. F. Fledge, *Geology of Lordsburg Quadrangle, Hidalgo County, New Mexico* (New Mexico State Bureau of Mines and Mineral Resources, Bulletin 62, 1959), 28.

43 The matter of *Oasis Mine v. Last Chance Mine* is covered in III of the present work.

44 C. L. and Grace Jackson, *Quanah Parker: Last Chief of the Comanches* (New York, 1963), especially Chapters 10 and 11. In June, 1874, Parker had led an Indian attack on a number of buffalo hunters intrenched at Adobe Walls, on the South Canadian River in the Texas Panhandle. Repulsed, he continued to scourge the white man for two years. He finally surrendered and adjusted to a new and useful life in the reservation at Fort Sill, Oklahoma. The town of Quanah, Texas, is named in his honor.

45 The route from Fort Worth ran westward via Thorp Springs, Stephenville, Dublin, Comanche, Brownwood, Coleman, Ft. Concho, Ft. Davis, Barrel Springs, El Muerto, Van Horn, Eagle Springs, Quitman, San Elizario and Ysleta to Franklin (El Paso). *Diary,* April 6-15, 1880. Williams later claimed that he made this journey on the last of the Overland stages. C. R. Wharton, *Texas Under Many Flags* (Chicago and New York, 1930, 5 vols.), V, 18. For a brief description of the route and a map, see Mrs. Tom Charles, "Route of the Overland Mail," *New Mexico Magazine* (No. 12, Dec., 1958), XXXVI, 48-50, 74.

46 Concord coaches traveled day and night, averaging about five miles an hour over bad stretches of road. On good expanses, the speed was much better. The stages carried as many as six passengers each, plus sacks of letters and express packages.

47 Regarding Fort Concho, see I, note 84.

48 Fort Stockton was established in 1859 near Comanche Springs as a frontier outpost. The springs had long been an important watering place for the Indians, especially during their raids into Mexico, and for wagon trains. The fort, which was to be abandoned in 1886, was still active when Williams passed through the settlement. At the time, Fort Stockton was a station on the Southern Stage Route, a road regarded as relatively safe from Indian attacks. Williams had no idea that the town would figure prominently in his later life. Conklin, *Butterfield Overland Mail*, I, 112, 365, 375; II, 13, 15-19. Clayton W. Williams, "Fort Stockton's First 100 Years," *Fort Stockton Centennial* (Fort Stockton, 1959), 28-43; C. G. Raht, *The Romance of Davis Mountains and Big Bend Country* (El Paso, 1919), 33, 86, 113, 139, 175, 217. For conditions in the 1860's and 1880's, see *Fort Stockton Pioneer*, Sept. 10, 1908; Jan. 27, 1928.

49 The old Leon Water Holes are located about eight miles west of Ft. Stockton. They had served as an important Indian campground, as a watering place on the Old Salt Trail running from the salt lakes of present-day Crane County to Presidio, Texas, and as the site of a stage stand used by the Overland stage line. Conkling, *Butterfield Overland Mail*, I, 366; II, 19-21; Raht, *Romance of Davis Mountains*, 87, 220-23.

50 Fort Davis was created in 1854 as a frontier post on the Lower Route from San Antonio to El Paso. The old fort is about twenty-five miles northwest of Alpine on Highway 118 in the heart of the Fort Davis Mountains. The fort was named for Jefferson Davis, who was United States Secretary of War when it was established. Barry Scobee, *Fort Davis, Texas, 1583-1960* (El Paso, 1963), *passim;* Conkling, *Butterfield Overland Mail*, II, 13, 16, 25-27; Raht, *Romance of Davis Mountains*, 159-60.

51 Barrel Springs was a stage station twenty-two miles southwest of Fort Davis, in Jeff Davis County. The name apparently came from the water collected in the barrels which soldiers from Fort Davis sank in the bed of the ravine nearby. Conklin, *Butterfield Overland Mail*, II, 30-31. The place was the scene of several Indian attacks. Raht, *Romance of Davis Mountains*, 148, 219.

52 El Muerto "is one of the worst places in Texas for Indians and is called Dead Man's Gulch." *Diary*, April 14. El Muerto ("The Dead Man") was located in Jeff Davis County on the north side of El Muerto Peak, a half mile west of Dead Man's Spring. It was officially known as Dead Man's Hole Station. Conkling, *Butterfield Overland Mail*, I, 374; II, 31-33; III, Plate 48. The place was noted for the Indian attacks on it. Raht, *Romance of Davis Mountains*, 88, 138, 163.

53 Van Horn's Wells lay thirty-two miles west of Dead Man's Hole. The wells were in the foothills of the Van Horn Mountains and were regarded as a dependable watering place. Near this station, in Bass Canyon, Mrs. Maggie Graham was killed (Oct., 1880) in an Apache ambuscade. Conkling, *Butterfield Overland Mail*, II, 34-35.

54 Eagle Springs was twenty miles from Van Horn's Wells on a stretch of road now abandoned. The site is in Hudspeth County, nine miles south of Eagle Flat, on the T. & P. Railroad line. A number of Indian attacks occurred here and the place was considered dangerous at the time Williams passed through. *Ibid.*, II, 36-39; Raht, *Romance of Davis Mountains*, 89, 138.

55 Regarding Fort Quitman, see Conkling, *Butterfield Overland Mail*, II, 13, 16, 18, 41, 42. The fort was established in September, 1858, and named for General John Anthony Quitman. It was evacuated during the Civil War, reoccupied in 1868, and permanently abandoned in 1877. Webb (ed.), *Handbook of Texas*, II, 630-31.

56 San Elizario (San Elceario) is located about twenty miles below El Paso, on the Rio Grande. It was founded in the 1780's when the older San Elizario Presidio was moved to the site at or near the present town. San Elizario was the county seat of El Paso County from 1850 to 1876. U. S. troops were stationed in the town in 1850. The famous Salt War of 1877 reached its climax here. The town's size and importance declined rapidly thereafter. *Ibid.*, II, 549-50. San Elizario has been the focus of much history, extending back to the time of Juan de Oñate. Between 1849 and 1853, it was a station on the route of the first horseback mail runs between Santa Fe and San Antonio. For interesting details about the place, see Bartlett, *Personal Narrative*, I, 193-94; Conkling, *Butterfield Overland Mail*, II, 47-53; E. O. Porter, "The Founding of San Elizario," *Password* (El Paso Historical Society, No. 3, Fall, 1964), IX, 87-98. Ysleta, now an eastern subdivision of El Paso, is one of the oldest settlements in the United States, with a Spanish mission dating back to 1682. The place had long been the home of the Tigua Indians. For some time before 1884, Ysleta was the county seat of El Paso County. J. M. Broaddus, *The Legal Heritage of El Paso* (El Paso, 1963), 3, 107, 143, 168. When Williams passed through, Ysleta was the largest town in the county, having a population of 1,453. Bureau of the Census, *Compendium of the Tenth Census of the United States* (Washington, 1883), 301.

57 Elephant Butte Dam is located twelve miles from Engle and five miles from Truth or Consequences, N. M. Completed in May, 1916, it provides a more even flow of water from the Rio Grande to the farming areas and towns downstream. H. H. Brok, *The International Aspects of the Rio Grande Project* (Las Cruces, 1926); P. L. Hayney, *The International Controversy Over the Waters of the Upper Rio Grande* (M.A. Thesis, Texas Western College, 1948); Ferguson, *New Mexico*, 354-58; "Elephant Butte Lake," *New Mexico Magazine* (No. 11, Nov., 1960), XXXVIII, 26-34.

58 The location mentioned is near the present-day center of El Paso at Mills and Oregon streets. The Mills building faces the main plaza. In 1880 when Williams visited El Paso, it was still a village, having only 736 inhabitants. Bureau of the Census, *Compendium of the Tenth Census of the United States*, 301. In May, 1881, however, the Southern Pacific Railroad completed its line into town, and thereafter population increased rapidly. Broaddus, *Legal Heritage of El Paso*, Chapters V and VI.

59 Dr. Edward W. Alexander, owner of the vineyard, was the son of an American wine merchant. Born May 2, 1832, he was educated at the Universities of Munich and Vienna. He became a medical officer in the U. S. Army and came to Texas in 1870. After serving at Fort Bliss for two years (1874-76), he resigned his post be-

cause of the illness of his wife. He then put in a grape orchard along the Rio Grande below El Paso. The vineyard and his spacious home became a showplace in the Valley. In 1888 Dr. Alexander was named an American quarantine inspector at the river boundary and later practiced medicine successfully in El Paso. He died in 1915 at the age of eighty-three. Data in Southwestern Room, El Paso Public Library.

60 The mission Nuestra Señora de Guadalupe was founded in 1659 by Fray García de San Francisco y Zúñiga. The civil settlement of El Paso del Norte (later Ciudad Juárez) evolved thereafter. Anne E. Hughes, *The Beginnings of Spanish Settlement in the El Paso District* (Berkeley, 1914), 295-391, *passim.* C. E. Castañeda, *Our Catholic Heritage in Texas, 1519-1936* (Austin, 1936-58, 7 vols.), I, 243-48.

61 The Hussmann Hotel faced the east side of the central plaza of town on the site of the old Hotel Orndorff. The Hussmann later became the Cortez Hotel. *El Paso Times,* Oct. 2, 1927; Aug. 9 and Oct. 12, 1935.

62 Mesilla is located two miles southwest of Las Cruces, N. M. It was once a part of the state of Chihuahua, Mexico. After the Americans occupied the Southwest, a group of New Mexicans settled at Mesilla in order to remain under the Mexican flag and thus protect their property from loss to Americans making claims on the basis of headright certificates. The Gadsden Purchase of 1854, however, placed Mesilla within the United States. Three years later the town became a stage station on the Butterfield route. During the Civil War, Confederate Lt. Col. John R. Baylor made the place his headquarters until Gen. James Carleton recaptured it for the Union. Billy the Kid was a frequent visitor and stood trial here while Williams was in New Mexico. Bartlett, *Personal Narrative,* I, 212-15; P. M. Baldwin, "A Short Story of Mesilla Valley," *The New Mexico Historical Review* (No. 3, July, 1938), XIII, 314-24; Grace Long, *The Anglo-American Occupation of the El Paso District* (M.A. Thesis, The University of Texas, 1931), 64-71.

63 Fort Cummings was a military post at Cooke's Springs on the northwest side of Cooke's Peak. It was also a stopping point between the Rio Grande and Silver City. Established on Oct. 2, 1863, it was named for Dr. Joseph Cummings, killed by Indians the preceding August. The fort was directly on the road from Mesilla to Tucson, in the heart of Apache country. Its garrison did much to reduce the danger of Indian attacks in the area. George Griggs, *History of Mesilla Valley or the Gadsden Purchase* (Mesilla, 1930), 55; Bancroft, *History of Arizona and New Mexico,* 726; W. A. Keleher, *Turmoil in New Mexico, 1846-1868* (Santa Fe, 1952), 266, 346, 489, 509.

64 The military activities of Lt. Col. John R. Baylor in the El Paso area are summarized in Broaddus, *Legal Heritage of El Paso,* 69-75; Mary Taylor and Nona Barrick, "The Confederates Invade Mesilla," *New Mexico Magazine* (No. 7, July, 1961), XXXIX, 20-23, 38. On the countermoves of General J. H. Carleton and his California Column, see Keleher, *Turmoil in New Mexico,* Chapter III.

65 The story of the Mills brothers centers around El Paso during the last half of the nineteenth century. The four brothers — Anson, Emmett, Ethan A., and W. W. — came from Indiana. They were Unionists during the Civil War in an area predominantly Confederate. The experiences of W. W. Mills are especially interesting as told in his autobiography: Rex Strickland (ed.), *W. W. Mills: Forty Years at El Paso, 1858-1898* (El Paso, 1962).

66 Emmett Mills was a Union sympathizer during the first months of the Civil War. To escape likely arrest by the Confederate forces under Col. John R. Baylor, he left El Paso by stage on July 20, 1861, hoping to reach California. The next day, however, Cochise and Mangas Coloradas, with a large band of Apaches, intercepted the stagecoach a mile beyond Cooke's Springs in New Mexico. A pitched battle ensued, in which a number of Indians and all the white passengers, including Mills, were killed. *Ibid.*, 53, 185, 195-96. For a contemporary account, see *The Mesilla Times,* July 27, 1861. More details will be found in E. G. W. Mahon and C. V. Kielman, "George H. Giddings and the San Antonio - San Diego Mail Line," *Southwestern Historical Quarterly* (No. 2, Oct., 1957), LXI, 220-39.

67 George M. Frazer, on orders from Colonel John R. Baylor, went with a detachment of fifteen other men to learn the details of the massacre. Later, Frazer gave Williams the facts on which his account is based. Williams' article was published in the *Southwest Sentinel,* Silver City, Jan. 31, 1885, and reprinted in the *El Paso Times,* Jan. 20, 1887. Frazer settled near Fort Stockton, where he became a leading rancher and citizen. He was a member of the board named by the Legislature of Texas to organize Pecos County in 1871. He also served as county judge and chairman of the first commissioners' court of the county. Frazer later operated a ranch on the border of Texas and New Mexico. Raht, *Romance of Davis Mountains,* 215-16, 226; *Fort Stockton Pioneer,* Sept. 17, 1908.

68 On Sept. 20, 1920, the mayor and council of El Paso authorized the erection of a white shaft to the memory of the seven men — all employees of the Butterfield Overland Mail Company — who were killed in the fight that Williams mentions. The shaft is located on the grounds of the El Paso Public Library. S. D. Myres has annotated Williams' letter to the *Southwest Sentinel,* filling in various details of the account from contemporary sources. *Password* (El Paso Historical Society, No. 2, Summer, 1965), X, 43 ff.

69 Cooke's Peak is named for General Philip St. George Cooke, a Virginian who was graduated from West Point in 1827. Later, in 1846, he led a battalion of Mormons from Santa Fe to California. En route, the party traveled down the Rio Grande to a point near Rincon, New Mexico, then over to Luna County, the site of Cooke's Peak and Cooke's Range. After passing Ojo de Vaca (Cow Spring) on the Mimbres River, they journeyed southwestward through Hidalgo County, and thence along Animas Creek, through the Guadalupe Pass in the Piloncillo Mountains and to Bernardino, Arizona. From there the party passed through the Pima Indian villages to the Gila River. They crossed the Colorado River in lower California, went on through the desert, and finally reached the camp of Gen. S. W. Kearny at San Diego, Jan. 27, 1847. The westward route they established was used later by emigrants, stage lines and railroads. Cooke's Springs, near the site of old Ft. Cummings, is still used for watering stock. Cooke retired from the Army and wrote a history of *The Conquest of New Mexico and California* (New York, 1878), detailing his experiences. See also O. E. Young, *The West of Philip St. George Cooke, 1808-1895* (Glendale, Calif., 1955), *passim;* R. P. Bieber (ed.), *Exploring Southwestern Trails, 1846-1854* (Southwest Historical Series, Glendale, 1938), VII, 27-30, 65-240.

70 The so-called California Column was a Union force under Gen. James H. Carleton which in 1862 marched 859 miles from Los Angeles to Mesilla for the purpose of

wresting New Mexico and Arizona from the Confederates. After accomplishing their principal objective, the Californians fought the Apaches and looked for gold. At the end of their military service, many settled in New Mexico and Texas. Keleher, *Turmoil in New Mexico*, 228-74, 304, 337, 344, 429, 450-53.

71 Regarding Roy Bean, see C. L. Sonnichsen, *Law West of the Pecos* (New York, 1943); Everett Lloyd, *Law West of the Pecos: The Story of Roy Bean* (San Antonio, 1941); Ruel McDaniel, *Vinegaroon: The Saga of Judge Roy Bean* (Kingport, Tenn., 1936).

72 The station on the Mimbres River was eighteen miles northwest of Cooke's Spring. It consisted of a large corral equipped with four rooms, a well and a blacksmith shop. The station was located a mile south of Old Town or Mowry City, one of the ghost towns of Luna County, New Mexico. Conkling, *Butterfield Overland Mail*, II, 118-20; *El Paso Times*, Dec. 20, 1964.

73 The Butterfield Overland Mail was one of the great American adventures in transportation before the building of the railroads. The stage lines of John Butterfield ran from St. Louis to San Francisco. Although the operation was abandoned during the Civil War, successors revived the stage service for a time. Williams was traveling over the Southern Route from Fort Stockton to New Mexico. Conkling, *Butterfield Overland Mail*, I, 121 ff; II, 332-59; III, endpiece, for map of routes. Muir, *Shakespeare*, No. 7, pp. 27, 52, 59; O. O. Winter, "The Southern Overland Mail and Stagecoach Line, 1857-1861," *New Mexico Historical Review* (No. 2, April, 1957), XXXII, 81-106, and map at back of this issue; J. W. Williams, "The Butterfield Overland Mail Road Across Texas," *Southwestern Historical Quarterly* (No. 1, July, 1957), LXI, 1-19.

74 Benjamin L. E. Bonneville (1795-1878) was a French-born graduate of West Point who earlier explored the Rocky Mountain area and wrote an account of his adventures, which Washington Irving edited and made famous: *Rocky Mountains: On Scenes, Incidents, and Adventures in the Far West — Digest from the Journal of Captain B. L. E. Bonneville* (Philadelphia, 1837, 2 vols.). After serving in the Mexican War, Bonneville became military head of the New Mexico Department. In New Mexico, he led campaigns against the Indians; he was on such a mission in 1859 at the time he and his party visited the places Williams mentions. Keleher, *Turmoil in New Mexico*, 100, 137, 191, 301, 303, 354, 446.

75 Leitendorf's Wells, located six to eight miles south of Shakespeare, was named for an early settler, Eugene Leitzendorfer. Driving a herd of cattle from Illinois, he could not find water in the vicinity and therefore dug a well to provide it. Later he became the first auditor of New Mexico after its Territorial government was established in 1851. The place named for him became a watering stop on the Overland route. It was later included in the Pyramid Mining District. The Superior (later the "85") Mine was located in this area. *Grant County Herald*, July 9, 1881; *The Lordsburg Liberal*, May 23, 1930; Muir, *Shakespeare*, No. 7, p. 7.

76 During Williams' days at Shakespeare, Lordsburg was only a convenient railroad stop, equipped with a few plank houses and walled-up tents. Passengers and freight to or from Shakespeare were carried by stagecoach and wagon train. *Lordsburg Liberal*, April 18, 1881. Regarding Cow Spring, see note 113, following.

77 Stein's Peak Station was on the Butterfield route, just east of Stein's Peak and the New Mexico - Arizona boundary. Built in 1858, it was named for the peak nearby bearing the name of Major Enoch Stein, commander of the dragoons who camped here in 1856 while en route to Tucson to occupy the old presidio under the terms of the Gadsden Purchase. The station was the scene of several bloody Indian attacks. Conkling, *Butterfield Overland Mail*, II, 129; D. L. Thrapp, "Stein's Pass: Gateway to Adventure," *New Mexico Magazine* (No. 6, June, 1961), XXXIX, 8-11, 30. A mining district was located nearby, in the northern extension of the Piloncillo Mountains, which from 1875 to 1930 consistently produced gold, silver, lead and copper. The Homestake Lode, discovered by Charles H. Fry, was the richest. Anderson, *Metal Resources of New Mexico*, 88-89. The San Simon station was located in Cochise County, Ariz., thirteen miles southwest of Stein's Peak. Conkling, *Butterfield Overland Mail*, II, 130.

78 Apache Pass Station was on the Butterfield route, across the New Mexico line in Arizona. It was deep in Indian country; hence its name. The area was infested by Apaches who mounted several attacks on the stages that passed through, notably one in February, 1861. In July, 1862, an army post — Fort Bowie — was established nearby, in an effort to insure protection to travelers. *Ibid.*, II, 132-39.

79 The Burro Mountains lie southwest of Silver City on the way to Shakespeare and Lordsburg. During Williams' stay in New Mexico, the Burros were the scene both of mineral strikes and Indian attacks.

80 In the early 1880's there were thirty-eight lines in New Mexico, covering approximately eight hundred miles of road. The longest of these was between Deming and Mogollon, a distance of ninety miles. After 1879, the stage lines became feeder operations for the railroads, which were rapidly extending their service. One of these stage lines connected Shakespeare with Silver City and another with Lordsburg. For routes and distances of these lines, see *Grant County Herald*, Nov. 27, 1880; W. S. Wallace, "Stagecoaching in Territorial New Mexico," *New Mexico Historical Review* (No. 2, April, 1957), XXXII, 204-11.

81 The Santa Rita copper mines, which are of the "open" type, are located in Grant County, east of Silver City. The mines have been worked since Spanish colonial times for their copper ore, which is of superior quality. Before the Apaches were finally confined to their reservation, they were a constant threat to miners and residents of the Santa Rita area. Much of the history of Southwestern New Mexico centers around this mining field. Bartlett, *Personal Narrative*, I, 178, 227-35; Dale Collins, *Frontier Mining Days in Southwestern New Mexico* (M.A. Thesis, Texas Western College, 1955), 10-24, 29-34. Regarding the mineral resources of Santa Rita, see New Mexico Geological Society, *Guidebook of Southwestern New Mexico* (Fourth Field Conference, 1953), 117-31.

82 The Old Chihuahua Trail, in the sense used here, was the route from Santa Rita del Cobre southward via Casas Grandes or the Valley of San Miguel, over which copper ore was carried to Durango for smelting. The refined metal was then sent to Mexico City or transported to Matamoros for shipment to Europe. The nearest Mexican settlement south of Santa Rita was the Presidio of Janos, Sonora, on the San Miguel River 150 miles away. Many of the supplies for the mines could be obtained only from Chihuahua, 400 miles distant. Wagon trains plied the trail in

both directions. Bartlett, *Personal Narrative*, I, 227-31. The Chihuahua Highway in Mexico extended from El Paso del Norte southward through Chihuahua City to Zacatecas and Aguascalientes. L. B. Bloom, "The Chihuahua Highway," *New Mexico Historical Review* (No. 3, July, 1937), XII, 209-16.

83 The Clifton copper mines, opened in 1872, are across the border of New Mexico in Arizona, north and slightly west of Lordsburg. They lie west of the town of Clifton, between the Francisco River and the Rio Bonito. Richard J. Hinton, *The Handbook of Arizona, 1877* (Reprint, 1954, Tucson), Chapter V; *Grant County Herald*, Dec. 13, 1879; *The Daily Southwest*, April 20, 1880.

84 San Carlos, in northern Chihuahua, Mexico, was the scene of several interesting incidents which Williams discusses in IV. The Dr. Flotte referred to may have been the man who left Mexico under duress, escaping with Bartlett's party. Bartlett, *Personal Narrative*, II, 425-26, 442-43.

85 Apache Tejo (Tejú) was on the road running southward from the Santa Rita mines to Janos in the interior of Mexico. Fort McLane was established here in 1860. A spring located in the area had been used for many years by Indians, Spaniards, and Mexicans. As Williams indicates presently, it was at this place that the Indian chief Mangas Coloradas lost his life in 1863. See Keleher, *Turmoil in New Mexico*, 292-95.

86 The Domesday Book was a survey of the lands and other resources of England at the time of William the Conqueror (1085). The records of the survey were published in two volumes of 760 and 900 pages, respectively. During the Middle Ages, evidence from these records was often used in the law courts to settle claims. The information in the Book is still of value to topographers and historians. Many of the terms used, however, are today archaic.

87 *Arrastra* is from the Spanish *arrastrar*, to drag, which in turn comes from the Latin *rastrum*, rake. The word refers to a rude drag-stone mill for pulverizing ores. It is listed in unabridged English dictionaries. *Veta* is a Spanish word in general use, referring to a vein of ore. *Petanque* is Mexican for a mineral rock containing hard silver that makes it shine notably. F. J. Santamaría, *Diccionario de Mejicanismos* (Méjico, 1959), 836.

88 Cochise was a Chiricahua Apache chief whose warriors ravaged New Mexico and Arizona from 1861 to 1874, when he died on the reservation in Arizona. Following numerous bloody forays, he and his men were pursued ruthlessly by U. S. troops. He finally surrendered in 1871. Mangas Coloradas was a Mimbreño Apache chief from the area near Santa Rita, N. M., who led attacks on the mining towns of the area. He joined with Cochise at Apache Pass to resist the California Column under General Carleton, moving to reopen communication between the Pacific Coast and the East. Mangas Coloradas was killed in 1863 while in custody. Frank C. Lockwood, *The Apache Indians* (New York, 1938), 89-95, 100-130, 137, 140, 143-45. F. W. Hodge, *Handbook of American Indians* (Washington, 1907), I, 317, 799.

89 The circumstances of Mangas Coloradas' death are not entirely clear. There are at least two conflicting versions. *Ibid.*, I, 799-800; Woodworth Clum, *Apache Agent: The Story of John P. Clum* (New York, 1936), 43-46; Lockwood, *The Apache Indians*, 143-45.

90 The Spanish word *pueblos* often refers to permanent Indian villages or towns and to the people in them. The Pueblos of New Mexico include the Tanoan, Keresan and Zuñian linguistic families. During the historical period, the Pueblo tribes have lived in an area extending from northeastern Arizona to the Pecos River in New Mexico, and from Taos, N. M., on the north to a few miles below El Paso, Texas, on the south. The ancient domain of these peoples, however, covered a much wider area. Hodge, *Handbook of American Indians*, II, 318-25; A. F. Bandelier and E. L. Hewett, *Indians of the Rio Grande Valley* (Albuquerque, 1937); E. L. Hewett and B. P. Dutton, *The Pueblo Indian World* (Albuquerque, 1945). Williams doubt-less consulted the following book in his library: Walter Hough, *Culture of the Ancient Pueblos of the Upper Gila Region, New Mexico and Arizona* (U. S. National Mu-seum, Bulletin No. 87, Washington, 1914). In 1918, Williams visited some pueblo ruins at Aztec and wrote an interesting account of what he saw. Letter to Clayton W. Williams, Sept. 19, 1918.

91 Silver City, county seat of Grant County, is located in a valley surrounded on three sides by mountain ranges — the Mogollon, the Pinos Altos and the Mimbres. On the south, the town opens onto rolling hills. The first permanent settlement was made in 1869 when four Americans arrived at "La Ciénega de S. Vicente," the Marsh of Saint Vincent, located much earlier by the Spanish explorers. In 1870, when silver was discovered in quantity, news of the strike drew many prospectors to the place. By the 1880's, when Williams arrived in New Mexico, Silver City was booming. For an excellent account covering the period that Williams lived in the area, see C. K. Naegle, *The History of Silver City, New Mexico, 1870-1886* (M.A. Thesis, University of New Mexico, 1943). Regarding the geology of the Silver City area, see New Mexico Geological Society, *Guidebook of Southwestern New Mexico* (1953), 138-40; Anderson, *Metal Resources of New Mexico*, 71-76.

92 Pinos Altos ("Tall Pines") is located eight miles northeast of Silver City. It may be described as a "semi-ghost" town, since it is still inhabited and continues to pro-duce small amounts of gold, silver, and copper. Although there was some yield from placer mining in the area during Spanish colonial times, the big strike occurred in 1860. The important Mountain Key lode was located in 1861. By 1867 a thousand men were at work on six hundred placer and lode claims within a radius of six miles. The town suffered from Apache raids in the late 1870's. By the early 1880's, when Williams came to New Mexico, Pinos Altos was in decline. Most of the miners had moved on to richer fields, especially those on the Upper Mimbres River. *Inventory of the County Archives of New Mexico*, No. 9, *Grant County*, 43-44; Collins, *Fron-tier Mining Days in Southwestern New Mexico*, 10, 68, 71; Anderson, *Metal Re-sources of New Mexico*, 70-71; Jones, *New Mexico Mines and Minerals*, 47-52; R. S. Allen, "Pinos Altos, New Mexico," *New Mexico Historical Review* (No. 4, Oct., 1948), XXIII, 302-32.

93 On July 21, 1895, two immense floods swept down on Silver City from the sur-rounding mountains. The second wave — twelve feet high and three hundred feet wide — was especially damaging. The floods, rolling down Main Street, converted it into a Big Ditch. The ditch is still there, but retaining walls have been built along its sides. Ross Calvin, "How Main Street Became the Ditch," *New Mexico Magazine* (No. 8, Aug., 1934), XII, 10-11, 37-41; *El Paso Herald-Post*, June 23, 1936.

94 The *Diary* does not record these details — only that Williams arrived at Silver City about 9:00 A.M. and at Shakespeare about 6:00 P.M. *Diary*, April 17, 1880.

95 Regarding Major S. A. Purington, see F. B. Heitman, *Historical Register and Dictionary of the United States Army*, I, 809. In the 1880's, Major Purington came to the Big Bend area and established a stock ranch some twenty miles northeast of Marathon. He and Williams continued their personal association until the early 1900's when Purington sold out his ranching interests. See *Fort Stockton Pioneer*, Nov. 26, Dec. 3, 1908.

96 Judge H. C. McComas was chairman of the board of commissioners of Grant County at the time of his death. On March 28, 1882, with his wife and six-year-old son Charley, he left Silver City by stage for Lordsburg. En route, near Knight's Station in the Burro Mountains some forty miles south of Silver City, the coach was overtaken by a roving band of Apaches under Chiefs Chato and Benito. The Indians killed the two adults and took the boy prisoner. He was never heard of again. This tragedy was especially shocking to Williams, since he and Judge McComas were friends and political allies. *Silver City Enterprise*, March 30, 1883; *Southwest Sentinel*, March 31, 1883; Davis, *The Truth About Geronimo*, 68; Lockwood, *The Apache Indians*, 264-65.

97 Hachita ("Little Axe") is in southern Grant County, near the border with Hidalgo County, in the Little Hatchet Mountains southeast of Shakespeare and Lordsburg. Southwest and southeast of it are several mining districts — the Hachita (Eureka), the Apache No. 2 and the Fremont. The Hachita district was opened in 1880 while Williams was in New Mexico. It has never achieved notable production. Anderson, *Metal Resources of New Mexico*, 84-85.

98 The Chiricahua Mountains are a small range in Cochise County, located in southeastern Arizona. They were the home of the Indians bearing the same name. One of the peaks (elevation 8,109 ft.) is said to resemble the face of Cochise. W. C. Barnes, *Arizona Place Names* (Tucson, 1960), 33-34.

99 North Pyramid Peak is one of the Pyramid Mountains south of Shakespeare. Leitendorf was often called Pyramid City because of the peak nearby. Regarding Piloncillo, see Bartlett, *Personal Narrative*, I, 364.

100 The Shakespeare Guards were organized Aug. 8, 1879, with J. E. Price as captain. R. P. Hart was 1st lieutenant and H. Cameron, 2nd lieutenant. The rank and file consisted of thirty-three men, a number of whom Williams mentions in his narrative. Williams, however, was not a member of the Guards. According to information supplied by Dr. Myra Ellen Jenkins, Senior Archivist, New Mexico State Records Center and Archives, the organization later became Company "C" and eventually Company "F" of the New Mexico Territorial Militia. For an interesting account of the Guards, see Emma M. Muir, "The First Militia," *New Mexico Magazine* (No. 10, Oct., 1952), XXX, 19, 41, 44-46.

101 The mansion of O. R. Smythe, being built in 1880 when Williams arrived, consisted of eight rooms, elegantly furnished. Other buildings in Shakespeare included the Grant House; the Stratford Hotel; the mercantile store of Smythe, Long and Price; and Roxy Jay's Saloon. The one street of the town —"Avon"— was named in

honor of Shakespeare's birthplace. Muir, *Shakespeare*, No. 9, pp. 41-43. Marjorie White, "Shakespeare: The West's Most Authentic Ghost Town," *New Mexico Magazine*, XL (No. 4), 5-9.

102 Roxy Jay's saloon in Shakespeare boasted a long mahogany bar, with a large mirror behind it. On occasion, as Mrs. Muir notes, dance-hall girls "contributed the refining influence of women. They did not live in Shakespeare, those girls, for Shakespeare had a high moral sense. They made their abode in Lordsburg, and were hauled in and out by buckboard." When Victor Gibson lost his horse in the Burro Mountains, he made a straight line to Roxy Jay's to quench his thirst. Mrs. Muir mentions Williams of Harvard and the Hart brothers of Yale as examples of culture in Shakespeare at the time. Muir, *Shakespeare*, No. 9, pp. 45-46.

103 Williams associated with these men on various occasions. *Diary*, April 28 and 30, May 8, July 1, Oct. 18, 1880; April 12 and 25, July 16 and 18, Aug. 7 and 9, 1881. Their enterprise was named the "Shakespeare Gold and Silver Mining and Milling Company." For an early report on General Boyle and Shakespeare, see *Grant County Herald*, Jan. 3, 1880.

104 Gage station is on the Southern Pacific Railroad about nineteen miles west of Deming, N. M. The Victorio Mountains lie a few miles farther west.

105 Uncle John Evenson spent twenty-two years of his life (until 1888) in Shakespeare. As stage keeper, he became well-known not only for his antelope steak dinners but also for his vivid stories of happenings in the mining camps. He served as the first postmaster of Shakespeare. Muir, *Shakespeare*, No. 8, p. 49.

106 The popular John Price was Captain of the Shakespeare guards. See note 100, preceding.

107 Williams refers to this trip to Chicago and other points, made in an effort to sell the Bremen mine, about which more is given later. *Diary*, Nov. 2, 1880 - Feb. 24, 1881.

108 After arriving in Shakespeare on April 17, 1880, Williams went into the mining field the next day and worked intensely in the area for several months before moving on to other mining districts on prospecting trips. *Ibid.*, April 18 - July 11, 1880.

109 Regarding the interesting history of these conflicting mining claims, see III, following.

110 Soon after Pettie had made the locations, Williams noted, "Pettie is to deed me a ½ interest in all his properties at earliest convenience. Considerable excitement in camp." *Diary*, April 25, 1880. The claims were in the Stonewall Mining District of southwestern Luna County. Although gold was found here in limited quantities, the mines have never proved commercially workable. Jones, *New Mexico Mines and Minerals*, 184.

111 Indian raids are mentioned in the *Diary* on May 2, 3, 6, 8, 11 and 12. In spite of such dangers, Williams continued his search for minerals. On May 15, for example, he set out alone for Cow Spring and went on to Carisalillo Springs, where he joined a party of prospectors. In July he and other miners went into the Tres Hermanas Mountains. Other excursions followed, despite the possibility of Indian attacks.

112 After Victorio had led raiding expeditions in the Candelaria Mountains of Mexico, some 125 miles south of the border, he would continue depredating in New Mexico, West Texas and Mexico until finally brought to bay in November, 1880. Lockwood, *The Apache Indians,* 226-33. Raht, *Romance of Davis Mountains,* 261, 269, 271. Among the outstanding prospectors killed at this time was James C. Cooney, who operated a prosperous gold mine in the Mogollon District. J. F. Dobie, *Apache Gold and Yaqui Silver* (Boston, 1939), 78; Anderson, *History of New Mexico,* I, 393; Neagle, *History of Silver City,* 95-97.

113 Cow Spring (Ojo de la Vaca) was a stage station sixteen miles north of the Mimbres River in Luna County. The spring had long been a watering place for travelers. Roads from California and Mexico crossed here. Cooke and Bartlett stopped at the spring to rest and obtain water. Today only a few' stones of the old stage building remain. A windmill is now used to lift water from the spring. An excellent early description of Ojo de la Vaca is found in Bartlett, *Personal Narrative,* I, 243-44, 361.

114 James O. Pattie and his father obtained control of the Santa Rita copper mines in the 1820's. The venture, however, proved quite costly to them. Timothy Flint (ed.), *The Personal Narrative of James O. Pattie of Kentucky* (Cincinnati, 1831), gives a full account. Williams doubtless referred to this book, which is in his library: J. E. Kirkpatrick, *Timothy Flint, Pioneer, Missionary, Author, Editor, 1780-1840* (Cleveland, 1911).

115 As to Lieutenant George N. Bascom's relations with Cochise, see Lockwood, *The Apache Indians,* 100-107. The dispute between Cochise and the white men is briefly explained in *The Mesilla Times,* Aug. 24, 1861. For a revised estimate of Bascom's responsibility in the affair, see Andrew Wallace (ed.), *Pumpelly's Arizona* (Tucson, 1965), 127-33.

116 J. J. Giddings and thirteen other men were in search of Cochise, with the purpose of persuading him to stop his attacks on the stage line. But at Stein's Peak, some 250 Apaches overtook the party and killed all but one man. G. H. Giddings estimated his total loss from the Indian attacks to have been $231,720. Mahon and Kielman, "George H. Giddings and the San Antonio - San Diego Mail Line," *Southwestern Historical Quarterly,* LXI, 220-39.

117 The details of this incident are given in James H. Wilkins (ed.), *The Great Diamond Hoax and Other Stirring Incidents in the Life of Asbury Harpending* (San Francisco, 1913), 191-259. For a summary see Muir, *Shakespeare,* No. 8, pp. 47-48.

118 With reference to the Adams "lost diggins," see Dobie, *Apache Gold and Yaqui Silver,* 3-46.

119 The Victorio Mountains and the Victorio Mining District are located near the present highway between Lordsburg and Deming, N. M.

120 The Stonewall (Carrisalillo) District is located in southern Luna County near the border with Mexico. Several other outfits, attracted by the prospects, were in the camp on the day that Williams arrived. *Diary,* May 17, 1880. For information on the Stonewall District as a mining area, see G. B. Griswold, *Mineral Deposits of Luna*

County, New Mexico (New Mexico State Bureau of Mines and Mineral Resources, Bulletin No. 72, 1961), 132-38.

121 Hermanas Spring is located near the village of Hermanas in the Carrisalillo Hills west of Columbus, N. M.

122 Williams arrived at Carrisalillo Springs on May 17. Russian Bill and Chamberlain left on the 18th.

123 Williams "dug into pioneer ground for minerals." *Diary*, May 20, 1880.

124 "Examined the Mexican smelter. Started south to prospect in the Hatchet Mts. ["Hachitas"] about 4 P.M. and camped on the road, leaving old Fry behind." *Ibid.*, May 22, 1880.

125 En route, they found no minerals of consequence. *Ibid.*, May 28, 1880.

126 The *Diary* does not mention this incident. For more details on the death of Fambro, see Muir, "The First Militia," *New Mexico Magazine*, XXX (No. 10), 46.

127 On June 1 Williams left for Silver City on horseback. En route, he stayed overnight at Hank Kramer's place, arriving at his destination around 11:00 A.M. the next day. On the 3rd he attended Bill Carroll's trial in Silver City, returning to Shakespeare on the 5th. *Diary*, June 1-5, 1880.

128 Martin W. Bremen's silver mill was one of the most important enterprises in Silver City. The mill was improvised from parts of two worn-out mills brought in from Pinos Altos and an antiquated engine previously used in sinking artesian wells. By September, 1871, the mill was in operation. Bremen used it chiefly to refine ore from his own mines. In one week alone — that of June 22, 1872 — the mill processed $2,422 worth of silver. In continuing the operation, however, Bremen faced many difficulties — a shortage of quicksilver used in the refining process, periodic breakdowns and costly thefts by his employees. Such problems may have motivated Bremen in his later decision to sell his mining interests. Naegle, *History of Silver City*, 121-267, 131-32. More about Bremen and his mill will be found in III, following.

129 See note 16, preceding.

130 "Currie goes off to Gila with some fellow after a bonanza, on burros." *Diary*, June 16, 1880.

131 Currie returned on June 20, bringing back "some fine ore." *Ibid.*, June 20, 1880. The East Camp at Steeple Rock, as the name indicates, was a settlement in the eastern part of the mining district located in Grant County near the Arizona line. While Williams was in New Mexico, the mines in this area produced gold and silver ores, principally. In time, production dwindled. After a period of relative inactivity, the mines were reopened in 1932 by the East Camp Exploration Syndicate, and continued to operate for twelve years. During this last period the mines produced 17,000 ounces of gold, 1,000,000 ounces of silver, 800,000 pounds of copper and 3,000,000 pounds of zinc. Anderson, *Metal Resources of New Mexico*, 76-78.

132 The Carlisle Mine is in the Steeple Rock District, western Grant County, four miles from the Arizona line. The mine, located in 1881, is the most important in the

area; it produced $3,000,000 worth of ore before it was temporarily closed in 1897. It was later reopened and worked successfully by Veta Mines, Inc. *Inventory of the County Archives*, No. 9, *Grant County*, 47, 76-77.

133 *Diary*, June 22, 27, 1880.

134 Poverty Flat was the *arroyo* on the west side of the only street (Avon) in Shakespeare. The settlement was the abode of miners and prospectors, who were proud of it. Muir, *Shakespeare*, No. 9, p. 43.

135 Mrs. Muir retells this story, which she says was "for years a classic." *Ibid.*

136 *Diary*, June 20 - July 8, 1880. Charlie Williams is not mentioned.

137 *Ibid.*, July 8, 1880.

138 *Ibid.*, July 11-13, 1880.

139 The party arrived at the Tres Hermanas on July 15. They were now prospecting in an area northeast of Carrisalillo Springs, where they had worked two months earlier. On the 16th they rode around the north side of the mountains in search of ore. *Ibid.*, July 15-16, 1880. The Tres Hermanas were named for three sisters — Alice, Kate and Lou. *Grant County Herald*, Dec. 4, 1880.

140 The *Diary* at this point does not mention Indians.

141 The "Faraon Apache" group is frequently referred to in Spanish documents of the 1700's. There is no etymological evidence to support the conclusion that the term *faraón* as used here is related to the Spanish *farol* (lantern) or *faro* (lighthouse).

142 The party arrived at Carisalillo early on July 17. While there, they examined their claims and put up four monuments. Some of the men were bitten by rattlesnakes. On the 19th the party left for Fry's camp, arriving there about 1:00 P.M. *Diary*, July 17-19.

143 The party prospected around the Tres Hermanas from July 20 to July 23. On the 24th they left early and arrived in Shakespeare about 1:00 P.M. *Ibid.*, July 20-24, 1880. Williams gives more details about the incidents of July, 1880, and the persons involved, in a letter to J. C. Williams, Dec. 15, 1924.

Part III

Refuge in Silver City

Hank Herrick of Arizona

The Hanging of Richard Remine

Oasis Mine v. Last Chance Mine

City of Refuge

REFUGE IN SILVER CITY

Hank Herrick of Arizona

ILLIAMS DID NOT COMPLETE the story of his mining ac- tivities in New Mexico. His account comes down only to July 23, 1880; however, he remained in Southwestern New Mexico, although not continuously active as a miner, for fifteen more months. In the winter of 1881, he finally returned to Dallas. For the period July, 1880, to December, 1881, his diary and four brief sketches supply enough data to outline his movements and ex- periences.

During several months beginning the last week of July, 1880, Williams was quite busy. He prospected in the mining fields near Mesilla, Mal Pais Springs, Tularosa and Carrisalillo, inspecting such mines as the Old Padre, the Sesnicky, the Superior and the Last Chance. At the same time, he conducted extensive and in- volved business transactions, acting as broker and lawyer in the mining area and in Dallas, Chicago and other places where in- vestors might be reached.[1]

His diary lists the names of various persons with whom he was associated in the mining fields: Grant, Pettie, Currie, Crittenden, Price, Graves, Campbell, Chamberlain, Richards, Bucher, Smythe, Dorsey, Osburn, Tierman, Fowler, Roadhouse — in the order of entries. In addition, Williams dealt with numerous investors, back- ers and prospects outside New Mexico. In Dallas he negotiated with Captain Webb and with McCutcheon, Prather, Daugherty, Powell and Gage. In Chicago he established connections with Haverly's Mining Exchange and with Ferris, Mason, Jewett, Lester and Colby. Several prospective buyers or investors arrived in the mining area from unidentified places: Foster, Huffacker, Weston, Welch, Brevoort and Wurtzbach.

From the business standpoint, Williams occupied himself in various ways: forming partnerships (the corporate structure was not used); raising money; selling ownership rights in mining prop- erties (usually one-half, one-third or one-fourth interest); draw- ing up deeds and contracts, and bonding mines to finance their operation. He thus acted as an operator, holding partnership interests in several mines; a promoter, bringing in capital; and a middleman, seeking to turn a profit by finding buyers for properties offered for sale. If he were active in Texas today, he doubtless would be described as a "wheeler-dealer."

One of Williams' most important undertakings was his commitment to sell the famous "76" Mine of Martin W. Bremen. The mine, opened in 1876 (hence its name), was located in Chloride Flat near Silver City. It soon became the largest producer in the district: within five years, it sent $900,000 in silver bullion to market. By the middle of 1880, however, the mine had reached its peak, and Bremen concluded that the time to sell had arrived, before production began to fall off. He commissioned Williams to find a responsible buyer for the property.[2]

Williams devoted much attention to this assignment. On November 2 he left Silver City, taking the stage to San Marcial.[3] Hank Herrick was one of the passengers. At San Marcial, Williams boarded the train to Kansas City and went on to Dallas. Williams remained in Dallas until the 22nd, meanwhile negotiating with business associates and visiting friends. On the 24th he arrived in Carthage, Illinois, where he saw members of his immediate family and more distant relatives. He was in Chicago by the morning of the 30th. Here he called on several prospects but aroused among them no interest in the Bremen mine. Disappointed, he returned to Dallas via Kansas City. He stayed in Dallas until February 7, 1881, when he again went north. He was in Kansas City on the 17th; while there, he again saw Hank Herrick during a stopover at the railroad station, caused partly by excessive snow on the rails. Leaving Kansas City after the delay, he was back in Shakespeare on February 26 and resumed his prospecting.[4]

In spite of his rebuffs in Chicago, Williams did not slacken his efforts to sell the Bremen mine. His diary for April 16 shows that on that day a Mr. Foster arrived to inspect the property. On the 18th an expert examined the mine and reported his findings to Foster and Williams. Ten days later, a Mr. Weston looked at the mine; a Mr. Welch showed up on May 6, and a Mr. Wurtzbach the following day. For several days it seemed that Welch would buy, and Wurtzbach also appeared to be well in tow. By the 22nd, however, it became clear to Williams that all his efforts had fallen flat.

Strangely, specimens from the mine — which was reported to be "completely gutted" — soon won all the mineral prizes at the

Albuquerque Fair, as Williams noted in his diary on October 12.[5] Even more unexpectedly, the mine eventually came back into full production, through the opening of new and richer lodes. During 1882, total production of the mine from the date of its opening in 1876 rose to $1,500,000, an increase of $600,000 since 1881, or within a year. Bremen's wealth and influence continued to grow.[6] He was elected mayor of Silver City three times — in 1879, again in 1880 and for the third time in 1884.[7]

Although Williams' efforts to sell Bremen's mine ended in failure, they were not entirely wasted. Again, he turned loss to profit — and again, his compensation was literary rather than monetary, as the following account of Hank Herrick demonstrates.

I spent the spring and summer of 1880 in prospecting for minerals in Southern New Mexico. By fall I had covered the territory from the Gila River to the Sacramento Mountains in the east and as far south as the Mexican border. I had had the assistance of two seasoned prospectors up to November of that year. The search, of course, was quite hasty and superficial, but it had produced no very encouraging results and had cost me the balance of my small resources. So I turned to another and, as it finally proved, just as bootless a method of helping out my finances from the mining game.

Martin Bremen had for some years previous operated his stamp mill in Silver City with ore mined from several mining claims near that town, principally from the "76" Mine, I believe. He had produced a large amount of bullion from this mine named for the Centennial year, and had in fact by this production insured the future stability of that mining town. He was worn and tired by some years of hectic life resulting from the consequent prosperity; and he greatly desired to close out his holdings and retire to a quiet life, which he thought he could enjoy fairly well with the sum of $400,000 cash. At least, that was the story given to me.

So when, by the help of Mr. Bremen's manager, I got the right to put the mine on the market at this price without paying down any sum of money, I went into a game which could not cost me much money — I did not have it to spend. I had nothing to preempt my time for the next four months; in the case of success, the reward would be princely. It was more exciting than a return to the hunt of the last summer under torrid skies over sand, malpais and mountain, and always under a *qui vive* for the lurking Apache. The worst enemies I could encounter were the brokers, with whom at least life would be safe.

With these preliminaries behind me, on the 2nd of November, 1880, I got on the eastbound Overland stagecoach at Silver City, New Mexico, bound for Chicago and other Eastern cities. With me went T. D. Pettie, one of my summer aids, who was to present my proposition to the mining men and capitalists of Denver, Colorado. Mr. Lawrence, reporter for the Denver *Mining News,* also boarded the same stage; he was bound for Denver. We found some other passengers already on board and routed to go to the railhead of the Santa Fe at San Marcial.

One of these passengers, Mr. Donoho, was an acquaintance of mine. He had spent the summer at the Shakespeare camp near the new town of Lordsburg and, although over sixty years of age, had put in his time there prospecting for minerals in the two camps of Shakespeare and Leitendorf's. No experienced prospector ever put in his search for a stake more diligently and faithfully than that old man accustomed to indoor life. He braved the sun, wind and storm for six months in the hills of the Pyramid Range, in the forlorn hope of bringing a mortuary legacy to his household. He had failed, and the failure had cut deep in a gallant soul; but not a word of grief or complaint passed his lips to mar the pleasure of his fellow passengers.

Another of those passengers attracted our attention at once because of the character of his baggage. Apparently he had only one piece, but that was so valuable that during his entire journey with us, he kept the two-gallon jug of whiskey between his legs, relieving his posture now and then by pouring out a pint cup more or less full and passing it to his fellow passengers. He appeared to regard this passing of the cup as a serious Office of State. Because neither Mr. Donoho nor I would partake, he seemed to bear considerable resentment toward us and to regard our action as a serious breach of frontier courtesy. But he was so mellow with repeated potations, and with the earnest observance of frontier courtesy shown by the other passengers, that little by little he came to drop his feeling against us.

The man's face bore testimony to long service in some out-of-door occupation. It was burned to a thick brick red, and his eyes were set in a corona of fine wrinkles that ran outwards, so characteristic of those who have lived much in the glare of fierce sunshine. But the general expression of the face, in spite of the mask built over it by the sun and wind, was kindly, and the tone of his talk was that of a man to whom the face of his fellows was welcome. So I think that every passenger on that coach made him the center of interest, and encouraged him in telling the story of his life and the occasion of his journey. By the time darkness fell on us, just after we had left the single house at Leasburg, New Mexico, with a sign over the door reading "Live and let live" (which was supposed to explain the charge for our supper), I think we had come to believe that we had brought out every salient feature of the man's life.

For the greater part of his manhood, he had lived in Arizona; he had, as stage driver generally and prospector occasionally, been in the open. The sun in summer and the cold wind in winter had seared his face, while the accidents of his business had marked him with scars. His home had been an adobe shack, at times; at others, the sky made his roof, the bare ground his bed. His comrades had been the rough, hardened men of frontier posts; his acquaintances with women were rare and usually brief; and in sickness, the crude care of his companions was sadly wanting in gentleness. His wages had been small, yet always on the road there had been peril from robbers and from Indians. Often, as he sat in the driver's seat, he had promised himself that soon he would go back to God's Country and lie down to rest once more under the shade of the old maple tree in the bluegrass lawn. But something was always happening to keep him longer in a country where he could find no real grass to camp on; and where, if he found a shady cottonwood that promised a cool rest to a tired man, the sandburs and the fleas were just too bad.

But now the old man's promise, made to himself so often as he rode the stage, was to be carried out. He and his partners had sold out their interest in the Copper Queen Mine for $20,000, and he had been paid for his one-quarter interest. Without further delay, he had gotten his one-piece baggage and had set out on his return to his particular part of God's Country, where he was going to spend the remainder of his life in quiet and comfort. No more would he ride the boot, with one eye on the wild Mexican mules and the other flickering from bush to rock on the wayside, with his heart disturbed by the least movement of leaf or bird, lest an Indian form might materialize. Now forever was passed the night drive in icy winds; and passed away for all time was the fear that he would never again lay eyes on his family and the friends of his youth. He was a free man once more.

The old stage driver would have his old friends visit him on his farm, and when they were not following the hounds, they would lie awake in bed at night telling stories, stories of youth common to them, and of his friends' later days at the old home, exchanged for his tales of the wild days of the mining camps, of the bullion robbers, of the feuds between the outlaws, and of the shadow of Indian raids which hung over outlaw and peaceable citizen alike. He would visit these old friends at their homes and would take their families into the same bond of old friendship that the elders had; so he would repay himself for the long, lonesome days of Arizona — and Missouri would make up to him for the default of the Desert State.

Finally, he told us that his name was Hank Herrick and that he was going to the little town of Fairmont in Clark County, Missouri, where his kin still lived. This brought me to the front. I told him that in the fall of 1871 I had been one of a crew of engineers on the construction of a railroad, stationed at that town. For two months I had boarded there with a widow named Herrick, who was having a hard time maintaining herself and two pretty little girls of about six and eight years of age.

"Bless their souls," said the old man with tears in his eyes, "they are nieces of mine; I will be their help, and at last I shall know children." From that time, no matter what was being talked over, he would break in with questions about those children, very few of which questions I could answer.

About dusk we came on the rolling plateau of the Jornada del Muerto.[8] The six great coach-horses were carrying us along at a clipping rate, and the conversation had died down in the body of the coach at about the hour of nine, when the horses suddenly veered out of the road with an increased rate of speed. At almost the same moment, the flash of a dark lantern for an instant showed me the wheels and a flapping curtain of our coach, with black darkness behind. Not a sound was heard nor a form seen by the roadside, but the driver called on his teams for greater speed and pulled them back into the road. The passengers, somewhat excited, concluded that we had barely escaped a holdup, as the driver said he had been warned of possible trouble before starting. Old Hank paid small attention, beyond remarking that he thought he had left that sort of thing in Arizona.

We all caught the train at San Marcial at 1:00 P.M. of the next day. Hank with his baggage got into the smoker, where he was a very popular passenger. We took our dinner at Las Vegas on the 5th, breakfast at Lakin, Kansas, on the 6th, and we were well into Kansas on the morning of the 7th. At Newton, Hank went out with an empty jug at dinner time and came back complaining because he could not fill it. He was reminded by Mr. Donoho that we were now in God's Country. At 6:00 P.M. we were in Kansas City, where Hank, perfectly sober, left us for the last leg of his journey. We supposed that none of us would lay eyes on him again, and we bade him good-bye with many expressions of good wishes and hope for his enjoyment of the last haven to which he was making sail.

I put in the next three months visiting city after city, trying to sell that Bremen mine, until at last in the dead of winter I came to Chicago. Owing to a previous short residence in that place, I had expected to find easy access to the class of people whom I might hope to be interested in such matters. It was very cold, and the stiff lake winds were hard on a man from the borders of Mexico. But the air blowing off the icebound shores of Lake Michigan was no colder than that which I found in the offices of brokers and mine investors when I mentioned my errand. I soon learned that some mining engineer had recently examined the mine and had reported it as worked out or, in his coarse but expressive wording, as "completely gutted." This report had been made public, and it was useless for me to waste more time on a hopeless quest. So I took the back track.

On the 17th day of February, 1881, I was in that old and dingy station at the foot of the hill in Kansas City, Missouri, which had for so many years been the point of departure for a multitude of fortune-hungry people going from God's Country in the hope of finding a paradise of hill, valley or plain somewhere in the Wild West. So shabby and forbidding was that long, low, sinister shack of a building that it must have turned back many a doubting soul just on the verge of stepping from the platform of safety to the darkness of the Great American Desert. But it could add no gloom to my frame of mind. I was on my way back to whatever silver lining there might remain to me in Southern New Mexico.

Needing a shine for my shoes, I was told that I would find a bootblack in the room of the "Big Horse," some eight or ten doors back from the waiting room along the track front. So I came to a door just inside of which I saw a large hobbyhorse saddled and bridled, with a man mounted on it having his shoes blacked in a kind of open stirrup. I passed this and another horse, and sat down to wait my turn. The man on the nearest horse was talking with a voice that sounded wobbly and uncertain, as if the owner had had some acquaintance with the bottle — and yet somehow it was familiar. I got up, walked over and looked up into the reddened eyes of — old Hank Herrick.

Old Hank remembered me and began at once to unfold a tale of woe. He was lonesome; he was homesick; he was on his way back to Arizona. There he had looked over the driver's boot all day long when no house but the keeper's station was to be seen, and all night with no one to talk with; but never had he been so forlorn and alone as he had felt back in his old childhood home. He had found only three old friends, but they had no time to visit with him and could talk about nothing but crops and weather when they met. He had been told that nobody but young fools hunted the coon and the opossum with hounds.

Hank had told his old friends his stories of life on the road in Arizona, but they looked at him as if he knew that they would not believe such wild yarns. His nieces were glad at first to meet their old uncle, but they had so many younger men to laugh and talk with, that they could spare little time for his questions. It was all so dull — so little to learn — so small an outlook! No Indians to talk about, no mines to hunt for, no fights, no robbers . . . Why, he was as lonesome as he would be in Sunday school! So he had sold his little place at a loss, and he was going back to Arizona on the next train with me. That was where he had a place in the sun.

When I got on the train that afternoon I could not find the face of Old Hank. Somehow he had missed out, and I never again saw him. I heard long afterward that some eight years later he was seen driving a small country stage out of Tucson, old and broken; and long ago he must have made that last voyage to God's Country from which no traveler ever returns. But whether his port of departure lay in the country or in the land of the maple, I can only believe that it must have lain where he had had a place in the sun.

Such an ending was characteristic of many of the waifs of civilization of that day and country. I have repeated in the story of Hank Herrick the experience of hundreds of early American settlers in Arizona and New Mexico, except only that unlike Hank very few of them ever had a stake to help out with the desired return to the old home. A life of forty years in a country with a wide horizon of sky and mountain among a people whose habits, ambitions and passions were greatly loosened from the conventions of civilization — such a life left the wayfarer helpless to rest content within the bounds of a small farming community.

The Hanging of Richard Remine

URING THE SPRING of 1881 Williams continued his perambulations in the region around Shakespeare and Silver City.[9] On March 1 he examined Currie's Eagle Mine at Steeple Rock. The following day he visited Grant's three mines nearby, and was so favorably impressed that he obtained one-quarter interest in them for Powell and Gage of Dallas.

Meanwhile, a serious legal question had arisen concerning Williams' title to his Oasis Mine; for this reason, on March 5 he journeyed to Silver City to discuss the problem with his lawyers, who had come in from Tucson. He spent several days going over the legal issues with them and attending to other mining business. Then, on the 14th, he made an entry in his diary saying laconically, "At 2½ P.M. attended hanging of Richard Remine, who met death calmly."

In the sketch that follows, Williams recounts the details of Remine's crime and describes the nature of imprisonment and punishment in New Mexico during those early days. In this story, it is somewhat difficult to separate fact from fiction. The sheriff's lax control of his prisoner is reasonably plausible, as are the opportunities for easy escape — even in the case of a convicted murderer under sentence of death. In the early West, jails were far from escape-proof, and sheriffs frequently regarded long-term prisoners as nuisances, to be rid of as soon as possible.[10] Also, the sheriff in this account may have had scruples against a legal hanging, a procedure only recently substituted for the more immediate and certain executions by self-appointed vigilantes.[11]

The influence of the devil-woman, however, is more difficult to accept. Granted that she had unequaled hypnotic power combined with demonic influence, poor Remine must have been unusually stupid in refusing to leave her; he must have known that if he stayed he would almost certainly die. Yet, what mortal can account for the influence of a woman over a man? Whether this part of the story is fact or fiction, it was widely current in Silver City at the time. Williams recounts it here as it was generally accepted.

 IN THE SPRING of 1881, I spent some days in Silver City, New Mexico, at what was then known as Timmer's Hotel. There was a stone coping in front of the hotel, marking the division between the sidewalk and the street. After meals, it was the custom of the guests and town idlers to sit out there with feet elevated on this coping and discuss such news and gossip as might be current in the town. While so engaged one evening after supper, I saw a man with a basket on his arm pass through a gate leading to the kitchen from the enclosure at the back part of the hotel. I had seen this man at other times pass through this gate with a basket on his arm, and always he

was alone. I asked my companions about his name and his purpose. I was told that his name was Remine and that he was carrying food to the prisoners in the jail some four blocks distant.

"Oh!" I said, "a deputy sheriff or a jailer." No, they replied, he was a prisoner under sentence of death. Now, it was almost dark at the time; the hotel building was at the foot of a hill at the extreme edge of the town buildings; there was a rocky canyon a few yards south where the hiding was good, and apparently the chance of escape for the prisoner was excellent. So it was with a good share of astonishment that I set out to learn the man's story.

This is what I was told: Remine and a man named Winterburn from Albany, New York, occupied a room in a building in the little burg of Central City [12] a few miles distant from Silver City. They cooked their food in this room and slept in a double bed. Winterburn seldom indulged in drink; but Remine drank to excess, and when intoxicated was a quarrelsome, evil-tempered man. One night late, on coming to the room much the worse for drink, he found Winterburn lying across the bed asleep in a position which interfered with Remine's attempt to lie down. Angered, he procured an axe, killed the sleeping man at a single blow, and in a tempest of rage continued to hack the dead body until it was cut to pieces. After this fury had been spent, the drunken man dropped asleep and was found later on the same bed with his victim. He was immediately arrested.

Afterward, Remine was tried for the murder in Silver City, the county seat of Grant County. His brothers back in Tennessee were poor men but they helped him with such money as they could scrape together, and an attorney was employed to defend him. Ordinarily this would have almost insured his final release in a community so engrossed in the pursuit of quick riches as to be almost indifferent to any crime that did not in some way directly take a dollar away from a citizen. For a peace officer to bring a criminal to justice, he had to take time and energy from the hunt for a mine and risk his life. He exposed himself to danger from the criminal's resentment, without any disposition on the part of any other citizen to aid, or even to sympathize with him. The doctrine of *laissez-faire* was carried out to a high degree in those frontier mining camps, except in the matter of adopting camp rules to protect the locations of mining claims in a new camp.

There were other notable exceptions to this rule of *laissez-faire*; the brutality of this murder made it one. The nature of the crime brought public attention to the deed in a very unusual degree. Then, too, Sheriff Whitehill was at that time trying to make a good record in his office. [13]

Also, Winterburn's brother back in New York, having hired an attorney to prosecute, put up money to assist in securing and holding the witness for the trial necessary for conviction. So the stars went out of their usual courses to fight against Remine.

In spite of the efforts of Remine's attorney and of the delays in coming to trial, which are considered by the lawyers to be a defendant's best defense, and in spite of the subsidence of the feeling against him, Remine was tried and found guilty, and was sentenced to be hung. His attorney appealed the case, but Remine was not allowed to give bail and was kept in the Silver City jail while his case took its leisurely course through the higher court at Santa Fe.

We sat out by the stone coping in front of Timmer's Hotel discussing the case some months after the appeal had been taken. Any day might bring the word over the military telegraph-line that stretched from Santa Fe to Silver City that the prisoner must be hanged. The best that Remine could hope for was a reversal and an order for a new trial. Yet, the sheriff appeared to be giving his prisoner every chance for escape that he reasonably could. It was stated that Remine was allowed to go out at nights to gamble in the town.

Having stayed out until after 11:00 o'clock one night, Remine was sternly notified by the sheriff that this could not be allowed, as it made too much trouble to the jailer to let him in after bedtime. Thereafter, he was warned, if he did not come back by 10:00 o'clock, he would "d----d sure be locked out." It was not understood why the prisoner had failed to make his escape under these circumstances. It was believed that he was relying on his attorney's opinion that the case would surely be reversed; and in the meantime life "in jail" was easy, and the fare of Timmer's Hotel was good.[14]

About a week later, I was told that the sheriff had received a telegram from Santa Fe stating that the upper court had approved the action of the lower court — and that the prisoner should be hung on the following Monday.[15] So when Remine came in that evening from gambling, he was locked in to await the day set for execution. The sheriff summoned me to become one of the legal witnesses required to attend the hanging and vouch for the execution of the sentence. Being possessed at the time with an itching curiosity to see how death would be met by a man who had flagrantly neglected his chances to escape from it, I accepted the invitation. That curiosity passed with Remine's death. I have never had it to return.

The decree of the court was to be executed within the palisaded enclosure around the jail and in the presence of about twenty men. The scaffold consisted of a platform of planks erected about five or six feet above the ground; it was large enough for the free movement on it of five or six men. There were steps on the north side to mount by, but nothing further was attached to the frame, save the simple skeleton of the gallows on the eastern margin of the platform. On this side there was a small sliding platform projecting from the main platform between two upright timbers. These supported on a crosspiece at the top the rope for execution. This slide could be suddenly pulled back under the main platform by means of a trigger set under the platform. We had ample time before the hour set for the execution to examine the machinery by which the drop was worked.

While waiting the hour of execution, Sheriff Whitehill told me that the prisoner had smoked up half a box of cigars and consumed five or six bottles of wine during the past twenty-four hours. Thus stimulated, Remine had expressed his determination to meet his fate quietly and without complaint. After learning that everything was in readiness at the gallows and that the man of God was present — in spite of the prisoner's refusal to call for his presence —Sheriff Whitehill went into the jail to bring out the condemned man. During quite a period of waiting, while the sheriff was in the jail, it was noticed that the hum of conversation died down to a few whispers among the bystanders. Death was near.

At last, the jail door opened and the sheriff stepped out, holding in his hand a box of cigars. Behind him came the prisoner, rather small and of insignificant presence, with a face covered by a ragged dark-brown beard. Clothed in ill-fitting garments, he presented a picture which one would have passed on the street without consideration as a poor specimen of physical humanity and probably of little moral significance. But standing in the shadow of death, he was invested with a strange dignity.

With carefully balanced and slow steps, Remine came out. With lusterless eyes, blinking in the bright sunshine, he gave an impression of one whose mind was little concerned with what was before him. The sheriff afterwards attributed this appearance to a measure of stupor brought on by the cigars and wine the prisoner had used up during the previous hours. To my mind, there was something more to it than mere smoke and drink.

After a few words with the sheriff — which I did not hear — Remine slowly ascended the steps, assisted by the officer. He now turned to gaze over the upturned faces, possibly hoping to meet a friendly glance. If the condemned man saw such a face, he gave no sign of response.

He refused some request of the clergyman with a mute shake of the head. Turning to the sheriff, he made a request which the officer seemed to grant. Remine then turned to his audience and began a slow, halting address, which became more animated as he proceeded. It was a declaration of innocence; an assertion of perjury on the part of the prosecuting witness; and a charge of prejudice leveled against the trial judge. His speech was rambling and disconnected, with so much repetition that it caused us to think that he was talking on to save a few wretched minutes of life. He left no message to friend or kin — no warning to young or old — and no word of hope in God or man.[16]

Remine was not checked or interrupted, but finally ended his talk with some inarticulate cadence deep down in the throat, as if the voice were dying before the body died. The preacher knelt down and prayed. If the prisoner heard a word of the prayer, there was no sign of it in his stooped shoulders or his faded eyes.

When the prayer ended, the deputy sheriff stepped forward and, with the aid of the sheriff, moved the man over so that he finally stood on the side between the two upright posts, under the noosed rope. Then the prisoner's ankles were bound together and his hands were tied behind his back. Next, the noose was let down and fastened around his throat. After that, the black cap was placed on his head and drawn over his eyes. As the last move, the knot of the noose was turned so that it rested just under the ear of the doomed man.

The deputy stepped back and looked at the sheriff, who gave a mute signal. We heard the sound of the trigger as it was unlocked. The sliding platform slipped from under the feet of the condemned man; his body shot down between the uprights and stopped with a thud that caused the beating of my heart to cease for a moment. I heard a sound of indrawn breath from the spectators as if their hearts, too, had halted life for a second. The bound legs of the prisoner drew up convulsively and pressed against his breast for a few moments with a curious quivering movement as if shaken by the passing of the soul of the dead man. Then, with a slow, gradual decline, the limbs lowered until the limp body hung straight down from the knotted rope.[17]

The sheriff looked at his watch, turned to the jail and went inside to make his report to the court: that at a certain hour on a certain day, in obedience to the mandate of the court, he had caused the defendant Remine to be hung by the neck until he was dead — all in the presence of the following-named witnesses, citizens of New Mexico.

I went away feeling that there was something in the story of the last days of Remine that had not come to me. Here was a man threatened with death, with the gates of safety in sight; yet he apparently had made no effort to pass through the portals. Around the town lay a wild world, a world of wooded hills and rocky canyons, with a few small mining camps scattered about in lonely places. The Indian and the mountain lion marauded the very borders of the parade ground in the solitary fort that guarded the foothills. It would have been an easy matter for Remine to escape into those hills. There, hunger or the Indians might get him, but the sheriff never. That chance was at least worth taking.

I made some effort to discover this fugitive element in the Remine story, and finally I caught the trail and followed it down. It reminded me of that part of the palaver of the fortune-teller who examines the palms of hands and tells you that a certain line in your hand which crosses another certain line at a certain place is the line of Mars crossing the line of Venus. It means that at a particular time you will meet the lady you will marry. In Remine's case it meant that in jail, under sentence, he was to meet a woman of sinister history, whose fascination led him to neglect his last chance for saving himself.

This woman was said to have come from California several years earlier; she bore a rather doubtful reputation. She must have had some personal attractions, considerable shrewdness and a devilish disposition, judged in the light of her career around Silver City.[18] She succeeded in getting a respectable man named Henry Granger[19] to make her his wife. He was a man past middle life, with a weak-minded son. It was believed that Granger had some money with him and some property back in Illinois. He owned a mining claim which he thought valuable, and had begun sinking a deep shaft on it with the aid of the feeble-minded son and of another man. This other person was known as "Silver Plate Dick," because he continually asserted that he had a silver plate in his skull to cover a fracture. After Dick was executed some time later, it was found that he had no such plate; this discovery confirmed the general impression that he, too, was mentally defective.[20]

Now, the woman planned to kill her husband; so she gradually acquired a hold on Silver Plate Dick, and even on Granger's son, until she made them confederates in the plot. The two younger men killed the old man at the shaft, threw his body in, and filled the shaft up with the rocks and earth taken from it, just as the woman had planned. She outlined the story that was to explain Granger's disappearance, but her weak-minded confederates could not sustain the story as could the woman.

In the end the men confessed. When they came to their trials, Silver

Plate Dick was tried first; after conviction, he was hung.[21] Next, the boy was tried and received some fifteen years in the penitentiary.[22]

When Remine went to jail, the woman was already an inmate awaiting trial. Although the apartments for men and women in the Silver City jail were considerably apart, there was a corridor in which both sexes walked for air, sunshine and exercise. Men and women were separated only by an iron railing the length of the corridor. Here Remine and the woman plotted and jested, swore and cried with each other through the iron bars as each told the other a tale of trouble and revenge — until Remine became another victim of the woman's evil influence.

When Remine's line crossed the line of Granger's murderess, it meant that the days of his life were to be cut off. He could not leave the woman — or would not do so — while the road to safety yet lay open. To him the world was lost for a woman. Possibly he thought it was well lost, but there was nothing in his dying talk to indicate such a belief. After his death, she was removed to Mesilla, where she was tried and sentenced for her crime.[23]

Oasis Mine v. Last Chance Mine

IN THE RECORDS of the District Court of Grant County, New Mexico (of which Silver City is the county seat), are found fragmentary details of a suit styled *Oscar Williams et al.* v. *Thomas Dunn et al.* The entries in the *Court Register and Cost Book, 1873-1884,* are prosaic: Cause No. 626 in Equity — Bill filed, May 24, 1881; amended bill filed, July 12; demurrer overruled, February 20, 1882; defendant's answer filed, April 1; stipulation filed, April 29; May 12 and June 19, replications filed; September 28, maps and exhibits filed; April 23, 1883, case dismissed in favor of defendants.[24]

Yet, these notations, brief as they are, had deep meaning for Oscar W. Williams at the time they were made. With his most important mining property in peril — and his future in New Mexico as well — he had filed the suit in a determined effort to protect his legal rights as he understood them.

In none of his writings does Williams make entirely clear the circumstances that led to the controversy. However, an hour's search of the records in the office of the Grant County Clerk, where mining locations are registered, has been sufficient to turn up the essential facts. These facts are as follows:

On September 4, 1879, Fred W. Smith, Thomas Dunn and William A. Downing filed their claim to Oasis Mine, located at Leitendorf in the Virginia Mining District, near Shakespeare.[25] The survey of the mine, however, was not completed and registered at the same time. Meanwhile, on June 17, 1880, the Last Chance Mine was located by metes and bounds; the claim was recorded in full on September 23.[26] Finally, on January 18, 1881, the survey of the Oasis Mine was registered in full. The plat of the Oasis registration shows that the survey of this mine overlapped and covered most of the Last Chance Mine.[27]

Williams and his partners, W. G. Currie and T. D. Pettie, in January, 1880, had acquired a one-half interest in the Oasis from Smith, Dunn and Downing, its original locators. The buyers thus relied on the claim registered September 4, 1879. Williams was surprised to learn on July 30, 1880 — as he noted in his diary — that "Crosby's Last Chance is our Oasis," Crosby being the manager of the Last Chance. Even though the Last Chance had been located on June 17, 1880, if Williams had acted promptly by surveying the property and registering the survey in the name of the Oasis, he could have safeguarded his interests. As it was, however, the Last Chance group jumped his claim by filing their survey on September 23, 1880, in advance of the Oasis survey. (See Appendix II for copies of the respective mining claims.)

Entries in Williams' diary show that he devoted much time to working on the lawsuit and worrying over it. Thus, he spent most of August 3, 1880, at the courthouse in Silver City examining the records of the two mines. By May of 1881, he had employed a lawyer, Amos Green, to handle the litigation. Williams met with him on May 23, 24 and 25 to draw up a bill of complaint. The plaintiffs filed *lis pendens* in the office of the Circuit Court on the 24th.

There was, however, no officer in Shakespeare authorized to serve the legal papers. Williams solved this problem by inducing Sheriff Harvey H. Whitehill to appoint a deputy who could act. After the plaintiffs had filed amendments to their original petition, the case was docketed for a hearing on general demurrer, and was argued initially on July 25. The judge, however, rendered no decision at the time, waiting until February 20, 1882, to overrule the demurrer.

Pending trial of the case on its merits, plaintiffs and defendants sought to effect a compromise. Williams' diary for September 30, 1881, refers to these negotiations thus: "Hear that Last Chance men are willing to give $10,000 to settle our suit." A notation dated October 1 reads: "Telegraphed Currie $5,000 would buy me out on Oasis — no less." Another entry, of October 17, says: "Parties trying to compromise Oasis." On the 25th, word comes from Currie that the compromise will "probably go." Finally, however, Williams records on the 28th: "Learned from Currie that Oasis compromise is off."

The case of *Oscar Williams* v. *Thomas Dunn* never came to trial, chiefly because the mine had proved unproductive during the pendency of the suit. Williams' claim was dismissed and judgment was entered in favor of the Last Chance owners some twenty months after Williams had turned his back on mining as a career. As the Silver City *Enterprise* reported when the curtain was rung down on the dispute: "This mine has been in litigation several years, and this decision fully settles the matter. Decision was rendered by Judge Bristol." The newspaper also stated that "Not a single blast has been fired in this mine for nearly thirteen months, work having been suspended in December, 1881."[28]

Many years later, Williams gave a fuller explanation of how the controversy ended and of what happened to the mine. In an interview with Mary Ethel Dunn on April 27, 1940, he said: "About two months after the judge granted his decision against us, we considered the proposition of taking an appeal. But during the course of those two months, a radical change had taken place in the progress of that mine over which we were fighting. At the time we brought the suit, about $50,000 worth of ore had been shipped from the mine to the smelter. But during the course of the suit, the pocket of ore had played out, and now, sixty years later, I find that it never was opened again. So it happens that we never appealed that case to a higher court."

The fiasco of the Oasis mine brought Williams' activities as a miner to a close. After moving to Silver City in July, 1881, he may have salvaged some of his interests, but there is no evidence of this fact. Williams did say later that he "went broke" in New Mexico.[29] Here are his comments on the case and the parties interested in its outcome.

I HAVE BEEN familiar with court procedure since 1871, and have attended several trials of note. Our case of the owners of the Oasis Mine versus the owners of the Last Chance Mine at Leitendorf was tried at Silver City in 1882. It was not, after all, a contention over a great property, although we thought so at the time; but it was carried on between adversaries of picturesque careers, and marked by peculiar incidents. Let us consider the figures on that stage. As we were the plaintiffs, I will begin with our side.

F. W. ("Bean Bellied") Smith claimed to be the son of "Extra Billy" Smith, Confederate War Governor of Virginia. Smith, Will Downing and Tom Dunn were the original locators of the Oasis Mine. After the location notice was recorded, Smith kept it in his possession. When I saw the document first, it had a bullet hole in it and bloodstains on it; he claimed he had received the shot in his duel with Ross Wood. We agreed on entering the suit that no one of us would sell out unless the others joined in, but Smith deserted us on a small offer, and carried away by night the bloodstained location notice.[30]

William Downing was a Kentuckian, about sixty-five years old — six feet one inch of erect manhood, with a snow-white mustache covering a firm mouth from which speech came like the sound of a blacksmith's hammer on the anvil. The man's bearing and record were such that after John Ringo was killed by some party unknown,[30a] it was believed that Downing was that party, having as a cause of grievance the stealing of mules from his Chiricahua lumber camp. He was an old associate of Senator William M. Stewart of Nevada,[31] had consulted him recently on our case and received the crisp legal maxim that "Possession is nine points of the law"; so Downing came up to Silver City before the trial to persuade us to take possession of the Oasis, which had practically the same boundaries as the Last Chance, and hold it with shotguns.

When we would not adopt this line of action, he went back to that lumber camp in the Chiricahua Mountains and, calling to his aid an anomalous character known as the "Irish Lord," brought him to Silver City to help in the trial.[32] Downing carried this man, dissolute but bearing himself with many of the social graces of a former Beau Brummel, and introduced him to every barroom in the town. Downing gave him unlimited credit for whiskey, wine, beer and cigars, when accompanied by Crosby, Tom Dunn or Dick Fitzgerald, witnesses for the defendants, but no others. This was a duty eminently pleasing to this lost scion of the Irish nobility, and he carried it out so zealously that, in spite of all precautions taken by the defendants' lawyers, these witnesses were drunk from the opening of the preliminary hearing until their evidence had been given in court.

The original locators — Smith, Downing and Dunn — had made a contract with W. G. Currie, T. D. Pettie and me in 1880, by which we became the owners of an undivided one-half interest in the Oasis location, in consideration of sinking a shaft on the Oasis vein. So, when suit was brought, the Oasis title was owned by the three original locators and Currie, Pettie and me. But Dunn had double-crossed his co-owners in the Oasis by making the Last Chance location directly over the Oasis ground, and later by selling the greater part of it to Bement, Nisbet and Mackay of Evansville, Indiana, who opened up a large chamber of good ore. So Dunn was not in the ranks of the plaintiffs, but was made a party defendant.

W. G. Currie was a native of some town in western New York. During the Civil War he was a member of some artillery company from that state; at the close of the War, he was discharged from the Union Army in northeastern Texas. He chose to remain in the Lone Star State. He was engaged in the real-estate business in Dallas in 1879, but in 1880, after acquiring his interest in the Oasis, he came out to Shakespeare and lived there for some time. Later he spent a year or more in what was known as the East Camp at Steeple Rock,[33] where the Davenports and some others of his old acquaintances were then located. Currie was a man of sensitive feeling and exceedingly conscientious conduct; during the trial of the case, he was so opposed to the movements of the Irish Lord that Currie was probably never informed of the greater part of those questionable activities. In old age he went back to his boyhood home and died there many years ago.

T. D. Pettie was a Georgian of good family, who had a brother in New York following the occupation of Wall Street broker when Thomas D. was a common miner in Colorado. From Georgetown in that state he came down in 1879 to a new camp near Santa Fe named Cerrillos, where I met him and employed him as a prospector to go down to Shakespeare in my interest. He was a bright, rather forceful man, but was afflicted with the drink habit. After a spell of abstinence he would break into a protracted period of drunkenness. Later he went to New York City, and I was informed by a letter from John E. Price several years ago that he was then living in London, England.

At the time, I, the third partner, was in charge of the post office at Silver City. It was my task during the trial to keep in touch with our lawyers and to watch the progress of the pleadings and evidence. I was too busy in the post office to do more than pick up what I could after office hours and send out what word might be necessary to our witnesses and now and then to one of our plaintiffs. These men might be in the outlands at Shakespeare, Steeple Rock or the Chiricahuas.

But of all the protagonists in this play, the fortunes of the attorneys in the cause unfolded greatest in story and grimmest in tragedy. Half of them met death by the Indians, while one lived for years under a cloud of rumor.

Amos Green was our senior attorney. He had previously been a practitioner at the St. Louis bar; he was an able man and a good lawyer. Before coming to New Mexico, Green had passed the Civil War years in the Midwest. At that time there had been much dissatisfaction with the Lincoln administration in the states of Illinois, Indiana and Ohio. It was charged openly — and I think generally believed — that there was a treasonable organization in those states, going under the name of the Knights of the Golden Circle.[34]

It was claimed that the members of the organization were drilled in arms on moonlight nights in preparation for the day when they should rise in revolt to aid the Southern States. However this may have been, in point of fact Union troops were stationed in many towns in Illinois as a precaution. Many Democrats were arrested as quietly as possible and taken to secret prisons far away, which seems to indicate there was fear of the existence of some such organization. Now, it was rumored later, when the War was over, that Amos Green had been the treasurer of the Knights of the Golden Circle, and that as such officer he had fallen heir to all of their golden circles — or greenbacks. All of this was nothing but rumor, and I mention it only as a tribute to the man's standing and prominence.

John P. Risque, our junior attorney, was a young man, recently married, of much promise and greatly liked in his adopted home, Silver City. He had lived formerly in St. Louis; I believe he was a graduate of the Catholic college at Georgetown, District of Columbia. Not long after he had filed the suit for us in the Territorial Court at Silver City, he and Captain Slawson (I believe that is the name) were ambushed by Indians near Clifton, Arizona, while on a visit to the copper mines. The mutilated remains were brought back to Silver City, where his fraternity stood guard as the public passed in solemn view of the body. One of the most vivid recollections that I have of those days is that of listening to the sobs of Risque's young widow as the choir sang the beautiful church songs at the funeral.[35]

The defendants' attorneys were Judge John D. Bail and Judge H. C. McComas. Judge Bail was an Old Timer, well-informed in the law. But in the public eye Judge McComas was the star figure for the defendants. He had had a previous career of some consequence in East St. Louis, Illinois, and in Fort Scott, Kansas. He was then a dominant leader in the politics of Grant County and Southern New Mexico, and a man of considerable force in court. The thread of his life was cut very shortly thereafter; his two little girls (who had taken music lessons from my wife) were left doubly orphaned when the Apaches waylaid their parents almost in sight of the ground fought over in the Oasis - Last Chance litigation. That story is classic; I do not need to repeat it.[36]

The defendants must have had a story worth telling, but I do not know it. Certainly W. J. Crosby's Panama experiences must have been worthwhile, and they left a life-burden on him, but I have not time to tell the little I know.[37]

City of Refuge

WILLIAMS' FAILURE to sell Bremen's "76" Mine and his involvement in the dispute between the owners of the Oasis and of the Last Chance mines were harbingers of more trouble. During the period from the middle of June to the first part of December, 1881, his fortunes declined rapidly; and the plans he had made so carefully, and worked so diligently to carry out, largely fell apart.

The spring of 1881 was an especially difficult time. First of all, Williams learned on May 2 that his friend James W. Bell had been killed a few days before, on April 28, by Billy the Kid. Bell, along with another peace officer, R. W. Ollinger, was charged with guarding the Kid, being held in Murphy's store at Lincoln while he awaited execution. According to a contemporary account, Ollinger "had just gone to his supper and Bell was sitting down on the floor, when the 'Kid' approached him, talking in his pleasant way. Quick as lightning he jumped and struck Bell with his handcuffs, fracturing the skull. He immediately snatched Bell's revolver and shot him through the breast." The Kid next shot Ollinger as he was returning to the improvised jail. Then the desperado forced a man to saddle a horse, and fled on it.[38]

Another death — that of U. C. Garrison, a lawyer friend, on June 4 — was also a depressing experience for Williams. Later, on June 6, he wrote to his fiancée, Miss Sallie Wheat: "I had the melancholy experience of closing the eyes of a lawyer who died here very suddenly. He was taken with a sudden hemorrhage of the lungs and died in five minutes without uttering a word. (He was buried nine hours after death, and that is the last I have heard of him.)"

The conduct of Williams' partner Pettie added to the increasing troubles. Pettie was in Denver on mining business for the partnership. On June 2, Williams noted in his diary: "Bad news from Pettie. More money wanted." Another entry—on the 10th—stated: "Telegram from Pettie wanting money immediately." Pettie asked for $500, but Williams sent him only $50, apparently all he could spare. Six days later, Williams received news that Pettie was on a drunken spree. Later on, Williams was told that Pettie had double-crossed him in the Oasis Mine matter.

On June 20, Williams wrote in his diary, "Affairs getting desperate with me in money matters." Then, on the 29th, he summarized his problems: "Pettie drunk in Denver, suit pending here on Last Chance — no work going on any of my property — no money and not able to get employment, in debt about $2,500 — everything, in short, against me, but I am determined to pull through somehow. My hopes that I can get employment of some kind so as to pay expenses and in the meantime sell something."

Williams first thought of returning to Dallas and working for Powell and Gage, his former employers in the land-surveying business. Next, he considered the offer from a mining company at Clifton, Arizona, of a job as engineer at $100 a month; but the job did not materialize. Then, finally, he applied for the deputy postmastership at Silver City. He was appointed to this position at $60 for the first month and $75 a month thereafter. He was also promised a position in the office of the District Clerk of Grant County if he wished it. By July 20, he was at work in the post office; on July 26 his appointment as deputy district clerk was confirmed.

Williams now turned his attention to his duties in the post office: he became preoccupied with things like the weather and the arrival and delivery of the mails. To salvage his mining interests, he also took such steps as he could, including the sale of his share of the Oasis Mine. He grubstaked one old prospector (Henry H.

Stevens), and as a result lost $41. He received a favorable report on a mine — the Honest Miner — and arranged for a manager, Preston, to work his claim at Carrisalillo Springs.

For some time now, Williams had corresponded with his fiancée in Dallas, Miss Sallie Wheat. He had found her sympathetic and helpful under all circumstances. Since Miss Wheat evidenced a willingness to become his wife, he decided to return to Dallas for their marriage. His diary on November 26 notes: "Draw on Cherville and Sholl of Carthage for $500 to defray expenses of the marriage." The next day, there is this entry: "Make arrangements to leave $100 to Currie's credit."

The final notations in the Diary relate to Williams' business affairs: the mines at Carrisalillo are reported as doing well; Williams agrees to sell his interest in the Oasis for $2,670, a prospect that is never to materialize; he pays his assessment of $25 on the Crittenden Mine the day of his departure for Dallas, December 1, 1881.[39]

Since Williams planned to bring his bride back to Silver City, he was naturally much concerned for her safety in the mining town. None too reassuring was the fact that the Apache Indians had recently resumed their destructive raids in Southwestern New Mexico. Late in August, 1881, they had ambushed and killed a number of white citizens at the head of Gavallan Canyon. The depredations had continued in the Victorio country and the Burro Mountains. Then, in October, they had killed three miners — York, Moon, and Purdy — in the Stein's Peak Range.[40]

Yet, in spite of these incidents, Williams regarded Silver City as relatively safe — as indeed it was in 1881. Although the residents had experienced much trouble from the Indians earlier, the final raid had occurred in February, 1871. It caused the townspeople, chiefly hardened miners, to retaliate with unusual severity. This action taught the Apaches a lesson, and they never again risked a direct attack on the well-armed and determined inhabitants of Silver City.[41]

Even so, the Indians had resumed their depredations in the vicinity. The Apache chief Victorio was especially troublesome during the time that Williams was in New Mexico, although he and his warriors never ventured into Silver City. On September 4, 1881, Williams wrote Miss Wheat that the town was not in danger and that families from the adjoining country were arriving in large numbers, seeking protection from Indian attacks. Thus confident of the safety of the town, the young couple took up residence here shortly after their marriage in Dallas on December 15, 1881.

Before the Williamses came to Silver City, the place had evolved from a mining camp, established in 1870, into a town of some consequence. Located in a charming little valley flanked by rolling hills filled with precious metals, it had been founded to endure. Its buildings were permanent, constructed of brick; it had recently become the county seat of Grant County, and it enjoyed special status under a charter granted by the Territorial Legislature.[42]

Of course the community possessed much wealth — and it enjoyed much culture also. The people were especially proud of their public school, opened in 1874; within a decade, Silver City would become the first independent school district in the Territory. In addition, two institutions of higher learning served the community: the Silver City Institute and the Academy of Our Lady of Lourdes.

Several churches — Catholic, Presbyterian, Methodist and Episcopal — were organized during the first year of the settlement. On May 4, 1880, the Silver City Library Association was incorporated. Lecture programs were provided by the Silver City Lyceum. The Silver City Dramatics Association gave its initial entertainment on January 1, 1878, and the organization continued to function during the Williamses' sojourn in the town.[43] Several good newspapers were published during these early years.[44]

The town government was reasonably efficient, although it had some problems with law enforcement, public health and water supply. As could be expected in any mining community, a rough element was present, but at no time did the outlaws take over and run the community.[45] As mining centers went, Silver City was notably clean, law-abiding and progressive, in spite of its share of "characters," some of whom are described in the following pages.

According to Williams, Silver City was for such persons a City of Refuge. But it was also a haven for Williams himself, who at the time needed a quiet and secure place where he could plan for the future. During his brief residence in Silver City, Williams without doubt welcomed the opportunity to clear away the wreckage of his failures in the mine fields and prepare resolutely for the next chance.

STAGE COACH OF EARLY 1880'S

This coach ran from Silver City to old Georgetown. It was typical of those on which Williams traveled in New Mexico.

SILVER CITY IN LATE 1880'S

Center of town shown in background. Built to endure.

MAIN STREET, SILVER CITY

As Williams knew it. In 1895 two floods swept down the street, destroying the buildings and converting it into the Big Ditch.

OLD COURTHOUSE, SILVER CITY

Williams worked here as deputy district clerk. Also, the case of Oasis Mine v. Last Chance Mine was decided in this building. It stood on the site of the present courthouse.

IN 1881 I was in charge of the post office at Silver City, New Mexico, under Dr. G. W. Bailey, postmaster. The town was then in this peculiar stage of existence: while not strictly cosmopolitan, yet it was composed of many people of different nationalities, and of many Americans of most distinct and marked types and of radically different antecedents. There were some Englishmen, Scotchmen and Frenchmen to whom the burr and the brogue obstinately clung. And there were Welsh and Cornish miners of the ancient Celtic blood, employed in the old Bremen mines above the city.

There were many Mexicans in the town — mostly employed in the lowest kinds of manual labor, and living scantily. Among them strutted as patricians the smugglers. Clad in wide-brimmed, high-pointed and beaded sombreros, and in short, gilded and fringed jackets of fustian, the *contrabandistas* stepped in time to the musical jingle of silver spurs, and apparently held the world in as much contempt as they did the revenue laws of Old Mexico.

The aristocrat of all the Mexican blood there — old Don Nepomuceno Acosta — now and then sedately sauntered to the post office, hoping to receive a letter that might feed his hopes of restoration of the princely gold mine in Old Mexico which had been confiscated in one of the many fruitless revolutions of that turbulent country.

The wide-matted umbrella hats and silk or cotton gowns of the Chinese could be met at any hour on the city streets. When the Southern Pacific Railroad was built through New Mexico by Chinese labor, Silver City caught much of the drift from its labor camps. The coolies especially took over the labor of raising vegetables on the flat below the town, where the springs provided the necessary water. And they were preferred over the Mexicans in most kinds of manual labor.

One day a procession of Chinese, afoot and widely separated, marched downstreet in front of the post office, to the noise of incessant firecrackers. There they halted and began tossing into the air a great number of paper slips, which I found carried the slashes, angles and curves of Chinese hieroglyphics, all very much of the same pattern.

Curious about the meaning of those slips, I called on Sam Lee for an explanation. Sam was an educated Chinaman who wrote in good English script and was a kind of nabob among his Chinese people. He owned a store near the post office. He told me that the paper slips contained prayers to the Chinese deities to return the slip-tossers safely to their Chinese homes with pockets full of money. Soon after this, Sam Lee came into my office with another Chinaman, who, he told me, was to be Sam Lee from that time on. "For," said Sam,"I have sold him my store, my goods and my name." He was going home to China with his "pockets full of money."

I was told that a few years before, Billy the Kid had started his career of outlawry by robbing and pistol-beating a Chinese gardener in the city. He was arrested and put in the old city jail, built of huge pine logs. His place of confinement was a large room with a huge fireplace topped by a small, narrow chimney. Billy, being a small, narrow-bodied person, managed to climb out, and made his way to Globe, Arizona. There he started his major career in crime by killing a man in a saloon. It was believed that he had never returned at any time to Silver City, although his mother and stepfather lived there. I never saw his mother, but his stepfather, whose name was Antrim, called often at the post office for his mail.[46]

Prostitutes in silks and diamonds walked the streets to meet the courteous salutations of the general public. Gamblers were the most aristocratic and distinguished-looking of the restless men who passed up and down the sidewalks; their names always headed a contribution list, whether for public improvements or private charity. When an Army officer came in from the neighboring Fort Bayard,[47] mounted and clad in the gilt and blue of his troop, he was ranked in public estimation as worthy to associate with the gentlemen of the velvet cloth.

At times a silent string of half-naked men would pass into the city in single file. Headed by an American, the men were marked with a red cotton band tied around each copper-colored forehead to show that they were Army scouts. The quick birdlike motions of the heads and the restless glittering eyes told me that they were noting everything — perhaps in anticipation of the time when they would take the warpath under old Geronimo, to rob and plunder in a carnival of bloodshed. For those were the days when the Apaches were leaving a trail of fire and blood as they passed from their fastnesses in the Mogollon Mountains through the Burros to their *rancherías* in the Sierra Madre and then, after a brief rest, back through the Floridas and the Black Range to their nest in the Mogollons.[48]

This tale was told to me in the post office day by day as mail sacks came in from one place and then another — empty, gashed and covered with the blood of some faithful guardian. I could note the march of the Apaches by those silent testimonies of their evil work. But that march was too rapid for soldiers mounted on heavy, grain-fed horses — unused to grass only, and not accustomed to climbing precipitous mountains. So the Government tried to help by hiring Apaches. It supplied them with arms and munitions, which later were to be used against us on occasion by these same Apaches. For the time, though, they were good Indians, and the people on the street gave passage to these mercenaries.

But notable as was the difference in nationalities, greater yet was the contrast in the social history and conditions of the Americans who came to that feverish little city. There were always many prospectors — so called from their habit of hunting mines — who had known nothing for long periods but the gold pan, the pack-mule, and pick and shovel, varied only with brief periods of violent debauch — "oases" that marked epochs in their lives. Many would fall finally under the scalping knife of the Indian in some lonely canyon, perish of thirst in some wide desert or pass away in a drunken dream of a wonderful strike.

But among them were always some adventurous men of action and thought — men who had made their mark somewhere and somehow — possibly for evil, often for good. In the town there were two places where all such men met on common ground: the gambling house and the post office — and before my eyes passed in turn, in front of the little delivery box, most of those characters, rapidly as in a kaleidoscope.

There was George Daly, debonair and high-spirited, who had earned laurels at Leadville, Colorado, as an iron-hearted leader of men fighting for law and order, and in the same fight later at Lake Valley, New Mexico. When the Apaches raided and murdered at Long Mountain, seven miles from Silver City, he was foremost in pursuit, urging on the soldiers; and he finally laid down his life in a reckless lone charge up the walls of a steep canyon against entrenched Apaches. And that heart which had beaten high among his fellows was torn out of his body and eaten by the savages within sight of the soldiers in the valley below, in tribute to his courage.[49]

Then came Du Chaillu, author and traveler, anxious to test his hand against the monster "Silver Tip" of the Gila Bend country, as he had tested it and found it sure and steady against the gorilla and elephant in the Dark Continent. We never heard of any success on his part, but we did hear that he had bought from a professional hunter the hugest grizzly bearskin known in all that country.[50]

And there for a time, in the wake of better men, lived as a sycophant a huge, uncouth monster of a man, with the mouth of a gorilla and the fangs of a wolf, known as "Big Mike" Grace. He boasted that he had gotten in bad while employed as a section boss on a railroad near San Antonio, Texas, and had run away by night. He had come west on the old Overland stage road, and traveled it afoot most of the way to Silver City when the Apaches infested the route. A few years later the hyena trail of this man came to an end in Arizona near the border of Mexico when the same Indians, who had marched through Silver City as Army scouts, murdered him and dismembered that huge bulk.

Now and then came to the city a character known as the "Irish Lord," said to be an expatriate from his native Ireland because of some connection with the Fenian troubles. He would come from his little horse-ranch in Arizona to spend his remittances from the old country among flatterers and to waste the silken courtesy of his manners upon the drunken boors of many nations.[51]

There, too, walked Judge H. C. McComas in the sedate pride of manhood, deadening physically but still wise and ripe in the charms of intellect and experience. It was but a few months later that the light went out of those kindly old eyes in that Burro Mountain canyon where his wife also died under the inhuman hands of the Apaches; and in this same attack, their rosy-cheeked boy, the idol of his old age, disappeared from the light of the white race. The same fate awaited the young lawyer Risque, whose pleasant face and erect form were a pleasure to meet on the city streets, and who had been educated in his profession in St. Louis, Missouri, and Washington, D. C. His life was ended by the same Apache outlaws near the copper mines of Clifton, Arizona.[52]

Some of the city's wanderers came close to me in one relation or another. One day there came to my window Adolphus B. Preston from my boyhood home in Carthage, Hancock County, Illinois. He was Judge McComas' field man in matters of mines and prospecting. And I occupied a room in a building whose owner was born in Michigan and who for some years was captain of a boat on the Great Lakes. The rigors of the winters on those northern waters drove him to Silver City, where his life was probably extended by several years.

My most intimate friend was a soldier of the U. S. Army who served in the city as telegrapher on the transcontinental Army line, under the name of James B. Wallace. But he told me that he was born in New York City under the name of James B. Dye, and that his family had given the name to a street in lower Manhattan Island, running from the Hudson to the East River; further, that his father had been an employee of the religious periodical published in Brooklyn by Henry Ward

Beecher; [53] also that at nineteen years of age he had married a young woman, and three months later, after a bitter quarrel with his wife, he had run away and enlisted in the Army. There he had been trained as a telegrapher and sent to Santa Fe, and later to Silver City.

Many and diverse in race, profession, character and physique were the notable figures who marched in the human procession of that small burg during those feverish days. To one who came from the well-ordered and time-honored organizations of those days, it seems like the hazy, unnatural progression of a dream, or the farce of some carnival of masks. Under the stimulus of that impression, one could hardly meet the most commonplace-looking individuals without the suspicion arising in the mind that this common, placid face was a mask too, and that behind it lay a distorted image, remarkable for some deformity or wearing a livery of some unnatural woe. For this was a City of Refuge.

NOTES

(for PART III)

1 *Diary,* July 25 - Oct. 31, 1880.

2 Bremen's "76" Mine was located about a mile and a half west of Silver City. It actually consisted of four properties — the Bremen, the Backbone, the Chloride and the Victoria mines — connected by shafts, levels and drifts some twelve thousand feet in extent. The combined mine covered about seventy-five acres of surface ground and reached a maximum depth of 198 feet. After failing to sell the mine, Bremen discovered a new vein, the ore from which was assayed at $2,360 a ton. *The Daily New Mexican,* Dec. 14, 1881. Regarding Bremen's mill and his other interests and activities in Silver City, see C. K. Naegle, *The History of Silver City, 1870-1886* (M.A. Thesis, University of New Mexico, 1943), 121-25, 130-32, 177.

3 San Marcial, founded in 1854, was a junction point of the stage line and the railroad. The town is located in Socorro County, five miles off the American Central Highway between Truth or Consequences and San Antonio, New Mexico. The ruins of Fort Craig are nearby. In the early 1880's San Marcial was the scene of much lawlessness. It was almost destroyed by fire on April 19, 1881. After the town had been largely rebuilt, another fire damaged it materially. *The Daily New Mexican,* April 20, Nov. 16, 1881; Jan. 17, Feb. 13, 1883.

4 *Diary,* Nov. 2, 1880 - Feb. 26, 1881. Williams carried a railroad pass which enabled him to travel at minimum expense.

5 *The Daily New Mexican,* Oct. 13, 1881, published a detailed and glowing account of Bremen's exhibit at the Albuquerque Fair.

6 H. H. Bancroft, *History of Arizona and New Mexico* (San Francisco, 1890), 753.

7 Naegle, *History of Silver City,* 177.

8 Jornada del Muerto (Dead Man's Journey) is the desert area in south-central New Mexico lying between the San Andres and Caballo mountains. It is some ninety miles long; it was a serious barrier to early overland travel. In earlier days, those who journeyed along El Camino Real, and later those who followed the Santa Fe Trail, entered this stage of their journey with serious misgivings. J. M. Broaddus, *The Legal Heritage of El Paso* (El Paso, 1963), 21, 39; Alice Wright, "Jornada del Muerto," *New Mexico Magazine* (No. 9, Sept., 1937), XV, 18, 40; Margaret P. Hood, "Jornada Spells Adventure," *ibid.* (No. 9, Sept., 1945), XXIII, 14-15, 39-42.

9 After returning to Shakespeare from his visit to Chicago, Williams made several excursions to the mining fields: Steeple Rock Camp (March 1), Lake Valley (March 22), Hillsboro (March 23), Chloride City (March 26), Apache Tejú (April 2). He also attended to a number of business matters during the first part of 1881. *Diary,* Feb. 28 - June 1, 1881.

10 Contemporary newspaper accounts show that the jails of New Mexico were far from secure, and that officers in charge of prisoners were often careless in guarding them. After six prisoners had picked the locks of the jail at Las Vegas and walked away unhindered, a newspaper reporter said succinctly, "Jails of New Mexico are little more than so many farces." *The Daily New Mexican*, Nov. 13, 1880.

11 The courts of New Mexico were slow to adopt hanging as a legal means of execution. *Ibid.*, Feb. 2, 1881. Many citizens preferred lynching to the relatively slow and uncertain process of trial by jury. *Ibid.*, Feb. 27, 1881; Aug. 29; Sept. 23 and 26, 1882. The fact that New Mexico was infested with outlaws encouraged summary methods against them. *Ibid.*, Sept. 23 and 26, 1882; Jan. 1, 1883. *Thirty-Four*, April 30, July 2, 1879.

12 Central City was a thriving gold-mining town across the road from Fort Bayard, on the route from Silver City to Santa Rita. *Grant County Herald*, Feb. 26, 1881; *The New Southwest and Grant County Herald*, May 28, 1881.

13 Harvey H. Whitehill became sheriff of Grant County in 1875, just as rough and rowdy men began drifting into Silver City and its environs. Fortunately, he was one of the most capable sheriffs in the Southwest. He served eight years, during the height of the mining boom, and did much to maintain law and order in the area. George B. Anderson (ed.), *The History of New Mexico* (Los Angeles, 1907, 2 vols.), II, 722.

14 In spite of Sheriff Whitehill's integrity and fearlessness as a peace officer, he appears to have been negligent in keeping prisoners in custody. A few months after the hanging of Remine, the Grant County grand jury censured Whitehill for permitting the escape of one John Gilmo, indicted for murder. *The New Southwest*, July 30, 1881. Yet, despite this warning, another dangerous prisoner – William Dwenger, who had killed his father in cold blood – easily broke jail some eight months later. *Ibid.*, March 25, 1882. See notes 19 and 22, following.

15 On March 11, 1881, Governor Lew Wallace refused to grant any further extension of the reprieve and authorized Remine's execution on the following Monday, March 14. *Grant County Herald*, March 19, 1881. The original death warrant is in the Secretary of the Territory Papers, State Records Center, Santa Fe.

16 A contemporary account describes Remine as entirely repentant at the time of his death. *Grant County Herald*, March 19, 1881.

17 "The hanging of Richard Remine, last Monday, passed off very quietly. A large crowd was present but there was little or no excitement and no demonstrations. The doomed man was remarkably cool, and except for an occasional nervous twitching of the fingers, gave no outward sign of emotion. He was smoking a cigar as he ascended the scaffold, and this he retained in his possession until Father Stagnon was prepared to administer the last rites of the church . . . he [Remine] stated that during the four years he had been in confinement he had been treated with uniform kindness by Sheriff Whitehill and his deputies. The Sheriff and Deputy Tucker stood upon the scaffold until the drop fell, about a quarter before four o'clock. The body remained hanging some twenty minutes, when life was pronounced extinct." *Ibid.*

18 Sheriff Whitehill identified the woman as Kate Bender, notorious criminal from Kansas. She was arrested shortly after the crime and held in jail at Silver City. *Ibid.*, Oct. 20, 1879. This woman may have been one of several wrongly identified as the notorious Kate Bender, who was actually lynched in Kansas in 1873. See Glenn Shirley, *Toughest of Them All* (Albuquerque, 1953), Chapter IV.

19 The local newspapers used the names Granger, Downger, and Dwenger in referring to this man. His son was known as William Dwenger. *Grant County Herald*, Oct. 20, 1879; March 19, 1881; *The New Southwest*, March 25, 1882.

20 "Silver Plate Dick" was actually William Young, alias "Parson" Young, known locally as a half-witted drifter. *Grant County Herald*, Oct. 20, 1879. According to a Dr. Wood who examined Young for evidence of insanity: "He [Young] said he had met with an accident during the war, in which his head was injured and that [a] silver plate had been put in his skull. I made an examination by moving the hair and searching, but found nothing of it." Secretary of the Territory Papers, Santa Fe.

21 Young was executed, by order of Governor Wallace, on March 25, eleven days after the hanging of Remine.

22 The half-witted son, William Dwenger, was sentenced to life imprisonment, but one day while awaiting transfer to prison he opened the door of his iron cage, located outside the jail at Silver City, and escaped. *The New Southwest*, March 25, 1882.

23 The woman, according to the same account, was sentenced to ten years in prison. *Ibid.*

24 Grant County, *Court Register and Cost Book, 1873-1884*, 215-16, 302.

25 Grant County, *Mining Claims*, I, 597.

26 *Ibid.*, III, 72.

27 *Ibid.*, III, 510.

28 Quoted in *The Lordsburg Liberal*, May 23, 1930. After winning the lawsuit, the owners of the Last Chance Mine sank the shaft 105 feet deeper (from 75 ft. down to 180 ft.) and struck a rich lode of silver. Between 1882 and 1890, the mine produced some $100,000 worth of the metal. W. Lindgren, L. C. Groton and C. H. Gordon, *The Ore Deposits of New Mexico* (Washington, 1910), 334. Records in the possession of Miss Ima Fairly of Lordsburg, N. M., now part owner of the mine, indicate that it operated off and on until 1917. By this time, the shaft had reached a depth of 375 ft. In general, the ore in both the Pyramid and Virginia districts lay well below the surface and beyond the reach of miners equipped only with picks and shovels. The shafts that the early miners sunk around Shakespeare ranged from 10 ft. to 54 ft. in depth. Later, well-equipped mining companies — such as the Superior, the "85," the Atwood and the Henry Clay — went much deeper (as deep as 2,000 ft.) and found minerals, especially copper, in well-paying quantities. On the geological structure around Shakespeare, see E. C. Anderson, *The Metal Resources of New Mexico and Their Economic Features Through 1954* (New Mexico Bureau of Mines and Mineral Resources, Revised Bulletin No. 7, 1947), 87. A detailed description of the mines during Williams' day will be found in *Grant County Herald*, Dec. 13, 1879; Jan. 3, 1880.

29 Letter, O. W. Williams to J. C. Williams, Oct. 16, 1942.

30 Since the location of the mine had been registered in the Clerk's office of Grant County, there appears to be no legal significance in the disappearance of the original location notice.

30a Johnny Ringo (Ringgold?), a dangerous gunman, came to New Mexico from Texas about 1879. He soon established a reputation as a cattle rustler. In 1881 he, along with Curly Bill Brocius, was suspected of killing the Haslett brothers at Hachita, located southeast of Shakespeare. In July, 1882, Ringo was found dead, of gunshot wounds, in Turkey Creek Canyon, Southeastern Arizona. The identity of his killer was never determined. W. M. Raine, *Famous Sheriffs and Western Outlaws* (New York, 1926), 100-101; Ed Bartholomew, *The Biographical Album of Western Gunfighters* (Houston, 1958).

31 Senator William Morris Stewart of Nebraska was born in New York, Aug. 9, 1827. After the discovery of silver in Nevada, he moved west to Virginia City and Carson City and specialized in mining law. He received a fee of $500,000 for successfully defending the interests of the original claimants to the Comstock Lode. After Nevada was admitted to the Union, in 1864, he was elected to the U. S. Senate, where he wrote the Fifteenth Amendment to the Constitution in its final form. Between 1875 and 1887, Stewart devoted his time to the practice of law and to his extensive mining interests. He was again elected to the Senate in 1887 and served continuously until 1905. He was an ardent champion of the silver cause during his years in Congress. Dumas Malone (ed.), *Dictionary of American Biography* (New York, 1936), XVIII, 13-15.

32 The "Irish Lord" had aroused the enmity of the Fenians in Ireland, who threatened him with death. He had taken refuge in the West and was living on remittances from his native country until the danger should blow over. All three defense witnesses who made the rounds with the Irish Lord were addicted to alcohol. O. W. Williams, interview with Mary Ethel Dunn, April 27, 1940. Led by the redoubtable Parnell, the Irish Fenian revolutionaries caused many disturbances and seriously menaced British control of Ireland. The newspapers of New Mexico were full of accounts of the trouble. See, for example, *The Daily New Mexican*, Jan. 1 and 7; Aug. 8 and 17, 1882.

33 Regarding the East Camp at Steeple Rock, see II, note 131.

34 The Knights of the Golden Circle were also known as the Sons of Liberty. This secret society, active in the Midwestern states during the Civil War, opposed the Union cause. For a time, the group gained strength, and some observers feared that it would seriously undermine the Union war effort. Lincoln, for his part, held the organization in contempt. Eventually, in 1864, the arrest of some of its leaders, and the flight of others, broke up the conspiracy. J. F. Rhodes, *History of the United States from the Compromise of 1850 to the Final Restoration of Home Rule in the South in 1877* (New York, 1909; 7 vols.), V, 315-38; C. A. Bridges, "The Knights of the Golden Circle: A Filibustering Fantasy," *The Southwestern Historical Quarterly* (No. 2, 1940), XLIV, 287-302. In addition to practicing law, Amos Green, who came directly from St. Louis, invested in the mines of New Mexico. *Grant County Herald*, Jan. 1, 1880.

35 John P. Risque, a well-known lawyer in Grant County, was killed in the spring of 1882, near Clifton, Arizona. While on the way to visit a mine about seven miles from the town, he and four other men, including Captain Slawson, were suddenly ambushed by Indians. A volley of rifle shots killed Risque, Slawson, and one Triscott immediately. At Risque's funeral, his wife was reported to have suffered near-collapse. *The Daily New Mexican,* May 4, 1882. For fuller details about Risque and his death, see *The New Southwest,* April 29, May 6, 1882.

36 On the death of Judge H. C. McComas, see II, note 96. Judge Bail served one term as mayor of Silver City, in 1887. Naegle, *History of Silver City,* 177. For more about John D. Bail, see Arie Poldervaart, *Black-Robed Justice* (Santa Fe, 1948), 33.

37 "Crosby was the manager of the mine for the defendants and had a habit of getting on a drunk about every three months. When De Lesseps was building the Panama Canal, Crosby was one of the clerical force employed in that country of swamps and mosquitoes. He had contracted what was known as Panama fever, and when a spell of that fever came on him his only cure was to go on a spree." O. W. Williams, interview with Mary Ethel Dunn, April 27, 1940.

38 Details of the attack and escape are given in *The Daily New Mexican,* May 1, 3 and 5, 1881. After his escape, the Kid remained at large for about two months, during which time he continued his depredations. *Ibid.,* May 19 and June 10, 1881. Sheriff Pat Garrett eventually overtook him at the home of Pete Maxwell in Fort Sumner and shot the fugitive to death on July 14. *The New Southwest and Grant County Herald,* July 23, Aug. 20, 1881. See also M. G. Fulton (ed.), *Pat F. Garrett's Authentic Life of Billy the Kid* (New York, 1917), 200-25. See also, C. W. Breihan, *Badmen of the Frontier Days* (New York, 1959), Chapter VII; G. W. Coe, *Frontier Fighter* (Albuquerque, 1934), *passim.*

39 *Diary,* Nov. 29-30; Dec. 1, 1881. These were indeed the final entries. Williams did not keep the *Diary* after his marriage.

40 *Ibid.,* Aug. 20, 22 and 24; Sept. 27 and 28; Oct. 13, 1881.

41 On Feb. 23, 1871, while the citizens of Silver City were enjoying their regular *fandango* (dance), the Apaches slipped silently into town and stole all the horses and mules in the Whitehill corral. This act caused the local militia to take stern measures against the Indians, who never again invited the reprisals that a raid on the town would surely set in motion. Naegle, *History of Silver City,* 71-75.

42 *Ibid.,* Chapter I.

43 *Ibid.,* Chapter IV.

44 The residents of Silver City did not lack for news and editorial opinion. The following newspapers appeared during the early history of the town: *Mining Life, Tribune, Grant County Herald, Silver Record, Daily Southwest, Telegram, Mining Chronicle, Grant County Sentinel, Watch Dog, New Mexico Mining Gazette, Enterprise,* and *Daily Silver Citizen.* Some of these publications were short-lived. Others were merged into longer-lasting publications. Naegle, *History of Silver City,* 156-63.

45 *Ibid.,* Chapter V.

46 On Billy the Kid, see II, note 21. An account of W. H. Antrim will be found in Mary H. Brothers, "The Stepfather of Billy the Kid," *New Mexico Magazine* (No. 10, Oct., 1950), XXVIII, 22, 52-53.

47 Fort Bayard was located some ten miles east of Silver City. It was established in 1866, being garrisoned originally by two companies of the 5th Infantry, one company of the 125th Infantry (Colored) and one troop of the 3rd Cavalry. The number of cavalrymen was increased materially by 1879. The fort was active during Williams' years in New Mexico, primarily to protect the miners around Silver City, but it was abandoned early in 1900. It then became the site of an Army hospital, which was later taken over by the Veterans Administration. Albion Smith, *Southwestern Frontier Army* (unpublished manuscript, El Paso, 1960), 290-91; F. D. Reeve, "The Federal Indian Policy in New Mexico," *New Mexico Historical Review* (No. 3, July, 1938), XIII, 288; Ruth Thurman, "Here's Health," *New Mexico Magazine* (No. 3, March, 1943), XXI, 17-19; Grant Maxwell, "Sentinels on the Frontier," *ibid.* (No. 9, Sept., 1940), XVIII, 13-15, 39-42; Emma M. Muir, "We Lived Under the Forts," *ibid.* (No. 5, May, 1954), XXXII, 26, 48-49.

48 Victorio and his band had been wiped out in October of 1880 in Mexico by Col. Joaquín Terrazas, an event that caused much rejoicing along the Border. *The Daily New Mexican*, Oct. 23 and 30; Dec. 2, 1880. The Apache chief Nana fell heir to the remnants of Victorio's forces. He proceeded to lead a number of raids in Socorro County and its environs, to which Williams here refers. In March, 1883, Chato and Benito, daring and able Apache chiefs, ran amuck, entered the Silver City area, and killed Judge and Mrs. H. C. McComas. There was no further trouble locally until May, 1885, when Geronimo and Nachee went on the warpath. They operated from the Mogollon and Black Range mountains, endangering all settlements within striking distance, until they too were subdued by superior military forces. Geronimo finally surrendered to General N. A. Miles on September 4, 1886. Hodge, *Handbook of American Indians*, I, 491; F. C. Lockwood, *The Apache Indians* (New York, 1938), 256 ff.; Naegle, *History of Silver City*, 102-109. Regarding the problem of the Apaches, see Bertha Blount, "The Apache in the Southwest, 1846-1886," *The Southwestern Historical Quarterly* (No. 1, July, 1919), XXIII, 20-38; Francisco R. Almada, *Diccionario de Historia, Geografía y Biografía Sonorenses* (Chihuahua, n.d.), 68-77. The Mexican version of the campaign against Victorio is given in Joaquín Terrazas, *Memorias* (Cd. Juárez, 1905), *passim;* also, E. G. Flores, *Chihuahua de la Independencia a la Revolución* (México, 1949), 174-79.

49 George Daly was killed in August, 1881, with some eight or ten other white men in a fight with the Indians at the head of Gavallan Canyon. *Diary*, Aug. 20-21, 1881. The preceding year Daly had led in opposing a strike of miners at Leadville. D. L. and J. H. Griswold, *The Carbonate Camp Called Leadville* (Denver, 1951), 181-88, 196-97. For a contemporary account of Daly, his activities and his death, see *The New Southwest and Grant County Herald*, Aug. 27 and Sept. 3, 1881.

50 Paul Belloni du Chaillu (1835-1903), born in France, emigrated to the United States in 1852. Four years later the Philadelphia Academy of Sciences employed him to conduct an extensive scientific expedition through Africa. In 1861, two years after his return to America, he published an account of his journey, *Explorations and Adventures in Equatorial Africa*. Other travels and other books followed, establish-

ing Du Chaillu as an authority on the lands and peoples of the Dark Continent. He next turned his attention to Scandinavia, publishing the *Land of the Midnight Sun* in 1881, and *The Viking Age* in 1889. He wrote nothing of importance regarding the Southwest. Allen Johnson and Dumas Malone (ed.), *Dictionary of American Biography* (New York, 1930), V, 475-76.

51 Regarding the Irish Lord, see note 32 of this chapter.

52 On the death of McComas, see II, note 96. On the death of Risque, see note 35 of this chapter.

53 The religious periodical referred to was apparently *The Christian Union,* founded in 1870. It later became *The Outlook.*

Part IV

Letters and Stories from the Big Bend

ALPINE, 1890

County seat of Brewster County. Formerly known as Murphyville.
Located in foothills of Davis Mountains. Gateway to Big Bend.

FORT DAVIS, 1890

Established in 1854 as post on Lower Route from San Antonio to
El Paso. Located about twenty-five miles northwest of present-day
Alpine. Until 1891, when inactivated, the fort was important in
protecting American settlers in the Big Bend.

LETTERS AND STORIES FROM
THE BIG BEND

FTER HAVING PASSED several uneventful months in Silver City, Williams and his wife returned to Dallas in October, 1882. A short time later, while Mrs. Williams remained at the home of her parents in Dallas, he went on to East Texas. Here he worked during most of 1883 and 1884, identifying and classifying pine lands for his former associate, J. S. Daugherty.[1]

In December, 1884, Williams—again worried about his health—moved to Fort Stockton in arid West Texas, where he had found an opening as deputy surveyor of Pecos County. His wife and their oldest son, O. W., Jr., born in Dallas, April 14, 1883, soon joined him to make this small frontier town their permanent home. In his new position, Williams made several surveys for the county, including Block O.W., a strip four and a half by twenty miles, today the site of several producing oil fields.[2]

On February 6, 1886, Williams was appointed a surveyor and land agent of the University of Texas; he served in this capacity until the middle of October.[3] While thus employed, he discovered that a large tract of public land in El Paso County (in Block L, University lands, near Fabens) had been improperly surveyed and wrongly transferred to individuals. He reported this discrepancy to the Board of Regents of the University, who on receiving his report ordered an investigation.[4] After long delay, the Attorney General of Texas filed suit in the District Court of Travis County for the return of the land.[5] Williams eventually appeared as a witness for the State during the trial, held in November, 1902, and assisted in recovering the property to which the University was legally entitled.[6]

On November 2, 1886, Williams was elected county judge of Pecos County at a salary of $50 a month, plus certain fees. Since the income was insufficient for a livelihood, and since the duties of the office were light, he supplemented his earnings by completing several surveys in the county for private clients. Recognizing the potential value of the land surveyed, he acquired and registered in his name several large tracts, thus initiating a program of investment that would become increasingly important.[7]

Williams was defeated for reelection in 1888. He again turned
to surveying; in addition, he did clerical work at the courthouse
and took on odd jobs. Making a further effort to establish himself financially, he bought the Francis Rooney irrigation project
on the Pecos River. By 1892 he had put into cultivation between
640 and 1,000 acres, chiefly in cotton.[8] But this venture failed,
leaving him deeply in debt.[9]

Fortunately for him, Williams was reelected county judge in
1892, and continued in office for eight years. Both his duties and
his fees of office were now greater. The court dockets for the period
indicate that he presided over a number of civil and criminal
trials of some importance.[10] He also served as probate judge and
as presiding officer of the county commissioners' court, charged
with managing the business affairs of Pecos County. In addition,
he was preoccupied with the bitter feud involving Sheriff A. J.
Royal, which led to the mysterious death of that official.[11]

Meanwhile, during these early years in Fort Stockton, Williams
enjoyed a great deal of leisure time — part of it rest periods prescribed by his doctor. As soon as Williams was firmly settled in
the town, he began to use some of these hours to study and to
write. In 1885 he prepared and submitted to the *Southwest Sentinel* an account of early Grant County, New Mexico, which the
newspaper duly published.[12] In 1899 he completed an article about
the route of Cabeza de Vaca in Texas, which appeared in the
Texas Historical Association Quarterly.[13] During the years between, he wrote several other pieces.[14] He began, at the same
time, to buy books — only a few at first, but more as the years
passed — and to lay the foundation for the best private library in
Pecos County.[15]

Williams was defeated in the election of 1900 and returned
permanently to private life.[16] Lacking other prospects of income,
he once again accepted employment as a surveyor — this time in
the southwestern region of the Big Bend. Since the new assignment would take him far from home and would require much of
his time, he sent his older children to Carthage, Illinois, to live
with their grandparents and to attend school there during 1901
and 1902. This arrangement, while not ideal, proved productive
in a special sense: It prompted Williams to write the letters included in the first part of this chapter, which give a distinctive
picture of the Big Bend country in the early 1900's.

In March, 1900, Williams and two other surveyors were named by the district judge in Brewster County — the large county at the lower extremity of the Big Bend on the border with Mexico — to conduct an official survey. The survey was ordered on behalf of W. W. Turney, a prominent lawyer, rancher and land owner who was seeking to clear the title to his property. The land in dispute was located in the quicksilver-mining district, a short distance west of Terlingua, a town about fourteen miles north of the Santa Elena Canyon of the Rio Grande. Because of the complexity of the lawsuit, it could not be settled immediately.[17]

Meanwhile, toward the end of February, 1901, Williams and T. H. Bomar of El Paso made a survey for Howard E. Perry, the eccentric and astute owner of a fabulous quicksilver mine at Terlingua. The purpose of the project was to establish the true location of Surveys 295 and 296, Block G4, in the heart of the Terlingua mining district. Using the measurements and field notes that the survey by Williams and Bomar provided him, Perry later successfully defended his title in court.[18]

During August, 1901, Williams worked on another survey for the University of Texas. In El Paso County, a change in the course of the Rio Grande south of San Elizario raised some difficult legal issues. Involved was the question of whether this change affected adversely the rights of grantees under the historic grant of 1853. The issues were settled in a lawsuit tried in November, 1902, with Williams appearing as an expert witness.[19]

In December, 1901, Williams joined the Texas State Mineral Survey. This was a group of scientists from the University making a field study of the minerals and the plant and animal life around Marfa and Alpine. The party went into the future oil fields of Pecos and Reeves counties and the mining area of Brewster County. In January, 1902, Williams switched briefly to a party of the United States Geological Survey. This second group was working in the area of the Agua Fria Mountains in Brewster County north of Terlingua and the Chisos Mountains, located in the present-day Big Bend National Park. Early in March, Williams resumed his work for W. W. Turney, who needed additional evidence in the lawsuit that had been under way for two years.

During the last months that Williams spent in the Big Bend, a man destined to assume considerable importance in this narrative — as it turned out — joined the surveyors. This was Natividad Luján, the story-teller, who held forth around the campfire after work each night, and provided the raw materials for Williams' well-known stories of the Big Bend. Natividad was an old, weather-beaten Mexican from the town of San Carlos, across the Rio Grande in Chihuahua. He knew the people of the Big Bend intimately; he was full of the fantasy and folklore that had enriched their lives from the earliest times.

Williams' party was now working west of Terlingua. While in the area, he spent a few days in Lajitas, on the Texas side of the Rio Grande, just above Santa Elena Canyon (Grand Canyon). Then after a brief visit to the mines at Terlingua, he took the stagecoach back to Marfa. By the middle of March, he was in Alpine, and two months later, back in Fort Stockton.

The Big Bend in which Williams worked in 1900-1902 is an immense domain embracing much of the southwestern bulge of Texas. It includes the large counties of Jeff Davis, Presidio, Brewster and Pecos. The area received its name from the bend the Rio Grande makes along the border with Mexico as it flows towards its junction with the Pecos River to the east. It first follows a southeastward course from Porvenir to Santa Elena Canyon and on to Mariscal Canyon. Then it turns northeastward as it moves through Mariscal Canyon; it continues in this direction through Boquillas and Reagan canyons. At Isinglass Canyon, the river again changes its course, now to flow southeasterly. The Big Bend is the area within the loop which the Rio Grande thus describes.

In Williams' day the Big Bend country was largely untamed; it lay beyond the limits of civilization and was inhabited mostly by backward natives of Indian or Mexican descent. Only twenty years earlier, Victorio and his Apaches had harried the area at will, and remnants of the Indian tribes were still at large. A few towns in the north — Fort Davis, Marfa, Alpine and Marathon — formed a line of outposts facing the vast, sparsely settled domain that extended to the Rio Grande. Along the river itself, several villages — Presidio, Redford, Lajitas — served as points of contact between Americans and Mexicans.[20]

In the great stretch of land between the villages of the Rio Grande and the towns to the north, only a few hardy American ranchers had established permanent homes. Land was plentiful and cheap for those tough enough to endure the hardships of Nature — arid climate and soil unfriendly to cultivated plants — plus the dangers of assaults by outlaws from both sides of the river and depredations by natives of the region who rustled cattle and horses.

Geologically, the Big Bend area is unique. Dr. Robert T. Hill, head of the first United States Geological Expedition to explore the area (in 1899), described it strikingly. He characterized the Big Bend as " 'hard country,' that is, one in which, through lack of water, civilization finds it difficult to get a foothold." The country, he continued, "is weird and strange and of a type unfamiliar to the inhabitants of civilized lands. The surface is a peculiar combination of desert plain and volcanic hills and mountains, the proportions of which are increased by the vast distance which the vision here reaches through the crystalline atmosphere. There is no natural feature that can be described in familiar words."[21]

The few travelers who had entered the lower reaches of the region — the area now included in the Big Bend National Park — were commonly impressed with its eeriness, as if it were part of another planet. At that time, much of the territory remained unknown. It had been only broadly surveyed; the government in Washington had just recently begun to take an interest in it.

While on his various surveying trips in the Big Bend, Williams wrote letters regularly to his children back in Carthage, Illinois. The letters, pertinent excerpts of which are printed in this chapter, give many details about the early scientists and surveyors with whom he was associated, as well as much information about the natural history and the people of the area.

Williams paid special attention to the stories of Natividad Luján. He made detailed notes as Natividad told the stories, and later published them in a series of brief pamphlets. The setting of the stories is the country extending from the northern parts of Chihuahua and Coahuila, Mexico, into Brewster and Presidio counties, Texas. These stories, which are included in the second part of this chapter, have found a special place in the folklore of the Southwest.[22]

LETTERS FROM THE OPEN COUNTRY

Terlingua, Texas

February 23, 1901

WE HAVE BEEN a week out with our pack outfits, and I will write something of our experiences. We have carried the chain — or steel tape, rather — from Agua Fria Springs[23] to the mines, a country which Waldo will remember we thought so impassable that we made measurement by triangulation rather than by chaining. This year we have chained it, but I think hardly as correctly as we triangulated; and the going was certainly not so easy or comfortable.

This country is the land of the sotol and lechuguilla.[24] We can truthfully say that the sotol is "monarch of all the country we have surveyed" for the past six or seven days. And we have paid our tribute to this monarch, for our clothes are all frayed and worn; and here and there a piece of skin has been left behind as an offering to the reigning power.

Now, the sotol is not only abundant here, but it grows larger than I have ever seen it anywhere else. You know, the leaf of the sotol is lance-shaped, with teeth on each side of a curving catclaw. It reminds me of the saw of the sawfish or the sword of the swordfish. This leaf lives five or six years before it dies, judging from appearances. But when it dies, it does not drop off and decay like most leaves. It wilts and slowly droops down from an erect to a fallen position. In that state it dries hard.

As the leaves of the sotol drop down from every side, they form a sort of thatched roof, and shed the rain that falls; the dead leaves never decay but remain on the plant, dry and hard, for maybe a century. The plants must live a long time, as there are many here five to seven feet high, with a base of dried leaves larger than a big barrel. So, an old sotol is a collection of fuel that has been growing for many years. On a cold day or night, it makes a magnificent fire to warm by, and it is used by both Mexicans and Anglos for that purpose.

I must give you an idea of our daily routine while working with a packtrain. In many respects it is as Waldo will remember the work with the wagon. But there are some differences. About the first streak of daylight I call "Chapo," our valiant pygmy of a cook. He gets up, and by sunrise has our breakfast ready for us. This is not luxurious fare, as we cannot carry much besides bacon and flour in a packtrain. At breakfast I give directions to the master of the train on where to go to get his water. This water may be two or three miles away from our route. There are no springs near our route. But there are *tinajas*.

Now, a *tinaja* is a peculiarity of this Southwestern country. The rocks of the country are mostly limestone and sandstone in regular strata, occasionally disarranged by a dike of some volcanic rocks or by dipping in different ways, owing to some disturbance at some time. Some of the strata are of very hard rock, with softer rock just below it. In a draw or wash, the hard rock soon forms a dry shelf, owing to the rapid washing away of the softer rock just below it. The water falls over this shelf after a rain and soon forms a deep hollow or hole just below it. This pit, if it is in rock that will hold water, gathers water after a rain, which water may remain there until it dries away by evaporation or is used. This rock pit is a *tinaja*.

Now, the trainmaster takes his burros with the water kegs to the *tinaja*, waters the burros and fills the kegs. He then comes back to camp, loads up the beds and starts after us. He follows us by means of fires (sotol) which we have set to guide him; he catches us by noon, when we have our dinner. After dinner, he gets the same instructions and comes back to us at supper.

After supper the Major[25] and I smoke a pipe or two and tell a yarn or two, at which pastime the Major is a past master. Our men spread out and begin to make bonfires out of the sotols, sometimes having set twenty or thirty on fire at one time. As the flames begin to mount and the green leaves to crack like firecrackers, the Mexicans get enthused and go to singing and shouting. We generally camp in a cave or glen; and the blaze of the burning bushes lighting up the dark walls of the hills, and the sound of the shouts echoing back from the same walls — the combination suggests the idea of some forbidden revelry, such as Rip Van Winkle had with the dwarfs upon the Catskills when they played that great game of ninepins.

Today, however, we have ended our work with the packtrain, and tomorrow we go back to the wagon. I shall be glad of it, as I am tired of the pack and want some of the luxuries of the wagon. We go then to Cigar Springs and will run a line of seven or eight miles, after which we take our road to Alpine. I think that March 1 will see us ready to start for Alpine. I am now at the first post office I have seen in five weeks.

Fort Stockton, Texas

August 4, 1901

I AM EXPECTING to go out with the Mineral Survey, a party sent out by the State of Texas to examine her mineral lands. My party will arrive here the last of this week. They are going out under the auspices of the University of Texas, with Dr. W. B. Phillips, Field Geologist of the University, at their head.[26] They have asked me to join them — on a salary — and I will probably do so. We expect to be out three months. We will examine the oil fields in Pecos and Reeves counties, and the quicksilver mines and black marble granite in Brewster County and possibly other sections.

Respecting a lawsuit in which the University is interested, involving the San Elizario Grant, I will give you the conclusion at which I have arrived. The Legislature of Texas, intending to validate an older Spanish grant of four leagues (17,752 acres) to the inhabitants of San Elizario, in February, 1853, granted them four leagues "more or less." The grant described the tract as beginning on the Rio Grande above San Elizario at its border with the town of Socorro. It extended thence easterly to the foothills on the east bank of the Old River channel, thence down the Old River to the junction with the Rio Grande. From the junction, the boundary ran up the Rio Grande back to the beginning.

Now the present junction (the upper) has been the junction for a long time — so long that the Mexican government claimed title to the land lying below it on the east side of the river bed of 1852. Above this junction there are more than four leagues of land — about twenty thousand acres — obviously included in the San Elizario Grant. The University of Texas claims that the grant did not extend to the lower junction, and thus that the University is entitled to some twenty thousand acres between the two junctions. On the face of the matter, the claim of the University would seem to be just. But my examination leads me to think the claim of the San Elizario people will hold, although they get more than eight and a half leagues instead of four.

The point is this: When the State — or anybody else — makes a deed or grant to certain lands and describes them in two ways: first, by acreage and, second, by metes and bounds — and the two descriptions do not tally — the metes and bounds will always hold, if they can be identified on the ground. Now, the Legislature made this grant in 1852; and whatever can be proven to have been the junction of the two rivers at that time will hold today as the south boundary of that grant.

Well, I find that in 1852 the Rio Grande ran differently than it does now — to the south and west of its present channel. And the people can prove, they say, that the river broke a new channel across to the Old River and made a new junction in 1854 and 1855 — after the grant was made. Consequently, the new junction cannot be the one referred to in the grant; so the San Elizario people will hold all that eight and a half leagues of land.[27]

Marfa, Texas

December 12, 1901

OUR PARTY LEFT Fort Stockton on Saturday the 7th. It was composed of Dr. William B. Phillips, Professor of Field Geology at the University of Texas, Chief of the Mineral Survey; Dr. William M. Wheeler, Professor of Biology in the same school,[28] and myself. Dr. Phillips and I did the cooking until we got to Alpine, where we secured the services of "Chapo" ("Shorty"), the lilliputian cook, who had been *chef de cuisine* for Major Bomar and me on our trip to Terlingua last spring. We carried along the big wagon, the black mules, Rex (our dog) and the three saddle horses, including Waldo's pony.

Dr. Phillips examines the rocks and minerals of the country through which we move. I pass on the question of what lands these minerals are found upon, while Dr. Wheeler examines plants and insects in the country, as our expert on biology. Now, biology includes both the study of vegetable life — botany — and that of animal life — zoology. Dr. Wheeler devotes himself especially to zoology. Dr. W. L. Bray, son of an old acquaintance of your grandfather's living near Burnside, devotes himself to botany.

Dr. Wheeler is a highly educated man. He was a student at Chicago University, studied sea life at a famous school near Woods Hole in Massachusetts and at the Marine Observatory in Naples, Italy, and spent some time studying in Germany. He is not only a good scientist, but I find him also well versed in classics. He knows little about frontier "roughing" and makes some awkward mistakes, although he is always willing to help out all he can. When he gets a moment of leisure, he starts out with a trowel, a bottle of alcohol, a pair of tweezers, and a dozen or so open-mouthed bottles about the size of a cartridge.

Dr. Wheeler hunts up any kind of animal life but pays more attention to insects. He devotes special attention to ants, which are his hobby. In about the first conversation I ever had with him, he asked me if I knew anything or had heard anything of the ant known as the *Myrme-cocystus*.[29] Since I did not know the name, he explained that it is a large ant, somewhat like the red ant in size, with a black head and body, and it has workers, males and bottle-holders. The workers gather honey and sweet juices and carry them into their holes and deposit them in the bodies of the ants called bottle-holders, who serve no other purpose than that of holding these sweets. In the course of time these bottle-holders swell to a large size. He went on to say that in time of scarcity the other ants go to the bottle-holders and feed from them. Finally, he told me that in certain parts of Mexico the natives hunt up these ants, dig out the bottle-holders and butter their bread with them.

This sounded to me like a production of a very imaginative mind; but I remembered that a Mexican (whom I had at once set down as an outrageous liar) had once told me some such story; and besides, I have heard of and found so many extraordinary things in natural history that I am not much surprised at anything. But I had never seen the *Myrmecocystus*, nor had any knowledge of the bottle-holder in this country. The Doctor, however, said he had some hopes of finding it, as he had heard of it as far north as the Rio Grande.

So at every camping place, he sallied out, dug up ant nests with his trowel, picked the ants up with his tweezers, put them in the little bottles, put alcohol in the bottles and stoppered them up for future examination under the microscope. He carried a cartridge belt, and as fast as he filled up a bottle he placed it in his belt. Looking at him from a distance, you would imagine that he was armed for Indians or desperadoes. And possibly the alcohol in his bottles might be as dangerous as powder and ball in a genuine cartridge. Finally, in Paisano Pass,[30] the Doctor was very much delighted to find a nest of what he thought was the *Myrmecocystus*, and he subsequently found elsewhere a number of nests of the same kind of ant. But up to the present time, he has never been able to find a bottle-holder. Still, he never lets up.

We have just gotten to Marfa in a windstorm.[31] It is an exceedingly dusty town, and a windstorm raises a tornado of dust. Yet, we had hardly arrived here, when Dr. Wheeler took his implements of warfare and started out to hunt up his quarry. He is "The Doctor in Search of a Bottle-Holder" and he intends to find it.

Thus, ants are the Doctor's special pets. An old classification that he uses is to call some ants carnivorous: these ants store up spiders, bugs and scraps of meat. Others he calls agricultural: they store up seeds of grasses and pieces of leaves. Now, if he can discover a species or two of ants that have never been discovered and named by scientists, his

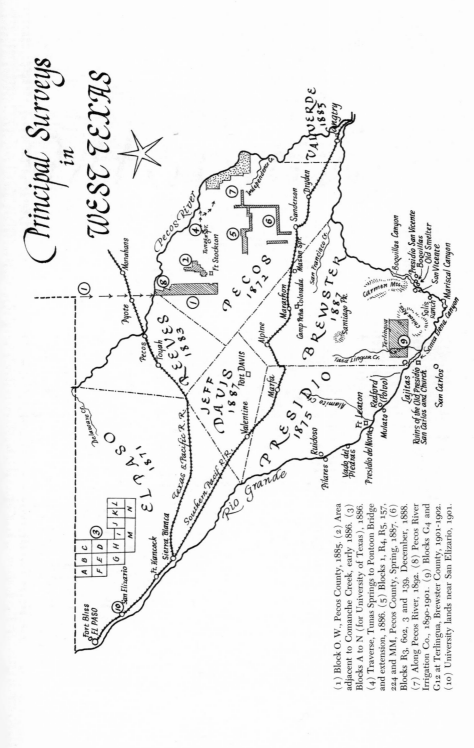

Principal Surveys in WEST TEXAS

(1) Block O. W., Pecos County, 1885. (2) Area adjacent to Comanche Creek, early 1886. (3) Blocks A to N (for University of Texas), 1886. (4) Traverse, Tunas Springs to Pontoon Bridge and extension, 1886. (5) Blocks 1, R4, R5, 157, 224 and MM, Pecos County, Spring, 1887. (6) Blocks R3, 602, 3 and 139, December, 1888. (7) Along Pecos River, 1892. (8) Pecos River Irrigation Co., 1890-1901. (9) Blocks G4 and G12 at Terlingua, Brewster County, 1901-1902. (10) University lands near San Elizario, 1901.

FREIGHT WAGON, ALPINE TO TERLINGUA

Supplies for the Terlingua mines were hauled overland in wagons like this one. Note spare horse behind.

OLD POST OFFICE, TERLINGUA

Williams frequently came here to send and receive letters. Note construction of houses: flagstone and adobe. Roofs were of wood, now mostly removed.

cup of happiness will be full, and he will stand the hardships of the trip without murmur.

There is a party of United States Engineers at work running a line of levels from Marfa to Terlingua.[32] We have not seen them yet, as they were out at work when we got in. We are to work in conjunction with them for probably five or six months. We expect to turn our cook over to them tomorrow while we go on to Terlingua to examine the mines there. We will return from there about January 1, and will go to Austin for two weeks, more or less. Then we will return and work back towards Alpine and the Glass Mountains.[33]

We have had, up to the present, a remarkably mild and open fall. If it should continue, we will not suffer much from cold. This country about Marfa and Alpine, being quite elevated (about five thousand feet above sea level), is at times quite cool on winter nights. But the Terlingua country is one to two thousand feet lower and one hundred miles farther south, and both these things cause it to be warmer.

Terlingua Creek
2 Miles above the Alpine Crossing
January 25, 1902

Mr. McDowell, the river guard, and I left Marfa Tuesday the 21st, on a cool, clear morning. We arrived at the Alamito that evening without incident.[34] On my former trip I had found no fireplace and no bedding in the cabin on the creek. As we carried no blankets except under the saddle, we rather expected trouble at night; but in this we were agreeably disappointed. There was no fireplace, but we found a nice bed with good covers, and we went our way Wednesday morning feeling pretty well. We made thirty-two miles that day along a road with not a house on it. Still, it is a well-traveled road, and we met with a good many freighters carrying goods between Marfa and Terlingua.

We went off the road about a mile and a half into a deep canyon, to a place called Alamo Cesaria, where we found living a man named Rawles and his family. He had lived in Pecos County on Independence Creek, and had some knowledge of me; we fared very nicely. While there, I inquired how the place — which was a bunch of cottonwoods and other trees — happened to bear the peculiar name of Alamo Cesaria and was told one of the many stories which are laid in different localities of this country.

This place in early days had been the home of a band of Apaches, probably of the Mescalero tribe. In a raid into Mexico, they captured and carried away with them a Mexican girl named Cesaria. The Apache band brought her back with them to this place. While unloading and dispersing their plunder here, they tied her to a cottonwood tree (which you know the Mexicans call *álamo*). But friends and relatives of the girl had been quietly but diligently following on the trail, and in a very short time made an attack on the Indians. The Indians were driven away and the girl rescued. So the cottonwood tree, which was easily the king of the little forest around, received the name of "Alamo Cesaria" or Cesaria's cottonwood. In time this name became fastened to the locality around it.

I found at Alamo Cesaria a very thrifty growth of bois d'arc[35] or osage orange trees, about thirty in number. Now, in West Texas I know of but two places where they are found — and only a few at those places. One of these is at Fort Stockton, where we know they were planted by Government soldiers; another is about thirty miles south of Stockton, where there are thirty or forty young trees. When I first saw them sixteen years ago, they were about three feet high and apparently all of about the same age, there being no old ones and no very young ones. They gave me the idea that all had been planted at about the same time. The Old Timers said that the Indians planted them for bows.

Well, the bois d'arc does make a famous bow. The name means "wood for bows" in French. But did the Indians have thrift and business management enough to plant trees and then to wait ten years or more for the bows? In this country the trees grow very slowly, not rapidly as in Illinois. Again, while we know that the Indians carried on considerable intertribal trade, yet this requires us to believe that the trade was much more far-reaching than we have been disposed to believe. The bois d'arc grows wild about Dallas and on the Red River north of Dallas but is not found growing wild very much west of those points. I am familiar with the Pecos River: the tree is not found there.

So if the Indians planted the trees for a purpose, the seed must originally have come from a country at least three hundred miles to the east. This was a long stretch, particularly as the intervening country was inhabited by alien and generally hostile tribes. Again, if the A-paches, so far west, planted the seed for a purpose so absolutely necessary to all Indians, how does it happen that the Indians in the country nearer to the bois d'arc did not plant it? These are reasons which make me skeptical about this story and I am inclined to hold the Mexicans responsible for the theory. I find you cannot place the most implicit faith in Mexican stories.

Since my business requires me to see the country, I decided to leave the road at Rawles' place and cut across the country to the mines.[36] This is an exceedingly rough country, and without trails except in the neighborhood of the quicksilver mines. I thought I could make it, and I did; but the pony and I had a rough time of it before I got in. At one time I thought I should have to camp out by the light of the huge sotols. And it was cool, too. But just after sunset I caught a trail. As the moon rose early and brilliant, I was able to keep going until nine o'clock, when I trotted into the camp exceedingly glad to get under a roof for the night.

The next thing the following day was to find my party. On the way, I heard many conflicting stories about their whereabouts, but finally I recognized the tracks of my mule in the road. I followed them, and at three o'clock in the afternoon I caught up with the party twenty-five miles from the mines. That was Friday, and today we are on the road to the Agua Fria Spring. Our U. S. party is small, consisting only of levelman and rodman. When the levels are finally finished (in two or three weeks probably), then Dr. Phillips and I will have everything to ourselves.

Since I was last in the mines in August, 1900, considerable improvements have been made. There are now probably three hundred men working there in the mines — hauling wood, hauling water, hauling ore or working in the furnaces. Freight wagons pulled by two, five, six or ten mules come in every day. The place is doing a good deal of business; as yet, however, the strata of ore have only been scratched on the surface.[37]

In camp near Agua Fria Mountain

January 30, 1902

I HAVE RECENTLY BEEN with a party running a set of levels for the United States. They have my wagon and team, for they are working under a sort of agreement with Dr. Phillips, by which he turns over to them for a time his entire outfit. We are now running to the Agua Fria Spring. Yesterday I went to the top of Agua Fria Mountain,[38] built a monument for triangulation and set a tablet at its base in solid rock. The mountain is over a mile long at the top. It was a foggy, cool morning, and long before I got there the mist hung about the top. I found snow or ice up there — it was hard to tell which — but there was none on the ground. It was on the west side of bushes and of sotol stalks, and was evidently the condensation on the high warm stalks, of the mist driven by the west wind. It was nearly one and a half inches in thickness. The mountain was quite steep: we found only one place to get up and down, yet in that place I found the tracks of a horse leading nearly to the summit. We scared up an enormous blacktail deer with horns on his head like a small forest. Evidently animals do live there, yet I would not trust a horse of mine there.

It is a sunny, pleasant day today; as I sit here writing I can hear the hum of numerous bees buzzing around our camp and more particularly near our water barrel, where they are sipping. Evidently there is a bee cave in some of the rock bluffs near our camp; if I could only find it, we might have honey for breakfast. The pleasant weather has brought the bees out to get a drink. They are the ordinary black bees which were first brought to this country before apiarists found out the superior value of the Italian bee.[39] They have been wild in North America for perhaps two hundred years and have found their way this far west. Two things are necessary for their wild life — first, plenty of water and, second, a good safe place to build their nests. Pecos County is deficient in these things in most of its territory; so we have no bees there except down in the south part and in the canyons of the Pecos River.

While looking for the bee cave, I found a species of lantana in bloom.[40] I have found only one species of this flower here — a shrub growing to about the size of a red-currant bush. It seems to bloom in the late fall and early winter. It is one of the few shrubs in this country which do not bear a thorn or spine; its protection against animals must lie in its leaves, which must be bitter or unsavory to the taste. It is quite abundant in places here, yet I do not find evidence that any animal feeds on it. The deer browses on many kinds of shrubs but apparently not on the lantana.

Yesterday, on the mountain I found a place where some animal had dug up the lechuguilla and eaten its roots. This may have been a deer, as I have heard that this animal eats the lechuguilla roots. The Indians are said to roast these roots and eat them. An old ranger who was with John Gano when he went through the Grand Canyon of the Rio Grande twenty-one years ago told me that they broke up a camp of Indians just after passing through the canyon. On going up to it, they found that the Indians had been dining on these roots, which they had roasted.

Gano's party tasted some of the roots, but finding them bitter, let them alone, with the remark that they might do for Indians but would not do for white folks. Indians seemed to like some things which do not set well on our stomachs. For instance, roasted grasshoppers were quite a delicacy to them, something like oysters are to us. Indians considered snakes pretty fair eating; and by way of change of diet, they took to lizards when they could catch them.[41]

Yesterday as I went to the mountain on an old Indian trail, I noticed at one place a great number of flint flakes. When I got down and began to examine them, I found them in great profusion and of all kinds and colors, on the brink of a ledge ten or twelve feet above the valley level. Among them I found several broken or incomplete arrowheads, and a tiny white one suitable for a child. Among the loose flakes and small rocks, the earth was very black, and finally I found some charred wood.

Then it dawned on me that this was the site of an old Indian blacksmith shop. The ancient Indians had no metals to work with, and they probably did not know the use of charcoal. Yet, a blacksmith shop it was — such as blacksmith shops were before man learned the use of iron. Here evidently lived one of the Tubal-cains who fashioned arms and utensils before the use of iron was known. The first smith who worked in iron simply made in metal the arms and implements which had before been made in stone and bone, and which in some parts of the world are still made in stone and bone. The smith's trade was here long before iron was known, but it was confined to chipping and fashioning stones and bones. The flint was heated in what served as a forge (perhaps the smith's lungs furnished the bellows) and was then trimmed and chipped in some way not very well understood now.[42]

Neither is it understood how Hannibal blasted a part of his passage over the Alps without powder, although it is said that he did do something of that kind. But the marks on old arrowheads show plainly that they were worked by men skilled in the process. And this was probably the highest art known among the Indians; it was the result of their necessities. So on this ledge of rock was probably located a primordial Indian's workshop or perhaps several of them. To this center the Indians brought flints from many places. In the hunt, when an extra-promising flint was found, it was picked up and brought here to be fashioned by the skilled hand into a weapon of life and death.

Here Indian youths brought especially beautiful flints to be made into articles beautiful and useful, designed as presents for their primeval sweethearts. Here came the father or mother to have made for their children the tiny arrowheads and knives with which the infants were to receive their first lessons in the art of making a living. And here, too, came the old warriors, now almost in the valley of the shadow of death, to have the cunning hand of the smith form for them the mortuary weapons and utensils which were to be buried with them and were even to serve them in the Happy Hunting Ground.

These shops must have been the epitome of savage life. They were the common loafing place where gossip was circulated, and where hunts were arranged and ancestral stories handed down, while the gossipers looked on at the deft hands of the artist as he formed into shape the weapons of their livelihood. There must have been here a Lodge of State where questions of war and statecraft were treated with more solemnity than our Senate discusses such things. The social life of the ancient village must have had its heart in and about such shops as this, for apparently there were no other such gathering places.

In favored localities these shops may have produced, and probably did, more arrowheads than were necessary for that immediate village. If so, then traders went out and exchanged these arms to other tribes for bows, hides, vessels of woven willow and such other things as might serve as savage barter. Then on their return, the village traders naturally disposed of their wares and opinions at the smith's shop. If continued, this process would naturally accumulate in one spot a multitude of flakes and chips and old broken arrowheads, just as about a blacksmith's shop of today we find a lot of iron filings and broken iron scraps — a waste heap that is noticeably large and that may furnish speculation for some 30th-century writer.

In Camp near Chisos Mountains

Brewster County, Texas

February 9, 1902

WE ARE NOW NOT FAR from the western foot of the Chisos Mountains. On Tuesday we expect to get to Gano Springs, which lie at the foot of the Chisos. These springs were named after John T. Gano, surveyor, an old Dallas friend of mine. Now dead, he was the son of General R. M. Gano, an ex-Confederate general, now a preacher in the Christian Church.[43]

We have been having mild but cloudy weather. The cardinal birds have been very much in evidence this week, and are apparently on their way north to their summer habitat. The flowers of some early-blooming plants are beginning to open, but the moisture in the ground at this season of the year is so slight that it will not support growth of the larger flowers.

During this week we have been coming up the bed of a dry creek called Rough Run. It is well named, as the country bordering the creek bed is very much cut up. It is, or was at one time, a country of Cretaceous beds of limestone, lying one above the other as in Pecos County. But when these Chisos beds were deposited, the bottom here was not so deep under the seas as it was in Pecos County. So there are some differences between the beds deposited here and those in Pecos County, though both were laid down at approximately the same time.

For example, the rock is not so firm and hard here. Not being so deep undersea, the deposit was not so purely of lime and seashells. There were some washings from the land mixed up in it (as sand, soil etc.); so it is a looser, shalier rock. Then again, some parts of it were entirely above seawater. In such parts there were swamps where fresh water gave growth to luxuriant grasses, sedges, trees. In time, peat beds were formed at the bottom of these swamps and were finally covered up with the sea again, and a deposit was laid down on top. Still later, the pressure from the deposit caused these peat beds to become coal.

We are camped now near an outcropping of one of these transformed peat beds, and I have dug into it with my prospector's pick. On the outside where it is exposed to the air, the bed is nothing but a lot of finely pulverized dirt of various colors, with occasionally a little shaly rock. The presence of iron in two or three different forms in or near the coal has caused a development of various colors where the carbonic acid in the rainfall, or oxygen in the air, has had a chance to work on it. There are places where oxides have resulted, giving various shades of red to the decomposed dirt. In other places, the presence of sulphur has given a tinge of yellow to the decaying rock—and many other shades of colors result. This all comes from the exposure of the vein. On exposure, the coal itself breaks up into very minute particles so that it shows very little; only after you have dug twenty to fifty feet below the surface do you begin to find coal in the form that we use it.

But the coal of the Cretaceous period is generally not so good as the coal of the older Carboniferous formation. This difference is supposed to be due to the presence of a class of vegetation in Carboniferous times, in larger quantity and of a class better suited to make good coal, than existed in Cretaceous times. According to science, there have been progressive stages of growth on the earth, or at least a series of changing types of vegetation. In Carboniferous times there was apparently little, if any, "hardwood" on earth. The oaks, maples and elms had not evolved then. But the pines were here and so were the palms.

It is largely out of the palms and a family known as club mosses (which must have looked very much like the dagger plant, only larger) that our coals were made in the Carboniferous period. To these must be added sedges like the bulrushes which grow at Fort Stockton. In Cretaceous times the vegetation had somewhat changed, and the change made inferior coal.

While coal was forming here — for how long no man can make any good guess — there was a great disturbance of the earth's surface. Earthquakes came on, breaking the smoothness of the ground. Amid all of this (and probably causing it all), lava broke through to the surface. But not in the way I have always been accustomed to think it came out. I imagined it pouring out of a volcano down on the lower country, running slowly in channels of red-hot melted rock, gradually hardening as it got away from the volcano. Nowadays, we read something like this about Vesuvius or Mauna Loa after an eruption.

Yet, I have never heard of any extinct crater in the Big Bend country. The lava must have poured out here in some few places, as I have seen a few instances of what seems to have been a stream of lava that once flowed over the surface. But no circular vents or extinct pits have been found, while a great many dikes have been discovered; so it seems probable that the lava made its way out in dikes.

Dikes occur in two shapes. First, there is the upright dike. This type seems to have worked up transversely through the strata of rock — at right angles to the surface of the earth. Such a dike must have extended from the surface down to the melted rock below; through it the lava must have flowed up to the top. Forming the other sort of dike, the lava on its way up would sometimes flow out sideways. It would work its way out between two strata, lifting one up or pushing one down and crawling between, very much as if you would imagine a layer of jelly to push its way in between two layers of cake — if you could imagine such a thing. This is called an "intrusive" dike, and we have many such dikes on the Rough Run.

Now, the lava rock is so firm and so solid that water filters through it only with great difficulty. So when a dike crosses the Rough Run we have a spring, or "sipe," of water. The water which has been working its way down the creek bed, hidden deep under gravel and rock, meets the lava and is forced to rise up here and flow over this rock, and as a result we have a spring. Then it sinks again until it meets the next dike, when it has to rise up again.

Wherever we have crossed a dike in coming up this run, there we have found water. There also I have almost invariably found the remains of an old Apache village: numerous fragments of flints — broken arrowheads, broken flint hatchets, broken flint knives, broken fire drills, broken needles. I have found also some very nice whole implements. These places must have been deserted for at least twenty-five years now; yet I find some paved floors, circular in form and almost intact. They were apparently the floors of the tepees in which the Indians lived. The remains are round, about six feet in diameter, and consist of stones nicely fitted to each other, a little higher at the outside than at the center. Over this the lodge poles were set up, tapering to a center; and around the outsides were wrapped the hides or covering. These must have been the more permanent houses of the Indians in their *rancheria* or headquarters. The Indians also had a form of house made by sinking willow poles in the ground, bending them over in a loop and fixing the other end in the ground. A habitation of this kind must have resembled a covered wagon from the bed up. But as I find no flat paved floors in this shape, I conclude that this was not the more permanent form of habitation here. However, the Apaches may have used the willow poles over the round floors instead of letting them taper to a center as was the fashion with the Sioux and others, the former scheme making a mosque-shaped or dome-shaped house.44

In Camp near Peña Spring

February 19, 1902

 We have slowly moved over and around the southwest shoulder of the Chisos Mountains toward the Grand Canyon of the Rio Grande. When I came back from the Terlingua post office last week, I had to pilot the wagon over a divide into the Blue Canyon at the southwest corner of the Chisos, while the levelmen took a shortcut over the divide by a trail known as "Smugglers' Trail." It was a steep trail, difficult to travel; it had been used a number of years ago to smuggle goods over the border. For some time a regular business was carried on over this trail. A Mexican merchant intending to smuggle would order a car of goods to be shipped to him at Marathon or Alpine. The goods would be put up in parcels of a certain size and weight, no matter whether it was muslin, calico, flour or whatever it might be.

These parcels were made up suitable for quick and convenient loading and unloading on mules or burros, for the packages were to be carried across country on pack saddles. The railway car containing the goods would be placed upon a sidetrack at, say, 8:00 o'clock in the evening. The packtrain, which had been somewhere nearby in hiding, would come in after nightfall. The smugglers would unload the car, load the packs, and be ten or fifteen miles on the way before the morning sun revealed an empty car on the siding. Americans of course knew what was going on, but they cared not how much Mexico was cheated of her customs duties.

These smugglers would later take their way on lonely routes not likely to be traveled — making a trail of their own in many places — until they approached the Rio Grande. Then they would hide out near some spring until someone came to them according to previous arrangement and notified them how and where to cross, so as to avoid the Mexican officers. Finally, some moonlit night, the train would take its way, silently crossing the Rio Grande, going up to a hiding place on the Mexican side and waiting there for a suitable opportunity to unload the contrabrand goods at a Mexican dealer's house or store.

This is now a business of the past. Of course, a little smuggling still goes on, but the old days of the wholesale smuggler are over. Mexican officials began to learn of this secret traffic. New and more officers were put on guard; fights between the officials and the smugglers became frequent, and some men were killed. Then, too, treachery became common. Sometimes for a reward, a member of a packtrain would convey to the officers information of the movements of the train, so the officers could capture it. Men supposed to be faithful spies for the smugglers would secretly get word to the officers about the spies' movements, until finally the trade was broken up.[45]

Today, about the only things to remind one of the old days are the occasional sight of a river guard patrolling the river with a loaded gun, and the further infrequent sight of packsaddles and pack animals. For during those days every Mexican in this country received an education in the art of driving pack animals.

While our levelmen were crossing over Smugglers' Trail, I was engaged in carrying the wagon around by some easy route to where we could again catch a road. In doing so, I was puzzled to find in some places what appeared to be a wagon road. But on closer examination, the tracks or trail, or what looked like a wheel track, proved to be of unequal width. It might be six inches wide here, and two inches wide ten feet farther on. Sometimes the parallel tracks would be three feet apart, sometimes five feet. Finally, it was explained to me that these trails were made by Mexicans carrying pine poles out of the Chisos Mountains. For the pitiful sum of $1.75 for each pole, they go up to the summits of the mountains — eight thousand to nine thousand feet high, for they can't find the poles any lower. They proceeded to cut pine poles eighteen to twenty feet long, ten to twelve inches in diameter at the big end, carry or drag them down fifteen miles to where a wagon can get them, and then finally haul them in the wagon fifteen or twenty miles to their destination.

This is cheap labor. Yet the Mexican manages to make a living at it. He will carry up eight or ten burros. He will load each burro with two poles that it can well carry down. His manner of loading and carrying is peculiar — a relic of primeval times. He puts his burros into shafts, so to speak, having a pole fastened on each side. The poles are fastened to a backband that goes over the back. A cinch goes under the breast, from pole to pole. Finally a strap is passed around the neck against the shoulders, and this is fastened to the backband, in order to keep it from slipping back too far. The heavy end of the pole is fastened in this way to the animal, while the little end drags down on the ground. In this manner one man will drive a whole array of burros, each loaded with two poles and leaving a trail behind it somewhat resembling a wagon road. But this method is archaic transportation. It carries one back to the most ancient accounts we have of such things.

I have among my books one in French by a man named Le Page du Pratz, with the title, *History of Louisiana,* printed about 1740. Among the interesting things told, I remember his description of Indians moving their personal effects and plunder from place to place. They had no horses then — or at least exceedingly few. The Indian was not then *facile princeps* at horse stealing, as tribesmen afterwards became — simply because there were no horses convenient to steal. But the Indians had a beast of burden just the same: it was the dog.

When those Indians in French Louisiana changed their place of living, their principal chore was to move a tepee or wigwam. When that was the task at hand, they called up their dogs and fastened two tepee poles to each dog, as the Mexicans here fastened two pine poles to each burro. But the Indian made a slight improvement on the method of the Mexican. The red man fastened a hide from one pole to the other behind the dog, and on this he carried some of his household goods — if he had any. Afterwards, he applied this same method to the horse, when he had such an animal. The old Indian trails in those days must somewhat have resembled a dim wagon trail.

If we can imagine some spirit of an Apache Indian, dead now some four hundred years or more, hovering about some peak of the Chisos and looking down upon our party of Mexicans using burros to drag pine poles down from the mountains, we can well understand the old fellow musing something like this: "Oh, there go some of my people now. See the dogs harnessed to the tepee poles. But what big dogs they are, and what large tepee poles! I suppose that dogs and tepees have grown larger in the four hundred years since my spirit came to the Happy Hunting Ground. But why don't they stretch the hide between the tepee poles? They could carry so many *metates* to grind corn and so many *papooses* that way. But it must be that *papooses* have grown so big in the little four-hundred-year pilgrimage of mine that they cannot get into a *gamusa* stretched between two tepee poles. What wonderful babies they must have now! But can we accommodate them when they get up here in this Happy Hunting Ground, which is already crowded?"[46]

Terlingua Post Office

February 20, 1902

I WAS RAISED in a country where trees of a fair size were not uncommon, and where the prevailing and general hue was green or yellow in spring, summer and fall, and white in winter. The everlasting neuter grays and browns of this arid country, not relieved by any trees, have for many years been monotonous to me. Yet, this dry, drab country charms one in its own way. The air is generally clear, the sunsets gorgeous, and the general scope of view large. But to get at its greatest beauty, it must be looked at through its details, the smallest of which is often the most interesting. Our vegetation is generally a miniature of that thriving in moister climates. Our walnuts, buckeyes, mulberries and persimmons are shrubs, difficult to detect at first glance. The acacias and mimosas are dwarfs. Our only giants in the forests are ocotillos, sotols, allthorns — all strangers to the Eastern floras.

I will leave the Government work tomorrow and go back for a time to surveying, until about April when I join the State Mineral Survey again. I expect to be in Fort Stockton about March 20 for two weeks.

AERIAL VIEW OF SANTA ELENA CANYON

Rio Grande cuts through the Mesa de Anguila, making canyon 16 miles long, 1,500 feet deep, and about 600 feet wide in upper part.

STAGE FROM MARFA TO LAJITAS AND TERLINGUA

Hacks like these were the usual means of travel in the Southwest during the early 1900's. Williams entered and left the Big Bend by this means.

QUICKSILVER MINE AT TERLINGUA

Williams surveyed nearby in 1901-02. All mining was by Mexican hand labor. Most workers received 50¢ to $1.00 a day (10 hours). Silicosis was a common ailment.

Terlingua, Texas

March 7, 1902

I QUIT the Mineral Survey — for a time at least — and went to surveying for Mr. Turney in the county between here and Agua Fria Spring to give evidence in the suit over mining property located in this camp, on which suit I did some work nearly two years ago. The case still hangs undecided in the courts, and may become a *cause celebre*.

I had a rather peculiar surveying party, made up almost entirely of old men and men of varied experience. There was my flagman, Mr. Lowe, born in Mississippi about sixty years ago, who has been prospecting for mines nearly ten years and who owns a number of claims in this mining camp. He was slow, genial, good-humored, and troubled with some kind of kidney trouble which made it advisable for him to drink mescal — so he said! But we carried no mescal with us, and in its place he gathered an herb that grows here and made a tea of it. When freshly gathered, the herb smells like pitch; when the old gentleman had his tea boiling, it gave out a pungent, peculiar smell, like boiling tar; it did not add much to my appetite.

Then there was Mr. King, the cook. He was born in California about forty-seven years ago, of Tennessee parents. He had mined around Silver City, New Mexico, and knew many men there whom I knew. He had ranched in Uvalde County, Texas, and he "went broke" there. Finally he drifted in here. He was active, lively, talkative and jovial, and had followed nearly every calling known in the West. He was a handy all-round man.

Next, there was Mr. Woods of Maine. He came here from Colorado to look after a prominent man's mining property. The man, a Mr. Perry of Portland, Maine,[47] owned a section of land which would have been almost worthless in this country, barren of everything on its surface except rocks, sotols, ocotillos, tasajillos,[48] lechuguillas, and a few other "-illas" — all thorny and all representing pointed and barbed edges and faces. But on this land, or rather under it, there was found some *azogue*, as Mexicans call it — "quicksilver," as we call it. Perry happened to hear of it; so he sent Woods down to see that nobody stole it. Now Woods took a very serious view of his duties and he tried to protect not only the *azogue* under the ground, but also the grass and all "-illas" on top of it.

As no land is fenced here, and as animals are turned loose, you can imagine that Woods had a time of it; and as it was not "good hunting" to run after these animals on foot among all those thorns and barbs, after prayerful consideration he determined to buy a horse to ride. This involved an outlay of $25 to start with — a very serious matter to a Maine man — and a further after-expense for corn. But what troubled him most was the fact that he had never ridden a horse. He had an idea that it was a performance something like taming a lion, for which only a few men were specially fitted by Nature, and he was pretty sure that Nature had not equipped him very well in that line. And he was right. Woods and his horse became a subject for camp humor for quite a time, and I have heard several good stories about them. I will give you one.

Woods established his camp on the land he was guarding. Across this land ran a number of roads, headed for all points of the compass. Now, Woods, when he wished to ride anywhere, would lead his horse to the particular spot from which he wished to go, face him in the right direction, then (after infinite patience and perseverance) he would get on and start the horse at whatever pace the animal saw fit to take. But one of these starts did not prove a success.

One day a Mrs. Cartwright, who lived with her family about six miles away from the mines on a road which crossed over the land Woods was guarding, looked up the road towards the mines. She saw a man on horseback coming down the road towards her place at an exceedingly slow and terrapin-like gait. After quite a time he got to her place, and she saw that it was Woods and his horse. She invited him to get down. He thanked her but said he was afraid that if he did so, he could not get up again. However, he said, if she would loan him one of her boys to turn the horse around, he would be very much obliged. He went on to explain that he had intended to ride the other way, but that after he had faced the horse on the right course, the horse had turned around while he was mounting and had started the wrong way, and that this was the first chance he had had to turn him the other way.

The Cartwright boy turned the horse around and started the pair back. Late that afternoon, a Mexican with a burro met the two on a road the other side of Woods' place. Heeding signs which Woods made, the Mexican stopped the horse. Then Woods took the reins in his hands and started off leading the horse — and, it is supposed, reached home safely after an exciting day's experience. He carried his horse with him on the trip with us, but as his duties compelled him to go afoot, he had very little chance to display his horsemanship. The horse was fat and impudent-looking, if I can properly use such an expression about an animal. I managed, however, to get a little of the fat and impudence out of him in a way I will shortly relate.

Then, there was Andrew Kennedy, the darky — one of my chainmen. He had been a chainman for John T. Gano on this land about twenty-seven years ago.[49] Andrew had been living for some years in El Paso, driving a cart, and had become old, pretty fat and quite lazy. He had been sent down by Turney's lawyers to identify some old landmarks, and I was instructed to use him any way I could. So I made a kind of chainman of him — no little to the discontent of the head chainman, who claimed that he had to drag not only the chain but also the darky at the end of it.

When we got into camp, I borrowed Woods' horse for Andrew to ride. I took Andrew off with me, telling him we would go to Agua Fria Spring — about six miles away — in order that he might identify certain places. I intended to carry him much farther; in fact, I carried him about twenty-five miles in all — but I did not tell him anything of that in advance. We rode across the country, seldom finding any trail — and it is a very rough country. We climbed mountains that the Negro declared a horse could not possibly go up. The result was that Andrew began to get used up pretty soon, and from his groans and lamentations you would think he had a dangerous case of colic.

But we kept on going, Andrew praying and swearing alternately. Night struck us six miles from camp — no moonlight, no trail, and very rugged mountains between us and home. I was afraid to tell Andrew how far away we were, for he might have camped right there by the light of a sotol. So I kept encouraging him, telling him we were almost there. This led him after a time to suspect that I was lost, and then his lamentations became loud.

Finally, as we were moving along in the dark, my horse refused to go any farther. I got down to see what was the matter — and found that we were on the brink of a rocky precipice a hundred feet high. I knew where we were, for it was the place I was heading for. Right under us were a *tinaja* and a tent, which I could make out by a sort of milky appearance in the darkness. But Andrew was panic-struck when I told him of the precipice in front, and I could hardly keep him from running back in the darkness.

I said to him, "Andrew, can you holler?" — "Yes, Boss." — "Can you holler real loud?" — "I kin, Boss, I feel mightily like it right now." — "Well," said I, "Andrew, if you will holler right loud now, somebody might hear us and we will get out." Now, just such a roar as Andrew let out then — you never heard anything but a lion to equal it. In an instant the answer came back, right from under our feet. "Thank the Lord, Boss," said Andrew most fervently.

We were a mile and a half from our camp, but there was a trail leading almost directly to our place, and we went in without any further trouble. After we got in and he had a chance to examine his injuries, Andrew told me confidentially that there were blisters two inches "acrost" inside the seat of his pants. I suspect it was true, for he got a lot of grease to use for some purpose shortly afterwards.

Woods' horse? Well, King told me next day that we must have used that horse pretty bad, for he looked like he had been put through a sausage grinder. But Woods didn't notice it. In fact, he complimented himself as having brought the horse along, for he said that the horse "had gotten so much tamer and gentler since he had associated out in camp with men and a lot of gentle animals." I suppose he still thinks this, for I never tried to give any other explanation of the horse's unexpected gentleness.

Then there was old Emilio Benaventes, a Mexican born in the state of Durango, and carried off a captive by the Comanches when he was ten or twelve years old. He was kept among the Comanches two or three years while they lived near the head of the Red River in the western part of Indian Territory. He was finally ransomed by a Captain Jeffries (as near I can make out the name), who took the Mexican boy to Seguin, Texas, where he remained twelve or fifteen years. Then he worked for a time with T. F. Hock on a cattle ranch near the Pontoon Bridge on the Pecos River. He is about sixty years of age.

Finally, there was old Natividad Luján. He said he thought he was about sixty or seventy years of age but did not know exactly. He told me that his brother, seven years older than he, was a younger man. I asked how he made that out. His reply was that his brother was not so gray as he was. Natividad was born at San Carlos, the Mexican town across the Rio Grande from here, and had lived there most of his life. He knew a great deal about Indians, as any man who had lived at San Carlos needs must; for that town was for fifty or a hundred years a point of contact between Mexicans and Indians, more particularly Comanche and Apache Indians. At last, according to his story, life became too hot in Mexico for him, owing to an unrighteous grudge against him on the part of an influential Mexican, and he had to transfer his scene of action to Texas.[50]

Alpine, Texas

March 16, 1902

WHILE I WAS WAITING two days for the stage to start for Marfa, I decided to go down to Lajitas on the Rio Grande, eight miles southwest of the post office at Terlingua. I wished to examine a place where a number of skeletons had been found nearly two years ago. I had seen six skulls that were taken from that place, exhibited over the mantlepiece in the office of the Marfa and Mariposa Company as a cheerful welcome to visitors. Some people imagined the bones to be those of Spaniards killed by Indians and thrown into a cave. Such a practice of course would have been contrary to Indian custom, as Indians leave their dead to the elements and the wild animals.[51] Then there was another theory that there had been an Indian battle here; and there were other theories that were much more fanciful.

I had a very strong suspicion that this was an Apache graveyard. I have examined many Apache graves, and I thought I recognized many things that indicated this one to be of that class. So I went to verify my suspicions if I could. On my way down, I passed a small spring known as Comanche Springs. Near this spring there were a number of red paintings on the face of a limestone ledge. One represented a buffalo, with the curl of the tail peculiar to any angry buffalo. The painting was exceedingly well done and immediately recognizable by anyone who has ever seen at close range that animal when enraged. The balance of the figure was oval and blurred so as to be indistinct, but the tail "told the tale at once."

Now, the Apaches did not live in buffalo country: the buffalo, I am satisfied, rarely ranged west of the Pecos. But the Comanches were emphatically a buffalo tribe. So it seems to me probable that this was a Comanche pictograph and meant to convey some idea about a Comanche chief named "Buffalo Tail." Near it were quite a number of red dots side by side, meant to convey the idea, possibly, of the number of men with him, or possibly the number of days he had been on the road to this place. There were various other pictographs on the rocks, but this one will illustrate all.

Passing the Comanche Spring, after some three miles or more I caught sight of a flag glistening and shimmering in the afternoon sun. Then I knew that Lajitas was near. For it is a customs town, and the U. S. flag is as regularly run up at dawn and hauled down at sunset over a customs office as it is at any frontier Army fort. I soon rode up in front of the office, which stood on a high but level-topped bluff of gravel on the brink of the Rio Grande.

A store, a saloon and a few adobe houses made up the town; the customs office with its colorful banner flying was the center of interest. I had known the Deputy Collector of Customs (in charge), Mr. Wark, for some twelve or fifteen years; he received me quite cordially. The River Guards were here also, and I met my former companion on the road from Marfa to the mines, young McDowell, the River Guard.[52] I also met his brother, who has recently been appointed captain of the River Guards from Presidio to Eagle Pass. I found him a pleasant gentleman.

From Wark and the McDowell brothers I learned that the Indian bone-cave was located about a mile and a quarter from town. As it was then about 4:00 o'clock in the afternoon, I set out immediately to examine the cave before sunset. I was told that I would find Bill Taylor camped near the spot, and that he would show it to me. Now, I had no acquaintance with Bill, but I was aware that he was known in this country as "Lying Bill"; I had some misgivings on the subject as I rode up to his *jacal* and inquired of his Mexican wife if Bill was "at home" to me. "*Sí, Señor,*" she said, and called him out. Well, to cut matters short, I found Bill as "mild-mannered a man as ever scuttled a ship or cut a throat." He went with me to the cave, showed it to me, told me how it was found and what was found in it. If he told me any lie, it was not a very big one.

The cave is in the side of a mountain, looking down on the small cove or valley in which Lajitas is situated. It is not very high on the mountainside, probably not over seventy-five feet above the valley level. It is oval-shaped, dips into the mountain almost perpendicularly, is about eight feet deep and six feet in diameter. It reminds me in shape of one of those Mexican water *ollas*. You might fancy that an enormous *olla* had been jammed into the mountainside at a slight angle from the perpendicular and left there.[53]

The cave had been filled with a fine loose dirt, together with some fairly large rocks of ten- to twenty-pound weight. It was hollowed out in limestone rock and had been made by the wearing away of a weak spot in the rock by exposures to air and moisture. The Indians had evidently used it for sepulture. The cave had been excavated, and numerous splinters and fragments of arm and leg bones lay around where they had been thrown aside during excavation.

There were no skulls left, but Bill Taylor informed me that twenty-seven skulls had been taken out of the cave and carried away. The bones were very light and dry, having lost substance until a sort of reticulation or network could be distinguished in them. Bill said that four other skeletons had been found on a ledge about a hundred yards away where, he explained, there was an ancient fortification, giving evidence of a fight. He then went on to outline to me his theory of an ancient massacre of one Indian people by another coming down on the victims from the high mountain. I did not presume to contradict such a man.

But I did lay away back in my mind a good-sized grain of doubt. This rocky ledge projects out into the valley above Lajitas from the high mountains like the ram of a warship, and it offers the ideal location for an Apache burying ground. The opened graves lay along the center of the crest — four in number; and they were all more or less caves. I examined the ledge and came to the conclusion that I recognized six or eight more graves, but I had no time to open them. What Bill called a fortification was a pile of rocks about two feet high, built semicircularly around one of the graves. A portion of this wall had fallen. The wall itself was ancient, the rocks on top being weather-stained to the same degree as the solid rock in place nearby. But I did not consider it a fortification. I thought it simply a part of the external work around a grave.

Evidently these graves are ancient. The Mexicans at San Carlos, Mexico, twelve miles distant, a town dealing more or less with these Indians for at least a hundred years, have no knowledge and no tradition about this place, so Bill says. Then, too, the "fortification" shows from its weather stain that it has been undisturbed for many, many years. In the graves were found the customary arrowheads of stone, a spear head of flint, but no metals. Now, an Apache was usually buried with his customary implements of war and the chase; whether they were of iron or flint or bone — no matter what — in they went. So these early people had not yet procured iron or beads from the whites, and were still in the Stone Age.

How close to the present day the manufacture and use of these flint implements remained among the Apaches, I have been unable to learn. But old Luján says that his people in San Carlos, as far as he can remember, did not know the Apaches of the flint implements. Fifty years ago he was shot by an Apache arrow, the shaft being of *membrillo* (quince wood) but the head of iron. And he says that his people always spoke of *La Gente Antigua* ("The Ancient People") as the Cholomos, the people of the "Pedernales" — people of the "Flints." What "Cholomos" means he did not know, nor have I been able to find the term used anywhere; I do not find it in any dictionary or in any book. I suppose it to have been a tribal name, possibly applied to them by some other tribes, and long ago out of use.[54]

When I got back to town, supper was ready. I ate as the guest of the Deputy Collector and the River Guards. A Mexican dance, a *baile*, was held that night and it was the principal topic of conversation. However, I did not attend.

The next morning early I went back to the mines. On the following morning I left on the stage for Marfa, carrying the Negro, Andrew Kennedy, along with me. We had a windy, cold and stormy trip, camping out on the road that night and getting to Marfa in a furious dust storm in the evening of the 11th. There I received a letter from Dr. Wheeler which will amuse you.

The Doctor, you will remember, is a great ant collector. He sent me sometime back a lot of small bottles filled with alcohol and a pair of tweezers, and asked me to collect some ants for him if I got the opportunity. Well, I filled his bottles and sent them back to him. Now it seems that I sent him some kinds of ants called *Pheidoles* which had not been found and classified before. There are two entirely new species and they have to be named. So the Doctor wrote me that with my permission he would name one of the species after me; he asked me to take my choice, the blonde or the brunette.

My father had a good many children named after him; I have had very few. But I will go him one better when I get an entire species of ants named after me. Some of his namesakes have been rather lazy and trifling and have not reflected much credit on the name, but I shall not have any uneasiness of this kind about mine.[55]

For Stockton, Texas

May 25, 1902

THIS LETTER CONCERNS my recent trip to San Carlos, Mexico. I found while at Terlingua that I could spare two or three days for the visit; so on the 15th of May, I drove down to Lajitas on the Rio Grande, about ten miles from Terlingua and just above where the river enters the Grand Canyon. I arrived in time for supper and was invited by Mr. Wark, the Deputy Collector at that place, to put up with him for the night. Mr. Wark had just hauled down his customhouse flag when we heard four or five shots. Looking down the line of Mexican houses towards the place from which the sound came, we saw a small bonfire and what appeared to be six or eight Chinese lanterns.

"Ah, some saint's day," said Mr. Wark. "I wonder what saint it is." Well, as I could not tell him, we asked a Mexican, who informed us that it was the day of "San Ysidro de los Labradores" — San Ysidro of the Farmers. Now, I had been farming on the Pecos, and I remembered the saint; for my Mexican tenants had told me all about him, and had tried several times to celebrate in his honor on my ranch.

San Ysidro was supposed to be the farmers' friend, and if properly propitiated would surely send rain on or about May 15th every year. The Mexicans had told me of some customs down in Mexico, used to set the saint in good humor. Among these customs I remember one — of a procession headed by a two-wheel wagon drawn by two white bulls. This procession reminded me of a similar one in use among the pagan Romans; and, in fact, I suspected the celebration of being a survival of some pagan custom.

But the ceremonies at Lajitas were not so elaborate. The shots fired in the air, the bonfire, the Chinese lanterns, and sundry potations of mescal or sotol completed the list. The lanterns were unique to me. A common paper bag such as you may see in any grocery store was procured; the bottom was filled with sand to make the bag bulge out evenly on each side; then a tallow candle was lit and set in the center of the bag — and behold, you had a Chinese lantern. Such lanterns (*faroles* or *luminarias*) are used on traditional festive occasions all along the Rio Grande.

But no rain came that night nor for several days after; so there was something lacking in the honors given San Ysidro. I judge from the remarks of the Mexicans next day that they gravely suspected they had not drunk enough mescal.

The next morning I began looking for a saddle horse to carry me to San Carlos, for there is no wagon trail from the river to that place. I was going over the old trail used by the Comanches fifty years ago, and I understood it was nothing but a bridle path over a country quite rough in some places. After some searching, I located an old Mexican who agreed to lend me his horse to ride on this journey. After dinner, I saddled the horse and crossed the river to a trail, which was pointed out to me, on the Mexican side.

The trail proved to be tolerably plain, and I had no difficulty in following it. It led over a rough country — over boulders and rocky pebbles all the way to San Carlos. On the way down, my horse was always slipping, sliding and lurching on those round pebblestones. I never saw so many round pebbles, apparently waterworn, anywhere except in the beds of creeks and rivers. Yet here they lay in the high lands as well as the low — on the crests of mountains as well as in the hollows of valleys. A question was always in my mind. How were these apparently water-worn boulders and pebbles strewn over the country in this fashion? I met nobody on the path, but saw three *Rurales* (Mounted Police) leaving it about halfway on my journey.

About 6:00 o'clock I came to a *hacienda* near the crest of the mountains. Nature made it a beautiful spot, and man had done a little to help out. The ranch house was built in a grove of trees. When I rode up to it. I was delighted to find a nice orchard. There were apples, pears and peaches, but what most attracted my attention was a row of pomegranate trees — about fifteen in number next to the house, their rounded mass of green leaves set off with those large red cup-shaped blooms, with an occasional small fruit showing up from the more mature blossoms. The trees had an elegant outline, bushy and rounded, about six feet high and uniform in shape. The fruit I have never tasted.

This ranch bore the name of "Matadero" ("Place of Killing") and, I was told, got its name from frequent killings there forty of fifty years ago when the Comanches and Apaches warred against each other and against the white men. It is not a dulcet name but very suggestive.

Here I inquired the distance to San Carlos and was informed that it was *cerquita* ("nearby"). As a matter of fact, it was six or eight miles. It has always been difficult for me when traveling to get any definite idea from a Mexican of any distance ahead. In Mexico, when one does finally get something of a definite estimate of distance from a Mexican, it is sure to be in leagues, not in miles; and it is about as sure to be anywhere from 50 to 150 per cent in error.

But I trotted on, pretty sure that San Carlos was not *cerquita* and that I must hurry my horse up, to get there before nightfall. It was dark and my horse was about fagged out, when the trail dropped from a hill of boulders into a deep wash where I heard the sound of falling water. Ahead of me on the other side of the wash, skylighted on top of a hill, evidently lay the town. Yet, not a light was visible, and I could only occasionally hear the bark of a cur. When I rode up to the top of that hill, I was in the town. I found two streets running parallel to the wash, and going down one of them I soon found a store open.

I got down from my horse, went into the store, and in the best Spanish I could command I asked the proprietor if there was a hotel or restaurant in the town, as I was a stranger and wanted to stay all night. In better English, the man informed me that there was no hotel or restaurant in the town but that I could put up with him while in town. I was only too glad to do so. He was Don Fermín Flotte, owner of the

Matadero Ranch, an old frontiersman of mixed blood. His grandfather McKnight went from St. Louis to Chihuahua in about 1810, there marrying a Spanish woman. McKnight's daughter married a Dr. Flotte from Cincinnati, evidently of Pennsylvania Dutch blood, and she was Don Fermín's mother. Don Fermín himself married a daughter of John Spencer, from Presidio del Norte; so you see the whole family had American blood.[56]

Don Fermín invited me to sit down, then called a Mexican servant and told him to take my horse and feed it. A moment later I heard a door open in a room adjoining the store; a Mexican seemed to be persuading a horse to enter, which the beast finally did. When later I heard a burro ushered through the same way, I decided that the only entrance to the stable or horse lot was through the sitting room. This seemed a little odd to me, but I presume was a result of the days when Indians and thieves were so abundant that every man locked up his animals at nightfall.

But what seemed more strange yet was the method of carrying water to the houses. For the burro that I have mentioned was a water carrier, bringing the daily supply of water to the Flotte household. Across his back was laid a very large pair of canvas sacks, resembling immense saddlebags. The water was carried in equal quantity on each side in the heavy pockets of ducking. This was peculiar enough, but the method of letting the water out when delivering it was stranger yet.

Any hole at the bottom that could be corked up at will would do, and the device for a stopper was a "corker."[57] There was a round hole cut at the bottom in one corner of the pocket. Now, the point was to put a stopper in that. What do you suppose they put there? Why, they put a cow's horn — pointed end out. The pressure of the water on the inside always forced the horn out as far as it would go, thus stopping the flow of water through the round hole. When they wanted to let the water out, they caught the cow's horn on the outside and pushed it in, thus letting the water out into the bucket quickly.

You have only to go a short distance from a 19th-century railroad to find customs and appliances that remind one of those we read about in the Bible. I imagine that some of the skins used to carry water and wine, about which we read in that Book, must have had horn stoppers such as the San Carlos Mexicans now use.

SANTIAGO PEAK

AFTER A LONG CLIMB through artemisias, fouquierias, yuccas and other thorny plants of thorn-infested country,[58] we arrived late in the after-noon at the summit of the hill towards which our burros had all day been headed. As the burros were stopped to gain a breathing spell, I looked around me at the extensive view. It was a goodly sight, for on three sides of me the peaks and mountains of two thousand square miles of territory were visible.

To the south could be seen a crevice in the gigantic wall of limestone, out of which crept the Rio Grande, trembling as if it had been doing penance in its tortuous long and dark course through the Grand Canyon.[59] To the east the circled tips of the Chisos (Ghost) Mountains[60] glistened in the western sun like the pearly points of a coronet. Sixty miles away to the north stood up the square, mesa-like top of Santiago Peak,[61] towering among the plains and smaller hills around it like Saul among his brethren. I had often fancied that it was a relic of the Cretaceous Age,[62] eroded by untold centuries of sun and storm from a large mesa to a narrow, flat-topped peak, and left on guard among the convulsions of nature, like the Roman sentinel at Pompeii. I had imagined that the very name must have come from some adventurous Hidalgo[63] of the old times, when the Spaniards carried their lances and morions to the ends of the wilderness in search of the fabulous El Dorado.[64]

So I turned to our guide and said to him, "Natividad, how does yonder peak get the name of Santiago Peak?" Now, Natividad had a face in color and texture like his deerskin jacket. The wind and sun for sixty years had been hardening and tanning and dressing its surface until by no possibility could any passion throw the red blood to the outer part of the epidermis. And of man's usual facial expression, there were left to him only a pair of keen black eyes under shaggy eyebrows and some archaic wrinkles about the mouth, which showed feebly when he attempted to laugh. But it seemed to me that Nature, by way of compensation, had given to his crown of red hair a sort of limited expression, and that it grew deeper or lighter according to the various emotions that might move the soul inside that leathern mask.

And now at this question, the eyes flashed, the archaic wrinkles deepened, and even his poll seemed to flush a deeper red as he replied,

"*Señor*, that peak was named after my uncle." Pride was plainly audible in his voice, and one might have thought from his manner that he considered the peak to owe its notoriety and possibly even its dimensions to the fact that it was named for his uncle. It was patent that one of Natividad's stories lay ahead of me; so I said to him, "Very well, as soon as we get into camp, you shall tell it to me."

The jaded burros were set in motion along the trail down the hill, and soon we were setting up our night camp in a diminutive park near the customary *tinaja*.[65] When supper had been disposed of, the beds made down and the sotol torches lit,[66] Natividad, with a good deal of importance, made up an unusually large cigarette and proceeded thus with his story:

"*Señor*, my uncle Santiago was a great man of war when he lived in Presidio del Norte[67] some fifty years ago. When the Indians raided, or killed any of the *norteños* — as we call the people of Presidio del Norte — it was my uncle who must lead in the pursuit. He had led the chase after Apaches into their *rancherías* near where Fort Davis now stands,[68] and had fought the Comanches on their retreats into the Staked Plains.[69] So when the Indians came in the dead of night and took away the horses of Gregorio Jiménez from the corral at his very door, it was to my uncle that Gregorio went for help to trail the thieves. My uncle gathered five men, and with Gregorio took up the pursuit.

"The trail led to the east, and it was at first thought that the Indians must be Apaches from the Chisos Mountains. But on the second day it turned to the north, and began to point towards the great peak that afterwards bore my uncle's name. By this time they had learned from the signs around the campfires that it was a small party, and they pushed on with the pursuit rapidly. On the evening of the fourth day, when almost under the shadow of the peak, the signs were plain that they were close upon the Indians; so they camped early and sent out two scouts who located the Indians' camp about dark.

"Very early the next morning my uncle and his men saddled up their horses and rode until the scouts of the evening before warned them that they were very near the Indian camp. Here they got down, tied their horses and took their way on foot silently and cautiously. Light was breaking in the east, and by it they saw a small column of smoke from the Indian campfire, and also made out a small *caballada*[70] on a hill about a mile to the east. Very quietly they slipped up an *arroyo* and soon got where they could see six Indians eating a breakfast of horsemeat.

"At a word from my uncle, the *norteños* fired upon them and killed three of the Indians. The others ran away. My uncle did not follow them, for he was an old Indian fighter and knew that his men must get back to their horses. As his party started back, they heard a shot and the yell of an Indian from the hill to the east where they had seen the *caballada,* and at times they could see a mounted Indian riding furiously from there towards them. They had barely mounted their horses when this Indian came riding at them, yelling and shooting, followed at a short distance by three more on foot. By his actions he showed that he meant to kill or be killed. Now, the *norteños* are not bred to this kind of fighting; so they began to ride away — all except my uncle, who was shooting at the charging Indian.

"All at once my uncle fell from his horse, shot through the hips and at the mercy of the Indian. As the Indian rode up to give my uncle his death-wound, the *norteños* heard him call out in good Spanish, 'Santiago,' (for he must have known my uncle) 'why do you cry, when you have killed three of our side, while you have lost only one of your own?' With that, he killed my uncle, and then rode away with the other Indians, and the *norteños* never saw them again. And I feel it necessary to explain to you, *Señor,* that the Indian did not put the matter about my uncle fairly. For my uncle did not cry only because one of his side was killed, but rather because he had to be that one.

"So the *norteños* buried him there, and put up over him a great pile of stones, and called the peak by his name. And whenever I go by that pile of stones, I pick up another and add to it, saying as I do so, 'Do you still weep — *Tío Mío* (Uncle Mine) — for that one of your side who was lost in the fight?' And always the mockingbird calls out to me from the bushes nearby — and nothing else. But how am I to know what the bird says? Only, the priest says that my uncle has long since ceased to weep, as his soul is among the blessed who have died for the Faith among the heathen. And surely the holy father knows, for did not Gregorio Jiménez pay him to say masses for the soul of Santiago in Purgatory? And did not I — more than twenty years afterwards — pay the *padre* again to say more masses? For Gregorio was a poor man, and I feared he had not paid the father enough to get my uncle's soul entirely out. If the father does not know, who does?"

MESCAL

THE SUN HAD BEEN shining bright and warm all that February day, but it was now about to go down behind the ragged peaks that hang over the Fresno Canyon,[71] and the air was getting quite chill. So my thoughts turned naturally toward the prospects for our night camp. The requisites for a good night camp were grass, water and wood. I had no uneasiness about grass, as there was plenty of it on every side to supply our six small, tired burros. Water we carried for ourselves — but when I looked around for wood, the prospect was not inviting.

No mesquites or junipers[72] — the giants of this miniature arboreal world — were to be seen, but the mesa was covered with a growth of small shrubs with limbs about the thickness of a man's finger, which would provide poor material to make a good fire for a cool night. The old Indian trail was then leading us along the top of a comparatively flat mesa, after a day of wandering through deep, dark canyons and climbing along the edges of ragged precipices, where we were in continual fear that a burro or two would drop over. While looking at the shrubs on the mesa, I noticed that some of them in a sheltered spot had a few flowers in bloom. When I went up to them, you may imagine my surprise on finding them to be lantanas. Here we were, one might say, in a forest of lantanas.[73]

Still, the question of fuel for the night was uppermost in my mind; so I said to our red-headed Mexican guide, "Natividad, have we a good camping place close ahead?" — "Sí, Señor, in a few moments we will come to it," was the reply.

Just then I noticed a peculiar cactus whose star-shaped top sat squarely level with the surface of the ground so that the plant itself was an inverted cone with the point down in the ground, while its base was at the ground level. I had seen such before, but I did not know its Mexican name. So I said to Natividad, "What do you Mexicans call this cactus?"

The reply came, " 'Peyote,' but the Apaches call it 'mescal'."[74] This was very interesting to me, for I had thus located the famous intoxicating plant of the Apaches which has given the modern name to the drink manufactured by Mexicans — a drink common on the Mexican border, but drawn from a different plant.[75]

"How do you know that the Apaches call it 'mescal' "? said I. — "If the *Señor* will kindly wait until we get into our night camp, I will then tell him, for it is a long story." So I waited, for it is useless to think about getting a Mexican to abbreviate a long story.

In a few minutes we descended from the mesa into a small cove or amphitheater, three sides of which were surrounded by high walls of Cretaceous limestone, while on the fourth lay a small gulch or ravine through which the water, after rainfall, ran off to the lower country. In the cove were some small mesquite trees — shrubs, I had better call them — but large enough for the cook's fuel, while most conspicuous were a number of large sotols, the largest that I have ever seen.[76] They were six to eight feet in height and three to four feet in diameter. The crowns of green and serrated slender leaves reminded one of the spiral tops of palm trees.

These sotol leaves never drop off but simply droop down at the end when dead, remaining attached to the trunk. These ancient sotols for a hundred years or more had been accumulating bulk, not so much in living as in dead material. And I was soon to find that this accumulation of dead leaves would furnish a most comfortable campfire for perhaps a half hour.

Here Natividad called a halt, and the *arriero* (burro driver) proceeded to unload the burros and, last of all, to take off the *aparejos*,[77] which all well-regulated Mexicans use rather than packsaddles. The cook commenced to build a fire and to prepare supper while Natividad directed the way to the *tinaja*, where the burros were to be watered. After the burros were watered, which had to be done by hand, we returned to the camp, where we found supper about ready.

When supper was over, some of the Mexicans proceeded to set a sotol on fire; and as fast as the fire from one got low, another was lit. The heat was great, and the green leaves of each crown popped like the report of guns. While this was going on, I reminded Natividad of his promise; so lighting a cigarette and seating himself comfortably on an *aparejo*, he commenced.

"*Señor*, my grandfather was a soldier of Spain, born, I have been told, in Estremadura.[78] That must be a country of fair-skinned men, because from him I inherit my color of hair. You seldom see such in this country; and on account of it the Comanches called me 'Peyote,' the Mexicans 'Alazán,' while you *americanos* call me 'Sorrel-Top,' which my *amigo americano*, Don Juan Humphris,[79] tells me is a name of honor among your people. My grandfather was sent to serve in Mexico, and after a time came with his company to the old Presidio of San Carlos, just across the Rio Grande from us, in Chihuahua. The presidio was built as an outpost against the Indians of the north — Apaches, Comanches and Lipans — and was then far out in the Indian country.[80] He married there."

Here followed an account of his grandfather's life, his father's life and that of some other relations, which was dealt out in excruciating detail; but finally he got around by a devious route to his own life.

"Here in San Carlos I was born and raised among wild Indians, many of whom lived temporarily in and about the presidio. When a tribe was in danger from their enemies, they would at times make a treaty with our people of San Carlos, in which they would promise to be good to our people of the town and not to rob or kill any of them, no matter what they might do to other peoples; and we would for our part let them live among us.[81]

"The people of Santa Rosalía used to talk hard about us, because some of these Indians while they lived with us went in a war-party to that place, and killed and robbed many of them. But, Señor, ¡Santo Dios! we could not stop them when they started out on the warpath, nor did we know where they were going. Besides this, we sometimes ransomed a captive from them who otherwise must have stayed with them. Then, too, we bought from them many pieces of plunder, good to us but which would have been wasted among infidel Indians, and we got in that way some fine curtains from Santa Rosalía for our council house. But the people of Santa Rosalía are gentes ingratas.[82]

"Thus, many kinds of Indians lived among us. I remember when at one time there were among us Kiowas, Comanches, Apaches Mescaleros, Apaches Gileños, Pananas and Cionabas;[83] so I grew up to know much of the Indian languages, but most of all, the Apache tongue. This was because my special amigo was an Apache boy named Güero Carranza. Güero, you know, Señor, means a light-colored person, and this boy was the lightest-colored Indian that I ever saw. I think he prided himself on it. At any rate, he was always partial to white people — so much so in his later years as to prefer the scalp of a white man to that of a dreaded Comanche.

"Now, Güero was always a great friend of mine, but he was too often remarking what a pretty scalp mine would be. After he had left us and gone back to his people in the Chisos Mountains and along Terlingua Creek,[84] he sent for me to come and visit him; so I went over and stayed with him for some time. Together we hunted the cimarrón (bighorn) in the Grand Canyon of Santa Elena and stalked the antelope in the valleys (clothed in the skin of its own kind). From him I learned to strike a fire out of the dried bloom stalk of the sotol by whirling the sharp point of the chaparro prieto[85] in the pitch of the sotol stalk until it took fire. Then, too, I learned to eat the powdered flour of the roasted sotol. He told me how the mescal buttons were sun-dried and hid away in a cool place to await the time of the *mezcal fiesta,* when the wise men and warriors went away in the mountains to eat them and to dream dreams and to have talks with the spirits while under the spell of the potent plant.

"Some of this I one day saw. Güero and I were following a black-tailed deer which he had wounded with his arrow. We became separated and I lost the trail. I went up on top of a rather high mountain to look for him. While up there I saw some Indians in a cove below me and, as their numbers and their quietness aroused my curiosity, I slipped easily down the mountainside until I got to a place where I could overlook them. They were sitting on the ground in a circle and were quiet and motionless. I watched them for a long time and, getting tired, was about to go away, when I saw one of them rise and go to a cave at the foot of the high rock on which I was lying. In a few moments he came back, carrying a basket of willow bark in which were a number of round black objects, which I took to be dried mescals. Without a word, he offered this basket in turn to the other Indians, who each took out a mescal and, after taking a bite of it, then put it down by his side.

"The first Indian then carried the basket back to the cave, and returning, without a word sat down in the circle. I waited a long time to see something more, but finally became tired and silently slipped away. When I found Güero again, I told him what I had seen. He seemed disturbed and told me never to tell anyone at any time what I had seen; that the Great Spirit would be very angry with me and do me great harm, and that I had better go back to my home at once. I was never much afraid of Mexican spirits, except when they took the shape of border guards in the days when I was smuggling. But I am not much acquainted with Indian spirits; so I took his advice, went back home and kept my secret for many years. Now, the Indians left this country more than twenty years ago and took their spirits with them; so it comes about that I tell you tonight how it happens that I know that the Apaches called that cactus 'mescal'."

I had some doubts about the correctness of that conclusion as applied to Natividad's premises, but it was getting late and I was afraid to start him again, for I might have had to hear the genealogy of the remainder of his family. I may mention in conclusion that the Mescalero Apaches derive their name from this custom of the mescal feast.

In the May, 1902, number of the *Popular Science Monthly* will be found an article by Havelock Ellis describing the physical effects of this use of the plant and of the religious rites connected with it.[86]

ALSATE

As we sat down to our open-air breakfast, the sun came up over the serrated outline of the Sierras Fronterizas [87] and dissipated the chill of a March morning almost instantly. I called attention to the sunrise.

"Ah," said Natividad, "the Great Spirit of Alsate coming up over Alsate's old home."—"Who was Alsate?" said I.—"The last chief of the Apaches who made their home on the Rio Grande borders," was the reply.—"Do you know his history?"—"I know his story, and I knew him," said Natividad.—"Then tell his story to us." [88]

"The *rancheria* of the Apaches might one week be up near your Fort Davis, on 'The Clear Waters'; [89] the next week where the great gray deer lies under the shadow of the Chisos, [90] and the next among the strawberry-clad canyons of the Santa Rosas. [91] So I do not certainly know where Alsate was born, but I think he first saw light in the *sierras* under yonder sun, for it was ever his favorite home in the days of his manhood. But a part of his young days he spent in San Carlos. The *Señor* must know that fifty years ago the people of San Carlos were on good terms with most of the Indians of this country.

"The Comanche might rob and kill in Chihuahua and Durango; but he had a home in San Carlos, and the man of San Carlos was to him a brother. We bought his captives to send back to their people, if they had any people left alive, and we sold him powder for his guns and iron for his arrowheads. As it was with the Comanches, so it was with other Indians — except maybe for a few small and short wars. And it comes that I remember the time when people of seven Indian tribes lived together in our little town. These were Comanches, Kiowas, Pananas, Cionabas (Shawnees), Rayados, Apaches Gileños and Apaches Mescaleros.

"The Rio Grande Apaches were of the Mescalero tribe; and there was nothing strange in that Alsate lived among us for a time with his father. Here I knew him and played with him as a boy. However, he soon left us and went back to his people in the hills, and for a long time I heard but little and saw less of him. But after a time the Apaches began to give trouble, first to the *americanos* over in Texas and afterwards to us. They would attack wagon trains over in Texas, run off stock from the forts over there, and carry the plunder into their hiding places in the

Rio Grande mountains. Then I began to hear often of Alsate, who was coming to be thought the best and boldest warrior in the tribe.

"Among others, a story came to us that Alsate had attacked a large wagon train at a place now called Charco de Alsate,[92] near your town of Alpine. He had kept it in corral for nearly a week, until some of the imprisoned men stole out at night on horses with hoofs muffled in shoes of rawhide, and by hard riding brought help in time to save the train. For quite a while during these raids into Texas, they left us in peace and safety. But it came about in time that when they needed horses to use in these raids, they stole our horses; or that if they were hungry and saw our cattle, they killed and ate them. So the complaints began to go up against them to our government. The Apaches steadfastly denied these charges and claimed that while they warred against the *tejanos* (Texans), yet they themselves were of Mexico and fought not against their own people.

"However, the charges went up so often to our government and from so many different people, and were so well proven, that finally our *Presidente* determined to take steps to stop the troubles. These steps were taken quietly, and the Indians were left to think that their pretenses of friendship to our people were believed. Without any warning they awoke one morning in their *ranchería* in the Sierras Fronterizas to find themselves surrounded by Mexican soldiers. All — men, women and children — were carried to Santa Rosa (Músquiz), Coahuila, where they were kept a few days while the soldiers were preparing to carry them to the City of Mexico.

"Here at Santa Rosa, so Alsate told me, his father, who was old and also blind from a wound in his head, took him aside and told him that he had sent for a great man of the place, Don Manuel Músquiz, to come to see him.[93] For Alsate's father was a Mexican who had been stolen in his youth by the Apaches, and Don Manuel was his brother. When Don Manuel came to him, Alsate's father told him that they were brothers, told how and when he (Alsate's father) had been stolen; told his own original name (Miguel) and also the name of their mother. But Don Manuel doubted, for the Indian might have learned these things from someone else. After some thought, he said to the Indian, 'If you are Miguel Músquiz, you have six toes on your right foot.'

"Then the blind man, stooping, took the moccasin off his right foot and said, 'Brother, because the mountain trails are rocky and hard to travel, long ago I cut off the sixth toe. But see, here is the scar where the sixth toe once rested.' And Don Manuel then knew him for his brother, and set about to help him and his people.

"Now, Don Manuel was a great friend of General Blanco, who was a member of the *Ayuntamiento*[94] and he bethought him that General Blanco might be of great aid to him in seeking to help his brother and his brother's people. But first he claimed his brother as an Indian captive, and the soldiers gave him up. Alsate they would not give up, as he was not only an Indian by birth and raising, but he had now come to be known as the war chief of his people. Then Don Manuel wrote a letter to General Blanco and gave it to his brother Miguel.

"Miguel took his son (Alsate) aside when they were about to set out with the still-captive Alsate for the City of Mexico and said to him, 'My son, here is a paper which my brother has given to me, to help you when you come to your journey's end. Keep it so that no one will know that you have it, and when you come to see General Blanco, give it to him — and to no one else — and he will help you.' Alsate then put the letter inside his *faja*[95] and kept it from the sight of everyone else during his long journey. The Apache captives went by wagon and, as the soldiers gave them wine to make them drunk and laughed to see them fall under the wagon wheels, they rode many a mile with aching heads, limbs and hearts.

"But after a long time they came to the great City of Mexico and after some days in prison were called before the *Ayuntamiento*. A great number of soldiers stood in two lines facing them as they marched between the lines — dirty, ragged and sore — up to the Council, sitting in their great chairs. Here Alsate stepped to the front and, addressing them, said, 'We are brought here, I am told, charged with having robbed and killed your people. If we have robbed, where is our plunder? Did your soldiers find any cattle or horses or gold or silver or fine clothes with us when they took us captive in our homes? Here we are — sore, naked and poor — the poorest of your people. All that we ask is to live and breathe the air of our mountains, where the oak and the sotol, the mescal and the lechuguilla are our friends and give us to eat and to drink. We want not your fine clothes, your wines and your foods. We want only our friends of the mountains, and we ask to be let go back to them.'

"Alsate then asked if General Blanco were there; and when he knew him, he handed to him the letter of Don Manuel Músquiz and asked him to be their friend for the sake of friendship alone, as they had neither money nor help to give him. They were soon taken back to prison. After some days they were again taken in wagons and sent back towards their homes. They were to be taken back to their *ranchería*, they were told. But they knew not what faith to put in this; so when they had gotten back among hills which they knew, they leaped from the wagons at a signal from Alsate and took to the hills like quails scattering before a hawk.

"For a time after their return, they did well. But the young bloods grew restive. They had tasted the foray and warpath, and soon the wildest and most lawless began again their old life — against the counsel of the old men, who well knew that they too would feel the punishment sure to follow the deeds of the young men. Alsate, as the acknowledged war chief, was soon drawn in with the young warriors. Then again the complaints began to go up to the government, and once more it was determined to capture the Indians and to put it out of their power to keep up their life of plunder and murder. So instructions were sent to the military chief at Chihuahua to capture the entire tribe if possible.

"Now, the military chief knew this would not be easily done. The Indians were now wary and could not be caught as before. If he marched against them with his soldiers, he might as well try with his hands to catch the birds in the treetops. Long before his soldiers could get to them, the keen-eyed Indians from their mountain summits would see them, the signal fires would be lit on the peaks; and when the soldiers would at last get to the *rancheria,* no living thing would be there — the campfires would be cold and the trails of the departed Indians would lead to every point of the compass. It was but a few miles for them to cross into Texas, and once there, they were safe from pursuit by the Mexican soldiers.

"It was too plain that this plan would not do. So the Mexican chief called in his officers to council. At this council it was decided to draw the Indians into San Carlos under a pretense of making a lasting peace with them and of giving to them on the first day of each month a lot of supplies and food just as, I am told, you *americanos* do with the Comanches and the Kiowas.[96] Then, when satisfied that all the Indians were in the town, they would surround and capture them there.

"To carry this out, one company of the Eleventh Cavalry and a company of the Eleventh Infantry were sent to Presidio del Norte, sixty-five miles from San Carlos, to await the proper time. It was feared that the Indians might learn of this and fail to make their appearance at San Carlos, if the troops were brought any nearer before the proper time. But there was yet one serious matter to arrange. Who should be the messenger to the Indians? Who should toll them into San Carlos? A soldier would not do, for the Indians would then suspect the presence of other soldiers. A messenger must be chosen who for some reason would be likely to gain the ear of the Apaches. At this point, someone thought of the name of Leonicio Castillo.

"This was a man in whom there was no good. He had nothing of his own to eat, yet he went always full fed; he had no money and he never worked, yet he went always well clothed. To feed and to clothe him, his neighbors' property went, sometimes by day, oftener by night. Thus it came about that he was often in jail — and when he was not in jail, the officers were hunting him to put him there. He was well known to the Apaches, and it was believed that he had been with them more than once on their raids — always, however, at times when he was not in jail.[97] At this time he lay in jail with an old one-eyed Indian. He and his comrade were taken out of prison and carried to Chihuahua, where the plan was made known to him alone, and he agreed to carry out his part.

"Leonicio and his Indian partner were then given a pardon for all past offenses (and some say for all future ones as well), under the Great Seal of the State of Chihuahua. They were then sent to San Carlos. They hunted up the Apaches, and Leonicio told them (as he had been instructed) that a sort of millennium had come around; that the government had forgiven all past crimes and wrongs of everybody; that everyone was now to be fed by the government; that the Apaches in particular had been pardoned and would be fed and clothed, if only they would go to San Carlos on the first of every month to receive the food and clothing.

"The Indians naturally wanted some assurance of this; so with great pride Leonicio brought out his pardon and that of the old one-eyed Indian to show them. The Apaches of course could not read, but they could admire the beautiful yellow-and-green seal and, more than this, they saw for themselves that for some cause Leonicio and the old Indian were out of prison. After a short parley among themselves, it was agreed that Alsate and two other chiefs would go to San Carlos on the first of the next month to find what truth there might be in what Leonicio had told them. After arranging with them the day of the new moon when they would come to San Carlos, Leonicio went back and made his report.

"On the first day of the month, Alsate and the two other chiefs of his tribe came to San Carlos. Here they were treated in the kindest manner. They were taken to the stores, and each received the best blanket and the best bridle that could be had, as well as many other things which they were told were given to them by the government. At the same time they were told that the government wished to make peace with every man, woman and child of the tribe, to each of whom would be given the same presents as the chiefs had already received, as well as many others.[98]

"But when the chiefs asked for the presents to carry back to these

Alpine

Marfa

Paisano Pass

PRESIDIO COUNTY

Chinati Pk.

Ruidosa

Alamito Ck.

Fresno Canyon

BREW

Terlingua Ck.

Presidio Fortin
(Ft. Leaton)

Ojinaga

Polvo
(REDFORD)

Rio Grande

Terlingua

Lajitas

San Carlos
Presidio

Santa
Elena Can

San Carlos

TO CHIHUAHUA CITY
AND DURANGO

Comanche Trail Return

Lake
Jaco

C H I H U A H U A

J. CISNEROS

TEXAS

PECOS CO.

Marathon

TERRELL COUNTY

San Francisco Cr.

...OUNTY
Persimmon Gap

Reagan Canyon

Carmen Mts.

Boquillas
Boquillas Canyon

Sierra del Carmen

San Vicente

Mariscal Canyon

COAHUILA

GREAT COMANCHE TRAIL

Indians, they were told that the government would give presents only into the very hands of those who were to receive them. The Indians then agreed that all the tribe would come to San Carlos on the first day of the following month to receive their presents and to make the treaty. In order to know how many presents should be ready, Alsate was asked to give the number of men, women and children in his tribe — which he gave according to his fashion. The Indians then departed, highly pleased.

"A few days before the time set, Leonicio again went to the Indians and told them on what day of the moon they were to come to San Carlos, for they knew not the days of the month as we count them. So on the day set, the Apaches came trooping into San Carlos, every soul from every *ranchería* along the Rio Grande. Here they were met with feasting and every sign of great joy. Oxen, sheep and pigs were killed and barbecued for them; the stores gave out sweets and drink to them without stint and without price, while Leonicio and others made talks to them about the presents they were to receive and the treaty they were to make on the morrow. The day was spent in feasting, dancing and drinking; and by nightfall nearly all of them, even the children in arms, were very drunk,[99] and gathered together in the little plaza, which the *Señor* knows lies between the Town House and the Church, and very near to the *barranca* of the creek.[100]

"Now, on this day the soldiers were marching to San Carlos from Presidio. The cavalry had come to San Carlos Creek above the town, where they lay hidden in a deep canyon; while the infantry had come on the broad road until a short time before nightfall, when they stopped several miles from the town at a point where they could not be seen.[101] When night came and the whoops and yells of the drunken Indians began to die out, the cavalry again set up march and quietly during the night placed themselves around the east side of the town, where there is level ground. The infantry at the same time placed themselves at the foot of the *barranca* of the creek on the west side of town. The *Señor* knows that the town is set on a mesa, close against the *barranca* where the mesa drops into the creek on the west.

"At daylight the infantry climbed up this *barranca* to the town's edge, while the cavalry closed in from the mesa — so that the Indians were caught in a trap, from which not one escaped. Most of them were taken and tied in drunken sleep, but a few died fighting. This was the treaty Leonicio had promised them and the presents that were to follow.

"That day the troops started back to Presidio with the prisoners: sixty-three warriors, of whom two died on the road from wounds, and about one hundred and fifty women and children. At noon the next day they came to Presidio. Here three chiefs — Alsate, Colorado and Zorrillo — were taken from the rest and put at once in prison to themselves. Later in the day, a guard of soldiers came for them and marched them to the outskirts of the town. As he was carried out in this way, Alsate saw a Mexican named Gonzales whom he knew, and he called out a good-bye to him, for he knew he was going to his death. But Gonzales pulled his sombrero down over his eyes and answered him not. When the soldiers came to a stop, they began to tie handkerchiefs over the eyes of the Indian chiefs.

"But Alsate with his hands put away the handkerchief, saying to the soldiers, 'No, it is not good so; when the Great Spirit,' and he pointed with his hand to the declining sun, 'tells me to lay down anything here,' and with his finger he marked a cross in the dust at his feet, 'right here I lay it down, arms free and eyes open.' And a few moments later, at the fire of the soldiers he laid his body down on the dusty cross, and gave up to his Great Spirit the chieftainship of the Rio Grande Apaches. And nevermore has there been, or will there be, another chief of these Apaches. Nor has the Rio Grande seen one of them again, chieftain or child. For the rest were marched to Chihuahua and from there to the City of Mexico,[102] where, I am told, they were scattered in ones and twos into slavery in different places. In this way the very tribe was exterminated, and no one of them ever again saw his tribal hunting ground."

I learned later that, on the decision of the Díaz Cabinet, the Chisos Indians were separated and given out among different families in different towns in far Southern Mexico, in order that none of them should ever escape from this slavery to return to their former home.[103] This order was rigidly carried out, and the *rancheros* about San Carlos and the Rio Grande Valley rejoiced in the belief that they had seen the last of the Chisos Apaches. It was impossible, they all agreed, that any one of the band should ever be able to make his or her way back from Southern Mexico over the deserts and mountains, through the lands of their enemies, to their haunts in the Chisos Mountains — and it was almost certain, they said, that all of the Chisos Apaches, under the hardships of slavery and in an evil climate, would soon perish.[104]

But after a time a sinister rumor began to creep over the old frontier of the Chisos Mountains. It was told by the campfires at night among the shepherds and *vaqueros* (cowboys) that the ghost of Alsate had made its appearance in the old haunts of the Chisos Apaches. One man had seen it as evening began to fall, walking up the slopes of the Carmen Mountains.[105] Another had seen it standing on a rocky point overlooking the Río Bravo (Rio Grande). And several had seen it in different places about and near another mountain on the Mexican side of the river. It was always seen alone.

The rumor became so persistent that people became afraid to be out at night in the vicinity of the chosen haunts of the ghost. Finally, the San Carlos authorities sent out the *Rurales*,[106] that the ghost stories might be laid. They hunted out the neighborhood of every place where it had been reported as seen, but the ghost was too wary to permit these mounted officers to catch even a glimpse of its shape. But in searching about the mountains where it had most often been seen, they found a cave with signs of recent occupancy by some animal which was able to gather and carry in grass for a bed, to slay and eat birds, rabbits and other animals, and to build a fire for cooking. It was hardly supposed, however, that a ghost would have occasion for fire and food, and the search passed on.

Now and then the ghost was again seen, and always in the neighborhood of this cave, which soon became known by the name of the "Cueva de Alsate," or Alsate's Cave. As the ghost harmed nobody, it was not thought worthy of further pursuit officially. So in time, while the fact of the existence of Alsate's ghost became recognized over the land, it was accepted as a natural and inevitable occurrence which need trouble no one. It did, however, trouble one man — the poor *ratero* Castillo. As soon as the report became current that Alsate's ghost was at large in his former homes and haunts, Leonicio found occasion to depart from that country. When the *Rurales* reported that they could find no evidence of Alsate's presence, Castillo again turned up in San Carlos. But shortly afterwards the ghost was again seen, and again Leonicio disappeared.

For something like a year or more, first one person and then another was favored with the sight of the ghost. Finally, there came a time when the stories ceased, and people began to pluck up courage to pass in broad daylight near Alsate's Cave. And still later, a small band of the curious took their lives in their hands and ventured in fear and trembling to search the cave. There, in a dark corner lay the mummied remains of Alsate, near the charcoal remnants of a fire, and signs of a very frail bed. The ghost was laid.

And so it comes that while there may be a few hybrids in a few scattered towns in the far south of Mexico, in whose veins runs the blood of the Chisos Apaches; nevertheless, when Alsate died in the darkness of that cave alone, there passed away the last of the Chisos Apaches.[107]

GÜERO CARRANZA

"The first i heard of Güero Carranza," said old Natividad Luján, with his after-supper cigarette in full blast, "was when the Comanches long ago in a brief spell of anger attacked our old town of San Carlos because we had with us some ancient enemy of theirs. The town was always a place of refuge for Indians of various tribes, although at that time there were only thirteen or fourteen families of them, along with five or six Mexican families. Among the Indians there was an Apache warrior who had with him a son some nine or ten years of age. When the Comanches attacked, this boy fought bravely; and although crying all that time, he did not receive a scratch. The fight was desperate; several of the townspeople were killed, and a number wounded. Only the houses and fortifications saved the day for them.

"This battle was young Güero Carranza's introduction to a life of rapine and murder. The boy's father did not remain long in San Carlos after that fight. Something or other had taken him away from his people for a time — the killing of some fellow Apaches, the enmity of the Medicine Man, or some dream in which the Spirits warned him. At last the cause died away, and Güero's father went back to them with his son. But he did not entirely desert his town friends. His people lived in the mountains near where you *americanos* have your Fort Davis, and now and then young Güero came back with his father to visit his boyhood friends in San Carlos.

"So it happened that when Güero — then well grown — had arranged to trade old Chocte ten horses for his daughter Hupa, and when the time for the wedding was set, Güero thought of his boyhood friends in San Carlos, where he had made his first fight. He sent them bids to that marriage feast; each bid was a leaf of *fresno* (ash tree), cut in the form of a raven and a crow. For Güero was of the Raven clan, while Hupa belonged to the Crows; so each leaf was an invitation from both of these families to attend a wedding at the next new moon.

"The young men who received these ash leaves saddled their horses and, guided by an Indian sent for that purpose, made their way over the mountains and plains to the *ranchería* of Güero's people. They had a great experience for several days, feasting after the Apache fashion. The Indians each day killed a horse or a mule and roasted the fresh meat in plenty for all. Their women dived into their caves and brought out their delicacies, which had been stored away in cool dry places for use in just that kind of ceremony.

"There was the dried, roasted and powdered sotol — roasted in those rockpiles that you have so often seen in this country, and powdered in deep holes in solid rock by the rock pestle — and laid away in tightly wrapped skins in some shaded place, safe from rains, sun and insects. Then also came out the fruit of the pitaya,[108] gathered when ripe, put into willow baskets chinked and sealed with clay. As a special honor, guests were offered a number of honey ants dug freshly from their earthen nests. For drink, there came the Indian mescal. Thus Güero and his clan gave his friends a high-class feast, about which they long boasted in San Carlos, and memories of which stay with us who live now, nearly forty years after Güero died.

"For Güero soon came to be what we of the frontier call a *guapo,* a name common to us and to those Apaches, meaning a "bad man" to you *americanos.* And he was a *guapo* of *guapos,* a very, very bad man. He robbed and murdered Mexicans everywhere — everywhere except near San Carlos, either because of his boyhood friends in that town or, as some said, because so many Comanches (powerful warriors and tribal enemies to him) had come to make homes in that town, and might take his trail.

"But while Güero thus kept away from San Carlos, his hand fell heavily upon the people of Presidio del Norte. They were sixty miles away from San Carlos, and had begun to plume themselves with many feathers. Why, they had two companies of *soldados valientes*[109] stationed there! Did not they have in town six officers strolling by their houses with caps tied on with gold lace, brought down under the chins of the six heads tilted away back?

"However, these companies were a part of the 'condemned regiments' recruited from the prisons of Mexico, where criminals convicted of robbery, murder and other crimes were enlisted.[110] Instead of being hanged or serving time in jail, they were allowed to go into service in the Army and were sent out to face the hostile Indians in the deserted, uninhabited parts. Yet, these men, capable of murdering a man in his sleep for a *real,*[111] were almost certain to run when they saw a hostile enemy. The *norteños,* however, found the sound of the bugle call at sunset just as sweet as if their presidio were in the hands of the finest soldiers of the Republic; and the flag, with its cactus, eagle and snake, fluttered just as bravely in the breeze between the Conchos River and the Rio Grande.

"But Güero cared little for the bugle that blew or for the flag that fluttered. Hiding among the thickets in the river bottom within hearing of the bugle, he would murder and plunder the unwary soldiers or citizens who strayed too far from the outskirts of the city. Or rushing down from the hills in broad daylight, he would carry away the soldiers' horses — in sight of the flag. A scalp or a few horses — these were to him worth living for, and he risked his life often to get one or the other. Pursuit followed such a foray, either by the soldiers or by the *norteños,* or by both; but always it happened that he got safely away — until it came to be said that the Devil helped Güero, and until even he began to claim that it was so.

"Now this very belief brought him to his end. As a good comrade, he felt that the Devil was bound to help him against everybody, while it is easy to see now, *Señores,* that while the Devil did intend to help him as a good comrade, he, the Devil, would do so against everybody except the *americanos.* For the Devil had been a friend to them longer than to Güero, and he felt that he owed them more than he owed Güero.

"Some *americanos* had built a very large adobe house with corrals and outhouses about eight or ten miles down the river from Presidio del Norte, on the Texas bank. We knew the place as the Fortín.[112] The owners traded generally with both Mexicans and *americanos,* but it was also said that they sometimes traded with Indians for stolen horses; and that when the owners made claim, the *americanos diablos* held on by the strong arm. When once property had come into their hands, no matter by what road, they held it as theirs. So they must have profited from many a raid made by Güero, and he relied on their friendship and their help. Again, others say that these *americanos* began to suspect that he was stealing from them as well as from others, and therefore laid plans to trap him; but as for me, I believe that the people of Presidio agreed to give the *americanos* a large reward for capturing him and delivering him to them.

"However that may be, word was had one day at Presidio that the *americanos* had captured Güero, who was lying bound in the Fortín, and that they were willing to make arrangements with the *norteños* to turn him over to the Presidio people. Just here, the Devil, in a belated comradely feeling for Güero, came near to releasing him. When the *norteños* got to the Fortín, they found that their prisoner had rolled down the high bank to the river's edge and had wetted his rawhide bonds. In a few moments more, he would have freed himself, for the rawhide ropes would have loosened.

"The *norteños* picked him up, carried him up to the Fortín, and made their arrangements, whatever they may have been, with the *americanos*. They then held a council among themselves. They needed no council to determine what would be done with Güero, but they did need it to know when and by whom it should be done. They decided that my Uncle Mariano should kill him then, but in his own way. So Uncle, gravely considering the matter, slowly and deliberately drew his knife from its sheath. Güero watched his approach with keen eyes, but said nothing. He may have expected that his bonds would be cut, or he may have known the fate at hand — we cannot say which end he expected. He simply watched and waited in quiet.

"My uncle came near to him, then gave a quick thrust of his knife into the Indian's heart. Güero made no outcry — laughed in the face of my uncle — called out the word *guapo,* and his face froze in death. Now, some people say that his dying word meant that he saluted my uncle as a bad, brave man — to kill one bound and unable to move a limb in defense. I do not believe that it was so. I think he meant something like this: 'See! I am a *guapo,* for I die without fear or groan, with a smile on my face.' But, *¿Quién sabe?*"

The Fortín (Fort Leaton)

Located five miles south of Presidio. Origin not fully established but building may date back to 17th century. Ben Leaton occupied it in 1850's. Güero Carranza was executed here.

AN INTERNATIONAL KIDNAPPING

ⓦ WE HAD CAMPED for the night by the foot of a cliff which presented to us a front of rock as regular as that of a wall laid in Flemish bond.[113] Our campfire had dwindled down to feed on one or two sticks, the flickering light from which threw the shadow of a small *agrito* bush [114] on this wall in some sort of fantastic resemblance to a jumping jack or a dancing human being. To our comrade given to dolorous memories, it suggested recollections of the convulsive movement of a man dying under the hangman's attentions. This in turn suggested to someone the *Juez de Cordado* [115] of the other side of the river (the Rio Grande), whose title and whose summary power of inflicting death without hearing or trial hinted to us strongly of the cord or rope. After some discussion I asked of Natividad the name of the present *Juez de Cordado* at San Carlos, some thirty miles away from us in Mexico.

"*Señor*, they haven't any; they have not had one since I caught the last one." There was plainly a story behind this — a story in which Natividad delighted, if one could judge from the twinkling of the little black eyes and the wrinkles about that big mouth.

"The *Señor* must know that I keep very closely to the American side of the river; and that even when General Naranjo was about to sell his land on the other side and was carrying around those *indios* to show it to those wanting to buy, and sent for me to come over and show some corners, saying by his messenger that I would be safe, for he would protect me — for all that, I did not go. Yet, *Señores*, I was born in that land; the *amigos* of my youth are scattered over it, and I know those *terrenos* [116] as a bird knows the *chaparro chino* [117] in which its nest is built. But it comes about that I do not go there now, just because I knew it so well in my time.

"Your Honors know that the dividing line between the states of Coahuila and Chihuahua runs into the Rio Grande at the Paso de Chisos (Vado de Chizos). This was the *paso* which the Comanches used in the times long ago when they came to Mexico to rob and to kill.[118] I was a boy then at San Carlos, and many a time have I seen them there. I remember old Tave Peté, the old woman *capitana*, so old that when she rode she had to wear a thong that extended over her head and under her chin to keep her jaws from clattering together.[119] Often have I heard her call out her commands to her people from the belfry of the church in front of the *plazita*[120] in San Carlos, and often seen the warriors disperse to do her commands. There I saw her two sons, the *pelones,* so called by our people because they cut their hair short instead of wearing a long scalp-lock like the other Indians.[121]

"There have I seen the two sons, Mauwe and Tave Tuk,[122] contend to see who could shoot the strongest arrow. Ah! Tave Tuk was a *guapo!* We called him 'Bajo el Sol' (which means 'Under the Sun' in English), which was the Spanish for Tave Tuk, and he made his boast that there was no man like to him for courage under the sun. I have heard that he died in the Sierra del Carmen, as became a *guapo* of the *guapos,*[123] fighting Apaches single-handed; and that no one saw this last fight of his, save his enemies and their captive for whom he fought.

"These Comanches from the north came into Mexico over the great mines of *azogue,*[124] by the pass at Lajitas[125] to San Carlos in the light of the September moon every year. Some said they came in September because it was the time of *elote* (roasting ears), for which they had a great liking. Others said that they came then, because it was the time when the fall rains began; so when they went back with their plunder, they would find water on the great dry plains over which they had to pass. And the Comanches stayed until they had robbed and plundered to their fill — and were ready to go back. By this time they had captives, horses, mules and even cattle to carry back in great numbers; so they had to travel slowly. To return by the pass at Lajitas was to bring them within sixty miles of the soldiers at Presidio, and as they did not wish to have the soldiers following them, they took to crossing the river farther east — forty miles farther away from the soldiers. This carried them back on a trail on the east side of the Chisos Mountains, and so the pass came to be known as the Paso de Chisos.

"I saw this pass after I was a full-grown man; at that time the trail leading to and from the *paso* was a great wide trail covered with the bones of animals in great numbers. I thought then that this trail could be followed by the line of bones for a thousand years yet to come. But the Comanches ceased to come, and in time those who knew the Comanches and their ways died off, until now there are few of us living who have seen one of them ride into San Carlos with his *chimal*[126] on his arm and his spear across his horse.

"During this time, too, the bones along the old trail to the Paso de Chisos began to disappear — no one knew how. Some said the wind covered them with dust and the rain washed them into holes. Others said the wind ate them as we eat bread; that the bones flaked off into little thin pieces that those air snakes — the whirlwinds that come winding and twisting and grinding over the country in the springtime — picked up and ground into air. I do not know how this is, *Señores*, but the bones were missed long ago, so that nothing was left to mark the spot where the great trail once crossed the river at the Paso de Chisos. There are still a few of us left, however, who know where the old pass lay.

"So things were, when maybe some twenty-five years ago a surveyor came down to our country to survey out some land under a grant. He had to begin his work at the Paso de Chisos, which was at the corner of the two Mexican states, Chihuahua and Coahuila. He had to have someone with him who knew where that pass lay. It was in this way that I came to go with him, to carry the flag for him and to know where he built his corners. The work was finished, the surveyor went away and many years passed. Then there came up several years ago a dispute between General Naranjo and Don Celso González as to what point on the river was the Paso de Chisos.[127]

"The dispute came about in this way: Don Celso had a grant from the State of Chihuahua which called for it to begin at that pass. His land lay up the river towards the Canyon of Anguila, which you *americanos* call the Grand Canyon. General Naranjo had a grant from the State of Coahuila which was to begin at the pass and run down the river for many leagues. Each of these men had in mind a pass on the river which he called the Paso de Chisos. But General Naranjo said that the pass claimed by Don Celso to be the pass was too far down the river, while Don Celso said that the pass claimed by General Naranjo was too far up the river. Each of them said that his land near the *paso* was wrongly claimed by the other; so they were about to go to the courts over it.[128]

"Someone told Don Celso that I knew from my youth where the true *paso* lay; so he sent for me and I went. But it so happened that the *paso* which I knew to be the true Paso de Chisos was the pass claimed by General Naranjo. When Don Celso learned this, he was angry with me — in which Don Celso was wrong, for I had nothing to do with putting the pass where it lay. Since he was a man of importance on the Mexican side of the river and was on close terms with the officials, I felt that no good would come to me from his anger.

"I lived then on the Texas side of the river, and had done so for some years. I cultivated a little farm on the river bank. After this, one day in August while I was at work in the field, several men rode up to me. One of them, who was named Zúñiga, said to me that he was *Juez de Cordado* in San Carlos and that I must go with them.

"This was very bad news to me. The *Juez de Cordado* never tried men, but had authority from the Mexican government to execute them; and none of us knew how far that authority went. All we knew was that when he wanted help, he called on any and every one that he saw fit, and they had to go, for the government said so. Besides this, if anyone refused to aid, he did not know but that next the *Juez de Cordado* might call for him. Thus it was that everyone had a great respect for this judge, and when he asked anyone to go with him the man summoned went. When the judge commanded his helpers to hang or shoot anyone, they did so.

"I was unarmed and alone; so they bound me. I said good-by to my family, as I never expected to see them again, and they took me over the river into Mexico. Then they carried me to Presidio del Norte across the country — a long way it seemed to me — and put me in prison. Here, as I learned after a time, Juez de Cordado Zúñiga claimed that my name was on the books of the *Juez Primero*[129] as having been charged with theft and that if that was true, he had the right to execute me; it must have been that before the *Juez de Cordado* had the right to execute anyone, he had to find the prisoner already charged with some offense. But I had never stolen from anyone, and they did not find anything charged against me on the books; so after a time they turned me loose. If they had found anything charged up, my family would never have known what became of me.

"It was in November, 1894, following the August in which I was taken prisoner to Presidio del Norte, that I was paddling up and down the river and came near to Martín Solís' place[130] with three of my friends. We came to a wagon on the road; inquiring from the driver, we learned that it belonged to Zúñiga and that he was then riding to a house nearby to get his coat. After we rode by, my friend Juan said to me that here was a chance to catch Zúñiga, and that it was my duty to do so; that he had already been indicted for carrying me over the river, and that I was authorized to arrest him. But I was unarmed and told my friend Juan so.

"'No matter,' said Juan, 'Elijio and I have rifles, and we are your friends; if you will call on us to help you, we will arrest him.' With that, we hurried off in the direction Zúñiga had gone and caught up with him just before he got to the house that he was riding to. As I was unarmed, I passed him going towards the house, but my friends stopped to talk to him. Before getting to the house, I turned around and saw Zúñiga fall off his horse. Juan and Elijio had their guns drawn on him. I then turned back to help bind him. He called on us to say why we had done this thing. I answered that I would show him the papers; but he replied that he knew why, and that I need not do so. On him we found a list of names of men that he was to execute.

"We got such provisions as we could, and started to Polvo,[131] which was sixty miles away. It was a long, hard journey over the mountains. We had only four *almudas*[132] of corn and one pint of flour, and there were five of us — so it was only parched corn, and not much of that, at each meal. We camped to eat at the Mesa Prieta,[133] near where the mines of *azogue* now are. As the corn was not well parched and there was only a little of it, I said to Zúñiga: 'You must not complain of the parched corn, for it was all that we could get for you, and it is all we have for ourselves; and it is much better than you did for me when you took me to Presidio. I got nothing to eat from you on the road, depending entirely upon the charity of the *rancheros* that we passed. And while in jail at Presidio I was given a *medio*[134] each day and required to feed myself on it.' But Zúñiga made no complaint. He was afraid that we were going to kill him, and he was only too glad to live on a very little badly parched corn.

"When we got to Polvo, we turned Zúñiga over to Don Juan Humphris, who was a deputy sheriff. It so chanced that Don Juan's son was over the river in Mulato, which is just across from Polvo. When the *alcalde* of Mulato,[135] who was Zúñiga's brother, heard that Zúñiga was a prisoner of Don Juan, he arrested young Humphris and put him in jail. Then, when Don Juan heard of this, he went over to Mulato, where the *alcalde* arrested him also, and put him in jail with his son. But as the *alcalde* could find no way in all this to release his brother, he finally turned Don Juan and his son loose. Then we took Zúñiga up to Alpine, where he was tried and sent to the penitentiary for two years.[136]

"It so happened that Jesús Reyes, who now lives on Terlingua Creek, was sent to the penitentiary at the same time. He says that at first Zúñiga was sulky and mad, and made trouble — until one day the *mayordomo*[137] had a prisoner tied and in Zúñiga's presence had the man whipped with a lash on the bare back — after which the prison official called up Zúñiga. The *mayordomo* told him that he would be served in the same way if he did not behave himself. After this he gave no trouble; for he felt, I think, as he felt about the parched corn — that he would be satisfied if he fared no worse. When his term was served out, he returned to Mexico.

"In this way, *Señores*, it happens that they have no *Juez de Cordado* at San Carlos, for they appointed no other after they lost Zúñiga.

"In this way, too, it happens that I never go over the river into Mexico now, even if General Naranjo sends for me, because, you see, Zúñiga lives over there."[138]

MESCAL AS A DEFENSIVE WEAPON

 THE GRIZZLED LITTLE MAJOR (my companion, T. H. Bomar) had trudged steadily along all day from point to point, carrying his transit on his sunken right shoulder — sunken by the weight of transit and level in tunnel, on bridge and on line for twenty-five years — and now the day was drawing to a close. We had been coming up the valley of Terlingua Creek, a valley two or three miles wide in places. Once or twice during the afternoon he had called my attention to two men on horseback, riding parallel to and about a mile distant from our course. But we were running a line which was to be used in determining the boundaries of the district of the great quicksilver mines;[139] it was necessary that much care be taken, and our attention was so taken up with this work that we gave little heed to the strangers.

Now as the Major turned to look at the declining sun, he again noticed them, riding much nearer to us. This drew our attention to the fact that for about four hours they had been riding at the same pace with which we moved. Yet, we moved much too slowly for the ordinary pace of a horse; so we speculated a little about what had caused them to check their gait to conform to ours, finally concluding that they wanted to eat supper with us. With this agreed, we resumed our work until the setting sun sent us to our night camp.

As we made towards the camp, the two horsemen passed us, going in the same direction. As they passed us, they saluted us with *"Buenas tardes, Señores."* One of them was a tall rufous Mexican, a type rarely seen — but when seen, noticed. He had a bold, open countenance with large hazel eyes. His companion was a small, dark, sinister-looking Mexican. Both were heavily armed, carrying Winchester rifles in saddle scabbards and pistols buckled on the waist. Their appearance was such that we were not pleased at the idea of having them at our mess, which we then thought was inevitable, for any stranger is welcome at the way-farer's table in this country.

Our driver and our cook had selected for camp a sparse thicket of mesquites where there was good grass for the horses. As we came in, we saw the horses of the strange Mexicans grazing with ours — also the trappings of the strangers, but nowhere could we see anything of them.

The cook informed us that they had ridden up to the camp, and after a short salutation had dismounted.

After they had unsaddled and hobbled their horses, the strangers had taken their arms and left without any further parley. As our cook reported also that he had seen, in the direction which they had taken — about two miles distant — what appeared to be a Mexican *jacal*,[140] we took it that they had gone there for the night, and our uneasiness was laid.

After supper, the Major and I worked on our field notes until bedtime. Then the Major disappeared for a time in the depths of his baggage. When he came to my sight again, he appeared with a tin cup in one hand and a bottle of sotol — sometimes called mescal — in the other, inviting me to take a nightcap with him. The Major was a teetotaler, on principle. But regularly, just before going to bed at night, he laid aside his principles long enough to take a good-sized nightcap. After that, his principles resumed control again. This was his custom when he had anything out of which to construct a nightcap.

However, for some time prior, the Major's principles had not been laid aside after the customary manner, for the simple reason that he had had no liquor. He then explained to me that a Mexican whom I had that morning seen him hail and hold apart in mysterious consultation was a sotol smuggler and carried liquor in the innocent-looking water keg packed on his burro; and that he, the Major, had purchased some of the sotol, which on the word of the Mexican he assured me was good sotol.

Now, I have about as much liking for sotol as I have for a mixture of gin and kerosene, which it resembles in taste; so the Major's invitation did not tempt me to depart from my teetotal principles. And the Major, after a solitary nightcap, departed to his bed. I retired shortly afterwards.

After getting into bed, I heard a low conversation going on at a short distance away from me, between our tall flagman, Steve, and one of our Mexican hands. A few moments afterwards Steve came to my bed and told me that he had bad news for me. He said that our Mexican, Emilio, had just told him that he knew the two strange Mexicans; that one was the brother of Alvarado, the famous "White Mustache,"[141] and the other was a member of his gang; and that he was afraid that they planned to rob us that night.

This was truly bad news. For Alvarado was a notorious robber and murderer who had gathered around him a band of ruffians as desperate as he was. He had received the name of White Mustache (*Bigote*

Blanco) on account of the remarkable fact that his mustache on one side of his lip was white, while on the other side it was a dead black. He had been outlawed by the Mexican government and placed on the same footing with the wolf and the panther, which anyone might kill on sight. Shortly before our encounter with his brother, he had been killed while under the ban of outlawry, but his gang was said to be operating as boldly and ferociously as ever.

Of course, we had to make preparations for what might prove to be very serious trouble. We were seven men in all; but the two robbers might come back with a dozen confederates. What alarmed me most, however, was the fact that I could not find among my men a single firearm, and I had none myself. We hunted up axes, hatchets and iron bars, and placed them by our beds in readiness for use.

This done, I decided to wake up the Major, inform him of the situation, and ascertain how he was armed. But this was rather a serious matter, as the Major had some peculiar habits of his own, and decidedly objected to having his rest broken into at any time. When he went to bed, it was a labor of skill and experience for him to arrange his two extremities properly, and when they were once arranged, he was very averse to have to rearrange them.

First, my friend's two feet, clad in woolen socks, must be fixed at the proper slant out of the bed so that the cover just reached the top of the socks, leaving the wool-clad feet out to the night air. I have often seen those woolen-clothed feet sticking out of the bed, with the frost on them glittering in the early morning light. When I would see them thus, there always came to my mind the uncanny idea of a corpse partially buried, with the feet sticking up through Mother Earth.

Lastly, the covers must be properly arranged, not about his head but over, in the proper folds and of the proper thickness. He was bald-headed, and instead of using a bona fide nightcap, he preferred to cover his bald pate with the blankets and comforts of the bed. When these preparations were once completed, the Major was in for the night and resented anything which brought him out before the proper time in the morning.

But now it had to be done; so I went to his bed and, gently shaking him, called to him pretty loudly. There was a rustling of the bedclothes, a few serpentine and mystic moves of the top covers, then the face of the Major appeared. Very briefly and hurriedly I told him the news, and asked if he were armed. Sleepily and resentfully came the reply, "Lift up the top pillow."

Now, the Major had been a military cadet in youth, and had earned his title in the front rank of battle for the Lost Cause. I had no doubt in my mind that this man, "to battles bred," had carried arms down into this wild country, for what man of war would be as foolish as we civilians had been in a matter of that kind? I fully expected to see some powerful engine of war exposed to view when that pillow was lifted. I lifted it very gingerly.

Imagine my disgust, then, at making out the lines of the lower pillow lovingly fitted to the form of a — bottle of sotol!

Rather angrily I demanded of the Major how he was armed. He seemed now to be getting to understand matters, and he answered me that that was all he had. His brow began to knit in thought, and after a few moments he added, "And I believe it's better than anything the balance of you have."

Anyhow, the robbers never did make their appearance; when we left camp the next morning, their hobbled horses were still grazing in the mesquite thicket. I have since then come to the conclusion that the Major's statement was correct. Had the bandits come, I am inclined to think that Major Bomar's sotol would have done more execution among them than all our hatchets, axes and iron bars.

BAJO EL SOL

Bajo el Sol was a Comanche chief belonging to that division of Comanches known sixty years ago as the Southern Comanches, as distinguished from the Northern Comanches, who held their *rancherías* on the Purgatoire and other branches of the Arkansas River in Colorado. The Southern Comanches, from their homes on the Staked Plains in Texas, at the time of the war of Mexico with the United States, for many years had been incessantly raiding the Mexican border states. So long had this continued that the younger generations had been raised and trained in all the arts and practices of predatory war. They had become accustomed to consider raiding into Mexico as their future hope of gain and distinction, just as naturally as an American boy of the present time looks forward to becoming President or a John D. Rockefeller.

The scenes of their life of rapine lay in the semiarid Southwest. Now, in this country there is usually an abundance of rain in the months of

August and September, when the grasses start into vigorous growth and the *charcos* (pools of rainwater) are full of water all across the desert wastes. So in the month of September of each year when the moon became full, the war parties of young men and ambitious bloods began to trail across the four hundred miles of wild country which lay between the Llano Estacado and the homes of the *vaqueros* (cowboys) and the farmers in Chihuahua and Durango. Magnificent horsemen as the Comanches were, mounted on half-wild horses taken from some unbroken herd, they regarded the long trip over thorny plains and through stony mountains as a festival. They fitted their horses with a rawhide bit and rein for a bridle, and with a tanned sheepskin or a patch of buffalo hide for a stirrupless saddle.

With bow of Osage-orange wood and arrows of the river reeds or the *vara dulce* [142] slung over the shoulders in quivers of lynx hide — carrying a lance of ash wood shod in iron, resting across the saddle — with *chimal* (shield) of buffalo hide, fringed with turkey feathers—with now and then an old *escopeta* (musket) slung under the leg in a rawhide case — with a bowie knife from Texas or a *machete* [143] from Mexico, carried most anywhere — these Comanche raiders made up a picture of barbaric freebooters of the Highland type, ready to reive and to slay. Each year in the light of the "Mexican Moon" — for so they came to term the September full moon — the Comanche War Trail became a moving-picture show. Parties of these barbaric warriors, in troops of a half dozen to a hundred — Comanches, Kiowas, Plains Apaches, Utahs from the Rocky Mountains, outlaws from many other tribes, and even renegades from Mexico — all were hurrying forward to the Carnival of Rapine over the Rio Grande.

The trail carried the savage troops out over the southeastward shoulder of the great Llano Estacado,[144] where for a hundred miles nothing was to be seen but an open grassy plain tenanted only by the jackrabbit and the antelope, and sentineled by the buzzard and the hawk — down through the terraced pass of Castle Gap,[145] into the wide mesquite plains of the Pecos River; on by the noted Comanche Springs [146] and into the mesa-topped limestone hills; then into the mountains of burnt rocks — monuments of primeval fires — and over the Rio Grande into the Promised Land. Here the parties diverged, each to its own devoted area. One scourged the fertile valley of the Conchos River up to the very walls of Chihuahua City.[147] Another carried fire and lance into the confines of Durango.[148] Some went to the mines, some to the farming valleys, but most of them sought the *haciendas* where they might find horses and cattle, the great sources of savage wealth.

Along in the following November or December, the parties began to return. The great Comanche War Trail then presented again a picture of movement. A party here would be driving a herd of cattle; a party there, a troop of half-wild horses. At another place might be seen a small train of captives, laced like Mazeppa to a "Tartar of the Ukraine breed," and herded and driven as any other beasts devoted to man's use.[149]

Here and there by the trail might be seen a great prairie fire set by a party to escape pursuers, while the reivers themselves deflected from the main trail in order to shun the avengers of blood. But there was no way to cover or hide the Great Trail itself. It was worn deep by the tracks of countless travelers — man and beast — and whitened by the bones of animals. It was a great chalk line on the map of West Texas from the Llano Estacado to the Rio Grande.

Among the habitual tenants of this great trail, the Comanches were easily the chief ones. Their flag of sovereignty was lowered to one necessity only — the *lingua franca* of the trail was Spanish. This concession was granted because the Kiowa, the Utah, the Cheyenne, the Comanche — each in time learned some Spanish from Mexican captives, while many a captive became in time a good Indian and at the same time a good interpreter; so it came about, as it has so often happened among the languages of the world, that the language of the vanquished became the language of the war trail. This *lingua franca* was aided and supplemented in many ways by the sign language common to the Indians of the Southwestern Plains; so on the Trail, these Indians of diverse tribes and languages had a common language that was foreign to each one of them.

The forays of the Indian reivers into Chihuahua and Durango were most destructive to life and property. The country was being depopulated. The central government at the City of Mexico — when there was any central government there — was entirely occupied in trying to uphold itself against hostile factions, and had no time to aid its frontier states. These states themselves were more or less divided among the same factions — and all was confusion. The states were suffering both from the Comanche War Trail and the Mountain Apaches, who from their *rancherías* in the heights of New Mexico, Chihuahua and Western Texas descended in a separate warfare of their own upon the defenseless borders of Northern Mexico. The Comanches descended upon these frontiers once a year, but the Mountain Apaches — like the poor — were with them always.

In despair over the situation, the State of Chihuahua resolved to make a treaty with the Indians for that state alone; and as the lesser of two

evils, and also as offering probably a more reliable ally, the Chihuahua
government decided to treat with the Comanches. The treaty was made
with Bajo el Sol as the main chief, and with other chiefs of the War
Trail, by which treaty Bajo el Sol and his associates for a consideration
agreed to make war on the Mountain Apaches and to refrain from ravag-
ing Chihuahua. Bajo el Sol and his braves, however, were left free to
raid any other Mexican state.[150] To carry out the agreement more
effectually, the Indians of the War Trail removed into Chihuahua to
the borders of Lake Jaco.[151] From this seat they could more conven-

BAJO EL SOL

*From lithograph in Report of United States and Mexican Boundary
Survey, 1857. Cross around Bajo's neck and pious expression on his
face hardly symbolized his character.*

iently carry on the fight with the Ranchería Apaches, and at the same time raid Durango.

While this treaty was in force, Bajo el Sol, with his wife and her brother, was traveling near the Carmen Mountains in Trans-Pecos Texas, when they ran into a band of about thirty Ranchería Apaches, with a captive Mexican boy named Domingo Porras (who afterwards lived on my Pecos River ranch). Bajo's wife and her brother wanted him to go on and leave the Apaches unmolested. To this he replied, it was reported, that his treaty with Chihuahua bound him to fight the Apaches wherever he met them, and he would not have it said that he feared the face of any living man.

He sent on his wife and her brother, and prepared to make his lone fight against thirty Apaches. He tightened the cinch on his skin saddle and examined the bit in the mouth of his horse. He looked to see that the point of his ash-wood spear was well set, saw that his arrows were good and in place, strung his bois-d'arc bow, and placed his *chimal* (shield) of buffalo-bull hide in readiness.

Then Bajo el Sol, the Comanche chief, rode up to the Apaches and in the *lingua franca* of Southwestern Indians demanded the surrender of the captive boy. This was refused. Then he informed them that he would fight them, and that they must get ready. In reply, they taunted him. He set his spear firmly under his right armpit, and charged. The Apaches scattered to avoid the charge. Then rapidly drawing his bow and arrows, he began shooting at them as they ran and dodged among the bushes and rocks. In this erratic manner the fight continued for several hours, during which he killed two Apaches and wounded several others. After his arrows were all shot, he continued the fight with the spear alone — which the Apaches, owing to the broken nature of the ground, were easily able to avoid.

The Apaches had an *escopeta* (an old-style Mexican gun, with a bell-shaped mouth). According to Domingo, the owner had only one load, so he had to wait until he had a dead shot before firing. It was planned among the Apaches that this man should hide behind a certain rock, while the others continued to lure Bajo el Sol to charge them by the side of this rock. He charged as they intended him to. Then, just after Bajo el Sol had passed by, the Apache with the *escopeta* came out from behind the rock and fired at him. The slug struck the Comanche chief in the back of the head, and he fell from his horse. Thus ended in the foothills of the Carmen Mountains the last fight of Bajo el Sol, probably the most heroic of the Indians of the Comanche War Trail — a *guapo de los guapos.*[152]

NOTES

(for PART IV)

1 Personal letters, O. W. Williams to his wife, March 10, 13, 19, 20, 23, 25, 27 and 28, 1883; April 1 and 14, 1883. Letter, O. W. W. to his son Jesse C. Williams, Sept. 26, 1925.

2 See accompanying map for Williams' principal surveys in West Texas.

3 The conditions of his employment are indicated in Board of Regents, The University of Texas, *Minutes*, Jan. 29, 1886; *Report, Commissioner of the General Land Office*, Aug. 31, 1898 through Sept. 1, 1900, p. 36.

4 Board of Regents, *Minutes*, June 12 and 14, 1886. Williams' report is Document 26 in the records of the Board.

5 At its spring meeting of 1887, the Board of Regents requested Attorney General James Stephen Hogg "to take such steps as may in his judgment be necessary to recover said lands." *Minutes*, June 14, 1887. In spite of further prodding by the Regents (*Minutes*, Sept. 23, 1887; Dec. 10, 1894), the Attorney General's staff delayed action more than twelve years, at last filing suit on Nov. 16, 1899, in the 53rd District Court of Travis County.

6 The issues were finally settled in *The State of Texas* v. *Michael Meehan et al.*, Cause No. 16,282, decided by Judge R. L. Penn, 26th District Court, Austin, Nov. 24, 1902. Judge Penn ordered the tracts in question restored to the University. Williams' testimony is found in the transcript of the case, pp. 29-45, 135-36.

7 Pecos County, *Deed Records*, IV, 86 and 87.

8 According to the records in the office of the County Clerk of Pecos County, Williams registered eight water rights for Surveys 99½, 80 and 83, in Block 8, on Jan. 13, 1891. To finance his farm operations the following year, he executed on Jan. 22, 1892, a deed of trust to the City National Bank of Austin, covering Survey 99½ of Block 8, as security on a note of $4,660.50. Pecos County, *Deed Records*, V, 38; *Deed of Trust Records*, I, 391.

9 Williams was eventually obliged to sell (in 1899) most of the land he had acquired earlier in Pecos County. Pecos County, *Deed of Trust Records*, II, 7; *Deed Records*, VII, 62.

10 Excerpts from the docket of the County Court for 1895-1900 show that in addition to trying routine cases of misdemeanor, Williams held preliminary hearings on complaints involving such felonies as horse theft, abduction and assault with intent to murder.

11 Dean C. L. Sonnichsen discusses this feud in the Introduction.

12 The article appeared in the *Southwest Sentinel* (Silver City), Jan. 31, 1885. It was reprinted in the *El Paso Times*, Jan. 20, 1887. For an annotated version, pre-

pared by S. D. Myres, see *Password*, El Paso Historical Society (No. 2, Summer, 1965), X, 43-52.

13 O. W. Williams, "Route of Cabeza de Vaca in Texas," *Texas Historical Association Quarterly* (No. 1, July, 1899), III, 54-64.

14 These included the following pamphlets: *The Hawk and The Owl, The Ferrule of Pecos County, Panther Hunt Around Livingston Mesa,* and *The Honca Accursed* — all privately printed.

15 Williams' library, which unfortunately has not been kept intact, was built up to a total of some 4,000 volumes.

16 Williams' defeat resulted chiefly from his stand in favor of Prohibition, which a majority of the voters opposed as unrealistic in the lusty frontier town.

17 *W. W. Turney et al.* v. *Del Dewees et al.,* District Court of Brewster County, Cause No. 376, March Term, 1900. Information about Turney's activities in the Big Bend area will be found in Alice V. Cain, *A History of Brewster County, 1535-1934* (M.A. Thesis, Sul Ross State Teachers College, 1935), 46-51, 77-78, 225-27.

18 *Howard E. Perry* v. *W. M. Harmon et al.,* U. S. Circuit Court for the Western District of Texas, San Antonio, No. 133 Equity, May 13, 1901.

19 The issues were decided in favor of the San Elizario grantees in *The State of Texas* v. *Michael Meehan et al.,* which also settled the claims of the University to land in Block L, El Paso County. See note 6, preceding.

20 Standard books on the Big Bend are C. G. Raht, *The Romance of Davis Mountains and Big Bend Country* (El Paso, 1919); Mrs. O. L. Shipman, *Taming The Big Bend* (Marfa, Tex., 1926); Virginia Madison, *The Big Bend Country of Texas* (Albuquerque, 1955); and Virginia Madison and Hallie Stilwell, *How Come It's Called That? Place Names in the Big Bend Country* (Albuquerque, 1958). The historical background of the area is covered briefly but authoritatively in Clifford B. Casey, "The Trans-Pecos in Texas History," *Publications, West Texas Historical and Scientific Society,* II (1928), 6-50. Regarding legends of the area, see Haldeen Braddy, "Folklore of the Texas Big Bend," *The Journal of American Folklore* (Nos. 211-12, January - June, 1941), LIV, 60-67. See also, *Voice of the Mexican Border* (Marfa, Tex., Centennial Ed., 1936), *passim,* and especially the article by J. E. Gregg, "The History of Presidio County," pp. 10-55 and 77.

21 Robert T. Hill, "Running the Cañons of the Rio Grande," *Century Magazine* (Jan., 1901), LXI, 371-87.

22 Writers like C. G. Raht and Virginia Madison have drawn extensively on Williams for materials about the Big Bend.

23 The name of Agua Fria Spring, located north of Terlingua, derives from the Spanish words meaning cold water. The spring flows into Alamo Cesario Creek from the base of a 600-foot cliff covered with pictographs. The site was once a large Indian camp. See the place-name directory of the Big Bend by Virginia Madison and Hallie Stillwell, *How Come It's Called That?,* 81. The mines referred to were located at Terlingua.

24 As the term is used here, sotol is a desert plant of the genus *Dasylirion*, found along the southwestern border with Mexico. See note 76, following. Sotol is also the name of a distilled liquor made from the juice of the maguey (agave). From this same plant is also derived the potent drink mescal. The Big Bend (Chisos Mountains) can be said to have given its name to one of the magueys, *Agave chisosensis*. Lechuguilla is related to, but smaller than, other species. Its rigid leaves are about a foot long, armed with marginal hooks and stout terminal spines. There are several species of the plant. In the Southwest, ranchers consider it to be poisonous to most animals. The early explorers in the El Paso region reported that the Indians sometimes ate the heart of some varieties of the plant. O. W. Williams, *Historical Review of Animal Life in Pecos County* (Fort Stockton, 1908, pamphlet), 3-4.

25 Reference is to Major T. H. Bomar, Williams' surveying companion and close friend.

26 William Battle Phillips was born in North Carolina in 1857. He received the B.A. degree from the University of North Carolina in 1877 and the Ph.D. in 1883. He then studied at the School of Mines, Freiburg, Germany. From 1901 to 1905 he was director of the University of Texas Mining Survey. Later, between 1909 and 1914, he was connected with the Bureau of Economic Geology and Technology of the University. He was a prolific writer on scientific subjects, and at one time edited the *Engineering and Mining Journal* and *Mining Age*. W. P. Webb (ed.), *Handbook of Texas* (Austin, 1952, 2 vols.), II, 373. Note: The Texas State Mineral Survey party was delayed, finally leaving four months later — on Dec. 12, 1901.

27 There had long been much confusion over land surveys in Texas. Many early surveys were hastily and carelessly made, requiring re-surveys, and frequently leading to lawsuits. Williams spent considerable time correcting such errors. Regarding the problem, see Sue Wallace (ed.), *One League to Each Wind* (Austin, n.d.), 10-11 and 16. Williams conducted a re-survey and appeared as a witness for The University of Texas in the San Elizario litigation. See notes 6 and 19, preceding.

28 In time, Dr. Wheeler became a leading authority on ants, discovering and classifying several species that bear his name. W. M. Wheeler, *Ants: Their Structure, Development and Behavior* (New York, 1910); E. O. Essig, *Insects of Western North America* (New York, 1934), 857-69, *passim*.

29 Honey ants (*Myrmecocystus*) feed mainly on a honeylike substance secreted by galls produced by gall wasps. This substance is stored in the crops of certain of the workers. They are fed until the abdomen becomes so swollen that they remain helpless in the nest, unable to move as they hang from the ceilings of their vaulted chambers. When active members of the colony need food, they feed on the regurgitated "honey" from these bottle-holders. Wheeler devoted Chapter XX of his book on *Ants* to this species.

30 Paisano Pass is halfway between Marfa and Alpine. It is the site of the Paisano Baptist Encampment; also the highest point on the Southern Pacific Railroad in Texas. *Paisano* is the Spanish word for countryman. Madison and Stillwell, *How Come It's Called That?*, 98.

31 Marfa is in northeast Presidio County. Established in 1881 as a water stop on the Texas and New Orleans Railway, it was named sentimentally by the wife of the rail-

road's president for the heroine (Martha) of a Russian novel. In 1885 the county seat was transferred to Marfa from Presidio. The town is a center of cattle, sheep and mohair production, and a gateway to the Davis Mountains and the Big Bend National Park. Cain, *History of Brewster County*, 92-94.

32 Terlingua is in Brewster County; it lies northwest of the Chisos Mountains and about ten miles northeast of the town of Lajitas on the Rio Grande. Some twelve miles farther south of the river is the old Mexican town of San Carlos, which figures prominently in the stories that follow. White settlers were in the area of Terlingua as early as 1860, but there was no permanent settlement until 1890, the year that cinnabar was discovered in quantity. The townsite and the Chisos Mining Company were the property of Howard E. Perry of Portland, Maine. At and around Terlingua are the worked-out quicksilver mines which Perry was operating while Williams was in the area. This general vicinity of southern Brewster and Presidio counties is the setting for Williams' stories about the Big Bend. For a historical account of the Terlingua mines, see J. M. Day, "The Chisos Quicksilver Bonanza in the Big Bend of Texas," *Southwestern Historical Quarterly* (No. 4, April, 1961), LXIV, 427-50. A vivid first-person description of the Terlingua mines at the height of their operations will be found in C. A. Hawley, "Life Along the Border," *Publications, West Texas Historical and Scientific Society* (No. 3, Sept., 1964), XLIV, 7-88. For technical information about the mines and an extensive bibliography, see J. H. Johnson, "A History of Mercury Mining in the Terlingua District of Texas," *The Mines Magazine* (No. 9, Sept., 1948), XXXVI, 390-95.

33 Alpine is the county seat of Brewster County. Formerly known as Murphyville, the town changed its name in 1888, with the approval of the Post Office Department. The town, located in the foothills of the Davis Mountains, is the center of an extensive ranching area. It is the site of Sul Ross State College. Cain, *History of Brewster County*, 87-89. The Glass Mountains extend from Alpine eastward into Pecos County.

34 Alamito Creek is named for the poplar, or cottonwood, trees along it. *Alamito* is the diminutive of the Spanish *'álamo.'* The Alamito runs from the Davis Mountains through Marfa southward to the Rio Grande. John Davis, for whom these mountains were named, in 1870 established a settlement about thirty miles below Marfa along Alamito Creek. From this location, his ranch expanded into a large holding. Madison and Stillwell, *How Come It's Called That?*, 112; Raht, *Romance of Davis Mountains*, 156, 162, 168, 169, 202, 230, 231, 281.

35 French for bow-wood; noted for its strength with flexibility.

36 Williams refers to the quicksilver mines at Terlingua. Actually, the mines were strata of cinnabar, from which quicksilver was refined. The Chisos Mining Company, controlled by H. E. Perry, had discovered and was exploiting some exceptionally rich veins. Perry's fortunes eventually declined, and the mines were closed. They were later re-opened, but eventually stopped producing. Because of the fantastic prices today being paid for quicksilver, the mines in the Terlingua - Study Butte area may again be utilized. *The El Paso Times*, May 16, 1965.

37 The idea prevailed at the time that the entire area around Terlingua was rich in cinnabar. However, Nature had distributed the ore capriciously; and only in this one location was it found in paying quantities. For a number of years the production

at Terlingua was fabulous − an average of $30,000 a month, or 40% of all the quick-silver being produced in the United States. The mining district was some fourteen miles long and four wide. The height of production was reached about 1926. Madison, *Big Bend Country*, 187-89.

38 This mountain, the source of Agua Fria Springs, northwest of Terlingua, has an elevation of approximately five thousand feet. The spring is at the southern base. See note 23, preceding.

39 Italian bees have proved to be more popular for these qualities: they build few queen cells, do not run over the comb, keep out wax moth and are most resistant to European foulbrood. Essig, *Insects of Western North America*, 904.

40 Lantana: There are three species of this scrub plant found in southern and western Texas: *involucrata, macropoda,* and *camara*. The last-named is considered poisonous to sheep and cattle. John M. Coulter, "Manual of the Plants of Western Texas," U. S. Department of Agriculture, *Contributions of the United States National Herbarium* (No. 2, June 1, 1892), II, 329. See also note 73, following.

41 According to the standards of white men, the diet of the Apaches, Comanches, and Tonkawa of the Southwest was considerably below par. The food they used varied with time, place and other conditions. While they preferred the meat of the buffalo, eaten either cooked or raw, they also occasionally dined on horsemeat and the meat of young mules. They enjoyed such delicacies as insects, snakes, rats and horned toads. Their vegetable diet ranged all the way from the screwbean and maize to the cacti. They ate lechuguilla roots in areas where these were more palatable. W. W. Newcomb, Jr., *The Indians of Texas* (Austin, 1961), 113, 164, 189-90.

42 Regarding weapons used by the Indians in Texas, see *ibid.,* 117-18, 165-66.

43 General R. M. Gano was an early surveyor in the Big Bend who accepted land certificates for his services, thus acquiring many acres of the best land in the region. He leased adjoining sections in the vicinity of the Chisos Mountains. With his sons Clarence and John, he organized the Estado Land and Cattle Company, which gained control of a vast territory extending from Agua Fria Mountain on the north to the Rio Grande on the south, and from Terlingua Creek on the west to the Chisos Mountains on the east. When the ranch floundered in financial difficulties, Gano employed Jim Gillett, famous ex-Ranger, to take charge. Gillett saved the operation from failure. Madison, *Big Bend Country,* 113-15.

44 Most of Williams' information about Indians seems to have been acquired from three sources: his early observations on the Southwestern frontier; the writings of explorers, soldiers and hunters; and general reference works. His library contains the following books which he used: F. S. Dellenbaugh, *The North American Indians of Yesterday* (New York, 1901); J. W. Powell, *Annual Reports of the Bureau of Ethnology* (Washington: No. 1, 1881; No. 17, 1898); R. I. Dodge, *Our Wild Indians* (Chicago, 1884); and George Catlin, *North American Indians* (Philadelphia, 1913, 2 vols.). Regarding the geology of the Big Bend, see *inter alia* notes 59 and 62, following.

45 The smugglers, or *contrabandistas*, continued active for a number of years after Williams was in the Big Bend. While the traffic had normally proceeded from the

United States to Mexico, the current was reversed during our era of Prohibition. Liquor smugglers developed many ways to reach Alpine, Marathon and Marfa with their wares. But with the increased vigilance of customs officials on both sides of the Rio Grande, illegal traffic has now been reduced to a minimum. Madison, *Big Bend Country*, 76-79, 218, 225, 230.

46 The Apaches in this area were also known as Chisos. They found the mountains of that name to be a convenient center from which to launch their raids on the sparse settlements of the Big Bend and to be a place of refuge when they were pursued by soldiers, Rangers or sheriffs' posses. For many years Indian raids continued, reaching a climax with the depredations of Victorio in 1879. Later, with the capture of Alsate, the rapid decline of the Indians began; by 1891 it was considered safe to remove the troops from Fort Davis. Raht, *Romance of Davis Mountains*, 175-201, 261-79. See also, F. D. Reeve, "The Apache Indians in Texas," *The Southwestern Historical Quarterly* (No. 2, Oct., 1946), L, 189-219.

47 Williams refers to H. E. Perry, owner of the Chisos Mining Company, with headquarters at Terlingua. See notes 32 and 36, preceding. Regarding sotol and lechuguilla, see note 24, preceding.

48 Tasajillo is an arborescent prickly pear of the region, with slender cylindrical joints and greenish yellow flowers. Ocotillo, a desert shrub with thorny branches, blossoms with clusters of scarlet flowers during a rainy period. On the distinctive plant life of the Big Bend, see note 58, following.

49 John T. Gano was the son of General R. M. Gano. Beginning in 1881, the two surveyed much of the land around the Chisos Mountains and established a big ranch in the area, with the brand "G-4," named for the large block in Brewster County in which the ranch was located. Madison, *Big Bend Country*, 113-15.

50 The reasons impelling Natividad Luján to leave Mexico are given fully in "An International Kidnapping," which appears later in this chapter. Luján was also the immediate source of other sketches written by Williams and included in the book.

51 Williams does not clearly explain the burial customs of Southwestern Indians. For example, the Apaches, because of their extreme fear of ghosts, buried their dead quickly in shallow graves, the immediate family of the deceased moving its tepee promptly to another location. The Comanches preferred inaccessible crevices and caves for interment. Only occasionally did they use a tree or scaffold on which to lay away the body of the deceased. Newcomb, *Indians of Texas*, 122-24, 172-73; Raht, *Romance of Davis Mountains*, 72 and 77.

52 These River Guards were forerunners of the U. S. Border Patrol, which was established in 1924. The Patrol operates today under the administration of the United States Immigration and Naturalization Service. Mary Kidder Rak, *Border Patrol* (Boston, 1938), *passim*.

53 The Spanish word *olla* refers to a round earthen pot or wide-mouthed jar.

54 According to a recognized Mexican authority, Manuel Orozco y Berra, the Spanish on arriving in Chihuahua found *restos* (traces or remains) of the Cholomos and ninety-three other *tribus autóctonas* (indigenous tribes). Of these, only the Tara-

humara, Tepehuana, Uarojía, Pima and Tubari exist today. F. R. Almada, *Geografía del Estado de Chihuahua* (n.d.), 100-104. See also, Raht, *Romance of Davis Mountains,* 69, 75, 77. According to Mr. Rex E. Gerald, Curator of the Museum at Texas Western College, the Tepehuana are not presently found in Chihuahua, although they exist elsewhere in Mexico. The Uarojía have apparently become extinct.

55 Seemingly, no members of the genus *Pheidole* were named for Williams. See checklist, *Ants,* 563-64.

56 Regarding the Flottes, see II, note 84. John W. Spencer arrived in the Big Bend in 1848 and established a large farm on the Rio Grande. In the early 1860's he discovered silver in the Chinati Mountains; some twenty years later he joined others in successful mining operations in the region. Madison, *Big Bend Country,* 169-71.

57 Williams here indulges in a subtle pun. In his day, the word "corker" referred to anything apt and ingenious.

58 Artemisias are any of several plants of the genus *Artemisia,* common in the Western United States. Examples are wormwood and sagebrush. The plants grow one to two feet high, with silver-gray leaves that stand out conspicuously in green fields. Fouquierias are representatives of a small genus of scarlet-flowered shrubs and low trees of the family Fouquieriaceae (Ocotillo), having brittle wood and spiny stems. The plants are leafless most of the time. Yuccas, of the genus *Yucca,* have long, pointed, rigid, and often fibrous-margined leaves resting on a woody caudex; the shrubs bear a large panicle of white blossoms. Yuccas are widespread throughout the desert Southwest. Williams and his party were surveying in the quicksilver-mining district to the west of present-day Big Bend National Park. The entire region is luxuriant in semi-tropical plant life and may be described as a botanist's paradise. W. B. McDougall and O. E. Sperry, *Plants of Big Bend National Park* (Washington, 1951); O. E. Sperry, "A Check List of the Ferns, Gymnosperms, and Flowering Plants of the Proposed Big Bend National Park of Texas," *Publications, West Texas Historical and Scientific Society* (1938), XIX, 15-98; H. T. Fletcher, "Notes on the Vegetation of the Green Valley Region," *ibid.* (1928), II, 6-50.

59 The Grand Canyon (Santa Elena Canyon) is on the lower bend of the Rio Grande between the towns of Lajitas and Castolon. At this point, the river cuts sharply through the Mesa de Anguila, leaving perpendicular walls more than 1,500 feet high on each side. Dr. Robert T. Hill, leader of the first United States Geological Expedition to the Big Bend (in 1899), commented: "Why this particular cañon is called Grand is not known, for many of the cañons below were not only as deep, but far longer and in every way deserving of the name. But Texas is poor in topographic names; most of the features [of the Big Bend] are without names at all." The Mexicans in the area told the American explorers that the name of the adjoining mountain range was Sierra de Santa Elena; so the canyon is known today by the corresponding name in American usage. "Running the Cañons of the Rio Grande," *Century Magazine,* LXI, 378-79.

60 The Chisos Mountains are in Brewster County at the southern bend of the Rio Grande, in the heart of the Big Bend National Park. They form a circular mass about twenty miles in diameter. Because of their open structure, they are of special interest to geologists. Also, they are a kind of biological island in which are to be found

plants that do not grow elsewhere in the United States. The Chisos are heavily forested and are marked by a great variety of flora and fauna. One version of the derivation of the word "Chisos" is that it means "Ghosts." More recently, it has been suggested that the name is derived from the Spanish *hechizo*, meaning "enchantment." Dr. Hill described the Chisos as follows: "They are ragged points of reddish granite rock. . . . Wherever one climbs out of the low stream groove, these peaks stare him in the face like a group of white-clad spirits rising from the base of misty gray shadow and vegetation. Many are the weird forms and outlines that the peaks assume." *Ibid.*, 381. Williams uses this area as the setting for his stories of Alsate, Bajo el Sol and others to follow. For a general description of the country, see V. H. Schoffelmayer, "The Big Bend Area of Texas," *Texas Geographic Magazine* (No. 1, May, 1937), I, 1-25.

61 Santiago Peak is the highest point in the Santiago Mountains of central Brewster County. The peak is located about forty-five miles south, and a little east, of Alpine. It is a truncated cone with an elevation of 6,521 feet. On top of the peak is located the phantom townsite of Progress City, a map of which was filed for record in the office of the County Clerk of Brewster County. A number of lots were actually sold to outside "suckers." See Madison and Stillwell, *How Come It's Called That?*, 68-70.

62 The Cretaceous Age was the final period of the Mesozoic Era, during which were deposited the larger chalk beds, greensand marl, and most of the coal of the United States west of the Great Plains. Also, the period was marked by the stabilization of temperatures and plant life. On the complex geology of the Big Bend, see B. F. Hill, *The Terlingua Quicksilver Deposits* (Bulletin No. 15, University of Texas, Oct., 1902); J. A. Udden, *A Sketch of the Geology of the Chisos Country, Brewster County, Texas* (*ibid.*, No. 93, April 15, 1907); C. G. Moon, "Geology of Agua Fria Quadrangle, Brewster County, Texas," *Bulletin of the Geological Society of America* (Feb., 1953), LXIV, 151-95.

63 *Hidalgo* is Spanish for a nobleman – a person of noble descent, or one who is ennobled.

64 *Eldorado* is Spanish for an imaginary paradise of riches and abundance. Much of the Spanish exploration of America resulted from the search for gold, silver and precious stones.

65 *Tinaja* is Spanish, meaning "jar," and specifically a large earthen jar, bulging around the middle, originally used to receive and store water in the household. See also note 92, following.

66 The burning of sotol plants for heat and light is explained in Williams' next story.

67 Presidio del Norte was located near the junction of the Conchos River, flowing north from Mexico, and the Rio Grande. The place has had quite a history, dating from the time Cabeza de Vaca stopped here in his wanderings through Texas and erected a cross on the mountainside, calling the site Las Cruces. Later, the settlement became known as La Junta (The Junction). In time – about 1760 – a military garrison was established here and the name was accordingly changed to Presidio del Norte to identify the place as a military outpost. After the United States - Mexican War of 1846-48, the settlement was divided. The part on the Mexican side of the river became Ojinaga, the town on the American side, Presidio. Madison and Still-

well, *How Come It's Called That?*, 108; H. H. Bancroft, *History of North Mexican States and Texas* (San Francisco, 1890, 2 vols.), I, Chapter 13 and p. 593; H. E. Bolton, *Spanish Exploration in the Southwest, 1542-1716* (New York, 1908), 520-28; G. B. Eckhart, "Some Little Known Missions in Texas," *The Masterkey Quarterly of the Southwest Museum* (Oct.-Dec., 1962), IV, 127-36. In 1901 Presidio was described as "a village with a few miserable adobe houses, opposite the older and larger Mexican town of Ojinaga." Hill, "Running the Cañons of the Rio Grande," *Century Magazine*, LXI, 373.

68 *Rancherías* were the camps of the border Indians, generally found in the mountains along the Rio Grande. Fort Davis, located in the heart of the Davis Mountains of Jeff Davis County, was established in 1854 as a frontier post on the Lower Route from San Antonio to El Paso. The fort was named for Jefferson Davis, Secretary of War at the time it was created. For interesting accounts, see Barry Scobee, *Fort Davis, Texas, 1583-1960* (El Paso, 1963); J. H. Lundy, *The History of Jeff Davis County* (M.A. Thesis, Sul Ross State Teachers College, 1941), especially Chap. III.

69 After their raids into Northern Mexico during the periods of the "Mexican Moon," the Comanches returned to their camps on the Staked Plains, or Llano Estacado, an area extending from Horsehead Crossing on the Pecos River eastward and northward to the Panhandle of Oklahoma and embracing a portion of eastern New Mexico lying east of the Pecos River. See note 148, following.

70 *Caballada* is Spanish, meaning a group of horses, usually in charge of riders.

71 Fresno Canyon, located in eastern Presidio County, runs almost due south, to open into the Rio Grande a few miles west of Lajitas. Williams and his party were surveying Block G 12 in the vicinity of Terlingua, Brewster County, where the quicksilver mines were located. These were the property of the Chisos Mining Company, owned by H. E. Perry of Portland, Maine. See note 32, preceding.

72 Mesquite (from Nahuatl *mizquitl,* Spanish *mezquite*) is a hardy plant of the genus *Prosopis,* a spiny tree or shrub of the Southwest that bears pods rich in sugar, important as livestock feed. Juniper is an evergreen shrub or tree of the genus *Juniperus,* having a prostrate or shrubby habit, also found extensively in the Southwest. McDougall and Sperry, *Plants of the Big Bend National Park,* 23 and 98.

73 Probably *Lantana horrida.* A plant native to Texas, it is a shrub three to five feet tall, with ten to eighteen coarse teeth on each margin of a leaf, and yellow or orange flowers that turn red with age. It blooms most of the year in the Rio Grande country. H. S. Irwin, *Roadside Flowers of Texas* (Austin, 1961), 190-91. This plant is the wild and unculturated *Lantana camara.*

74 Peyote is described thus: "*Lophophora williamsii.* Cactus, Dry Whisky, Devil's Root, Mescal Button, Sacred Mushroom, 'Peyote': A spineless cactus, with flat, round, wrinkled top, two to three inches across, and bearing pink blossoms out of the tufts of silky hairs that appear in regular order, in place of the usual tufts of spine in other cacti." E. D. Schultz, *Texas Wild Flowers* (Chicago and New York, 1928), 256-57. The word comes from Nahuatl *peyotl,* which means "caterpillar." The plant produces the hallucinatory button, used by certain Indian tribes of the Southwest. See note 86, following.

75 This variety of mescal (aguardiente) is obtained from the maguey plant (genus *Agave*) by distilling the fermented juices.

76 "Dasylirion, Saw Yucca, Sotol: A large rosette of slender, arching leaves, the leaves one to three feet long, about one-half inch wide, the saw-toothed margins armed with sharp recurved teeth. . . . Flower stalk erect, not branched, five to fifteen feet tall, rising from the center and terminating in a large spike of inconspicuous flowers." The dried plants make excellent fuel. Schultz, *Texas Wild Flowers,* 52-53.

77 *Aparejo:* A heavy, clumsy packsaddle, "stuffed with hay to form a large pad on each side of the animal, to protect him from his heavy burden." The outfit weighs thirty to forty pounds. J. R. Bartlett, *Personal Narrative of Explorations and Incidents in Texas, New Mexico, California, Sonora, and Chihuahua* (New York, 1854, 2 vols.), I, 359.

78 Estremadura is a region of west-central Spain, near the border with Portugal, known for the relatively light complexion of its natives.

79 John Humphris, an Englishman known locally as "Don Juan," came to the Big Bend in 1883 and established a sheep ranch. He later engaged in other enterprises, becoming a leading figure in the area. Shipman, *Taming the Big Bend,* 115, 188-89; Madison, *Big Bend Country,* 148 and 170.

80 According to the best information available, the old Presidio of San Carlos and its church were located to the south of the Rio Grande between the mouth of Santa Elena Canyon and Lajitas, about six miles up the Río de San Carlos. The town of San Carlos is some twelve miles south-southwest of Lajitas. According to the *presidente municipal* (mayor) of Ojinaga, the military records of the old Presidio were destroyed by the Revolutionaries during the raids of 1915-16. The town of San Carlos is located in the *municipio* of Ojinaga, Distrito Morelos. F. R. Almada, *Diccionario de Historia, Geografía y Biografía Chihuahuenses* (Chihuahua, 1927), 632. The old Presidio, which the Spanish established in 1772 as a part of their system of frontier defense, was previously known as Cerro Gordo. S. B. Brinckerhoff and O. B. Faulk, *Lancers for the King: A Study of the Frontier Military System of Northern New Spain* (Phoenix, 1965), 80 and 94.

81 This anomalous situation led Major William H. Emory, United States Boundary Commissioner, to observe in his report of 1857: "The relations between the Indians of this region and several towns, particularly San Carlos, a small town twenty miles below [Presidio del Norte], are peculiar, and are well worth the attention of both the United States and Mexican governments. The Apaches are usually at war with the people of both countries, but have friendly leagues with certain towns, where they trade and receive supplies of arms and ammunition, &c., for stolen mules. This is undoubtedly the case with the people of San Carlos, who also have amicable relations with the Comanches, who make San Carlos a depot of arms in their annual excursions into Mexico. While at the Presidio we had authentic accounts of the unmolested march through Chihuahua, towards Durango, of four hundred Comanches under Bajo Sol. It seems that Chihuahua, not receiving the protection it was entitled to from the central government of Mexico, made an independent treaty with the Comanches, the practical effect of which was to aid and abet the Indians in their

war upon Durango." *Report on the United States and Mexican Boundary Survey* (Washington, 1857), I, 86.

82 Santa Rosalía de Camargo (now Cd. Camargo) is located in southeastern Chihuahua, on the Conchos River. For an early description of the *pueblo*, see G. F. Ruxton, *Adventures in Mexico and the Rocky Mountains* (New York, 1848), 147-48. Numerous other communities in Northern Mexico were subject to raids. Bartlett details the effects of Indian raids on Santa Cruz, Sonora. *Personal Narrative*, I, 407-09. The Indians bartered their booty in the region of San Carlos and Presidio del Norte. *Gentes ingratas:* ungrateful or unthankful persons – ingrates.

83 These members of diverse Indian tribes, who had entered Mexico in search of booty, had remained in the hospitable environs of San Carlos.

84 Terlingua Creek originates southwest of Alpine. Running southward, it enters the Rio Grande below Santa Elena Canyon. The name *tres lenguas* apparently refers either to the three tongues or branches of the creek, or to the fact that three Indian tribes once lived on it. Up the creek, fourteen miles from the Rio Grande, is the ghost town of Terlingua, former center of the quicksilver-mining district. Madison and Stillwell, *How Come It's Called That?*, 54.

85 *Chaparro prieto:* This plant, according to a Mexican source, is the *Mimosa laxiflora*, found along the Rio Grande and in Northern Mexico. Almada, *Geografía del Estado de Chihuahua*, 35. It is a low shrub producing white flowers in dense racemes two to four centimeters long and a long, oblong, glabrous pod four to five centimeters long. I. Tidestrom and T. Kittell, *Flora of Arizona and New Mexico* (Washington, 1941), 152.

86 Havelock Ellis first published his findings regarding the effects of mescal (peyote) in *The Contemporary Review*, Jan., 1898. For a summary of his conclusions, plus those of Aldous Huxley and others, see David Ebin (ed.), *The Drug Experience* (New York, 1961), 221-307. The word "mescal" is used variously in the Southwest. It may refer to (*a*) the plant *Lophophora* (peyote), or loosely as here, to the hallucinatory button it yields; (*b*) the drink distilled from the juice of the maguey or agave, and (*c*) the food prepared from the pulp of the maguey. The Mescalero Indians (Apaches) derived their name from their use of both *a* and *c*. B. F. Jenness, "Apache Name from Mescal: A Food, a Drink," *The Southwesterner* (No. 4, Oct.-Nov., 1964), IV, 1 and 3. Regarding these Indians in the Big Bend, see Raht, *Romance of Davis Mountains*, 152-53, 193, 197-98, 200-01. See also Newcomb, *Indians of Texas*, 104-31.

87 Sierras Fronterizas refers here to a range southeast of Boquillas, Coahuila, east of the Rio Grande in Mexico.

88 Alsate is probably a misnomer for Arzate. Joe Cordero of Fort Stockton, grandson of Captain Francisco Arzate, says that during the short term the Indian chief was first imprisoned at Presidio del Norte, the officers wanted to know his name. Upon seeing Captain Arzate of Presidio pass by, the Indian inquired his name, then said that he would take it as his own. Captain Francisco Arzate is buried at Balmorhea, Texas. Following the Civil War, Alsate, as chief of the Chisos Apaches, was active along the border as a renegade and freebooter. Raht, *Romance of Davis Mountains*, 375.

89 Fort Davis lies on a small stream named "Las Limpias," Spanish for "Clear Waters."— O. W. W. (This footnote, and others hereinafter designated O. W. W., were included in Williams' original version.)

90 At the southwest corner of the Chisos Mountains there is a spring known as Mule Ear Spring on account of two remarkable peaks having a strong resemblance to the ears of a mule, or as the Indians have it, to a mule-eared deer. – O. W. W. The two sharp peaks may be seen from the main road in the western part of the Big Bend National Park.

91 The Santa Rosa Mountains in Mexico, opposite Dryden, have canyons in which the strawberry grows, so I am told. – O. W. W.

92 *Charco* means a pond of water or water hole. – O. W. W. In another place, Williams explains: "The term 'charco' as used among the Mexicans in this section means a small pond of water with earth bottom, as distinguished from 'tinaja,' a pond of water lying on rocks." *Mendosa, 1684, In Pecos County, Texas* (pamphlet, n.d.), 6. Charco de Alsate is located at Alpine, where it is also known as Kokernot or Burgess Spring. Raht, *Romance of Davis Mountains,* 158 and 167. Capt. Francisco Arzate persuaded the Apache chief to abandon a siege of John Burgess' wagon train here. In his more factual account covering the same ground as this story by Natividad, O. W. Williams states that the wagon train was engaged in hauling salt to Presidio del Norte. *Alsate – The Last of the Chisos Apaches* (pamphlet, n.d.), 5. (Hereinafter cited as *Last of the Chisos.*)

93 The Músquiz family operated a large ranch east of the Sierra Hermosa de Santa Rosa in north central Coahuila, with headquarters at the town bearing their name. In 1854 Manuel Músquiz left Mexico as a political refugee and settled in Músquiz Canyon (named for him) near Fort Davis, Texas, soon after the post was established. In 1861 the Apaches attacked and destroyed his ranch, forcing him to leave the area. He returned to Mexico and again took up residence in the Santa Rosa country, where he was living when the episode recounted here took place. As a stark reminder of his misadventure in Texas, the remains of his ranch house and corral may be seen today on the road between Alpine and Fort Davis. Shipman, *Taming the Big Bend,* 26, 34-36, 108, 200; Raht, *Romance of Davis Mountains,* 136, 146, 276-77, 375. For location of the Sierra Hermosa de Santa Rosa and the town of Músquiz, see Secretaría de Agricultura y Fomento, *Atlas Geográfico de los Estados Mexicanos* (México, 1919-1921), "Coahuila."

94 *Ayuntamiento* – literally a [town] council, but here supposed to refer to the Mexican [President's] cabinet. – O. W. W.

95*Faja* – sash worn around the waist by Mexicans and by some Indians. – O. W. W.

96 United States policy toward the Indians was hardly consistent. It ranged from generosity to marked severity. At this time, the policy was relatively lenient. Newcomb, *Indians of Texas,* 361-63; R. H. Ogle, *Federal Control of the Western Apaches, 1848-1886* (Albuquerque, 1940), *passim;* E. Wallace and E. A. Hoebel, *The Comanches: Lords of the South Plains* (Norman, 1952), 311-53; E. E. Dale, *The Indians of the Southwest: A Century of Development Under the United States* (Norman, 1949), Chapters II, IV, VII, VIII.

97 Castillo had been somewhat intimate with Alsate. "He [Castillo] was what the Mexicans call a 'ratero' – a petty thief. As a Mexican who knew him once told me, he spent a great deal of his time in jail, and when not in jail, he put in his time trying to get back in again. At times when out on 'furloughs' he had cultivated the acquaintance of these Indians of the Chisos, and probably had joined and aided in their petty thievery." *Last of the Chisos,* 5.

98 ". . . they were escorted to the Town House on the Plaza, and were met in solemn council by a number of men in lace and gold uniforms. Here for two days with all seeming solemnity the farce was played." *Ibid.,* 6.

99 "Some of the Indians were aware of the danger of the white man's 'fire-water,' and endeavored to prevent the others from indulging in it. But in spite of this, by nightfall when the blankets were to be dealt out, nearly every member of the band was very intoxicated, and as the supply of 'fire-water' was apparently unlimited, they drank on into the night until stupefied." *Ibid.,* 6.

100 *Barranca* is a bank. Such banks in this country, where a mesa drops into a creek, are abrupt, steep, and remind one somewhat of earthen fortifications. – O. W. W.

101 "On the night before the day set, several companies of the Twenty-Fourth Mexican Infantry marched from the Presidio at the mouth of the Conchos River on the road to San Carlos. At daybreak the next morning they camped in a secluded spot to escape the keen vision of any sentinel of Alsate's Band, and there they remained during the day in readiness for the climax in the game then being played." *Last of the Chisos,* 6.

102 A number of the Indians died en route. *Ibid.,* 7.

103 This concluding section is appended from *ibid.,* 7-8.

104 Williams remarks that "in 1882 the Chisos Apaches were trapped by the insidious policy of Porfirio Díaz, and distributed as slaves, one by one, in various parts of Yucatán and Campeche," and that as a result "the Indian ceased to be a factor on the Texas Border." *Ibid.,* 3.

105 The Del Carmen Mountains (Sierra del Carmen), a subsidiary of the Sierra Madre Oriental, are located in northern Coahuila, Mexico. The spur extends northwestward for some distance in the United States, where it is known as the Carmen Mountains. It is cut by the awe-inspiring Boquillas Canyon on the eastern boundary of the Big Bend National Park.

106 *Rurales* were mounted Federal police used by Porfirio Díaz, beginning in 1877, to pacify Mexico, patrol the roads and villages, and enforce his will. A. M. Carreño (ed.), *Archivo del General Porfirio Díaz: Memorias y Documentos* (Colección de Obras Mexicanas, México, 1947-1959), XVII, 249; XIX, 154 and 193; XX, 9 and 187; XXIII, 146; XXV, 163; XXVI, 63 and 284; XXVII, 114. Later, these mounted patrolmen, dressed neatly in dove-gray uniforms trimmed with silver buttons, became symbols of oppression among the Indians and the poor. Not the least-feared power that the *Rurales* exercised was the right to shoot outlaws and malcontents on sight, and to apply the *ley fuga* ("escape law": "killed while trying to escape") to prisoners who might prove objectionable for any reason. F. J. Santamaría, *Diccio-*

nario de Mejicanismos (Méjico, 1959), 662; L. B. Simpson, *Many Mexicos* (Berkeley, 1959), 259-63; A. Brenner and G. R. Leighton, *The Wind that Swept Mexico* (New York, 1943), 8 and 22. See photo No. 9, *ibid.*, for a typical detachment of *Rurales.*

107 The story of Alsate as Williams related it has found a lasting place in the literature of the Southwest. See Raht, *Romance of Davis Mountains,* 273-79; Madison, *Big Bend Country,* 35-37; Madison and Stillwell, *How Come It's Called That?,* 26-27. The facts seem to challenge the popular accounts regarding the mysterious death of Alsate. According to Norberto Benigno Contreras, grandson of the late Colonel Norberto Contreras of the Mexican Army, Alsate was captured and shot at Ojinaga, despite the intercession of Captain Francisco Arzate in his behalf. Brave to the end, Alsate pleaded that he be given a gun to fight it out with those who were to execute him, declaring that he would gladly die in this manner. This request, however, was denied, and the prisoner was duly blindfolded and led before the firing squad. His body is said to be buried at Ojinaga.

108 Pitaya is any of several cacti of the southwest, such as *Lemaireocereus thurberi* or *Acanthocereus pentagonus,* which produce a bright red, juicy, edible fruit, sometimes called "desert strawberries."

109 *Soldados valientes* – brave soldiers.

110 Some twenty miles above Presidio, Texas, is a collection of adobe houses, now abandoned, known as the "City of the Condemned Regiment." Here were stationed Mexicans who had been convicted of serious crimes. They were assigned the dangerous mission of fighting off the Apaches and Comanches seeking to enter Mexico on their raiding expeditions. The arrangement served the double purpose: subjecting the prisoners to punishment and offering some measure of protection to the frontier settlements. O. W. Williams, Letter to Bascom Giles, July 2, 1943.

111 *Real* – the old monetary unit of Spain.

112 The ruins of the Fortín, the origin of which may date back to the 17th century, stand five miles south of Presidio, and a half mile east of the Rio Grande. In the 1850's Ben Leaton, an American, acquired the property, which for a time was known as Fort Leaton. As a trader, Leaton maintained friendly relations with the Apache Indians and was accused of furnishing them with arms and ammunition in violation of both American and Mexican law. Raht, *Romance of Davis Mountains,* 115-17; Shipman, *Taming the Big Bend,* 10-11, 18-19, 199; James Leaverton and Kathleen Houston, "Presidio County's Oldest Building, Fort Leaton," *Voice of the Mexican Border* (1936), 85-86.

113 Flemish bond is a masonry bond in which each course consists of headers and stretchers laid alternately, thus always breaking joints. Some of the mountain sides in the Big Bend resemble well-laid rows of masonry.

114 *Agrito* – A name (Mexican) applied to a shrub. The name means "sour" – I suppose – from taste of the leaves. The leaves are light green and shaped like holly leaf. As it bears a red berry, it may be an ilex and close kin to holly, but I have never studied it out. – O. W. W. This plant, known in English as agarita (*Mahonia trifoliata*) yields a yellow dye, a tanning extract, an ink and a berry used to make jelly.

115 *Juez de Cordado:* A corruption of *juez de acordada,* an office originally created (1710) in Spanish Mexico to apprehend and summarily judge highwaymen. In 1719 the authority of the official was extended by an *acuerdo* of the Royal Audiencia of Spain; hence the name *acordada.* In effect, President Díaz had revived the office to administer immediate and drastic penalties to known outlaws. Santamaría, *Diccionario de Mejicanismos,* 23.

116 *Terrenos* — lands or fields.

117 *Chaparro chino* refers to clumps of chino gramma grass that turn green during the spring and serve as nesting places for birds.

118 This is a pass on the Rio Grande marking the northermost boundary of Chihuahua and Coahuila. The Comanches used the ford (*Vado*) on their return from raiding expeditions in Northern Mexico.

119 Tave Peté was the mother of the Comanche chief Tave Tuk, known best as Bajo el Sol (in Comanche, the name meant "sun"). She was a kind of shaman, a dominant figure at the old Presidio of San Carlos, and she passed her courage and determination on to her war-making sons. Raht, *Romance of Davis Mountains,* 65.

120 Little *plaza.*

121 In Spanish, *pelón* is a colloquial word used to describe a person who is hairless or bald, or who has his hair cropped short.

122 Both were sons of Tave Peté. Mauwe, like Tave Tuk (Bajo el Sol), was a brave and daring warrior. But see Emory's estimate in note 152, following.

123 In Spanish, *guapo* sums up many fine masculine qualities: stout, courageous, valiant, bold, enterprising, good, clever, neat, elegant, vain, gay and fond of courting women. Along the Rio Grande, the term was also applied to a very dangerous man.

124 *Azogue* is Spanish for mercury. The Indians, coming from the north, passed through the Terlingua area, where the quicksilver mines were later developed extensively.

125 Lajitas is located a short distance up the river from Santa Elena Canyon. The old presidio of San Carlos lay about six miles south of the Rio Grande. The Comanche Trail going south crossed the river in this vicinity. The return crossing was farther down the river, the trail coming northward through the wide opening between the mountains of Chihuahua and Coahuila, to intersect the Rio Grande at the Vado de Chizos. This point lies between the town of Castolon and Mariscal Canyon, almost immediately south of the Chisos Mountains.

126 *Chimal:* A shield, usually made of buffalo hide and fringed with turkey feathers.

127 General Francisco Naranjo had been second in command (*jefe segundo*) of the Tuxtepecano Army of the north. He had joined the Díaz forces to overthrow President Lerdo and was now a landowner and rancher in Coahuila. Celso González was originally from Ciudad Guerrero. He had served as governor of Chihuahua several times between April, 1884, and July, 1888. Almada, *Diccionario de Historia,*

Geografía y Biografía Chihuahuenses, 295-96, 475-76; F. R. Almada, *Resumen de Historia del Estado de Chihuahua* (México, D. F., 1955), Chapter L.

128 The land in dispute was immediately south of the most pronounced bend in the Rio Grande, in the vicinity of the *pueblos* of San Vicente, Altures and Las Piedras, all north of the Bolsón de Mapimí. See Theodore Gentilz, Map of the Republic of Mexico (Library of Congress, 1882).

129 *Juez Primero:* A judge of the first instance, who received complaints, determined *prima facie* guilt, and bound accused persons over for trial.

130 The United States Geological Survey Quadrangle of the Chisos Mountains, 1903, shows the Solís Ranch on the American side of the Rio Grande. It was located between Mariscal Canyon and San Vicente, east of the Chisos Mountains.

131 Polvo, meaning "Dust," was a little settlement about sixteen miles below Presidio, on the Rio Grande. The place is now known as Redford, located in Presidio County.

132 The old Spanish word is *almud.* The measure is not exact, varying from two to twenty-one quarts. During Williams' days on the Mexican border, the *almud* measured 5/24 of a bushel.

133 Mesa Prieta (Black Mesa) is shown on the U. S. G. S. Map of 1903 as lying about nine miles west of the Terlingua mines.

134 *Medio:* Six cents of Mexican money, a *medio* being one-half of a *real* worth twelve and a half cents.

135 The mayor of Mulato, the Mexican village opposite Polvo (Redford) on the south side of the Rio Grande.

136 The District Court records of Brewster County indicate that the grand jury indicted Matías Zúñiga for kidnaping, a felony in Texas, and that he was tried on March 7, 1895. The verdict of the jury was "guilty," and Zúñiga was obliged to serve two years in the State penitentiary. *District Court Minutes,* I, 462-63.

137 *Mayordomo:* Superintendent.

138 Apparently, Natividad did recross the river — and once too often. According to Norberto Benigno Contreras, grandson of the late Colonel Norberto Contreras of the Mexican Army, Natividad was arrested in Mulato in 1918, taken to Ojinaga and hanged.

139 See notes 32, 36 and 37, preceding.

140 *Jacal:* a hut or small house, usually built of adobe and having a straw, reed or rough wooden roof.

141 Alvarado was a Mexican ranchman, a really bad *hombre,* who had terrorized the region for some time. He was at large when Dr. Robert T. Hill led the first United States Geological Expedition down the canyons of the Rio Grande in 1899. Hill, "Running the Cañons of the Rio Grande," *Century Magazine,* LXI, 375.

142 *Vara dulce:* a verbenaceous plant of the genus *Lippia,* which in Coahuila is called *altamisa.* Santamaría, *Diccionario de Mejicanismos,* 1107.

143 A *machete* is a large heavy knife, usually resembling a broadsword, two or three feet long. It is used in the Southwest to cut underbrush and small plants, and may serve also as a weapon.

144 Llano Estacado: See I, note 57.

145 Castle Gap is a canyon about a mile in length cutting through the Castle Mountains of Southwest Texas at the western extremity of the Plains, approximately twelve miles east of Horsehead Crossing of the Pecos River. The gap was the scene of an ambuscade of cattlemen and their herd by Indians in 1867. J. E. Haley, *Charles Goodnight, Cowman and Plainsman* (Norman, 1949), 129, 148-50. For a description of the gap, see Bartlett, *Personal Narrative,* I, 91-92. A legend about Castle Gap involving Emperor Maximilian of Mexico is retold by Sidney Turner in *Voice of the Mexican Border* (1936), 87-88.

146 Comanche Springs, at the site of present-day Fort Stockton, was a watering place on the old Comanche Trail. The name of the springs came from the Indians who stopped en route to and from Mexico during the course of their depredations. The place, however, was known to travelers as early as the time of Cabeza de Vaca (1535) and was long a point of historical interest. Eventually, irrigation wells were drilled in the vicinity, draining off the water and stopping the flow of the springs. Raht, *Romance of Davis Mountains,* 33, 86, 113, 175. See also M. L. Crimmins, "Fort Stockton 60 Years Ago," *Fort Stockton Pioneer,* Jan. 27, 1928.

147 Chihuahua City, capital of the State of Chihuahua, is located on the Chuvíscar River, a northern tributary of the Conchos, near the center of the state. It lies about two hundred and forty miles south of El Paso in a picturesque valley formed by spurs of the Sierra Madre. After the place had been occupied for a number of years, the governor of Nueva Vizcaya issued a decree in 1709 giving it the name San Francisco de Cuéllar. In 1718 the name was changed to San Felipe el Real de Chihuahua and the settlement was designated a *villa.* By a decree of 1823, it became a *ciudad.* Meanwhile, by 1763 the town had attracted some 5,000 inhabitants, owing chiefly to the valuable minerals in the vicinity. The population today is in excess of 175,000. Of special historical interest are the old parish church of San Francisco founded in 1721, the Cathedral of Chihuahua (1725), and the *calabozo* of the old Jesuit convent, now inclosed in the Federal Building, in which the Mexican national hero Miguel Hidalgo y Costilla was imprisoned before the Spanish executed him in 1811. For more details about this interesting and cultured city, refer to F. R. Almada, "La Fundación de la Ciudad de Chihuahua," *Boletín de la Sociedad Chihuahuense de Estados Históricos* (No. 1, May, 1938), I, 6-10; J. J. Lozano (ed.), *Chihuahua: Ciudad Prócer, 1709-1959* (Universidad de Chihuahua, 1959), *passim.* A view of Chihuahua at the time of the Indian depredations referred to in the text will be found in Ruxton, *Adventures in Mexico,* Chapter XIX.

148 The state of Durango (capital, Durango) lies immediately south of Chihuahua. These two states, plus Coahuila and Sonora — also in Northern Mexico — were within the perimeter of the Indian raids. The main trail of the raiders entered present-day Big Bend National Park at Persimmon Gap and, moving southward, then south-

westward, followed the general course of the present road through the park to San Carlos Ford above Santa Elena Canyon. The return route was via the Vado de Chizos. Compare Grieson's Map, 1881, and Big Bend National Park Map, 1964. Regarding two other trails into Northern Mexico and the extent of the Indian depredations, see Ruxton, *Adventures in Mexico*, 111-12. For more details about the trails and the depredations, see J. E. Haley, *Fort Concho and the Texas Frontier* (San Angelo, Texas, 1952), 1-4; Paul Horgan, *Great River: The Rio Grande in North American History* (New York, 1954, 2 vols.), II, 845-53.

149 A loose reference to Lord Byron's poem, "Mazeppa," about a hetman of the Ukraine and the horse that was a "Tartar of the Ukraine Breed" (line 360). P. E. More (ed.), *The Complete Poetical Works of Lord Byron* (Cambridge edition, 1905), 410.

150 In 1842, the governor of Chihuahua, García Conde, in desperation resorted to "the pusillanimous and dangerous expedient of buying peace." The policy included the supplying of rations to the Indians and granting them the right to sell their stolen booty. Mexican leaders in Sonora, which state was being victimized, protested loudly, and moved in force against the Indian bands. Other extreme measures were adopted against the Apaches, such as the payment of $200 for each Indian scalp taken. At the time, however, the strength of the invaders was so great that no effective protection could be devised for the towns and settlements of Northern Mexico. Bancroft, *History of the North Mexican States and Texas*, II, 600-03, 614-20. See also Almada, *Resumen de Historia del Estado de Chihuahua*, 197-98, 235-36. W. H. Emory, U. S. Boundary Commissioner, estimated that the Indian raids led by Bajo el Sol in the 1850's cost the people of Northern Mexico more than $100,000,000. *Report on the United States and Mexican Boundary Survey*, I, 86-87.

151 Lake Jaco (Haco, Jaqui), located on the border between Chihuahua and Coahuila, drains the Bolsón de Mapimí. In his report of 1856, Commissioner Emory described the lake and its environs as "the rendezvous and stronghold of the Comanches and Kiowas, who annually plunder Durango and the neighboring States of Mexico. It is here they collect and divide the plunder, consisting of women, children, and animals. Here also, they leave their rifles, depending alone upon the lance in their depredations upon the Mexicans." *Ibid.*, I, 89.

152 Commissioner Emory detected nothing heroic in this Indian warrior: Although Bajo el Sol "called himself 'Mucho Toro,' and represented himself as a Comanche . . . he was evidently an escaped Mexican peon. . . . 'Mucho Toro' paid me a visit in full dress, on which occasion he displayed great humility, exhibiting conspicuously on his person an immense silver cross, which he stated had been given him by the Bishop of Durango when he was converted to Christianity. He had, no doubt, robbed some church of it. His features showed the profile of the Mexican Indian peon, but the warriors he commanded had the bold aquiline profile of the Kiowas and Comanches. I present him as a type who, by affiliation with the wild Indians, have produced such irreparable ruin to the northern States of Mexico." *Ibid.*, I, 86-88.

SEGMENT OF CHISOS MOUNTAINS

Located at southern extreme of Big Bend (now in Big Bend National Park). The mountains vary greatly in shape and height. Some rise to more than 7,500 feet above sea level.

Epilogue

Lawyer at Fort Stockton

OSCAR WALDO WILLIAMS
in 1924 at age 71

EPILOGUE

Lawyer at Fort Stockton

BY MARCH OF 1902 Williams had completed his work in the Big Bend and was back in Fort Stockton. He now determined to remain in the town and establish himself in the practice of law — a decision he could not postpone much longer, for he had reached middle age. Having managed to save something from his earnings as a surveyor during the past eighteen months, Williams was in a stronger position financially than he had been for some time. Even so, he knew that the struggle to build up a practice would be hard and long — given Fort Stockton's small population and limited resources.[1]

It would have been much easier for Williams to move to a large city where law clients would come his way in larger numbers and more promptly. But he had become a part of the Southwest and of the little town that epitomized it. For personal reasons, including those of health, he could not leave; and for the remaining forty-five years of his life, Fort Stockton would be the center of his activities — of his personal struggles and accomplishments — and the point of reference of many of his writings.

There could be no doubt of Williams' qualifications as a lawyer. A quarter of a century before, he had earned the LL.B. from Harvard, with excellent marks in Real Property and good ones in Torts and Criminal Law.[2] His experience in the mining fields of New Mexico had been a practical education, supplementing his academic training. As a surveyor in Texas, Williams had gained an intimate knowledge of the lands of the Lone Star State, their resources and the laws governing them. Thus equipped, he needed only an opportunity to put his knowledge to use and sufficient time to establish himself as a lawyer. Yet what kind of opportunity could the village of Fort Stockton offer a lawyer just opening his office for full-time practice? How much law practice could it actually provide?

It was clear that Fort Stockton could no longer depend on the flow of money from Washington to sustain its economy, for the Army had abandoned the fort years before — in 1886. The town must thus look to its own resources and to those of the ranching and farming area it served. Fortunately, even before Williams decided to open his law office, the local economy had received a welcome stimulus.

Between 1875 and 1900 a number of cattle ranchers had moved into Pecos County with large herds — the T-5 outfit, the Mule Shoe and the TX people, Doak, Frazer, Young, Harris, Childers and others. In addition, sheepmen — Anderson, Downie, Purington and Paxton — had located their stock in the southwestern part of the county, where the animals were bedded down at night within brush corrals. Fort Stockton had become the headquarters of these and other landholders, and it profited increasingly from their presence.[3]

An indication of progress, the Riggs Hotel was completed in 1902. Drummers, travelers and a few local bachelors and married couples occupied its rooms. Soon the first automobile, with its two-cylinder engine located in the turtleback, appeared on the dirt streets of the town. Homesteaders moved in with money to invest and to put into circulation. Business conditions in Fort Stockton and its vicinity improved materially.

Williams was alert to all these developments. Already having connections with the Pecos County Cattlemen's Association, he was soon able to line up the leading ranchers of the county as clients — firms like Western Beef and Livestock, the 7d Ranch and others. He also arranged to look after the affairs of various homesteaders, doing all of their surveys, abstracts and legal work. In addition, he performed increasing services for nonresidents; eventually he would represent more absentee landowners than any other lawyer in Fort Stockton.[4]

While thus acquiring more and more clients, Williams was able also to salvage something from his ill-fated farming venture along the Pecos River. Aided by his friend and associate engineer T. H. Bomar, he promoted the Imperial Irrigation Company, which constructed a dam to catch the floodwaters of the Pecos and make them available to adjacent farms through canals crossing Williams' land. At the same time, he helped develop the Zimmerman irrigation project, the ditches of which also also crossed his property. He served as attorney for both enterprises.[5]

By 1905, although he still owed some money, Williams had his affairs well enough under control to begin buying land again. As he proceeded with his legal practice and surveying activities, he had many opportunities to locate and secure title to tracts which cost little but which had much potential value. These he selected with great care, almost as if he were making moves on a gigantic chessboard. His holdings were so distributed that any development in Pecos County would almost certainly benefit him and his heirs. The foundations of his estate, which attained considerable proportions following the discovery of oil near his properties, were laid at this time.[6]

On April 8, 1908, the town arrived at a milestone in its history when the first issue of the *Fort Stockton Pioneer* appeared. At the outset, the paper consisted of only four pages, but it grew in both size and coverage as time passed. Perhaps the most important item in the initial number was an article by O. W. Williams on the aborigines of Pecos County. Once started, Williams continued his contributions each succeeding week throughout the year, broadening them to include information about the plant and animal life of the county. This series not only promoted culture in the community but it also enhanced the reputation of the writer. This was "ethical advertising" to which no member of the bar could object.[7]

Within two or three years Williams had established himself as a leading lawyer in West Texas. His practice, though not yet thriving, provided for his family comfortably; what is more, his law business was steadily growing. Because of his first-hand experience with the problems of irrigation and his recognition of the important role of water in this arid region, Williams devoted increasing attention to the law of riparian rights. He eventually became a recognized authority in this field, and won for clients several important suits involving both surface and subsurface water rights.[8]

In his practice, Williams functioned as an "office lawyer." Disinclined to courtroom appearances because of his weak voice and distaste for histrionics, he preferred to prepare his cases thoroughly and have associates present them. He followed this procedure particularly in jury trials. The system was effective; Williams had learned procedure from the ground up during his tenure as county judge, and he kept a tight rein on the conduct of all cases entrusted to him. His interests naturally carried him into the field of civil, as opposed to criminal, law.

Among fellow lawyers in Fort Stockton, Williams was said to have one of the keenest and best-organized minds in the country and one of the most disorganized desks. His filing system was unique; he piled letters, documents and papers eighteen inches to two feet deep in apparent disorder on his rolltop desk and two tables. Yet, when he needed to find something, his hand usually went unerringly to the item required and took it out promptly.[9]

His colleagues of the bar often referred to him as "a walking abstract office" because of his extensive knowledge of surveys and land titles. He retained in his remarkable memory both the location and the title history of almost every tract in Pecos County. His knowledge extended back to his early surveying days, when he designated a number of blocks with the now-familiar initials "O. W." Williams organized one of the pioneer abstracting firms in Fort Stockton, the Shaw Abstract Company. Its files and books were afterward sold to Ellyson Guarantee Abstract Company, which continues to operate.

In less than a decade after Williams embarked on his legal career, the economy of Fort Stockton received a decided boost when surveyors of the Kansas City, Mexico and Orient Railroad began laying out a route through Pecos County. The arrival of the railroad was expected at last to bring the isolated town into touch with the outside world and thus stimulate business and increase property values. Anticipating this development, real-estate agents and promoters began to operate with enthusiasm. They bought the two largest farms near town — the 7d and the Rooney properties — subdivided them into forty-acre tracts, and sold these smaller plots to buyers all over the United States. When the railroad arrived on August 12, 1912, the future of the town seemed assured.[10]

Williams was at the center of developments during those days. His office became the legal headquarters of most of the land developers, including Belding, Lunger and Maxwell; William T. Shearer; the Union Land Company; the United States and Mexican Trust Company; the Orient Land Company, and others. In a short time he achieved the supreme award aspired to by lawyers practicing in small towns: He was appointed to represent the new railroad itself. A few years later he became the local attorney for the Southern Pacific.

Thus secure in his practice, Williams was able to branch out into business. He helped to organize, and was one of the owners of, several pioneer enterprises in Fort Stockton: an electric-power company, an ice plant, a laundry and a home-owners' loan company. He also continued buying land, acting always with fore-sight and calculation. He combined caution with skill in all these operations — proof that he was determined to avoid the risks that had brought him to ruin during his early mining days in New Mexico.

Now a mature, successful, and respected citizen, Williams faith-fully discharged the civic and social responsibilities of his position. He took the lead in raising funds for the first public-school library and for the school's athletic association. He was active in the Masonic Lodge of Alpine and the Woodmen of the World in Fort Stockton. He was a loyal member of the Christian Church; he regularly attended its services, supported it financially and par-ticipated in its religious programs.

Having been able to provide for the education of his own chil-dren, this loyal citizen of Fort Stockton now lent assistance to other young persons traveling the same road. He took enthusiastic interest in sports, especially baseball. As a booster of the local teams, he usually kept the official score when games were played at home, and he frequently attended out-of-town games when he could get away.[11]

From 1908 to 1923, Williams concentrated on his law practice. The legal records of Pecos County include many documents that attest to his activities during this period. With the exception of some personal letters and business records, these documents com-prise the major sources of information for these fifteen years.

In the fall of 1923, Williams resumed his routine of writing and continued it for the next twenty years. First, during this period he wrote most of the accounts of his earlier activities included in this volume. Second, he recorded a large number of current ex-periences and impressions — week by week — in a series of letters written to his son Jesse C. Williams, who was then in China with an American oil company.

Taken as a whole, these letters constitute a journal of special interest. They not only deal with Williams' personal activities; they also record in detail and interpret incisively the events in the Fort Stockton area. The letters tell much about the hard times of the early 1920's — the inability of even the most substantial citizens to pay their debts; the economic loss caused by the bank-ruptcy of the Orient Railroad; the distress that long drought caused the ranchman and the farmer. We sense also the depen-dence of the people of this arid region on rain as well as on fair weather — an almost fatalistic dependence on the elements for their livelihood and well-being.[12]

In addition, the letters give a close-up view of the effects locally of the stock-market crash of 1929 and the depression that followed it. Williams describes in detail the failure of the Pecos Valley Refining Company, the closing of the First National Bank and the financial plight of individual ranchers and prominent businessmen during that difficult period. He lists the unpaid notes held by him for collection and shrewdly appraises the causes of each default.[13]

The letters then trace the slow process of economic recovery in the 1930's. It is clear from them that recovery in Pecos County depended more on the development of the oil resources in the immediate area and the market price for oil than on any other factors. Although during July and August, 1930, the market price was low — due both to the general depression and to the overproduction of petroleum, especially in the East Texas field — a year later, the price had improved. Among other measures, the program of proration administered by the Oil and Gas Division of the Texas Railroad Commission had begun to have a stabilizing effect.[14]

When this final period of his life opened, Williams was in his early seventies; he therefore recognized the need to make a change in his habits and activities. In a letter dated September 8, 1929, he indicated the new policy he intended to follow:

Court is on, and while I go into it as little as possible, it is impossible to avoid some of the work and worry incident to a law firm in term time. I have absolutely quit all trials; yet I have to serve as a kind of sentry on guard or, maybe it is more correct to say, as a scout on reconnaissance. I do not want to encounter again the inevitable nervewracking experience of examining and cross-examining witnesses and wrangling with the opposing attorney. Youth can stand it, perhaps flourish on it — but age shrinks from it.

The oil game has greater rewards always in prospect, and so far I have not found its disappointments to be as bitter. Out of it, all I hope in the next two or three years is to find the leisure and strength to write out more of the experiences of my life for the use of my children. I still have diaries of my early years, which help greatly in this work.

And write he did — not only the detailed letters to his son Jesse, but also accounts of the early episodes of his life. The years 1930 through 1938 were especially productive of these miscellaneous pieces; from 1938 on, however, Williams confined his writing chiefly to the letters addressed to Jesse in China.

If Williams thought, as seems likely, that the oil business would be less strenuous than the practice of law, he was decidedly mistaken. The new career on which he embarked was in many respects the most exciting and exacting of his long, eventful life. The operation that he undertook involved much more than the negotiation and signing of leases and the collection of royalties. It involved also much strenuous physical work in the oil fields and a number of bitterly fought lawsuits, not only at Fort Stockton but also at Austin and in the East Texas oil fields.

Williams' activities in the oil-lease business were enough in themselves to call on all his energy and resourcefulness. They extended over a wide territory in Southwest Texas — through Pecos, Crockett, Reagan and Upton counties. He was concerned with all kinds of business details and legal problems: titles to land, leasehold rights, estates, partnerships, the relations between employer and employee, promotion and financing.

Here was grist for the mill of a resourceful lawyer, and Williams made the most of the opportunity. In particular, he took advantage of his intimate knowledge of surveys in Pecos County and of the investments in land he had made when it was plentiful and cheap. In his letters to his son Jesse, Williams reported from time to time that his profits from these sources were substantial.

Again, as had been true when Williams was on the Plains of Texas, in the mines of Southwestern New Mexico, and in the Texas Big Bend — he was on the scene at the historic moment, recording and interpreting what he witnessed. He visited and observed the oil fields of West Texas during the early days of exploration and discovery — the days of the wildcatter when fortunes were made overnight from the investment of a pittance, the big strike coming without notice — or, more often, when high hopes disappeared forever at the bottom of a dry hole.

Because of his extensive landholdings, Williams was vitally interested in the discovery of oil in Pecos County. Exploration and drilling had begun there in 1916, but only in a limited way — and without success.[15] Activities increased during 1919; however, no producing well was brought in.[16] In 1923, W. B. Troy and J. W. Grant aroused much interest with their drilling operations, but these failed, causing a loss to investors.[17]

At the same time, a new promoter appeared in Fort Stockton who would dominate the scene for the next five years — until 1927. This man was J. F. Quinby — robust, well-dressed, personable, astute and determined — who hailed from St. Louis and who was reputed to be backed by Eastern and British capital. Quinby was sure that vast deposits of oil could be found "west of the Pecos," in the area often described as "the graveyard of the wildcatter." He proceeded therefore to lease, in the name of the companies he headed, extensive oil acreage in Pecos County, and to sink test wells on the most promising locations.[18]

Williams followed Quinby's moves with intense interest and evaluated them each week in his letters. In Williams' appraisal, Quinby emerges as an operator of unusual resourcefulness, energy and audacity. Yet, like other wildcatters of the era, he was at heart a gambler who staked all on the big strike. Quinby did enlist some financial support, chiefly from associates in St. Louis,[19] but it proved inadequate for his grandiose plan. Within six months after beginning, he had run out of funds and was obliged to appeal in person to his Eastern backers to replenish them.

Some extra operating capital arrived, but not enough. Quinby was unable to pay his workers, and several of them sued him for past-due wages. He ran up heavy debts in town that went unpaid, including legal fees due Williams in the amount of $500. The venturesome promoter defaulted on obligations to lessors of land and suppliers of drilling equipment. He was repeatedly haled into court. Yet he shrugged off such harassments and — by one means or another — continued his operations for two more years.[20]

Williams reveals the unexpected resourcefulness and limitless gall of the man by recounting two episodes of Quinby's spectacular career at Fort Stockton.

By the middle of 1925 Quinby appeared to be almost certainly at the end of his resources — and of those of his associates. He had left town, and this time no one expected him to return. Yet, early in September, he suddenly reappeared, accompanied by a retinue of aides. The party engaged five rooms at the Stockton Hotel and passed out the word that Quinby had raised $250,000 with which to continue operating. This news called for a banquet in the dining room of the new Rooney Hotel and other appropriate festivities.

Yet, within a matter of weeks it became evident that something had gone wrong. Quinby had apparently relied on a vague promise

QUINBY No. 5

Located north of Fort Stockton on Section 6, Block 114, Pecos County.
Spudded in December, 1923. Ended as dry hole. The derrick was typical
of those used in the West Texas field during the 1920's.

FORT STOCKTON, CIRCA 1913
Principal downtown corner. New courthouse is shown on right.
Note the cars in use a half century ago.

of money from one or more of his "sources" in the East or abroad. At any rate, no money arrived, and he was without funds to pay even current expenses. What, under the circumstances, could he do? Quinby solved the dilemma quite simply. Feigning illness, he gathered together his party and their baggage, and Sunday at midnight, departed without notice for parts east. He left behind a thousand-dollar hotel bill, plus other debts. But Quinby apparently thought that these could be "consolidated" with the prodigious sums he already owed — and handled somehow.[21]

Work naturally faltered on Quinby's wells — in fact, his company was insolvent; but the promoter had not given up. Williams cites a second striking example of the wildcatter's fortitude in the face of insuperable odds. In May, 1926, Quinby showed up in Boston. There he listed the stock of his all-but-defunct oil company on the Boston Exchange.[22] Moreover, in the role of "Major" Quinby, he gave the Boston *Sunday Advertiser* of May 30, 1926, a long interview, which was published under the heading "New England Millionaire Is Oil King." Williams read a copy of the newspaper and commented that the interview was "full of lies — gigantic — so he must be very hard up."[23] A week later, Williams wrote that Quinby

made the most extravagant and, to us, ridiculous claims as to his properties and performances. Among them there was the story of one of his wells coming in and drowning two hundred ducks peacefully swimming on neighboring pools of water. Another story set up that a young man, his wife and their nine-year-old boy started *digging for potash*, struck a gusher and realized $16,000,000 from it. Some of our citizens are trying to locate this young man, whose acquaintance might prove valuable.[24]

In spite of Quinby's extravagant claims — claims of desperation, actually — he was unable to raise the capital needed to prevent the collapse of his grand design in Pecos County. Still undaunted, he returned to Fort Stockton for the last time, hoping to salvage his operation by bringing in a new well within the town limits — a well in which Williams had a sizeable interest. Unfortunately, in September, 1926, the drillers struck salt water; within a few months the well was abandoned as hopeless.[25] Quinby's creditors had meanwhile filed a series of lawsuits; these eventually wiped out the last traces of his projected oil empire.[26] Quinby left town and was never heard of again.

Quinby, despite his unorthodox methods, must be judged in the light of the conditions under which he operated. He entered the West Texas oil fields during the early days of wildcatting when the "play" was wide open, and rashness often paid off fabulously. He played a daring, reckless game according to the standards of the time, when the rule of. *caveat emptor* allowed promoters a wide latitude — provided they avoided outright fraud, especially in using the mails. He gambled on striking one or more gushers, but sunk only dry holes — for the prosaic reason that he drilled too far west and south of the Pecos River, near which the incredible Yates field was soon brought in.

If Quinby had succeeded in his venture, he no doubt would have ranked with Col. Albert E. Humphreys, "Dad" Joiner and other celebrated Texas oil barons. As it turned out, Fate decreed that the bold wildcatter of Pecos County was not to achieve even modest success. He will doubtless be remembered only as one of the most colorful persons who crossed Williams' path — a bold and intrepid adventurer who staked all on a turn of fortune — and lost.[27]

While following the activities of J. F. Quinby, mostly from the sidelines, Williams became increasingly involved in the oil business now developing rapidly in the area around Fort Stockton. Early in May, 1924, he expressed keen interest in the Santa Rita Discovery at Big Lake, to the northeast in Reagan County, and the drilling then under way on the Ira Yates ranch, just west of the river in Pecos County.[28]

Almost a year later — in April, 1925 — he visited the Santa Rita field and wrote this graphic account of what he saw:

Our first stop was at the place where the first well showed up oil, the famous Santa Rita No. 1. Here the Big Lake Oil Company has built fifty or sixty shacks to house its employees; and some thirty storage tanks, with from 500-barrel to 55,000-barrel capacity. There is also a gasoline-storage plant, plus some stores and supply houses. Our next stop was at the Group No. 1 headquarters, two miles farther east, where that company has built up a small city of shacks for its workers, with hospital, restaurant, dormitories, offices and small houses for married couples, along with various supply houses, oil tanks, warehouses, etc.

Two miles farther east we came to Best,[29] a town of about three hundred houses of lumber and sheet-iron — some of them two stories high — stores, offices, restaurants and homes. And all of these improvements, from Texon to Best, are built on five- and ten-year leases, as the

University is not selling its lands. Three miles farther east I saw the Marland Tank Farm, where fourteen 80,000-barrel tanks have been put up, with nine feet of circular earth wall around each, called a "fire guard."[30] Here there were some offices and homes on titled land.

I saw Big Lake No. 23 come in for some 2,500 barrels of oil, and No. 19 for over 25,000,000 cubic feet of gas. We waited some hours without success to see Group No. 1, Oil Corporation No. 5, come in. The well could have been brought in either in oil or in gas, as it was on debatable land — a gas structure on one side, an oil structure on the other. Finally, after the bailer had brought up water many times from the 1,200-foot level without lowering the water level in the hole, the driller announced that the water was coming into the hole as fast as it was being bailed out and that the drilling would be resumed.[31]

As we went away from Group No. 1, the last sight we had of the offset well on Big Lake No. 19 showed us the red cloud rising from the hole against the crow's nest in the top of the rig, and drifting away to the northwest to cover a mile of creosote bush with a red smudge. I wondered how that head of gas could ever be gotten under control. Yet it seems from the papers that two days later it had been completely shut off.[32]

As I knew that gas had caused several deaths in this field, I had supposed this gas to be deadly. I was told, however, that the deaths came from the gas thrown off from the 2,980-foot level; and that the gas coming from the 2,590-foot level was an innocuous "sweet" gas. When the gas from that level was first struck in the great 50,000,000-foot gas well, it was supposed to be deadly, and trains — engines, rather — were not allowed to pass near the well. The cars were shunted from one side of it by an engine, to be picked up by another on the other side of the well, while autos were forced to detour out a mile from the hole. Other extraordinary precautions were observed. Now none seem to be observed.[33]

About the middle of June, Williams returned to Big Lake to witness the opening of a new pool around World Oil Company No. 1, L. P. Powell. He reported his observations as follows:

The well rested on what seemed to be a rather long oil structure, with the highest point at the south end and with a surface of level strata at ground level where the well was drilled. The theory followed in drilling apparently was that the gas must be under that high south end, while the oil would be found near the roof of the structure on a lower level.[34]

We saw some waste oil about the slush pit and a little in a tank nearby. The driller had tied the bailer[35] off to one side and was unscrewing the joints of the drill bit while he was directing the scrubbing of the platform with warm water. After the casing had been set at 2,647 feet on the day before, a packer[36] had been set at the bottom to keep out more water. At the same time, oil was coming in below the casing. We left at 10:00 A.M., after people in some thirty automobiles arrived to learn what was going on. Later we heard that the well came in two hours after we left, with 500 barrels of production per day. The swab had been attached to the drill stem after we left. After some swabbing of the well, the oil rose rapidly to the top.[37]

Within twenty-four hours, the landowner had sold $150,000 of oil leases on his neighboring lands; and forty-eight hours afterwards, the World people had sold their well for $1,400,000, with 2,600 acres of lease around it. That is making money fast. After its sale, the well was capped. Arrangements were made to drill other wells — the plan being, I suppose, to get ready for additional pipelines to market the oil — and to that end, to find the oil and get it ready. The well was brought in by the Humble Company, a subsidiary of Standard Oil. Walter Teagle, President of Standard Oil of New Jersey, was present when the well came in.

While at the Texon camp, I saw a plat made by Clayton [Williams' son] that showed the underlying salt field through which the Big Lake wells are drilled to oil. It showed a dome — a salt dome — the highest point of which (in the center of the dome) was 1,065 feet below the surface. The edges of the salt dome would not be higher than 1,340 feet below the surface, nearly 280 feet lower than the central salt structure. Yet, on the surface there is no evidence of any kind of dome, the strata being laid down nearly level. The salt beds are 300 to 400 feet in thickness. It seems that the World well also found salt at about the same depth, and found oil in the same stratum as at Big Lake, but 200 feet higher up.[38]

Towards the end of September, 1925, another oil field was brought in — at McCamey in Upton County, a short distance northeast of Fort Stockton. Visiting the place later, Williams recorded these impressions:

I spent about an hour looking over a boom town in its infancy. Unpainted houses of one story with tin roofs, no lights and no water; narrow, boggy streets crowded and congested; autos and trucks carrying lumber, casing, oil and gasoline barrels, and household plunder —

all these things went to make up the boom town of McCamey. There were probably three hundred houses, interspersed with lumber yards; open lots filled with casing and drilling tools; restaurants galore and tents housing shows and movies. It was Sunday; I saw two or three men on the streets patently drunk and disorderly.

On coming back yesterday through McCamey, I was impressed again with the unpleasant features of residence or business in that town under present conditions. The dust on the roads and streets must lie three to four inches deep in the ruts worn by wheels; probably an inch deep on the level surfaces. The southeast trade winds blowing at this time of the year raise a yellowish-red cloud on the highways and streets; as a result, cars and persons are liable to accident, and the houses and tents nearby become filled with dirt. A single car streaking out of the town along a highway at a fair speed raises a yellow wall of dust. The dust cloud lines up against the sky as dense as the black front of a storm cloud.

Water simply is not to be found in the town, either in wells or in cisterns; it is brought in from Alpine or Big Lake, in tank cars over the railroad. The town lies in the flat valley of the Pecos River, where little water is found that even livestock will drink. I heard recently that for two days the water in the town was so scant that ice was shipped in and melted for drinking water. Working in dust, eating in dust, sleeping in dust, drinking bad water or getting none at all, dirty of face and hair and clothes — the average man must feel that life in McCamey is hard.[39]

Williams' letters contain many details about the oil fields of West Texas during this early period: descriptions of such devices as the torsion balance, the alidade, the core driller and a special radio-signal machine, plus explanations of how they were being used; vivid accounts of wells blowing in, of fatal accidents and costly fires in the oil fields; shrewd assessments of rumors about pending oil strikes; comments on the geological structure of the region; evaluations of oil developments as they affected the economy of Fort Stockton — plus regular reports on the complicated operations of O. W. Williams himself as landowner and as lawyer and leasing agent for an ever-increasing clientele.

The 1930's were in many ways the most satisfying period in Williams' life. Although he was now in his eighties — at an age when most men are inactive — he faced the future with unprecedented energy and assurance. Thanks chiefly to the developing oil fields, his law practice and leasing business grew rapidly, bringing in unexpected profits. His increased wealth, in turn, gave him additional leisure. This he devoted to study, writing and speaking. Using his diary as a source, he prepared accounts of his early experiences on the Staked Plains of Texas and in the mining fields of New Mexico, and published them in pamphlets for distribution among the members of his family and friends. He also wrote a number of shorter pieces — letters and recollections — filling in the details of his life story.[40]

Williams used some of the time of this period to travel. He made regular trips back to his old home at Carthage, Illinois, where he kept alive his contacts with relatives and friends. He visited places of historical interest in various parts of the United States. He took time to deliver an address to the boys and girls of the Fort Stockton schools; he also appeared, in 1939, as a principal speaker at a meeting of the West Texas Historical Association, held in Lubbock. From these activities he derived much satisfaction: he viewed them as the climax of his eventful career.

Many of Williams' acquaintances came to regard him during these twilight years as the Patriarch of the Trans-Pecos. In 1930 the *Fort Stockton Pioneer* reprinted his "History of Animal Life in Pecos County" from the first issues of 1908. The same newspaper, on March 16, 1934, celebrated Williams' eighty-first birthday with congratulatory headlines and an article that hailed him as "early-day citizen and leader."

As time passed, personal sorrows ensued, and age began to take its toll. In August, 1936, Mrs. Sallie Wheat Williams, his loyal and helpful wife for more than half a century, died.[41] As serious illness befell some other members of the family, Williams shared the worries stoically and did all he could to cope with them. Because his health remained good and his mind sharp throughout the decade, he was able to shoulder more than his quota of burdens and responsibilities.[42]

In the early 1940's, the old man suffered a reverse from which he never recovered. He fell while watering the lawn and struck his head on a concrete wall. The blow produced a brain concussion. Thereafter, Williams frequently blacked out or lost conscious contact with his surroundings. Realizing in his lucid periods that his death could not be far off, he began to distribute his extensive landholdings among his children. This process continued from the fall of 1943 through the middle of 1946.[43] In this interval, Williams' physical and mental condition worsened.

Bedridden at home for a number of months, he fell again after getting out of bed against doctors' orders. He suffered a broken hip in this fall and was taken to the local hospital, visibly feeble and emaciated. In this weakened condition, the nonagenarian soon contracted pneumonia, lapsed into a coma, and quietly expired. After ninety-three years and seven months, his lungs, which had worried him most of his life, finally failed him.

Williams died in the fall of 1946. Two days afterwards, the weekly *Pioneer* devoted two columns to the details of the funeral and to the "colorful career of Judge Williams." He was buried in the East Hill Cemetery, located a mile and a half east of Fort Stockton. A light-blue granite slab marks the grave.

For a special reason, the inscription on Williams' headstone is significant. During the years that he was engaged in historical research, he visited many old graveyards and copied data from many old grave markers. In so doing, he insisted that he was obtaining the most dependable source material available. First, he declared, these inscriptions always give accurately the dates of birth and death. Second, he maintained, the inscriptions usually tell in a few words who the deceased was and what he really achieved during his lifetime. Judged by these criteria, the words carved on his own gravestone at East Hill Cemetery serve fittingly to sum up Williams' life and to close this account of it.

WAITING IN THE FAITH

OSCAR WALDO WILLIAMS

SON OF JESSE CALEB WILLIAMS AND
MARY ANN COLLIER WILLIAMS OF CARTHAGE, ILL.

BORN MARCH 17, 1853, MT. VERNON, KY.

LAWYER, SURVEYOR, HISTORIAN, NATURALIST AND WRITER

DIED OCTOBER 29, 1946, FORT STOCKTON, TEXAS

NOTES

(for the Epilogue)

1 In 1900, Fort Stockton was a village of such scanty population that it was not mentioned in the Census for that year. In all of Pecos County, there were only 2,360 inhabitants. Bureau of the Census, *Thirteenth Census of the United States* (Washington, 1913), III, 790. Lacking railroad connections, the people of the area depended on horse-drawn wagons and coaches for transportation. While the Pecos River and Comanche Springs provided water for some agricultural production, the land and climate of Pecos County were suited essentially to ranching. At this early time, Fort Stockton was a small isolated community, only beginning to establish itself economically.

2 Letter, Austin W. Scott, retired Professor of Law, Harvard University, to Clayton W. Williams, June 4, 1964.

3 Clayton W. Williams, "Fort Stockton's First 100 Years," *Fort Stockton Centennial, 1859-1959,* p. 37. For a view of Pecos County in the formative 1880's, see *Fort Stockton Pioneer,* Sept. 10, 1908. (Hereinafter cited as *Pioneer.*) A brief survey for the year 1908 is found, *ibid.,* Sept. 17 and Nov. 5, 19 and 26, 1908. The outlook three years later is summarized, *ibid.,* April 4, 21 and 28, May 5 and 26, Aug. 4 and 25, Oct. 13, and Dec. 22, 1911.

4 Business letters in files of O. W. Williams.

5 Pecos County, *Deed Records,* Vol. 13, p. 85; Vol. 14, p. 24.

6 The Deed Records of Pecos County indicate that between 1905 and 1943, the year of his retirement, Williams handled many personal transactions relating to land in the county. Including purchases, sales, leases, releases, water rights, assignments, transfers, extensions, deeds of trust, etc., he registered with the County Clerk some three hundred legal instruments in his own name. These were in addition to the hundreds of transactions he handled for clients.

7 Williams later published these essays in a pamphlet, *Historic Review of Animal Life in Pecos County.*

8 Clayton Williams recalls attending some of these trials with his father, especially in adjoining counties. A number of the disputes were settled out of court.

9 Letters to Clayton Williams from Attorneys Maurice R. Bullock (Fort Stockton, July 30, 1964) and Ben G. Smith (Fort Worth, Sept. 29, 1964). Messrs. Bullock and Smith practiced law in Fort Stockton when O. W. Williams was a member of the bar there. Mr. Smith writes: "Judge Williams was, on all important subjects, the best informed man I have ever known."

10 Clayton Williams, "Fort Stockton's First 100 Years," *Fort Stockton Centennial,* 39. The coming of the Orient Railroad and its possible effects on the local economy are reviewed in the *Pioneer,* April 21 and 28, May 12 and 26, June 2, Aug. 25, Oct.

13, Dec. 22, 1911; May 5, 24 and 31, June 21 and 28, Sept. 13, Oct. 4, Nov. 19 and 20, 1912; Jan. 3, 1913.

11 This personal information about Judge Williams was supplied by Clayton Williams.

12 Letters, O. W. Williams to Jesse C. Williams: Sept. 16 and 23, Oct. 21, 1923; April 27, Aug. 10, Nov. 23, Dec. 21, 1924; May 3, 24 and 31, Nov. 11 and 18, 1925.

13 *Ibid.,* July 17, 1929; Oct. 26, 1930; Jan. 18, March 25, July 19, Sept. 27, Dec. 15, 1931. The files of the *Pioneer,* 1931-33, reflect in detail the conditions of the community during the Depression.

14 Letter, Aug. 30, 1931. By the beginning of 1933, the economy of Fort Stockton had become reasonably stable, thanks chiefly to the oil business in the area. *Ibid.,* Jan. 29, May 25, June 4, July 16, 1933; April 17, Dec. 3, 1934. Regarding the effects of proration on the oil economy, see C. C. Rister, *Oil! Titan of the Southwest* (University of Oklahoma Press, Norman, 1949), 298-99, 315 ff. (Hereinafter cited as Rister, *Oil!*)

15 *Pioneer,* Feb. 18 and 25, June 9, 16 and 30, July 7, 21 and 28, Aug. 4, 11 and 18, Sept. 1, Oct. 6, 1916.

16 *Ibid.,* May 16 and 23, June 6, July 25, Aug. 29, Sept. 26, Nov. 14, 1919.

17 *Ibid.,* Feb. 2 and 23, March 16, April 20, May 4 and 11, Aug. 17, Oct. 26, Nov. 11, 1923. The Troy-Grant well, reported to be a gusher, was actually "salted." *Ibid.,* Jan. 12, 1926.

18 That Quinby dominated the oil activity in Pecos County during this period is shown by Williams' letters to his son J. C. and by issues of the weekly *Pioneer.*

19 Backing Quinby were S. R. Francis, E. M. Metcalf and G. E. Minor, officers in his Trans-Pecos Oil Company. *Pioneer,* May 23, Nov. 16 and 23, Dec. 7 and 14, 1923; Jan. 11, 1924.

20 Claims were brought against Quinby's company in Causes 1572, 1622, 1623, 1624, 1625 and 1636, District Court of Pecos County. A series of judgments was entered against the company during the period of February to September, 1925.

21 Letters, O. W. Williams to Jesse C. Williams, Aug. 29, Sept. 6, 1925. *Pioneer,* Sept. 4, 1925.

22 Letter, May 30, 1926.

23 *Ibid.,* June 20, 1926.

24 *Ibid.,* June 27, 1926.

25 *Ibid.,* Sept. 19, 1926; Jan. 30, 1927.

26 Judgment by default was entered against Quinby in Causes 1710, 1731, 1740, 1742, 1754, 1755, 1756, 1771, 1900, 2111, 2655 and 2662, District Court of Pecos County.

27 The Texas wildcatter was a special breed. As Rister says: "Essentially he was a plunger and a gambler, an up-and-down, in-and-out operator, playing the game restlessly. Some early wildcatters made and lost several fortunes and are yet active, still following an oil will-o'-the-wisp. They prowl the little-known regions, swamps, hills, and valleys in their endless search for underground wealth. The urge of discovery draws them on; they seek hidden oil pools and formations whether the market is low or high. And it is through their wildcatting that great fields have been discovered." *Oil!*, 185.

28 Letter, May 4, 1924.

29 Best, a town located a few miles east of the Big Lake oil field, was overcrowded, with a population of some four thousand, during the oil boom, but today it is almost a ghost town. Big Lake, named for a large, shallow body of water nearby, is located fifteen miles east of the first bonanza oil field in West Texas, which was opened up by the discovery of Santa Rita Well No. 1. Rankin is west of this oil field, in Upton County, on the K. C. M. & O. Railroad. The Santa Rita well was located at a site in what is now Texon, a town named for the company that brought in the well.

30 The Marland Oil Company pumped oil from the Big Lake field into these tanks, from which the Humble Oil and Refining Company piped it to its refineries.

31 This well, located on Section 36, Block 6, University lands, Reagan County, was spudded in Feb. 23 and completed April 8, 1925, as a 1,318-barrel well at 3,019 feet.

32 In order to obtain the more prolific oil production at 3,000 feet, the shallower gas production was bypassed at this time by drilling through the gas horizon with the hole full of water.

33 Letters, April 5 and 12, 1925.

34 World No. 1 was the first commercial oil producer in Crockett County. It was brought in May 30, 1925, at a depth of 2,646 feet, in the Grayburg formation. The well was located about sixteen miles south of the Big Lake oil field. *Pioneer*, June 5, 1925. Up to 1953, wells in the World field produced 19,471,434 barrels of oil. F. A. Herald, *Occurrence of Oil and Gas in West Texas* (University of Texas Publication No. 5716, 1957), *passim*.

35 The bailer is a long cylinder attached to the sand line (cable), which is lowered into the hole of the test well during the process of drilling. It functions to bring up the drill-cuttings and thus clean the hole for further drilling. The lower end of the cylinder is closed by the tongue, which serves as a valve. When the bottom of the bailer strikes the mud or cuttings in the bottom of the hole, the tongue moves up into the cylinder a short distance, allowing the cuttings to go into the cylinder. Then when the cylinder is raised, the tongue drops down again, closing the bottom of the bailer. Thus, the bailer is used to collect and remove the drill-cuttings from a well — to bail them out of the hole, so to speak.

36 The packer is a hard rubber cylinder placed on the outside of the casing or tubing, fitting tightly against the walls of the drilled hole or the casing. The device holds back the fluid above and permits a test to be made in the hole below.

37 The swab, a device that fits snugly against the casing or pipe, contains a valve in its center. Attached to the sand line or drilling cable, it is lowered into the hole to collect fluid. As the swab descends, the fluid flows up through the valve. The device is then pulled up, lifting the fluid above it and creating a suction in the shaft below.

38 Letter, June 14, 1925.

39 *Ibid.*, July 26, Aug. 22, 1926.

40 For a list of Williams' writings, see Appendix III.

41 Mrs. Williams died of a heart attack, August 25, 1936. From the beginning of their marriage, she had shared with Judge Williams the responsibilities of the home and family. In addition to her household duties, she taught music, conducted a Sunday-school class, and was active in the Order of the Eastern Star and the Literary and Pioneer clubs of Fort Stockton. A few days after her death, Williams wrote: "Of the sixty-six years I have spent working for myself — hard times, most of them — she has spent nearly fifty-five of them with me, loyally and cheerfully, sunshine and storm . . . although I took her from a good home in Dallas, Texas, into a life of hardship and exposure in the Frontier for the remainder of her life. . . . If I did not think there is a reward for her hereafter I should blame myself for her hardships in this life, and feel that there is no such thing as Eternal Justice. God's mercy must surely rest on her." Letter, Aug. 30, 1936. See also, *Pioneer,* Sept. 4, 1936.

42 These family problems are discussed in a number of Williams' letters to his son Jesse during this period.

43 Williams executed a series of warranty deeds to individual members of his family, beginning Sept. 14, 1943, and continuing through July 9, 1946. See Pecos County *Deed Records* for this period.

Appendices

ACKNOWLEDGMENTS

APPENDIX I

CROSBY COUNTY, SKETCH 5

Statement of O. W. Williams relative to original corners to surveys in Crosby, Lubbock, Hale and Floyd Counties

In the summer of 1877 in conjunction with J. B. Ammerman I ran a line from Dewey's Lake (E end) in Crosby County up the Blanco Cañon to a point in the old McKenzie [Mackenzie] trail 4 to 6 miles N. W. of the (then called) Tasker house (now I think occupied by H. C. Smith). At this point (supposed to be on South Boundary line of Floyd County) we erected a small earth mound by the side of the trail. Continuing on up the trail some 20 miles more we erected a pretty fair sized earth mound close to where the McKenzie trail crossed a draw or arroyo which we supposed to be the draw of Upper Catfish Creek.

This was a corner (I think the N.W. cor. of Sur. 1) of a Survey in I & G. N. Ry Co. Block C. There were no bearings, no mark that I remember, except that it seems to me there were 1 or 2 small rocks in the mound.

Our Survey continued West along said McKenzie trail some 6 or 8 miles further to a dry lake about ½ mile North of the trail, which was then full of water and which was then named Julia Lake in honor or some sweetheart of Joe Ammerman's I think. On the West side of this small lake we erected a sod mound some 6 feet high capped with 2 buffalo heads. From this point we turned back to the earth mound on the County Boundary of Floyd Co.

From this point we surveyed West until we came to where the draw of North Fork of Yellowhouse Cañon crossed the North line of Lubbock County. Here on the divide about ¼ mile East of the draw we erected an earth mound. From thence we meandered the Yellowhouse as far as mouth of Plum Creek where we erected a stone mound on a hill just East of mouth of Plum Creek.

We started this Survey from East end of Dewey's Lake supposing it to be on East line of Survey 37 Block 28 I & G. N. Ry. Survey, and Surveys were made in Block C Floyd County, R and others Hale County and Blocks A & B [and O] Lubbock County based on this connection, & if Dewey's Lake is not on East line of Survey 37 Block 28 as its calls declare, then the Surveys in the Blocks I have enumerated tie to Dewey's Lake & not to Survey 37 Block 28.

In the Summer of 1878 I accompanied E. M. Powell of Dallas in a Survey which commenced in the center of Lubbock County at the forks of the Yellowhouse. We erected a rock mound at S.W. Corner of Survey 1 Block A as closely as we could approximate to the field notes of said Survey No. 1. From this as a starting point we ran South & East down the Yellowhouse, putting up rock corners every mile down the Yellowhouse, on Block S.

We then returned & beginning again at S.W. corner Survey No. 1 Block A we surveyed North up the North Fork, surveying entirely by right angles, East & North, & finally erecting an earth mound at N.W. corner of Survey No. 1 Block B, B. S. & F. Ry. at East side of Lamb Co. and just North of a sipe springs or water-hole in the draw of North Fork.

We then ran North across the Sand Hills to Upper Catfish Creek. Running down the creek we established corners on Survey 1 Block J. B. and some Surveys in Blocks K & K3.

From this it will be seen that Blocks S, E, E2, AK, JS, D, D2, D3, D4, D5, P, X, CK, & P in Lubbock County and Blocks DT, D10, K3 & K in Hale Co. — A & JB Lamb Co. tie really to a point 650 varas South of S.E. corner of Dewey's Lake.

In Dec. 1878 and Jany. 1879 Mr. Summerfield and I ran a joint line from Dewey's Lake to Blocks K & JK Hale County. We accepted Southeast corner of Dewey's Lake as being 650 varas North of S.E. corner Survey 37 Block 28 & established from that the relative position of certain Blocks in N.W. part of Hale Co. We supposed we were establishing this position relative to a point 650 varas S. of E. end of Dewey's Lake. This line was accepted at G. L. O. [General Land Office] as determining true situation of the Blocks N.W. part of Hale Co. & the L. O. [Land Office] maps of that portion of County are based on that line.

The Blocks thus certainly tied to Dewey's Lake instead of Survey 37 are O, O2, JK, SK4, O6, S1, S4, C3, JK2, JK3, M13.

It is my impression also that Blocks A1, A2, A3, A4, W, D7, D6, D8, N, CL, K, Hale County & C, RG, B9, D7, C2, H, Lubbock Co. & M, B, Crosby Co. are in the same condition, but as to this I am not certain. Mr. J. B. Ammerman or Mr. C. U. Connellee would probably know these facts.

O. W. Williams

October 6, 1887

APPENDIX II

OASIS MINE v. LAST CHANCE MINE

A. OASIS MINE: NOTICE OF LOCATION, 1879

The Oasis Quartz Mining Claim,   We the undersigned, Thomas Dunn, Fred W. Smith, and W. A. Downing of Shakespeare, County of Grant, Territory of New Mexico, Citizens of the United States, over the age of Twenty one (21) years, claim by right of location, under and in accordance with the revised Statutes of the United States, Chapter Six (6) Title Thirty two (32) Fifteen hundred (1500) feet linear and horizontal measurement on this vein or lode of copper and silver bearing Quartz or other rock in place, Together with all dips, Spurs, angles and variations of said lode or vein with surface ground Three hundred (300) feet in width upon each side of the center line of said vein or lode to be known as the "Oasis" Quartz Mining Claim, and further described as follows to wit: Beginning at a Stone Monument the same being situated on the West side of the Viola Shaft and being an extension of the Viola Mine running Southwesterly Fifteen Hundred (1500) feet, I further intend to hold and work said claims in accordance with local rules & customs of Miners, and the Mining Statues of the United States.

Dated upon the ground this twenty-eighth (28) day of August, A.D. 1879.

Witnesses	Fred W Smith
A. J. Thompson	Thomas Dunn
Henry C Harper	Wm A. Downing
	Locators.

Filed for Record in my office the 4th day of September A.D. 1879, at one Oclock P.M.

R. V. Newsham   *Probate Clerk*

B. LAST CHANCE MINE: MINING LOCATION, 1880

Territory of New Mexico
County of Grant

Know all men by these presents that the undersigned under the provisions of the laws of the United and for the purpose of amending Location to more definitely describe the same and reserving all rights heretofore acquired under former locations have located the Last Chance Mine situated in the Virginia Mining Dist County & Territory aforesaid which is Monumented and described as follows to Wit: Commencing at the East end centre monument of the Argonaut Mine, thence N 5° 25′ W 485 feet to Northeast corner of claim which is a monument of stone marked N.E.L.C. on the South line of the Ophir Mine. Thence S 83° 26′ W 600 feet to Northwest corner of claim, which is a monument stones marked W.W.L.C. on the South line of the Ophir Mine a stone monument set in the ground and marked Ophir No 3 bears S 83° 26′ W 385 feet distant thence S 5° 25′ E 542 feet to South West corner of claim which is a monument of stones on the Northwest line of the

Argonaut Mine marked SWLC Thence N 18º 0' E 521 feet to a monument of stones at the Northwest corner of the Argonaut Mine a prospect shaft 6x7x9 feet bears S 58º 12' W 138 feet distant Var 12º 37' E

Located on the ground this the 17th day of June AD 1880

Witness	*Locator*
Frank E Lyon	J E Price
John J Martin	

Filed for record September 23rd 1880 at 30 Min past 3 Oclock PM.

RV Newsham, *Probate Clerk*   By E Cosgrove, *Deputy*.

C. OASIS MINE SURVEY, 1881

I hereby certify that this is a correct plat of the boundaries of the Oasis Mining claim as surveyed by me the 8th day of January A. D. 1881.

Shakspeare, Grant Co.   Wilton R. Brown
lea. N. M.   U.S. *Mineral Deputy Surveyor*

OASIS MINE

Virginia District, Grant County N. M.

Located August 28th 1879. Surveyed Jan 8th 1881.

Field Notes of Survey. Commencing at the location monument and notice at the southwest end of Viola mine, and running S. 43º 32' E. (variation 13º 21' E) 300 ft to the northeast corner of claim. Monument marked O.N.E. thence S 46º 28' W 1500 ft to Southeast corner. Monument marked O.S.E. thence N 43º 32' W. 300 ft to

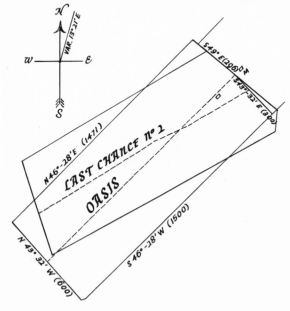

South west end center. Monument marked Oasis. S.W.E.C. and 600 ft to South west corner. Monument marked O.S.W.; thence N. 46° 28' E. 1471 ft to northwest corner. Marked O.N.W.; thence S 49° E. on end line of Viola to place of beginning. Location monument marked Oasis I.M.

Shakepeare N. M. Grant Co.
Jan 8th 1881.

Wilton R. Brown
U.S. Mineral Deputy Surveyor

Filed for record Jan. 18, 1881. at 1 P.M.
E Stine, *Probate Clerk*

D. Synopsis of the Mining Laws of the Territory of New Mexico Governing the Location and Relocation of Mining Claims

(By M. E. Hickey)

Dimension of Lode Claim

A lode claim may be 600 feet in width by 1,500 feet in length.

By Section 2324, Revised Statutes of the United States, the miners of each mining district may make regulations not in conflict with the laws of the United States, or with the laws of the State or Territory in which the district is situated, governing the location, manner of recording and the amount of work necessary to hold possession of a mining claim.

The local regulations of some of the mining districts in New Mexico make the lode claim 300 feet in width and 1,500 feet in length.

Dimension of Placer Claim

A placer claim may contain twenty acres.

The following references are to the Compiled Laws of New Mexico, except where otherwise noted.

Section 2286. It is necessary in locating a mining claim, to distinctly mark the boundaries of such claim, and to post in some conspicuous place on such location a notice in writing giving such a description as will identify the claim, and the names of the locator or locators, and his or their intention of locating said claim.

A copy of said notice must be recorded in the office of the recorder of the county in which said claim is located, within three months of the posting of such notice. No other record of said notice is necessary.

Section 2299 (as amended by the Session Laws of 1899, Section 1, Page 111). Within 120 days of the location of any mining claim in this territory, the surface boundaries of such claim shall be marked by four substantial posts or monuments, one at each corner of said claim.

Section 2300. The re-location of any mining claim which is subject to re-location, shall be made in the same way as an original location is required by law to be made.

Section 2301. If the original location is defective in any way or the requirement of law has not been complied with before, or if the owner of any mining claim shall be desirous of changing his surface boundaries, or of taking in any part of an overlapping claim which has been abandoned, such owner may file an amended or additional notice of location, provided such notice does not interfere with the rights of others.

Section 2302. Any person who shall take down, remove, alter or destroy any stake, post, monument or notice of location upon any mining claim without the consent of the owner or owners thereof, shall be deemed guilty of a misdemeanor, and on conviction, shall be punished by a fine not exceeding one hundred dollars or by imprisonment in the county jail not exceeding six months, or by both such fine and imprisonment.

Section 2311. Any person or persons, or the manager, officer, agent or employe of any person, firm, corporation or association, who shall in any manner alter, deface or change the location notice of any mining claim in this Territory, located under the laws of the United States or of the laws of this Territory, or any location regulation in force in the district wherein such claim is situated, thereby in any manner affecting the rights of any person, firm or corporation, to such claim or location, or the land covered thereby, shall be deemed guilty of a misdemeanor, and upon conviction thereof before any court of competent jurisdiction, shall be fined in a sum not less than one hundred dollars, nor more than five hundred dollars, or imprisonment in the county jail for not less than sixty days, nor more than one year, or by both such fine and imprisonment, in the discretion of the court trying the case. Nothing herein contained shall affect the rights of such locator or locators, to correct errors in such notices as provided in section two thousand three hundred and one, and the laws of the United States: Provided, such change shall not affect or change the date of such location notice, or affect the right of any other person.

Section 2298. The locator or locators of any mining claim shall within ninety days from the date of taking possession of the same, sink a discovery shaft, exposing mineral in place, or shall drive a tunnel, adit, or open cut upon such claim to a depth of at least ten feet below the surface.

Section 2300 (latter part of the section) . . . The re-locator of a mining claim shall sink a discovery shaft, exposing mineral in place or shall drive a tunnel, adit, or open cut upon such re-located claim to a depth of ten feet below the surface, or shall sink the original shaft ten feet deeper, or drive the original tunnel, adit, or open cut upon such claim ten feet further.

Section 2315. The owners of unpatented mining claims in New Mexico shall within sixty days from and after doing the assessment work which is required by law to be done upon said claim, cause to be filed with the recorder of the county in which such mining claim is situated, an affidavit setting forth the fact that all work required by law has been done.

The annual assessment work must be done each year not later than the 31st of December (Rev. Stats. U.S.).

On each claim, until patent is issued therefor, not less than one hundred dollars worth of labor shall be performed or improvements made during each year. . . . When five hundred dollars worth of labor has been performed, or improvements made, on any mining claim, the owner can get a patent from the United States for said claim upon compliance with the laws governing the issuance of patents, and upon payment to the United States of five dollars an acre for the land contained in said claim. (Rev. Stats. U.S.)   — From F. A. Jones, *New Mexico Mines and Minerals* (Santa Fe, 1904), 347-49.

APPENDIX III

CHECKLIST OF O. W. WILLIAMS' WRITINGS

A. WRITINGS INCLUDED IN THIS VOLUME

PART I
Surveyor on the Staked Plains

From Dallas to the Site of Lubbock. Pamphlet, 16 pp. No date. Probably written between 1930 and 1935.

"Muddy" Wilson and the Buffalo Stampede. Pamphlet, 8 pp. March, 1938.

The Big Snow of 1878. Pamphlet, 4 pp. (Letter to J. C. Williams, Feb. 13, 1933.)

PART II
Miner in Early New Mexico

In Old New Mexico, 1879-1880. Pamphlet, 48 pp., plus covers. Reprinted in the 1930's from the *Lordsburg Liberal* of Aug. 16, 23 and 30, Sept. 6 and 27, and Oct. 4 and 26, 1928.

PART III
Refuge in Silver City

After Many Years. Pamphlet, 4 pp. No date. Possibly written between 1930 and 1935. Reprinted in this book as "Hank Herrick of Arizona."

Letter to J. C. Williams, Jan. 25, 1925. Pamphlet, 4 pp. Reprinted in this book as "The Hanging of Richard Remine."

Letter to Mrs. John T. Muir, May 30, 1930. Pamphlet, 4 pp. Reprinted in this book as "Oasis Mine v. Last Chance Mine."

A City of Refuge. Pamphlet, 5 pp., plus covers. No date. Probably written in 1929. Reprinted in this book as "City of Refuge."

PART IV
Letters and Stories from the Big Bend

Letters of Jan. 25, March 7 and March 17, 1902 (all addressed to "My Dear Children") were printed in pamphlets. All other letters included in this book were taken from the originals. These originals were addressed to "My Dear Children," except the letter of Aug. 4, 1901, which was addressed to "My Dear Waldo." The series is reprinted in the book as "Letters from the Open Country." Note: Letter of March 7, 1902, summarizes the stories of Natividad Luján that Williams later wrote up in detail.

By the Campfire in the Southwest. Pamphlet, 28 pp., plus covers. No date. Written before 1919 and printed some years later. The following stories in this book were reprinted from this source: "Santiago Peak," "Mescal," "Alsate," "Mescal as a Defensive Weapon" and "An International Kidnapping." This pamphlet also contains a piece entitled "Poverty Flat on Darwin," which repeats a story related in Part II of the book.

Alsate — The Last of the Chisos. Pamphlet, 8 pp. No date. Written before 1914 and printed after 1919. Repeats the story told in *By the Campfire,* giving additional details included in the annotations to "Alsate" in this volume.

The Story of Guero Carransa. Pamphlet, 4 pp. No date. Written before 1914 and printed after 1919. Included in book as "Güero Carranza."

Baja el Sol. Pamphlet, 4 pp. No date. Written before 1914 and printed after 1919. Included in book as "Bajo el Sol."

B. WRITINGS NOT INCLUDED IN THIS VOLUME

(Note: Parts of some of the following have been quoted or cited in this book.)

1. Pamphlets Dealing with Williams' Family Background and Early Years

An Old Carthage Home. 16 pp., plus covers. Reprinted (1937) from *The Carthage Republican* of Dec. 6, 1922.

An Early College Year in the Hills. 12 pp. No date. Probably written about 1923.

Letter from O. W. Williams to His Son (J. C. Williams), June 3, 1925. 12 pp., plus covers.

Letter from O. W. Williams to His Son (J. C. Williams), March 10, 1930. 8 pp. (Contains some Southwestern material.)

Letter to Mrs. Jacob Pirkey, June 10, 1930. 4 pp.

Letter from O. W. Williams to His Son (J. C. Williams), March 8, 1931. 8 pp.

Letter to Mrs. Fernando Sanferd, Feb., 1943. 4 pp.

2. Pamphlets Dealing with Southwestern History

An Old Timer's Reminiscences of Grant County. Reprint of letter to *Southwest Sentinel* (Silver City, N. M.), Jan. 17, 1885. 8 pp.

"Route of Cabeza de Vaca in Texas." *Texas Historical Association Quarterly,* No. 1, July, 1899, III, 54-64. Reprinted in pamphlet, 8 pp. No date.

Mendosa — 1684 — In Pecos County. 24 pp., plus covers. No date. Probably written before 1919.

Pecos County — Its History. 24 pp. Reprinted from series of articles in *Fort Stockton Pioneer,* Dec. 11, 1923 — Feb. 29, 1924.

Crusoe or Jack: A Story for Our Boys. 4 pp. No date. Probably written about 1923.

Letter to Clayton W. Williams, Sept. 19, 1918. 16 pp.

Letter to J. C. Williams, Dec. 15, 1924. 8 pp.

Letter to G. F. Grant, June 30, 1930. 8 pp.

Letter to Judge J. W. Ballard, Dec. 8, 1930. 8 pp.

3. *Pamphlets Dealing with Natural History*

Letter to Kathryn Williams, Nov. 7, 1901. 2 pp.

The Honca Accursed. 4 pp. No date. Probably written about 1902.

Historic Review of Animal Life in Pecos County. 96 pp., plus covers. Reprinted from series of articles in *Fort Stockton Pioneer,* 1908.

The Ferrule of Pecos County. 4 pp. No date. Written about 1900.

Pecos County Panther Hunt Around Livingston Mesa. 12 pp. Story first printed in *Fort Stockton Pioneer,* Jan. 24, 1941. Reprinted as pamphlet, 1943. Written between 1902 and 1907.

To the Boys and Girls of the Fort Stockton Schools. 8 pp. January. 1930. Probably written between 1920 and 1930.

4. *Pamphlets and Articles Dealing with Miscellaneous Subjects*

Letter to "My Dear Children," 4 pp. Undated. Probably written in 1902 or 1903.

Letter of O. W. Williams to His Son (J. C. Williams), Nov. 21, 1926. 8 pp.

Letters to Fort Stockton Pioneer. Issues of March 1 and 8, 1929.

Letter to A. C. Harris, Sept. 7, 1931. 4 pp.

Letter to "My Dear Children," 4 pp. Undated. Probable date undetermined.

5. *Unpublished Essays*

Comparison between the Battles of Thermopylae and the Alamo. Undated. Probably written about 1889.

The Hawk & the Owl. Undated. Written about 1898.

Something About the Aryans. Undated. Probably written in the early 1900's.

Flanagan's Message. Undated. Probably written in the early 1900's.

6. *Unpublished Letters and Documents*

Statement in A. J. Royal Case, 1894.

Letter to Kathryn Williams, July 9, 1901.

Letter to George F. Lewis, Jan. 13, 1930.

Letter to George R. Bean, March 8, 1937.

Letter to J. H. Walker, Sept. 6, 1940.

Letter to Bascom Giles, July 21, 1943.

Letters to Jesse C. Williams, 1916-1943. A source of much information, some of which is used in this volume.

Personal and Business Letters, containing miscellaneous data.

Records of numerous legal transactions in files of County, Commissioners', and District courts, Pecos County.

ACKNOWLEDGMENTS

The persons and institutions whose names are listed below have contributed materially to the production of this book.

Dr. C. L. Sonnichsen, Dean of the Graduate School of Texas Western College, initiated the project, wrote the introduction to the book and gave helpful advice regarding its contents. Mr. Clayton W. Williams, son of Judge O. W. Williams, made available the writings of his father and did much of the research on which the study is based.

Dr. Joseph M. Ray, President of the College, took a personal interest in the book from the beginning. He arranged its financing, read the manuscript in full and offered valuable criticism. Mr. Carl Hertzog, Director of the College Press, devoted much attention to the distinctive design of the book; he also supervised all details of its production. Mr. José Cisneros made the attractive drawings and maps that illuminate the persons and places mentioned in the text.

Five specialists in Southwestern history read all, or essential parts, of the galley proof. Dr. Ernest Wallace, Professor of History, Texas Technological College, Lubbock, reviewed and criticized Part I. Dr. Myra Ellen Jenkins, Senior Archivist, New Mexico State Records, Santa Fe, performed the same function for Parts II and III; and Dr. Clifford B. Casey, Sul Ross State College, Alpine, for Part IV. Professors Rex Strickland and J. Morgan Broaddus of Texas Western College offered many constructive suggestions as work on the book progressed.

Several other members of the College staff rendered valuable assistance: Professors Haldeen Braddy (who read the entire manuscript), Anton H. Berkman, Rex Gerald, John H. McNeely, Edgar T. Ruff, John M. Sharp and Eugene M. Thomas.

These persons off the campus helped in clarifying a number of special points: Dr. Nettie Lee Benson, Latin American Collection, Library, The University of Texas, Austin; Mr. Maurice R. Bullock, Attorney, Fort Stockton; Sr. Norberto Benigno Contreras, Ojinaga, Mexico; Mr. Joe Cordero, Fort Stockton; Miss Ima Fairly, Lordsburg, N. M.; Mrs. Shirley Gonzales, El Paso; Mr. Berte R. Haigh, Consultant, University Lands, Midland; Mrs. Rita Hill, Shakespeare, N. M.; Professor William C. Holden, Texas Technological College, Lubbock; Mr. Douglas B. McHenry, Park Naturalist, Big Bend National Park; Dr. Benjamin Sacks, Director, Arizona Historical Foundation, Phoenix; Mr. Austin W. Scott, Professor Emeritus, Harvard Law School, Cambridge, Mass.; Mr. Ben G. Smith, Attorney, Fort Worth; Professor Barton H. Warnock, Sul Ross College, Alpine.

Essential documentation was supplied by Mr. James M. Day, Director of State Archives, Texas State Library, Austin; Mr. Roy Sylvan Dunn, Director, Southwest Collection, Texas Technological College, Lubbock; Mrs. Dorothy Gage Forker, Marathon; Messrs. Rex, William and John Kipp, the Emma Muir Collection, Lordsburg, N. M.; Mr. C. Boone McClure, Director, The Panhandle Plains Museum, Canyon; Miss Celia G. Padilla, County Clerk, Grant County, Silver City, N. M.; Miss Betty Anne Thetford, Secretary, Board of Regents, The University of Texas, Austin; Mr. Jerry Sadler, Commissioner, General Land Office, Austin; Mrs. Mary E. Steinberger, District Court Clerk, Silver City.

The following heirs of Judge Williams cooperated by permitting the use of his writings: Mrs. F. G. Walker, Clayton W. Williams, Jesse Caleb Williams, Mr. and Mrs. C. J. Berst, Mrs. Susan Olivia Coulter, Mr. and Mrs. W. K. Carnett and Mr. and Mrs. C. S. Schultz.

Mr. Baxter Polk, Librarian, and his staff at Texas Western College were especially helpful in providing books, maps, microfilms and documents. Additional materials came from the libraries of New Mexico Institute of Mining and Technology, Socorro; Southern Methodist University, Dallas; Sul Ross State College, Alpine; Texas Technological College, Lubbock; The University of New Mexico, Albuquerque; The University of Texas, Austin; Western New Mexico University, Silver City; and West Texas University, Canyon.

The staff of the El Paso Public Library made available many of the works cited in the notes. Other materials were supplied by the public libraries of Dallas, Albuquerque and Silver City, and by the History Library, State Museum of New Mexico, Santa Fe.

The College Committee on Research Professorships (Deans C. L. Sonnichsen, Ray Small and L. L. Abernethy) recommended the editior for an appointment that enabled him to undertake and complete the research on which the book is based. Members of the College Research Institute (Professors R. L. Schumaker, H. E. Alexander, W. E. Fuller, C. S. Knowlton and J. M. Richards) approved a grant for essential research assistance. The Editorial Board of the College Press (Vice President R. Milton Leech, Deans C. L. Sonnichsen and Ray Small, Professors J. H. Haddox, J. M. Sharp, W. H. Timmons and Mr. Carl Hertzog) supported the undertaking at all of its stages.

Mr. Richard Escantrias worked diligently on the manuscript and the proofs. The book owes much to his expertise as researcher and critic. Mrs. Winnie Middah typed the manuscript, and Mrs. Roberta Logerman and Mrs. Edward Anderson prepared the index. To Mr. J. E. Davis, Jr., Manager of the College Print Shop, fell the task of setting the book in type, a job he discharged with special competence.

Credit is due the following for the use of photographs: the heirs of Judge O. W. Williams; the Big Bend National Park; the H. H. Butz collection, Riggs Museum, Fort Stockton; the *Fort Stockton Pioneer;* the Lordsburg Chamber of Commerce; the Marathon Oil Company, Findlay, Ohio; the Emma Muir Collection, Lordsburg, N. M.; the Museum of New Mexico, Santa Fe; the *New Mexico Magazine;* the Pecos County State Bank, Fort Stockton; the Panhandle Plains Museum, Canyon, Texas; the Silver City Chamber of Commerce; Mr. W. D. Smithers, Alpine; the Southwest Collection, Texas Technological College, Lubbock; the Texas Surveyors Association; Mr. Herman Uhli, Silver City.

While expressing his gratitude to those mentioned, the editor assumes sole responsibility for the contents of the book, including any errors of fact or interpretation.

INDEX